A Field Guide to the Classroom Library G

A Field Guide to the Classroom Library Ⓖ

Lucy Calkins

and

*The Teachers College
Reading and Writing
Project Community*

HEINEMANN
Portsmouth, NH

Heinemann
A division of Reed Elsevier Inc.
361 Hanover Street
Portsmouth, NH 03801–3912
www.heinemann.com

Offices and agents throughout the world

Library of Congress Cataloging-in-Publication Data
Calkins, Lucy McCormick.
    A field guide to the classroom library / Lucy Calkins and the Teachers
College Reading and Writing Project community.
        v. cm.
Includes bibliographical references and index.
Contents: [v. 7] Library G : grades 5–6
ISBN 0-325-00501-X
    1. Reading (Elementary)—Handbooks, manuals, etc.   2. Children—Books and reading—Handbooks, manuals, etc.   3. Children's literature—Study and teaching (Elementary)—Handbooks, manuals, etc.   4. Classroom libraries—Handbooks, manuals, etc.   I. Teachers College Reading and Writing Project (Columbia University).   II. Title.
LB1573 .C183 2002
372.4—dc21   2002038767

Editor: Kate Montgomery
Production: Abigail M. Heim
Interior design: Catherine Hawkes, Cat & Mouse
Cover design: Jenny Jensen Greenleaf Graphic Design & Illustration
Manufacturing: Louise Richardson

Printed in the United States of America on acid-free paper

06 05 04 03   VP   4 5

This field guide is dedicated to

Isoke Nia

The Field Guides to the Classroom Library *project is a philanthropic effort. According to the wishes of the scores of contributors, all royalties from the sale of these field guides will be given back entirely to the project in the continued effort to put powerful, beautiful, and thoughtfully chosen literature into the hands of children.*

Contents

Acknowledgments

The entire Teachers College Reading and Writing Project community has joined together in the spirit of a barn-raising to contribute to this gigantic effort to put the best of children's literature into the hands of children.

There are hundreds of people to thank. In these pages, I will only be able to give special thanks to a few of the many who made this work possible.

First, we thank Alan and Gail Levenstein who sponsored this effort with a generous personal gift and who helped us remember and hold tight to our mission. We are grateful to Annemarie Powers who worked tirelessly, launching the entire effort in all its many dimensions. Annemarie's passionate love of good literature shines throughout this project.

Kate Montgomery, now an editor at Heinemann and a long-time friend and coauthor, joined me in writing and revising literally hundreds of the field guides. Kate's deep social consciousness, knowledge of reading, and her commitment to children are evident throughout the work. How lucky we were that she became a full-time editor at Heinemann just when this project reached there, and was, therefore, able to guide the project's final stages.

Tasha Kalista coordinated the effort, bringing grace, humor, and an attention to detail to the project. She's been our home base, helping us all stay on track. Tasha has made sure loose ends were tied up, leads pursued, inquiries conducted, and she's woven a graceful tapestry out of all the thousands of books, guides, and people.

Each library is dedicated to a brilliant, passionate educator who took that particular library and the entire effort under her wing. We are thankful to Lynn Holcomb whose deep understanding of early reading informed our work; to Mary Ann Colbert who gave generously of her wisdom of reading recovery and primary texts; to Kathleen Tolan who championed the little chapter books and made us see them with new eyes; to Gaby Layden for her expertise in the area of nonfiction reading; to Isoke Nia for passionate contributions to our upper grade libraries; and to Kathy Doyle who knows books better than anyone we know.

We thank Pam Allyn for her dedication to this effort, Laurie Pessah for working behind the scenes with me, and Beth Neville for keeping the Project on course when this undertaking threatened to swamp us.

Finally, we are grateful to Mayor Guiliani for putting these libraries into every New York City school. To Judith Rizzo, Deputy Chancellor of Instruction, Adele Schroeter, Director of Office of Research, Development and Dissemination, Peter Heaney, Executive Director of the Division of Instructional Support, and William P. Casey, Chief Executive for Instructional Innovation, we also offer our heartfelt thanks for contributing their wisdom, integrity, and precious time to making this miracle happen.

Contributors

Christina Adams
Lisa Ali Chetram
Pam Allyn
Francine Almash
Janet Angelillo
Liz Arfin
Anna Arrigo
Laura Ascenzi-Moreno
Maureen Bilewich
Melissa Biondi
Pat Bleichman
Christine Bluestein
Ellen Braunstein
Dina Bruno
Theresa Burns
Lucy Calkins
Adele Cammarata
Joanne Capozzoli
Laura Cappadona
Justin Charlebois
Linda Chen
Mary Chiarella
Danielle Cione
Erica Cohen
Mary Ann Colbert
Kerri Conlon
Denise Corichi
Danielle Corrao
Sue Dalba
Linda Darro
Mildred De Stefano
Marisa DeChiara
Erica Denman
Claudia Diamond
Renee Dinnerstein
Kathy Doyle
Lizz Errico
Rosemarie Fabbricante
Gabriel Feldberg
Holly Fisher

Sofia Forgione
Judy Friedman
Elizabeth Fuchs
Jerilyn Ganz
Allison Gentile
Linda Gerstman
Jessica Goff
Iris Goldstein-Jackman
Ivy Green
Cathy Grimes
David Hackenburg
Amanda Hartman
Grace Heske
Caren Hinckley
Lynn Holcomb
Michelle Hornof
Anne Illardi
Maria Interlandi
Erin Jackman
Debbie Jaffe
Helen Jurios
Kim Kaiser
Tasha Kalista
Beth Kanner
Michele Kaye
Laurie Kemme
Hue Kha
Tara Krebs
Joan Kuntz Verdino
Kathleen Kurtz
Lamson Lam
Gaby Layden
Karen Liebowitz
Adele Long
Cynthia Lopez
Natalie Louis
Eileen Lynch
Theresa Maldarelli
Lucille Malka

Corinne Maracina
Jennifer Marmo
Paula Marron
Marjorie Martinelli
Esther Martinez
Debbie Matz
Teresa Maura
Leah Mermelstein
Melissa Miller
Kate Montgomery
Jessica Moss
Janice Motloenya
Marie Naples
Marcia Nass
Beth Neville
Silvana Ng
Isoke Nia
Jennie Nolan Buonocore
Lynn Norton Manna
Beth Nuremberg
Sharon Nurse
Liz O'Connell
Jacqueline O'Connor
Joanne Onolfi
Suzann Pallai
Shefali Parekh
Karen Perepeluk
Laurie Pessah
Jayne Piccola
Laura Polos
Annemarie Powers
Bethany Pray
Carol Puglisi
Alice Ressner
Marcy Rhatigan
Khrishmati Ridgeway
Lisa Ripperger
Barbara Rosenblum
Jennifer Ruggiero

Liz Rusch
Jennifer Ryan
Karen Salzberg
Elizabeth Sandoval
Carmen Santiago
Karen Scher
Adele Schroeter
Shanna Schwartz
India Scott
Marci Seidman
Rosie Silberman
Jessica Silver
Miles Skorpen
Joann Smith
Chandra Smith
Helene Sokol
Gail Wesson Spivey
Barbara Stavetski
Barbara Stavridis
Jean Stehle
Kathleen Stevens
Emma Suarez Baez
Michelle Sufrin
Jane Sullivan
Evelyn Summer
Eileen Tabasko
Patricia Tanzosh
Lyon Terry
Kathleen Tolan
Christine Topf
Joseph Turzo
Cheryl Tyler
Emily Veronese
Anne Marie Vira
Marilyn Walker
Gillan White
Alison Wolensky
Michelle Wolf
Eileen Wolfring

Introduction: What Is This Field Guide?

Lucy Calkins

When I was pregnant with my first-born son, the Teachers College Reading and Writing Project community organized a giant baby shower for me. Each person came with a carefully chosen book, inscribed with a message for baby Miles. Since then, we have commemorated birthdays, engagements, graduations, and good-byes by searching the world for exactly the right poem or picture book, novel or essay, and writing a letter to accompany it. Inside the letter, it says "This is why I chose this piece of literature precisely for you." In this same way, the book lists and the written guides that accompany them in this field guide have become our gift to you, the teachers of our nation's children. We have chosen, from all the books we have ever read, exactly the ones we think could start best in your classroom, and with these books, we have written notes that explain exactly why and how we think these texts will be so powerful in your children's hands.

The book lists and guides in this field guide are the Teachers College Reading and Writing Project's literacy gift to New York City and to the nation. When, two years ago, patrons Alan and Gail Levenstein came to us asking if there was one thing, above all others, which could further our work with teachers and children, we knew our answer in a heartbeat. We couldn't imagine anything more important than giving children the opportunity to trade, collect, talk over, and live by books. We want children to carry poems in their backpacks, to cry with Jess when he finds out that his friend Leslie has drowned, to explore tropical seas from the deck of a ship, to wonder at the life teeming in a drop of water. We want our children's heroes to include the wise and loving spider Charlotte, spinning her web to save the life of Wilbur, and the brave Atticus Finch.

We told the Levensteins that for teachers, as well as for children, there could be no finer gift than the gift of books for their students. We want teachers to be able to read magnificent stories aloud as the prelude to each school day, and to know the joy of putting exactly the right book in the hands of a child and adding, with a wink, "When you finish this book, there are more like it." We want teachers to create libraries with categories of books that peak their students' interests and match their children's passions, with one shelf for Light Sports Books and another shelf for Cousins of the Harry Potter books, one for Books That Make You Cry and another for You'll-Never-Believe-This Books. With this kind of a library, how much easier it becomes to teach children to read, to teach them what they need to become powerful, knowledgeable, literate people!

Even as we embarked on the effort to design magnificent classroom libraries, we knew that the best classroom library would always be the one assembled by a knowledgeable classroom teacher with his or her own students in mind. But, in so many cities, twenty new teachers may arrive in a school in a single year, having had no opportunity to learn about children's books at all. Even though some teachers have studied children's books, they may not be the ones given the opportunity to purchase books. Or, too often, there is no time to make book selections carefully—funds are discovered ten minutes before they must be spent or be taken from the budget. For these situations, we knew it would be enormously helpful to have lists and arrangements of recommended books for classroom libraries. Even without these worries, we all know the value of receiving book recommendations from friends. And so, our commitment to the project grew.

Our plan became this: We'd rally the entire Project community around a gigantic, two-year-long effort to design state-of-the-art classroom libraries and guides, exactly tailored to the classrooms we know so well. Simultaneously, we'd begin working with political, educational, and philanthropic leaders in hopes that individuals or corporations might adopt a school (or a corridor of classrooms) and create in these schools and classrooms the libraries of our dreams. Sharing our enthusiasm, colleagues at the New York City Board of Education proposed that idea to the mayor. Two years later, that dream has come true—In his January 2001 state of the city address, Mayor Giuliani promised $31.5 million of support to put a lending library in every New York City classroom, kindergarten through eighth grade.

Hearing this pronouncement, educational leaders from around the city joined with us in our philanthropic effort. People from the New York City Board of Education reviewed the lists and added suggestions and revisions. The Robin Hood Foundation, which had already been involved in a parallel effort to develop *school* libraries, contributed their knowledge. Readers from the Teachers Union and from the Office of Multicultural Education and of Early Childhood Education and of Literacy Education all joined in, coordinated by Peter Heaney, Executive Director of the Division of Instructional Support, and Adele Schroeter, Director of the Office of Research, Development and Dissemination. The book selections for the classroom libraries became even more carefully honed, and the written guides became richer still.

Over the past few months, boxes upon boxes of books have arrived across New York City, and in every classroom, children are pulling close to watch, big-eyed, as one exquisite, carefully chosen book after another is brought from the box and set on the shelf. Each teacher will receive between three and four hundred books. With most of these books, there will be a carefully crafted guide which says, "We chose this book because . . ." and "On page . . ." and "You'll notice that . . ." and "If you like this book, these are some others like it. . . . " I cannot promise that in every town and city across the nation the effort to put literature in the hands of students and guidance in the hands of their teachers will proceed so smoothly. But I'm hoping these book lists and these ready-made libraries bearing a stamp of approval will catch the eye of funders, of generous patrons, and of foresighted school leaders. And, every penny that comes to the authors from the sale of these field guides will go directly back into this project, directly back into our efforts to get more books into children's hands.

In the meantime, we needn't be idle. We'll comb through the book sales at libraries, and we'll write requests to publishers and companies. In a letter home to our children's parents, we might say, "Instead of sending in cupcakes to honor your child's birthday, I'm hoping you'll send a book. Enclosed is a list of suggestions." We can and will get books into our children's hands, by hook or by crook. And we can and will get the professional support we need for our reading instruction—our vitality and effectiveness as educators depend on it.

About the Books

When hundreds of teachers pool their knowledge of children's books as we have here, the resulting libraries are far richer than anything any one of us could have imagined on our own. We're proud as peacocks of these selections and of the accompanying literary insights and teaching ideas, and can't wait to share them both with teachers and children across the country. Here is a window into some of the crafting that has gone into the book selections:

- We suggest author studies in which the texts that students will study approximately match those they'll write and will inform their own work as authors.

- In upper-grade libraries, we include books that are relatively easy to read, but we have tried to ensure that they contain issues of concern to older children as well.

- We include books that might inform other books in the same library. For example, one library contains three books about dust storms, another contains a variety of books on spiders.

- We know that comprehension and interpretive thinking must be a part of reading from the very beginning, so we include easy to read books that can support thoughtful responses.

- We try to match character ages with student ages, approximately. For example, we have put the book in which Ramona is five in the library we anticipate will be for kindergartners, and put fourth-grade Ramona in the library we anticipate will be for fourth graders.

- We include complementary stories together when possible. For example, Ringgold's *Tar Beach* and Dorros' *Abuela* appear in the same library, anticipating that readers will recognize these as parallel stories in which the narrator has an imagined trip.

- We have never assumed that books in a series are all of the same level. For example, we have determined that some of the *Frog and Toad* books are more challenging, and this is indicated in our libraries.

- We understand that books in a series cannot always be easily read out of sequence. Because we know the *Magic Treehouse* series is best read in a particular sequence, for example, we have been careful with regard to the books we select out of that series.

- We selected our libraries to reflect multicultural values and bring forth characters of many different backgrounds and lives.

■ We try to steer clear of books that will not meet with general public approval. We do not believe in censorship, but we do believe that books purchased en masse should not bring storms of criticism upon the unsuspecting teacher.

At the same time that we are proud of the work we've done, we also know that there are countless magnificent books we have omitted and countless helpful and obvious teaching moves we have missed. We are certain that there are authors' names we have inadvertently misspelled, opinions expressed with which we don't all agree, levels assigned that perhaps should be different, and so on. We consider this work to be a letter to a friend and a work in progress, and we are rushing it to you, eager for a response. We are hoping that when you come across areas that need more attention, when you get a bright idea about a guide or booklist, that you will write back to us. We have tried to make this as easy as possible for you to do—just go to our website and contact us!

Choosing the Library for Your Class

We have created seven libraries for kindergarten through sixth grade classrooms. The libraries are each assigned a letter name (A–G) rather than a grade-level in recognition of the fact that the teacher of one class of fourth graders might find that Library D is suited to her students, and another fourth grade teacher might opt for Library E or Library F.

In order to determine which classroom library is most appropriate for a particular class in a particular school, teachers need to determine the approximate reading levels of their students in November, after the teachers have had some time to assess their students as readers. Teachers can compare the book the middle-of-the-class reader tends to be reading with the books we note for each level, and choose the library that corresponds to that average text level. More detail follows this general description. In shorthand, however, the following equivalencies apply:

> **Library A** is usually Kindergarten
> **Library B** is usually K or 1st grade
> **Library C** is usually 1st or 2nd grade
> **Library D** is usually 2nd or 3rd grade
> **Library E** is usually 3rd or 4th grade
> **Library F** is usually 4th or 5th grade
> **Library G** is usually 5th or 6th grade

The system of saying, "If in November, your children are reading books like these," usually doesn't work for kindergarten children. Instead, we say Library A is suitable if, in November, the average student cannot yet do a rich, story-like, emergent (or pretend) reading of a familiar storybook, nor can this child write using enough initial and final consonants that an adult can "read" the child's writing.

It is important to note that all of the books in any given library are not at the same level of difficulty. Instead, we have created a mix of levels that tend to represent the mixed levels of ability of readers in the classes we have studied. The composition of the libraries, by level, is described on pages li–lx.

Once you have chosen the library that best corresponds to the average level of your students as readers, you will need to decide which components of the library best suit your curriculum. Each library is divided into components—a core and some modules. The core is the group of books in the library we regard as essential. Each library also contains six modules, each representing a category of books. For example, in each library there is a module of nonfiction books, and in the upper-grade libraries there are modules containing five copies each of ten books we recommend for book clubs. Each module contains approximately fifty titles. The exact quantity from module to module varies slightly because we have tried to keep the cost of each module approximately equal. This means, for example, that the nonfiction module that contains more hardcover books has fewer books overall.

There are a variety of ways to assemble a library. Some teachers will want to purchase the entire library—the core plus the six modules. Sometimes, teachers on the same grade level in a school each purchase the same core but different modules, so a greater variety of books will be available across the hall for their students. In New York City, teachers automatically received the core of their library of choice, 150 books, and then could choose three of the six possible modules.

The Contents of Each Library

Researchers generally agree that a classroom should contain at least twenty books per child. Obviously, the number of books needs to be far greater than this in kindergarten and first grade classrooms, because books for beginning readers often contain fewer than 100 words and can generally only sustain a child's reading for a short while. We would have liked to recommend libraries of 750 titles but decided to select a smaller number of books, trusting that each teacher will have other books of his or her choice to supplement our recommendations.

Because we predict that every teacher will receive or buy the core of a library and only some teachers will receive any particular module, we tried to fill the core of the libraries with great books we couldn't imagine teaching, or living, without. Because we know children will borrow and swap books between classrooms, it is rare for books to be in the core of more than one library, even though some great books could easily belong there.

Usually, these classroom libraries include enough books from a particularly wonderful series to turn that series into a class rage, but the libraries frequently do not contain all the books in a series. Often, more books in the series are included in Modules One and Two, which always contain more books for independent reading, divided into the same levels as those in the core. Our expectation is that once readers have become engrossed in a series, teachers or parents can help them track down sequels in the school or public library.

Within the core of a library, we include about a dozen books of various genres that could be perfect for the teacher to read aloud to the class. These are all tried-and-true read aloud books; each title on the read-aloud list is one that countless teachers have found will create rapt listeners and generate rich conversation.

In every library we have included nonfiction books. They were not chosen to support particular social studies or science units; that would be a different and admirable goal. Instead, our team members have searched for nonfiction texts that captivate readers, and we imagine them being read within the reading workshop. The nonfiction books were chosen either because their topics are generally high-interest ones for children (animals, yo-yo tricks, faraway lands, disgusting animals), or because they represent the best of their genre.

Each library contains about fifteen books that could be splendid mentor texts for young writers. That is, they contain writing that students could emulate and learn from easily since it is somewhat like the writing they are generally able to create themselves.

In each core library, an assortment of other categories is included. These differ somewhat from one library to another. Libraries D and E, for example, contain many early chapter books, but since it is also crucial for children at this level to read the richest picture books imaginable, the core contains a score of carefully chosen picture books. Some cores also contain a set of books perfect for an author study. The categories are indicated on the book lists themselves, and under "Teaching Uses" in the guides.

The vast majority of books in each library are single copies, chosen in hopes that they will be passed eagerly from one reader to another. The challenge was not to find the number of books representing a particular level, but instead to select irresistible books. The chosen books have been field tested in dozens of New York City classrooms, and they've emerged as favorites for teachers and children alike.

The few books that have been selected in duplicate are ones we regard as particularly worthwhile to talk over with a partner. We would have loved to suggest duplicate copies be available for half the books in each library—if libraries had more duplicates, this would allow two readers to move simultaneously through a book, meeting in partnerships to talk and think about the chapters they've read. The duplicate copies would allow readers to have deeper and more text-specific book talks, while growing and researching theories as they read with each other. Duplicates also help books gain social clout in a classroom—allowing the enthusiasm of several readers to urge even more readers to pick the book up. If teachers are looking for ways to supplement these libraries, buying some duplicate copies would be a perfect way to start.

Many of the libraries contain a very small number of multiple (four or five) copies of books intended for use in guided reading and strategy lessons. Once children are reading chapter books, we find teachers are wise to help children into a new series by pulling together a group of four readers, introducing the text, and guiding their early reading. Teachers may also want to offer extra support to children as they read the second book in a series, and so we suggest having a duplicate of this next book as well, so that each child can read it with a partner, meeting to retell and discuss it.

The Levels Within the Libraries

We've leveled many, but purposely not all, of the books in every classroom library. The fact that we have leveled these books doesn't mean that teachers should necessarily convey all of these levels to children. We expect teachers will often make these levels visible on less than half of their books (through the use of colored tabs), giving readers the responsibility of choosing appropriate books for themselves by judging unmarked books against the template of leveled books. "This book looks a lot like the green dot books that have been just-right for me, so I'll give it a try and see if I have a smooth read," a reader might say. It is important that kids learn to navigate different levels of difficulty within a classroom library on their own or with only minimal support from a teacher.

We do not imagine a classroom lending library that is divided into levels as discrete as the levels established by Reading Recovery© or by Gay Su Pinnell and Irene Fountas' book, *Guided Reading: Good First Teaching for All Children* (Heinemann, 1996). These levels were designed for either one-to-one tutorials or intensive, small group guided reading sessions, and in both of these situations a vigilant teacher is present to constantly shepherd children along toward more challenging books. If a classroom lending library is divided into micro-levels and each child's entire independent reading life is slotted into a micro-level, some children might languish at a particular level, and many youngsters might not receive the opportunities to read across a healthy range of somewhat-easier and somewhat-harder books. Most worrisome of all, because we imagine children working often with reading partners who "like to read the same kinds of books as you do," classroom libraries that contain ten micro-levels (instead of say, five more general levels) could inadvertently convey the message that many *children* as well as many *books* were off-limits as partners to particular readers.

There are benefits to micro-levels, however, and therefore within a difficulty level (or a color-dot), some teachers might ascribe a plus sign to certain books, signifying that this book is one of the harder ones at this level. Teachers can then tell a child who is new to a level to steer clear of the books with plus signs, or to be sure that he or she receives a book introduction before tackling a book with this marker.

When assigning books to levels, we have tried to research the difficulty levels that others have given to each text and we have included these levels in our guides. Fairly frequently, however, our close study of a particular text has led us to differ somewhat from the assessments others have made. Of course leveling books is and always will be a subjective and flawed process; and therefore teachers everywhere *should* deviate from assigned levels, ours and others, when confident of their rationale, or when particularly knowledgeable about a reader. You can turn to the tables at the back of this section, on pages xxxi–lxiv, to learn more about our leveling system.

Building the Libraries

When we started this project two years ago, we initiated some intensive study groups, each designed to investigate a different terrain in children's literature. Soon, a group led by Lynn Holcomb, one of the first Reading Recovery teachers in Connecticut, was working to select books for a K–1 library. Members of this group also learned from Barbara Peterson, author of *Literary Pathways: Selecting Books to Support New Readers* (Heinemann, 2001), who conducted groundbreaking research at Ohio State University, examining how readers actually experience levels of text complexity. The group also learned from Gay Su Pinnell, well-known scholar of literacy education and coauthor with Irene Fountas of many books including *Guided Reading*. Of course, the group learned especially from intensive work with children in classrooms. The group searched for books that:

- Represent a diverse range of shapes, sizes, authors, and language patterns as possible. The committee went to lengths to be sure that when taken as a whole, primary-level libraries looked more like libraries full of real books than like kits full of "teaching materials."

- Use unstilted language. A book that reads, "Come, Spot. Come, Spot, come," generally would not be selected.

- Contain many high frequency words. If one book contained just one word on a page ("Scissors/paste/paper/etc.") and another book contained the reoccurring refrain of "I see the scissors./ I see the paste." we selected the second option.

- Carry meaning and were written to communicate content with a reader. If the book would probably generate a conversation or spark an insight, it was more apt to be included than one that generally left a reader feeling flat and finished with the book.

- Represent the diversity of people in our world and convey valuable messages about the human spirit.

A second group, under the leadership of Kathleen Tolan, an experienced teacher and staff developer, spent thousands of hours studying early chapter books and the children who read them. This group pored over series, asking questions: Is each book in the series equally difficult? Which series act as good precursors for other series? Do the books in the series make up one continuous story, or can each book stand alone? What are the special demands placed on readers of this series?

Yet another group, led by Gaby Layden, staff developer at the Project, studied nonfiction books to determine which might be included in a balanced, independent reading library. The group studied levels of difficulty in nonfiction books, and found authors and texts that deserved special attention. Carefully, they chose books for teachers to demonstrate and for children to practice working through the special challenges of nonfiction reading.

Meanwhile, renowned teacher-educator Isoke Nia, teacher extraordinaire Kathy Doyle, and their team of educators dove into the search for the very best chapter books available for upper-grade readers. Isoke especially helped us select touchstone texts for writing workshops—books to help us teach children to craft their writing with style, care, and power.

Teacher, staff developer, and researcher Annemarie Powers worked full-time to ensure that our effort was informed by the related work of other groups across the city and nation. We pored over bibliographies and met with librarians and literature professors. We searched for particular kinds of books: books featuring Latino children, anthologies of short stories, Level A and B books which looked and sounded like literature. We researched the classrooms in our region that are especially famous for their classroom libraries, and took note of the most treasured books we found there. All of this information fed our work.

Reading Instruction and the Classroom Library: An Introduction to Workshop Structures

These classroom libraries have been developed with the expectation that they will be the centerpiece of reading instruction. When I ask teachers what they are really after in the teaching of reading, many answer, as I do, "I want children to be lifelong readers. I cannot imagine anything more important than helping children grow up able to read and loving to read. I want students to initiate reading in their own lives, for their own purposes."

There is, of course, no one best way to teach reading so that children become lifelong readers. One of the most straightforward ways to do this is to embrace the age-old, widely shared belief that children benefit from daily opportunities to read books they choose for their own purposes and pleasures (Krashen 1993, Atwell 1987, Cambourne 1993, Smith 1985, Meek 1988).

More and more, however, we've come to realize that students benefit not only from opportunities to read, read, read, but also from instruction that responds to what students do when they are given opportunities to read. I have described the reading workshop in my latest publication, *The Art of Teaching Reading* (Calkins 2001). The reading workshop is an instructional format in which children are given long chunks of time in which to read appropriate texts, and also given explicit and direct instruction. Teachers who come from a writing workshop background may find it helpful to structure the reading workshop in ways that parallel the writing workshop so that children learn simultaneously to work productively inside each of the two congruent structures. Whatever a teacher decides, it is important that the structures of a reading workshop are clear and predictable so that children know how to carry on with some independence, and so that teachers are able to assess and coach individuals as well as partnerships and small groups.

Many teachers begin a reading workshop by pulling students together for a minilesson lasting about eight minutes (unless the read aloud is, for that day, incorporated into the minilesson, which then adds at least twenty minutes). Children then bring their reading bins, holding the books they are currently reading, to their assigned "reading nooks." As children read independently, a teacher moves among them, conferring individually with a child or bringing a small group of readers together for a ten- to fifteen-minute guided reading or strategy lesson. After children have read independently for about half an hour, teachers ask them to meet with their partners to talk about their books and their reading. After the partners meet, teachers often call all the readers in a class together for a brief "share session" (Calkins 2001). The following table shows some general guidelines for the length of both independent reading and the partnership talks based on the approximate level of the texts students are reading in the class.

How Long Might a Class Have Independent Reading and Partnership Talk?		
Class Reading Level	*Independent Reading Duration*	*Partnership Talk Duration*
Library A	10 minutes	20 minutes
Library B	15 minutes	20 minutes
Library C	20 minutes	20 minutes
Library D	30 minutes	10 minutes
Library E	40 minutes	10 minutes
Library F	40 minutes	10 minutes
Library G	40 minutes	10 minutes

Periodically, the structure of the minilesson, independent reading, partnership, and then share time is replaced by a structure built around book clubs or "junior" book clubs, our own, reading-intensive version of reading centers.

Minilessons

During a minilesson, the class gathers on the carpet to learn a strategy all readers can use not only during the independent reading workshop but also throughout their reading lives. The content of a minilesson comes, in part, from a teacher deciding that for a period of time, usually a month, he needs to focus his teaching on a particular aspect of reading. For example, many teachers begin the year by devoting a month to reading with stamina and understanding (Calkins 2001). During this unit, teachers might give several minilessons designed to help children choose books they can understand, and they might give others designed to help readers sustain their reading over time. Another minilesson might be designed to help readers make more time for reading in their lives or to help them keep a stack of books-in-waiting to minimize the interval between finishing one book and starting another.

The minilesson, then, often directs the work readers do during independent reading. If the minilessons show students how to make sure their ideas are grounded in the details of the text, teachers may establish an interval between independent reading time and partnership conversations when children can prepare for a talk about their text by marking relevant sections that support their ideas.

Sometimes minilessons are self-standing, separate from the interactive read aloud. Other minilessons include and provide a frame for the day's read aloud. For example, the teacher may read aloud a book and direct that day's talk in a way that demonstrates the importance of thinking about a character's motivations. Then children may be asked to think in similar ways about their independent reading books. Perhaps, when they meet with a partner at the end of reading, the teacher will say, "Please talk about the motivations that drive your central characters and show evidence in the text to support your theories."

Conferences

While children read, a teacher confers. Usually this means that the teacher starts by sitting close to a child as he or she continues reading, watching for external behaviors that can help assess the child. After a moment or two, the teacher usually says, "Can I interrupt?" and conducts a few-minute-long conversation while continuing the assessment. A teacher will often ask, "Can you read to me a bit?" and this, too, informs any hunches about a child and his or her strengths and needs as a reader. Finally, teachers intervene to lift the level of what the child is doing. The following table offers some examples of this.

General Examples of the Conferring That Can Help Readers Grow	
If, in reading, the child is . . .	*Teachers might teach by . . .*
able to demonstrate a basic understanding of the text	nudging the child to grow deeper insights, perhaps by asking: ■ Do any pages (parts) go together in a surprising way? ■ Why do you think the author wrote this book? What is he (she) trying to say? ■ If you were to divide the book into different sections, what would they be? ■ How are you changing as a reader? How are you reading this book differently than you've read others? ■ What's the work you are doing as you read this?
talking mostly about the smallest, most recent details read	generalizing what kind of book it is, giving the child a larger sense of the genre. If it is a story, we can ask questions that will work for any story: ■ How is the main character changing? ■ How much time has gone by? ■ What is the setting for the story? If the text is a non-narrative, we could ask: ■ What are the main chunks (or sections) in the text? ■ How would you divide this up? ■ How do the parts of this text go together? ■ What do you think the author is trying to teach you?
clearly enthralled by the story	asking questions to help the reader tap into the best of this experience to use again later. ■ What do you think it is about this story that draws you in? ■ You seem really engaged, so I'm wondering what can you learn about this reading experience that might inform you as you read other books. ■ When I love a book, as you love this one, I sometimes find myself reading faster and faster, as if I'm trying to gulp it down. But a reading teacher once told me this quote. "Some people think a good book is one you can't put down, but me, I think a good book is one you must put down—to muse over, to question, to think about." Could you set some bookmarks throughout this book and use them to pause in those places to really think and even to write about this book? Make one of those places right now, would you?

Partnerships

When many of us imagine reading, we envision a solitary person curled up with a book. The truth is that reading is always social, always embedded in talk with others. If I think about the texts I am reading now in my life and ask myself, "Is there something *social* about my reading of those texts?" I quickly realize that I read texts because people have recommended them. I read anticipating conversations I will soon have with others, and I read noticing things in this one text that I have discussed with others. My reading, as is true for many readers, is multilayered and sharper because of the talk that surrounds it.

There are a lot of reasons to organize reading time so that children have opportunities to talk with a reading partner. Partner conversations can highlight the social elements of reading, making children enjoy reading more. Talking about books also helps children have more internal conversations (thoughts) as they read. Putting thoughts about texts out into the world by speaking them allows other readers to engage in conversation, in interpretations and ideas, and can push children to ground their ideas in the text, to revise their ideas, to lengthen and deepen their ideas.

For young children, talking with a partner usually doubles the actual unit of time a child spends working with books. In many primary classrooms, the whole class reads and then the teacher asks every child to meet with a partner who can read a similar level of book. Each child brings his bin of books, thus doubling the number of appropriate books available to any one child. The child who has already read a book talks about it with the other child, giving one partner a valuable and authentic reason to retell a book and another child an introduction to the book. Then the two readers discuss how they will read together. After the children read aloud together, the one book held between them as they sit hip to hip, there is always time for the partners to discuss the text. Sometimes, teachers offer students guidance in this conversation.

More proficient readers need a different sort of partnership because once a child can read short chapter books, there are few advantages to the child reading aloud often. Then too, by this time children can sustain reading longer. Typically in third grade, for example, individuals read independently for thirty minutes and then meet with partners for ten minutes to talk over the book. Again, the teacher often guides that conversation, sometimes by modeling—by entertaining with the whole-class read-aloud text—the sort of conversations she expects readers will have in their partnerships.

Book Clubs

Teaching children to read well has a great deal to do with teaching children to talk well about books, because the conversations children have in the air between one another become the conversations they have in their own minds as they read. Children who have talked in small groups about the role of the suitcase in Christopher Paul Curtis's book, *Bud, Not Buddy* will be far more apt to pause as they read another book, asking, "Might *this* object play a significant role in this book, like the suitcase did in *Bud, Not Buddy*?"

When we move children from partnership conversations toward small-group book clubs, we need to provide some scaffolding for them to lean on at first. This is because partnerships are generally easier for children to manage than small group conversations. It is also generally easier for students to read for thirty-minute reading sessions with ten-minute book talks than it is to read for a few days in a row and then sustain extended book talks, as they are expected to do in book clubs.

Children need some support as they begin clubs. One way to do this is to begin with small book club conversations about the read aloud book—the one book we know everyone will be prepared to talk about. Another way to get started with book clubs is for the teacher to suggest that children work in small groups to read multiple copies of, say, a mystery book. The teacher will plan to read a mystery book aloud to the class during the weeks they work in their clubs. Meanwhile, each group of approximately four readers will be reading one mystery that is at an appropriate level for them. The whole class works on and talks about the read-aloud mystery, and this work then guides the small group work. On one day, for example, after reading aloud the whole-class mystery, the teacher could immerse the class in talk about what it's like to read "suspiciously," suspecting everything and everyone. For a few days, the class can try that sort of reading as they listen to the read aloud. Meanwhile, when children disperse to their small groups to read their own mysteries, they can read these books "suspiciously."

Eventually the book clubs can become more independent. One small group of children might be reading several books by an author and talking about what they can learn from the vantage point of having read so many. Another group might read books that deal with a particular theme or subject. Either way, in the classrooms I know best, each book club lasts at least a few weeks. Teachers observe, and coach and teach into these talks, equipping kids with ways to write, talk, and think about texts. However, teachers neither dominate the clubs nor steer readers toward a particular preordained interpretation of a text. Instead, teachers steer readers toward ways of learning and thinking that can help them again and again, in reading after reading, throughout their lives.

Library **G** Contents Description

Library G consists of

I.	Independent Reading & Partner Reading			
	Chapter Books (Levels 10–14)	Level 10	27 Titles	31 Texts
		Level 11	34 Titles	40 Texts
		Level 12	99 Titles	108 Texts
		Level 13	57 Titles	60 Texts
		Level 14	26 Titles	26 Texts
	Nonfiction		68 Titles	68 Texts
	Picture Books		28 Titles	28 Texts
	Poetry		16 Titles	16 Texts
	Short Stories		14 Titles	14 Texts
II.	Guided Reading		8 Titles	32 Texts
III.	Book Club/Literature Circle		5 Titles	30 Texts
IV.	Author Study		10 Titles	20 Texts
V.	Read Alouds		9 Titles	9 Texts
VI.	Books to Support the Writing Process		2 Titles	2 Texts
	Total Number of Texts in Library G		**403 Titles**	**484 Texts**

(Because of substitutions made in the ordering process, this number may not be precise.)

Group Description	Level	#	Author	Title	ISBN	Publisher	Quantity	Heinemann Write-Up
CORE								
Independent Reading		1	Spinelli, Jerry	Stargirl	679886370	Alfred A. Knopf	1	Y
	10	1	Blume, Judy	Otherwise Known as Sheila the Great	440467012	Bantam Doubleday Dell	1	Y
		2	Boyd, Candy Dawson	Different Beat, A	140365826	Penguin Publishing	1	
		3	Christopher, Matt	Lucky Baseball Bat, The	316142603	Little Brown & Co	1	
		4	Dahl, Roald	Twits, The	141301074	Penguin Puffin	1	Y
		5	Ferguson, Dwayne	Kid Caramel Private Investigator, The (Vol. 1)	940975718	Just Us Books	1	
		6	Kinsey-Warnock, Natalie	Night the Bells Rang, The	141309865	Penguin Putnam	1	
		7	Manes, Stephen	Chocolate Covered Ants	590409611	Scholastic Inc.	1	Y
		8	Martin, Jacqueline Briggs	Snowflake Bentley	395861624	Houghton Mifflin	1	Y
		9	Prather, Ray	Fish and Bones	60251212	Harper Collins	1	
		10	Salisbury, Graham	Under the Blood-Red Sun	440411394	Bantam Doubleday Dell	1	
		11	Schultz, Irene	Circus Mystery, The	780272447	Wright Group	1	
		12	Spinelli, Jerry	School Daze Series/Report to the Principal's Office	590462776	Scholastic Inc.	1	
		13	Thayer, Ernest Lawrence	Casey at the Bat	590467336	Putnam Publishing	1	
	11	1	Banks, Lynne Reid	Indian in the Cupboard Series/ Indian in the Cupboard, The	380600129	William Morrow & Co	1	Y
		2	Bauer, Marion	On My Honor	440466334	Bantam Doubleday Dell	1	
		3	Brink, Carol Ryrie	Caddie Woodlawn	689713703	Simon & Schuster	1	
		4	Bruchac, Joseph	Eagle Song	141301694	Penguin Putnam	1	Y
		5	Dahl, Roald	Charlie & the Chocolate Factory	141301155	Penguin Putnam	1	
		6	Dahl, Roald	Esio Trot	141304642	Penguin Putnam	1	Y
		7	Myers, Walter Dean	Brown Angels	64434559	Harper Trophy	1	

Group Description	Level	#	Author	Title	ISBN	Publisher	Quantity	Heinemann Write-Up
		8	Paulsen, Gary	World of Adventure/Danger on Midnight River	440410282	Bantam Doubleday Dell	1	
		9	Paulsen, Gary	World of Adventure/Legend of Red Horse Cavern	440410231	Bantam Doubleday Dell	1	
		10	Peck, Robert	Soup	679892613	Random House	1	
		11	Pinkney, Andrea Davis	Silent Thunder	786804394	Hyperion Books	1	
		12	Wallace, Bill	Totally Disgusting!	671754165	Pocket Books	1	
	12	1	Alford, Jan	I Can't Believe I Have to Do This	698117859	Penguin Putnam	1	Y
		2	Babbitt, Natalie	Search for Delicious, The	374464537	Farrar Strauss & Giroux	1	Y
		3	Blume, Judy	It's Not the End of the World	440441587	Bantam Doubleday Dell	1	Y
		4	Boyd, Candy Dawson	Chevrolet Saturdays	140368590	Penguin Putnam	1	Y
		5	Brooks, Bruce	Wolfbay Wings/Woodsie, Again (#12)	64407292	Harper Collins	1	
		6	Burnett, Frances	Secret Garden, The	590433466	Scholastic Inc.	1	Y
		7	Byars, Betsy	Cracker Jackson	14031881X	Penguin Publishing	1	Y
		8	Clements, Andrew	Janitor's Boy	689818181	Simon & Schuster	1	
		9	Conly, Jane Leslie	What Happened on Planet Kid	805060650 (hc)	Henry Holt & Co	1	
		10	Cooper, Susan	Boggart, The	689801734	Simon & Schuster	1	Y
		11	Creech, Sharon	Bloomability	6440823X	Harper Collins	1	
		12	Creech, Sharon	Wanderer, The	60277300	Harper Collins	1	Y
		13	Cushman, Karen	Ballad of Lucy Whipple, The	64406849	Harper Collins	1	
		14	Cushman, Karen	Catherine Called Birdy	64405842	Harper Collins	1	
		15	Danziger, Paula	P.S. Longer Letter Later	590213113	Scholastic Inc.	1	
		16	Hamilton, Virginia	Cousins	590454366	Scholastic Inc.	1	
		17	Hesse, Karen	Music of Dolphins, The	590897985	Scholastic Inc.	1	Y
		18	Konigsburg, E.L.	From the Mixed-Up Files of Mrs. Basil E. Frankweiler	440431808	Bantam Doubleday Dell	1	Y

Group Description	Level	#	Author	Title	ISBN	Publisher	Quantity	Heinemann Write-Up
		19	Lewis, C.S.	Chronicles of Narnia/Lion, the Witch and the Wardrobe	64409422	Harper Trophy	1	Y
		20	Lewis, C.S.	Chronicles of Narnia/Magician's Nephew	64409430	Harper Trophy	1	
		21	Lewis, C.S.	Chronicles of Narnia/Prince Caspian	64409449	Harper Trophy	1	
		22	Lisle, Jane & Taylor	Afternoon of the Elves	698118065	Penguin Putnam	1	Y
		23	Lowry, Lois	Anastasia Again!	440400090	Dell Publishing	1	Y
		24	Lowry, Lois	Anastasia Krupnik	440408520	Bantam Doubleday Dell	1	Y
		25	Martin, Ann M.	California Diaries Series/Amalia	439095484	Scholastic Inc.	1	
		26	Martin, Ann M.	California Diaries Series/Dawn	590018469	Scholastic Inc.	1	Y
		27	Martin, Ann M.	California Diaries Series/Ducky	590298399	Scholastic Inc.	1	
		28	Nelson, Vaunda Micheaux	Mayfield Crossing	399223312	Putnam Publishing	1	
		29	Nina Bowden	Granny the Pag	140384472	Penguin Putnam	1	Y
		30	Paterson, Katherine	Flip Flop Girl	140376798	Penguin Putnam	1	Y
		31	Paterson, Katherine	Preacher's Boy	395838975	Clarion Books	1	
		32	Paulsen, Gary	Cookcamp, The	440407044	Bantam Doubleday Dell	1	Y
		33	Paulsen, Gary	Woodsong	590450522	Scholastic Inc.	1	
		34	Paulsen, Gary	Brian's Winter	440227194	Bantam Doubleday Dell	1	
		35	Pringle, Laurence P.	Animal Monsters	761450033	Marshall Cavendish, Inc.	1	Y
		36	Snicket, Lemony	Series of Unfortunate Events/Bad Beginning	64407667	Harper Collins	1	Y
		37	Spinelli, Jerry	Maniac Magee	64404242	Harper Trophy	1	Y
		38	Woodson, Jacqueline	Maizon at Blue Hill	440408997	Bantam Doubleday Dell	1	
	13	1	Alcott, Louisa M.	Little Women	140390693	Penguin Publishing	1	Y
		2	Alexander, Lloyd	Black Cauldron	440484839	Bantam Doubleday Dell	1	
		3	Alexander, Lloyd	Book of Three, The	440407028	Bantam Doubleday Dell	1	

Group Description	Level	#	Author	Title	ISBN	Publisher	Quantity	Heinemann Write-Up
		4	Alexander, Lloyd	Castle of Llyr	440411254	Bantam Doubleday Dell	1	
		5	Alexander, Lloyd	Gypsy Rizka	525461213	Dutton	1	
		6	Alexander, Lloyd	High King	440435749	Bantam Doubleday Dell	1	
		7	Alexander, Lloyd	Taran Wanderer	440484839	Bantam Doubleday Dell	1	
		8	Banks, Lynne Reid	Alice by Accident	380978652	William Morrow & Co	1	Y
		9	Bellairs, John	Dark Secret of Weatherend, The	14038006X	Viking Penguin	1	
		10	Brooks, Bruce	What Hearts	64471276	Harper Collins	1	
		11	Christopher, John	White Mountains, The	20427115	Macmillan Publishing	1	
		12	Cushman, Karen	Midwife's Apprentice	6440630X	Harper Collins	1	
		13	Flake, Sharon G.	Skin I'm In, The	786813075	Hyperion Books	1	Y
		14	George, Jean Craighead	My Side of the Mountain	140348107	Penguin Publishing	1	Y
		15	Giff, Patricia Reilly	Lilly's Crossing	440414539	Bantam Doubleday Dell	1	
		16	Griffin, Adele	Dive	786804408	Hyperion Books	1	Y
		17	Hermes, Patricia	Calling Me Home	380791005	Avon Books	1	
		18	Hickman, Janet	Jericho	688133983	Greenwillow Books	1	Y
		19	Hinton, S.E.	That was Then, This is Now	140389660	Viking Penguin	1	
		20	Johnson, Angela	Heaven	689822901	Simon & Schuster	1	Y
		21	King-Smith, Dick	Spider Sparrow	517800438	Crown Publishing	1	
		22	Konigsburg, E.L.	View from Saturday, The	68980993X	Simon & Schuster	1	Y
		23	Levine, Gail Carson	Ella Enchanted	64407055	Harper Trophy	1	Y
		24	Lowry, Lois	Gathering Blue	618055819	Houghton Mifflin	1	Y
		25	MacLachan, Patricia	Facts & Fictions of Minna Pratt	64402657	Harper Collins	1	
		26	McGraw, Eloise	Moorchild, The	590035584	Scholastic Inc.	1	Y
		27	Mohr, Nicholasa	Going Home	141306440	Penguin Publishing	1	
		28	Mohr, Nicholasa	In Nueva York	934770786	Arte Publico Press	1	
		29	Osborne, Mary Pope	Adaline Falling Star	43905947X	Scholastic Inc.	1	Y

Group Description	Level	#	Author	Title	ISBN	Publisher	Quantity	Heinemann Write-Up
		30	Paulsen, Gary	Nightjohn	440219361	Dell Publishing	1	Y
		31	Paulsen, Gary	Soldier's Heart	440228387	Bantam Doubleday Dell	1	Y
		32	Pullman, Philip	Clockwork: Or All Wound Up	590129988	Scholastic Inc.	1	Y
		33	Rowling, J.K.	Harry Potter Series/The Chamber of Secrets (#2)	59035342X	Scholastic Inc.	1	
		34	Rowling, J.K.	Harry Potter Series/The Prisoner of Azkaban (#3)	439136350	Scholastic Inc.	1	
		35	Rowling, J.K.	Harry Potter Series/The Sorcerer's Stone (#1)	59035342X	Scholastic Inc.	1	Y
		36	Soto, Gary	Pacific Crossing	590489968	Scholastic Inc.	1	
		37	Speare, Elizabeth George	Witch Of Blackbird Pond, The	440495962	Bantam Doubleday Dell	1	Y
		38	Spinelli, Jerry	Crash	679885501	Alfred A. Knopf	1	Y
		39	Taylor, Sydney	All of a Kind Family	440400597	Bantam Doubleday Dell	1	
		40	Taylor, Theodore	Cay, The	38000142X	William Morrow & Co	1	
		41	Warner, Sally	Sort of Forever	37580207X	Alfred A. Knopf	1	Y
		42	Woodson, Jacqueline	Between Madison & Palmetto	440410622	Bantam Doubleday Dell	1	
		43	Yep, Laurence	Hiroshima	590208330	Scholastic Inc.	1	Y
		44	Yolen, Jane	Devil's Arithmetic	140345353	Penguin Publishing	1	Y
	14	1	Brooks, Bruce	Vanishing	64472345	Harper Collins	1	Y
		2	Cooper, Susan	Dark is Rising Sequence/Over Sea, Under Stone	689840357	Simon & Schuster	1	Y
		3	Hamilton, Virginia	Bluish	590288792	Scholastic Inc.	1	Y
		4	Hamilton, Virginia	Mystery of Drear House, The Conclusion of the Dies Drear Chronicle	590956272	Greenwillow Books	1	
		5	Henkes, Kevin	Birthday Room, The	688167330	Greenwillow Books	1	Y
		6	Hesse, Karen	Letters from Rifka	440830508	Henry Holt & Co	1	Y
		7	Hesse, Karen	Time of Angels, A	786812095	Hyperion Books	1	Y

Group Description	Level	#	Author	Title	ISBN	Publisher	Quantity	Heinemann Write-Up
		8	Horvath, Polly	Trolls, The	374377871	Farrar Strauss & Giroux	1	Y
		9	Jacques, Brian	Redwall	441005489	Penguin Putnam	1	Y
		10	Johnson, Angela	Toning the Sweep	590481428	Scholastic Inc.	1	Y
		11	Lawson, Robert	Ben and Me	316517305	Little Brown & Co	1	Y
		12	L'Engle, Madeleine	Wrinkle in Time, A	440998050	Bantam Doubleday Dell	1	Y
		13	Lowry, Lois	Autumn Street	440403448	Bantam Doubleday Dell	1	Y
		14	Myers, Walter Dean	Hoops	440938848	Bantam Doubleday Dell	1	
		15	Myers, Walter Dean	Monster	380600129	Avon Books	1	Y
		16	Myers, Walter Dean.	Scorpions	64470660	Harper Collins	1	Y
		17	Naylor, Phyllis Reynolds	Sang Spell	689820062	Simon & Schuster	1	Y
		18	Peck, Robert	Day No Pigs Would Die, A	679853065	Random House	1	
		19	Pullman, Phillip	Subtle Knife, The	345413369	Ballantine Books	1	
		20	Taylor, Mildred	Let the Circle Be Unbroken	140348921	Penguin Publishing	1	
		21	Taylor, Mildred	Roll of Thunder, Hear My Cry	14034893X	Penguin Publishing	1	Y
		22	Tolkien, J.R.R.	Hobbit, The	345339681	Random House	1	Y
		23	Whelan, Gloria	Homeless Bird	60284544	Harper Collins	1	Y
		24	Woodson, Jacqueline	Lena	385323085	Delacorte Press	1	Y
Anthologies of Short Stories		1	Delacre, Lulu	Salsa Stories	590631187	Scholastic Inc.	1	Y
		2	Fleischman, Paul	Graven Images	64401863	Harper Collins	1	Y
		3	Fleischman, Paul	Seedfolks	64472078	Lee & Low Books	1	Y
		4	Gallo, Donald, ed.	Sixteen Short Stories: by Outstanding Writers for Young Adult Writers	440977576	Bantam Doubleday Dell	1	
		5	Grimes, Nikki	Jazmin's Notebook	141307021	Penguin Putnam	1	
		6	Hurwitz, Johanna	Birthday Surprises	688131948	William Morrow & Co	1	Y
		7	Myers, Walter Dean	145th Street: Short Stories	385321376 (hc)	Delacorte Press	1	

Group Description	Level	#	Author	Title	ISBN	Publisher	Quantity	Heinemann Write-Up
		8	Soto, Gary	Baseball in April & Other Stories	152025677	Harcourt Brace	1	Y
		9	Spinelli, Jerry	Library Card, The	590386336	Scholastic Inc.	1	Y
Teaching Writing		1	Cisneros, Sandra	House on Mango Street, The	679734775	Random House	1	Y
		2	Paulsen, Gary	Winter Room, The	440404541	Bantam Doubleday Dell	1	Y
Nonfiction		1	Denenberg, Barry	Stealing Home: Story of Jackie Robinson	590425609	Scholastic Inc.	1	Y
		2	Greenberg, Jan	Chuck Close Up Close	789426587	DK Publishing	1	Y
		3	Hausman, Gerald	Coyote Bead, The	1571749926	Hampton Roads	1	Y
		4	McDonough, Yona Zeldis	Sisters in Strength	8050061029	Henry Holt & Co	1	Y
		5	Murphy, Jim	Great Fire, The	590472674	Scholastic Inc.	1	Y
Picture Books		1	Alexander, Lloyd	Fortune-Tellers, The	140562338	Penguin Putnam	1	Y
		2	McKissack, Patricia	Mirandy & Brother Wind	679883339	Random House	1	Y
		3	Paterson, Katherine	King's Equal, the	6443396X	Harper Trophy	1	Y
		4	Steptoe, John	Mufaro's Beautiful Daughters	688040454	William Morrow & Co	1	Y
		5	Wood, Audrey	Moonflute	152553371	Harcourt Brace	1	Y
Poetry		1	Angelou, Maya	Life Doesn't Frighten Me	1556702884 (hc)	Stewart Tabori & Chang	1	
		2	Fleischman, Paul	Joyful Noise	64460932	Harper Collins	1	
		3	Nye, Naomi Shihab	I Feel a Little Jumpy Around You	689813414	Simon & Schuster	1	
		4	Rylant, Cynthia	Something Permanent	152770909	Harcourt Brace	1	
		5	Thomas, Joyce	Brown Honey in Broomwheat Tea	64434397	Harper Trophy	1	
Read-Aloud Texts		1	Babbitt, Natalie	Tuck Everlasting	374480125	Farrar Strauss & Giroux	1	Y
		2	Conly, Jane Leslie	While No One was Watching	6440787X	Harper Trophy	1	
		3	Cooney, Caroline	Burning Up	440226872	Bantam Doubleday Dell	1	
		4	Fenner, Carol	Yolanda's Genius	689813279	Simon & Schuster	1	Y
		5	Lasky, Kathryn	Monarchs	152552979	Harcourt Brace	1	Y

Group Description	Level	#	Author	Title	ISBN	Publisher	Quantity	Heinemann Write-Up
		6	Lowry, Lois	Giver, The	440219078	Bantam Doubleday Dell	1	
		7	MacLachlan, Patricia	Baby	440411459	Bantam Doubleday Dell	1	Y
		8	Morrison, Toni	Big Box, The	78682364X	Hyperion Books	1	Y
		9	Rylant, Cynthia	Missing May	440408652	Bantam Doubleday Dell	1	Y
		10	Sachar, Louis	Holes	440414806	Bantam Doubleday Dell	1	Y

MODULE 1: More Independent Reading: Filling in the Lower Portion of the Library

Group Description	Level	#	Author	Title	ISBN	Publisher	Quantity	Heinemann Write-Up
	10	1	Cherry, Lynne	River Ran Wild: An Environmental History, A	152005420	Harcourt Brace	1	
		2	Creech, Sharon	Pleasing the Ghost	64406865	Harper Trophy	1	
		3	Davis, Ossie	Just Like Martin	140370951	Penguin Puffin	1	
		4	Hill, Kirkpatrick	Toughboy and Sister	689839782	Simon & Schuster	1	
		5	Morris, Judy	Nightwalkers	60272007	Harper Collins	1	
		6	Porter, Connie Rose	American Girls Collection/Meet Addy	1562470752	Pleasant Company	1	
		7	Sandler, Martin	Pioneers			1	
		8	Siegelson, Kim	Terrible, Wonderful Tellin' at Hog Hammock, The	60248777	Harper Collins	1	
		9	Sobol, Donald	Encyclopedia Brown Series/E B and the Case of the Dead Eagles	553481673	Bantam Doubleday Dell	1	
		10	Sobol, Donald	More Two-Minute Mysteries	590447882	Scholastic Inc.	1	
	11	1	Boyd, Candy Dawson	Circle of Gold	590432664	Scholastic Inc.	1	Y
		2	Ellerbee, Linda	Get Real Series/Girl Reporter Rocks Polls 3	64407608	Harper Collins	1	
		3	Giff, Patricia Reilly	Case of the Cool Itch Kid, The	440401992	Bantam Doubleday Dell	1	
		4	Henkes, Kevin	Zebra Wall, The	140329692		1	
		5	Howe, James	Nighty-Nightmare			1	
		6	Jackel, Molly	Fast Breaks WNBA Superstars	590120816	Scholastic Inc.	1	

Group Description	Level	#	Author	Title	ISBN	Publisher	Quantity	Heinemann Write-Up
		7	Jackson, Donna	Bone Detectives, The	316829617	Little Brown & Co	1	
		8	Lenski, Lois	Strawberry Girl	64405850	Harper Collins	1	
		9	Naylor, Phyllis Reynolds	Beetles, Lightly Toasted	440401437	Bantam Doubleday Dell	1	
		10	Skolsky, Mindy	Love from Your Friend Hannah	64407462	Harper Trophy	1	
		11	Snedden, Robert	Yuck! A Big Book of Little Horrors	689806760		1	
		12	Sobol, Donald	Two-Minute Mysteries			1	
		13	Taylor, Mildred	Gold Cadillac, The	140389636	Penguin Publishing	1	
11; 12; 13		1	Facklam, Margery	And Then There was One	316259829	Sierra Club Books	1	
	12	1	Avi	Ereth's Birthday	380977346	Harper Collins	1	Y
		2	Cooper, Susan	Boggart and the Monster, The	689822863	Simon & Schuster	1	
		3	Fletcher, Ralph	Live Writing	380797011	Avon Books	1	
		4	Fox, Paula	Maurice's Room	689712162	Simon & Schuster	1	
		5	Getz, David	Thin Air	64404226	Harper Collins	1	
		6	Hamilton, Virginia	Second Cousins	590473697	Scholastic Inc.	1	
		7	Juster, Norton	Phantom Tollbooth	394820371	Random House	1	Y
		8	Paulson, Gary	Brian's Return	385325002	Bantam Doubleday Dell	1	
		9	Snicket, Lemony	Series of Unfortunate Events/ Reptile Room	64407675	Harper Collins	1	Y
		10	Snicket, Lemony	Series of Unfortunate Events/ Wide Window	64407683	Harper Collins	1	
		11	Woodson, Jacqueline	Last Summer with Maizon	440405556	Dell Publishing	1	
		12	Yep, Laurence	Magic Paintbrush, The	60281995	Harper Collins	1	

MODULE 2: More Independent Reading: Filling in the Upper Portion of the Library

Group Description	Level	#	Author	Title	ISBN	Publisher	Quantity	Heinemann Write-Up
		1	Travers, Pamela	Mary Poppins	152017178	Harcourt Brace	1	Y
	12	1	Brooks, Bruce	Throwing Smoke	60289724	Harper Collins	1	
		2	Brooks, Bruce	Wolfbay Wings/Reed (#9)	60280557	Harper Collins	1	

Group Description	Level	#	Author	Title	ISBN	Publisher	Quantity	Heinemann Write-Up
		3	Dahl, Roald	Witches, The	141301104	Penguin Putnam	1	Y
		4	Danziger, Paula	Cat Ate My Gymsuit, The	698116844	Putnam Publishing	1	
		5	Erickson, Gerald L.	Hank the Cowdog/It's a Dog's Life (#3)	141303794	Gulf Publishing Company	1	
		6	Erickson, John	Hank the Cowdog Series/The Further Adventures of Hank the Cowdog (#2)	141303786	Penguin Publishing	1	
		7	Erickson, John	Hank the Cowdog Series/The Original Adventures of Hank the Cowdog (#1)	141303778	Penguin Publishing	1	
		8	Fitzhugh, Louise	Harriet the Spy	64403319	Harper Collins	1	
		9	Herman, Hank	Super Hoops/In Your Face	553482742	Bantam Doubleday Dell	1	
		10	Herman, Hank	Super Hoops/Out of Bounds	553484761	Bantam Doubleday Dell	1	
		11	Murphy, Jim	Call of the Wolves, The	590419404	Scholastic Inc.	1	
		12	Myers, Walter Dean	Me, Mop & the Moondance Kid	440403960	Delacorte Press	1	
		13	Paulsen, Gary	Amos Gets Famous	440407494	Bantam Doubleday Dell	1	
		14	Paulsen, Gary	Amos's Killer Concert Caper	440409896	Bantam Doubleday Dell	1	
		15	Stolz, Mary	Ballad of the Civil War, A	64420884	Harper Trophy	1	
		16	Van Draanen, Wendelin	Sammy Keyes/and the Skeleton Man	375800549	Alfred A. Knopf	1	
	13	1	Cameron, Ann	Secret Life of Amanda K. Woods, The	141306424	Penguin Putnam	1	
		2	Dorris, Michael	Morning Girl	786813725	Hyperion Books	1	
		3	Edwards, Julie	Last of the Really Great Whangdoodles, The	64403149	Harper Trophy	1	
		4	Gantos, Jack	Joey Pigza Swallowed the Key	64408337 (pbk)	Harper Trophy	1	
		5	Ibbotson, Eva	Secret of Platform 13, The	141302860	Puffin	1	Y
		6	Paterson, Katherine	Lyddie	140373896	Penguin Putnam	1	

Group Description	Level	#	Author	Title	ISBN	Publisher	Quantity	Heinemann Write-Up
		7	Paulsen, Gary	Call Me Francis Tuckett	440412706	Bantam Doubleday Dell	1	
		8	Raskin, E.	Westing Game			1	
		9	Schlein, Miriam	Year of the Panda, The	64403661	Crowell	1	
		10	Van Draanen, Wendelin	How I Survived Being a Girl	6440725X	Harper Trophy	1	
	13; 14; 15	1	Fleischman, Paul	Bull Run	64405885	Harper Collins	1	
	14	1	Brooks, Bruce	Moves Make the Man, The	64405648	Harper Collins	1	
		2	Christopher, John	Tripods Trilogy/City of Gold and Lead	20427018	Macmillan Publishing	1	
		3	Cooney, Caroline	Face on the Milk Carton	440220653	Bantam Doubleday Dell	1	
		4	Cooper, Susan	Dark is Rising Sequence/Greenwitch	689840349	Simon & Schuster	1	Y
		5	Hamilton, Virginia	Girl Who Spun Gold, The	590473786	Scholastic	1	
		6	Hamilton, Virginia	M.C. Higgins the Great	68971694X	Simon & Schuster	1	
		7	Hesser, Terry Spencer	Kissing Doorknobs	440413141	Bantam Doubleday Dell	1	Y
		8	Jones, Tim Wynne	Maestro, The	140387056	Penguin Puffin	1	
		9	LeGuin, Ursula	Wizard of Earthsea, A	553262505	Bantam Doubleday Dell	1	
		10	L'Engle, Madeleine	Arm of the Starfish	644401117	Harper Collins	1	
		11	Myers, Walter Dean	Mouse Rap	64403564	Harper Collins	1	
		12	Naylor, Phyllis Reynolds	Jade Green	689820054	Simon & Schuster	1	
		13	O'Dell, Scott	Island of the Blue Dolphins	440940001	Bantam Doubleday Dell	1	Y
		14	Paterson, Katherine	Jacob Have I Loved	64403688	Harper Collins	1	
		15	Smith, Roland	Jaguar	786813121	Hyperion Books	1	Y
		16	Sperry, Armstrong	Call It Courage	590406116	Scholastic Inc.	1	Y
		17	Woodson, Jacqueline	I Hadn't Meant to Tell You This	440219604	Bantam Doubleday Dell	1	Y

MODULE 3: Multiple Copies for Small Group Work

Group Description	Level	#	Author	Title	ISBN	Publisher	Quantity	Heinemann Write-Up
	10	1	Christopher, Matt	Spike It!	316134015	Little Brown & Co	2	

Group Description	Level	#	Author	Title	ISBN	Publisher	Quantity	Heinemann Write-Up
		2	Giff, Patricia Reilly	Love from the 5th Grade Celebrity			2	
		3	Scieszka, Jon	Time Warp Trio Series/The Not So Jolly Roger	590981242	Scholastic Inc.	2	
		4	Spinelli, Jerry	School Daze Series/Do the Funky Pickle	59045448X	Scholastic Inc.	2	
	10; 11; 12	1	Markle, Sandra	Outside & Inside Spiders	689826834	Aladdin	2	
	11	1	Ellerbee, Linda	Get Real Series/Girl Reporter Snags Crush!	64407586	Harper Collins	2	Y
		2	Henkes, Kevin	Sun and Spoon	141300957	Penguin Puffin	2	Y
		3	Mohr, Nicholasa	All for the Better: A Story of El Barrio	811480607	Steck-Vaughn	2	
		4	Park, Barbara	Operation: Dump the Chump	394825926	Alfred A. Knopf	2	
	12	1	Blume, Judy	Are You There God? It's Me Margaret	440904196	Bantam Doubleday Dell	2	Y
		2	Fox, Paula	Monkey Island	440407702	Yearling Books	2	Y
		3	Hansen, Joyce	Gift Giver, The	89919852X	Clarion Books	2	Y
		4	Paulson, Gary	My Life in Dog Years	440414717	Bantam Doubleday Dell	2	
		5	Van Draanen, Wendelin	Sammy Keyes/and the Sisters of Mercy	679888527	Random House	2	
	13	1	Choi, Sook Nyul	Year of Impossible Goodbyes	440407591	Dell Publishing	2	
		2	Erdrich, Louise	Birchbark House, The	786803002	Hyperion Books	2	
		3	George, Jean Craighead	Julie of the Wolves	64400581	Harper Trophy	2	Y
		4	Getz, David	Frozen Girl	805051538	Henry Holt & Co	2	
		5	Klise, Kate	Regarding the Fountain	380793474	Avon Books	2	
		6	Philbrick, Rodman	Max the Mighty	590579649	Scholastic Inc.	2	
	14	1	Bloor, Edward	Tangerine	15201246X	Harcourt Brace	2	Y
		2	Blume, Judy	Deenie	440932599	Bantam Doubleday Dell	2	Y
		3	Cooper, Susan	Dark is Rising Sequence/Dark is Rising	689829833	Simon & Schuster	2	Y

Group Description	Level	#	Author	Title	ISBN	Publisher	Quantity	Heinemann Write-Up
		4	Greene, Bette	Philip Hall Likes Me, I Reckon Maybe	141303123	Penguin Publishing	2	
		5	O'Dell, Scott	My Name is Not Angelica	440403790	Bantam Doubleday Dell	2	
		6	Voigt, Cynthia	Homecoming	449702545	Ballantine Books	2	
MODULE 4: Enrichment								
Author Studies		1	Polacco, Patricia	Babushka Baba Yaga	69811633X	Putnam Publishing	2	
		2	Polacco, Patricia	Butterfly, The	399231706	Penguin Putnam	2	Y
		3	Polacco, Patricia	Mrs. Katz & Tush	440409365	Bantam Doubleday Dell	2	Y
		4	Polacco, Patricia	Pink and Say	399226710	Putnam Publishing	2	Y
		5	Polacco, Patricia	Thank You Mr. Falker	399231668	Penguin Putnam	2	Y
		6	Soto, Gary	Crazy Weekend	590478141	Scholastic Inc.	2	Y
		7	Soto, Gary	Neighborhood Odes	590473352	Scholastic Inc.	2	
		8	Soto, Gary	Off and Running	385321813	Delacorte Press	2	
		9	Soto, Gary	Skirt, The	440409241	Bantam Doubleday Dell	2	
		10	Soto, Gary	Summer Life, A	440210240	Bantam Doubleday Dell	2	
Memoir		1	Byers, Betsy	Moon and I, The	688137040	William Morrow & Co	1	
		2	Caines, Jeannette Franklin	Just Us Women	64430561	Harper Collins	1	Y
		3	Santiago, Esmeralda	When I was Puerto Rican	679756760	Vintage Books	1	Y
Nonfiction		1	Ammon, Richard	Conestoga Wagons	823414752	Holiday House	1	Y
		2	Bishop, Nic	Digging for Bird-Dinosaurs	1395960568	Houghton Mifflin	1	Y
		3	Burleigh, Robert	Flight	698114256	Penguin Putnam	1	Y
		4	Getz, David	Frozen Man	805046453	Henry Holt & Co	1	
		5	Govenar, Allen	Osceola: Memories of a Sharecropper's Daughter	786823577	Hyperion Books	1	Y
Qualities of Good Writing		1	Jimenez, Francisco	Circuit, The: Stories from the Life of a Migrant Child	826317979	Univ. of New Mexico Press	1	
		2	MacLachlan, Patricia	What You Know First	64434923	Harper Trophy	1	Y

Group Description	Level	#	Author	Title	ISBN	Publisher	Quantity	Heinemann Write-Up
		3	Manning, Mick	Ruined House, A	1564029360	Candlewick Press	1	
		4	Merriam, Eve	Wise Woman and Her Secret, The	689823819	Simon & Schuster	1	Y
Short Stories		1	Cisneros, Sandra	Woman Hollering Creek	679738568	Vintage Books	1	
		2	Hamilton, Virginia	Her Stories: African American Folktales, Fairy Tales and True Tales	590473700	Scholastic Inc.	1	
		3	Jones, Diane Wynne	Believing is Seeing	688168434	Greenwillow Books	1	
		4	Richardson, Sandy	Girl Who Ate Chicken Feet & Other Stories	803722559	Dial Books	1	
		5	Wynne-Jones, Tim	Some of the Kinder Planets	531094510	Orchard Books	1	Y

MODULE 5: Multiple Copies for Book Clubs

Group Description	Level	#	Author	Title	ISBN	Publisher	Quantity	Heinemann Write-Up
		1	Yolen, Jane	Wings	152015671	Harcourt Brace	4	
	10	1	Blume, Judy	Blubber	440407079	Bantam Doubleday Dell	4	
		2	Osborne, Mary Pope	Spider Kane/Mystery at Jumbo Night Crawler's	679808566	Random House	4	
	11	1	Hurwitz, Johanna	Baseball Fever	380732556	William Morrow & Co	4	
		2	Paulsen, Gary	World of Adventure/Creature of Black Water Lake	440412110	Bantam Doubleday Dell	4	
	12	1	Byars, Betsy	Cracker Jackson	14031881X	Penguin Publishing	4	Y
		2	Hansen, Joyce	Yellow Bird and Me	395553881	Clarion Books	4	
		3	Henkes, Kevin	Words of Stone	140366016	Penguin Putnam	4	
	13	1	Curtis, Christopher Paul	Watsons Go to Birmingham, The	440414121	Bantam Doubleday Dell	4	Y
		2	Holt, Kimberly Willis	My Louisiana Sky	440415705	Random House	4	Y
	14	1	Lowry, Lois	Autumn Street	440403448	Bantam Doubleday Dell	4	Y
		2	Voigt, Cynthia	Dicey's Song	449702766	Random House	4	Y
		3	Wolff, Virginia	Bat 6	590897993	Scholastic Inc.	4	

Group Description	Level	#	Author	Title	ISBN	Publisher	Quantity	Heinemann Write-Up
MODULE 6: Nonfiction								
		1	Arnold, Caroline	Killer Whale	688120296	William Morrow & Co	1	
		2	Batten, Mary	Anthropologist	618083685	Houghton Mifflin	1	
		3	Getz, David	Life on Mars	80503708X	Henry Holt & Co	1	
		4	Hoose, Philip M.	We Were There Too!	374382522	Farrar, Straus & Giroux,	1	
		5	Mochizuki, Ken	Basball Saved Us	590808052	Scholastic Inc.	1	Y
		6	Parker, Nancy Winslow	President's Cabinet & How It Grew, The	64461319	Harper Trophy	1	Y
		7	Pollard, M.	Amazing Structures	76070290X	Barnes & Noble Books	1	
		8	Settel, Joanne	Exploding Ants	689817398	Simon & Schuster	1	Y
		9	Stanley, Jerry	Digger	517709511	Crown Publishing	1	
		10	Thomas, Joyce	I Have Heard of a Land	64436179	Harper Collins	1	Y
		11	Yee, Paul	Tales from Gold Mountain: Stories of the Chinese in the New World	888990987	Everbest Printing Co. Ltd.	1	
	10; 11; 12	1	Aronsky, Jim	Wild and Swampy	688171192	Harper Collins	1	
		2	Cobb, Vicki	Dirt and Grime	590926667	Scholastic Inc.	1	
		3	Jenkins, Steve	Hottest, Coldest, Highest, Deepest	395899990	Houghton Mifflin	1	
		4	Lewin, Ted	Elephant Quest	688141110	Harper Collins	1	
	11; 12; 13	1	Krull, Kathleen	Lives of the Athletes	152008063	Harcourt Brace	1	Y
		2	Lauber, Patricia	Hurricanes	590474065	Scholastic Inc.	1	Y
		3	Lewin, Ted & Betsy	Gorilla Walk	688165095	Lothrop Lee & Shepard	1	Y
		4	Monceaux, Morgan	My Heroes, My People	374307709	Farrar Strauss & Giroux	1	
		5	O'Connor, Jim	Jackie Robinson & the Story of All Black Baseball	394824563	Random House	1	Y
		6	Pinkney, Andrea Davis	Let It Shine: Stories of Black Women Freedom Fighters	15201005X	Harcourt Brace	1	

Group Description	Level	#	Author	Title	ISBN	Publisher	Quantity	Heinemann Write-Up
		7	Pringle, Laurence	Extraordinary Life, An: The Story of a Monarch Butterfly	531300021	Orchard Books	1	
	12	1	Hughes, Langston	First Book of Jazz	880015527	Harper Collins	1	
	12; 13; 14	1	Dewey, Jennifer Owings	Mud Matters	761450149	Cavendish	1	
		2	Freedman, Russell	Immigrant Kids	590465651	Scholastic Inc.	1	Y
		3	Jarrow, Gail	Naked Mole Rats	1575050285	Lerner Publishing Group	1	
		4	Lasky, Kathryn	Think Like an Eagle			1	
		5	Peck, Ira	Life and Words of Martin Luther King, Jr., The	590438271	Scholastic Inc.	1	Y
	13	1	Burleigh, Robert	Black Whiteness: Admiral Byrd Alone in the Antarctic	68981299X	Simon & Schuster	1	
		2	Murphy, Jim	Blizzard!	590673092	Scholastic Inc.	1	
	13; 14; 15	1	Armstrong, Jennifer	Spirit of Endurance: True Story of the Shackleton Expedition to the Antarctic	517800918	Crown Publishing	1	Y
		2	Bachrach, Susan	Tell Them We Remember: The Story of the Holocaust	316074845	Little Brown & Co	1	
		3	Bartoletti, Susan Campbell	Kids on Strike!	395888921 (hc)	Houghton Mifflin	1	
		4	Colman, Penny	Girls: The History of Growing Up Female in America	590371290	Scholastic Inc.	1	
		5	Cox, Clinton	Come All You Brave Soldiers: Blacks in the Revolutionary War	590475762 (hc)	Scholastic Inc.	1	
		6	Freedman, Russell	Life and Death of Crazy Horse, The	823412199	Holiday House	1	
		7	Freedman, Russell	Wright Brothers, The	82341082X	Holiday House	1	
		8	McKissack, Patricia	Black Diamond: The Story of the Negro Baseball Leagues	59068213X	Scholastic Inc.	1	
		9	McKissack, Patricia	Black Hands, White Sails	590483137	Scholastic Inc.	1	

Group Description	Level	#	Author	Title	ISBN	Publisher	Quantity	Heinemann Write-Up
MODULE 7: More Great Books								
		1	Anderson, Janet	Going Through the Gate	014130698X	Penguin Putnam	1	
		2	Anderson, Laurie Halse	Speak	374371520 (hc)	Farrar Strauss & Giroux	1	Y
		3	Buck, Pearl	Big Wave, The	64401715	Harper Collins	1	Y
		4	Fletcher, Susan	Shadow Spinner	689830513	Simon & Schuster	1	
		5	Jiang, Ji Li	Red Scarf Girl	64462080	Harper Trophy	1	
		6	Peck, Richard	Long Way From Chicago, A	141303522	Penguin Putnam	1	
		7	Pullman, Philip	Golden Compass, The	679893105	Alfred A. Knopf	1	Y
		8	Rylant, Cynthia	I Had Seen Castles	152380035	Harcourt Brace	1	
		9	Snicket, Lemony	Series of Unfortunate Events/ Austere Academy	64408639	Harper Collins	1	Y
		10	Snicket, Lemony	Series of Unfortunate Events/ The Miserable Mill	64407691	Harper Collins	1	Y
		11	Tashjian, Janet	Multiple Choice	805060863	Henry Holt & Co	1	
		12	Woodson, Jacqueline	Miracle's Boys	399231137	Putnam	1	Y

Benchmark Books for Each Text Level

TC Level	Benchmarks: Books that Represent Each Level
1	*A Birthday Cake* (Cowley) *I Can Write* (Williams) *The Cat on the Mat* (Wildsmith)
2	*Rain* (Kaplan) *Fox on the Box* (Gregorich)
3	*It Looked Like Spilt Milk* (Shaw) *I Like Books* (Browne) *Mrs. Wishy-Washy* (Cowley)
4	*Rosie's Walk* (Hutchins) *The Carrot Seed* (Krauss) *Cookie's Week* (Ward)
5	*George Shrinks* (Joyce) *Goodnight Moon* (Brown) *Hattie and the Fox* (Fox)
6	*Danny and the Dinosaur* (Hoff) *Henry and Mudge* (Rylant)
7	*Nate the Great* (Sharmat) *Meet M&M* (Ross)
8	*Horrible Harry* (Kline) *Pinky and Rex* (Howe) Arthur Series (Marc Brown)
9	*Amber Brown* (Danziger) *Ramona Quimby, Age 8* (Cleary)
10	*James and the Giant Peach* (Dahl) *Fudge-A-Mania* (Blume)
11	*Shiloh* (Naylor) *The Great Gilly Hopkins* (Paterson)
12	*Bridge to Terabithia* (Paterson) *Baby* (MacLachlan)
13	*Missing May* (Rylant) *Where the Red Fern Grows* (Rawls)
14	*A Day No Pigs Would Die* (Peck) *Scorpions* (Myers)
15	*The Golden Compass* (Pullman) *The Dark Is Rising* (Cooper) *A Wizard of Earthsea* (Le Guin)

Descriptions of Text Levels One Through Seven

TEXT LEVEL ONE

This level roughly corresponds to the following levels in other systems:

Reading Recovery© (RR) Levels 1–2
Developmental Reading Assessment (DRA) Levels A–2

Text Characteristics for TC Level One

- The font is large, clear, and is usually printed in black on a white background.

- There is exaggerated spacing between words and letters. (In some books, publishers have enlarged the print but have not adjusted the spacing which can create difficulties for readers.)

- There is usually a single word, phrase, or simple sentence on a page, and the text is patterned and predictable. For example, in the book *I Can Read*, once a child knows the title (which is ideally read to a Level One reader) it is not hard for the child to read "I can read the newspaper," "I can read the cereal box." These readers are regarded as "preconventional" because they rely on the illustrations (that support the meaning) and the sounds of language (or syntax) and not on graphophonics or word/letter cues to read a sentence such as, "I can read the newspaper."

- Usually each page contains two or three sight words. A Level One book *may* contain one illustrated word on a page (such as "Mom," "Dad," "sister," "cat") but it's just as easy for a child to read "I see my mom. I see my Dad. I see my sister. I see my cat." because the sight words give the child a way into the text.

- The words are highly supported by illustrations. No one would expect a Level One reader to solve the word "newspaper." We would, however, expect a child at this level to look at the picture and at the text and to read the word "newspaper."

- Words are consistently placed in the same area of each page, preferably top left or bottom left.

Characteristics of the Reader

Readers in this group will demonstrate most of these behaviors.

- Remember the pattern in a predictable text
- Use picture cues

- Use left to right directionality to read one or two lines of print

- Work on matching spoken words with printed words and self-correcting when these don't "come out even"

- Rely on the spaces between words to signify the end of one word and the beginning of another. These readers read the spaces as well as the words, as the words are at first black blobs on white paper

- Locate one or two known words on a page

Benchmarks

The following titles are representative of the kinds of books found in this grouping.

> *A Birthday Cake*, Joy Cowley
> *Cat on the Mat*, Brian Wildsmith
> *The Farm*, Literacy 2000/Stage 1
> *Growing Colors*, Bruce McMillan
> *I Can Write*, Rozanne Williams
> *Time for Dinner*, PM Starters

Assessment

The following titles can be used to determine if a reader is ready to move on to the next grouping of books. This type of assessment is most effective if the text is unfamiliar to the reader. If these titles will be used as assessment texts, they should *not* be part of the classroom library.

> *My Home*, Story Box
> *The Tree Stump*, Little Celebrations
> DRA Assessments A–2

We move children from Level One to Level Two books when they are consistently able to match one spoken word with one word written on the page. This means that they can point under words in a Level One book as they read and know when they haven't matched a spoken word to a written word by noticing that, at the end of the line, they still have words left on the page or they've run out of words. When children read multisyllabic words and compound words and point to multiple, instead of one, word on the page, we consider this a successful one-to-one match.

TEXT LEVEL TWO

This level roughly corresponds to the following levels in other systems:

> Reading Recovery© (RR) Levels 3–4
> Developmental Reading Assessment (DRA) Levels 3–4

Text Characteristics of TC Level Two

■ There are usually two lines of print on at least some of the pages in these books, and sometimes there are three. This means readers will become accustomed to making the return sweep to the beginning of a new line.

■ The texts are still patterned and predictable, but now the patterns tend to switch at intervals. Almost always, the pattern changes at the end of the book. The repeating unit may be as long as two sentences in length.

■ The font continues to be large and clear. The letters might not, however, be black against white although this is generally the case.

■ Children still rely on the picture but the pictures tend to give readers more to deal with; children need to search more in the picture to find help in reading the words.

■ High frequency words are still helpful and important. The sentences in Level One books tend to begin with 2 to 3 high frequency words, for example, "I like to run. I like to jump." At this level, the pages are more apt to begin with a single high frequency word and then include words that require picture support and attention to first letters, for example, "A mouse has a long tail. A bear has a short tail."

■ Sentences are more varied, resulting in texts that include a full range of punctuation.

Characteristics of the Reader

Readers in this group will demonstrate most of these behaviors.

■ Get the mouth ready for the initial sound of a word

■ Use left to right directionality as well as a return sweep to another line of print

■ Locate one or two known words on a page

■ Monitor for meaning: check to make sure it makes sense

Benchmarks

The following titles are representative of the kinds of books found in this grouping.

All Fall Down, Brian Wildsmith
I Went Walking, Sue Williams
Rain, Robert Kalan
Shoo, Sunshine

Assessment

The following titles can be used to determine if a reader is ready to move on to the next grouping. This type of assessment is most effective if the text is unfamiliar to a reader. If these titles will be used as assessment texts, they should *not* be part of the classroom library.

The Bus Ride, Little Celebrations, DRA 3
Fox on the Box, School Zone, DRA 4

We generally move children from Level Two to Level Three texts when they know how to use the pictures and the syntax to generate possibilities for the next word, when they attend to the first letters of unknown words. These readers will also read and rely on high frequency words such as *I, the, a, to, me, mom, the child's name, like, love, go*, and *and*.

TEXT LEVEL THREE

This level roughly corresponds to the following levels in other systems:

Reading Recovery© (RR) Levels 5–8
Developmental Reading Assessment (DRA) Levels 6–8

Text Characteristics of TC Level Three

It is important to note that this grouping includes a wide range of levels. This was done deliberately because at this level, readers should be able to select "just right" books for themselves and be able to monitor their own reading.

- Sentences are longer and readers will need to put their words together in order to take in more of the sentence at a time. When they are stuck, it's often helpful to nudge them to reread and try again.

- The pictures are not as supportive as they've been. It's still helpful for children to do picture walks prior to reading an unfamiliar text, but now the goal is less about surmising what words the page contains and more about seeing an overview of the narrative.

- Readers must rely on graphophonics across the whole word. If readers hit a wall at this level, it's often because they're accustomed to predicting words based on a dominant pattern and using the initial letters (only) to confirm their predictions. It takes readers a while to begin checking the print closely enough to adjust their expectations.

- Children will need to use sight words to help with unknown words, using parts of these familiar words as analogies, helping them unlock the unfamiliar words.

- The font size and spacing are less important now.

- Words in the text begin to include contractions. We can help children read these by urging them to look all the way across a word.

Characteristics of the Reader

Readers in this group will demonstrate most of these behaviors.

- Reread and self-correct

- Read with some fluency

- Cross check one cue against another

- Monitor for meaning: check to make sure what has been read makes sense and sounds right

- Recognize common chunks of words

Benchmarks

The following titles are representative of the kinds of books found in this grouping.

Bears in the Night Stan and Jan, Berenstain
The Chick and the Duckling, Ginsburg
It Looked Like Spilt Milk, Charles G. Shaw
Mrs. Wishy-Washy, Joy Cowley

Assessment

The following titles can be used to determine if a reader is ready to move on to the next grouping. This type of assessment is most effective if the text is unfamiliar to a reader. If these titles will be used as assessment texts, they should *not* be part of the classroom library.

Bread, Story Box, DRA 6
Get Lost Becka, School Zone, DRA 8

We move a child to Level Four books if that child can pick up an unfamiliar book like *Bread* or *It Looked Like Spilt Milk* and read it with a little difficulty, but with a lot of independence and with strategies. This reader should know to reread when she is stuck, to use the initial sounds in a word, to chunk word families within a word, and so on.

TEXT LEVEL FOUR

This level roughly corresponds to the following levels in other systems:

Reading Recovery© (RR) Levels 9–12
Developmental Reading Assessment (DRA) Levels 10–12

Text Characteristics of TC Level Four

- In general, the child who is reading Level Four books is able to do more of the same reading work he could do with texts at the previous level. This child reads texts that contain more words, lines, pages, and more challenging vocabulary.

- These texts contain even less picture support than earlier levels.

- Fluency and phrasing are very important for the Level Four reader. If children don't begin to read quickly enough, they won't be able to carry the syntax of the sentence along well enough to comprehend what they are reading.

- These books use brief bits of literary language. That is, in these books the mother may turn to her child and say, "We shall be rich."

- These books are more apt to have a plot (with characters, setting, problem, solution) and they tend to be less patterned than they were at the previous level.

Characteristics of the Reader

Readers in this group will demonstrate most of these behaviors.

- Reread and self-correct

- Read with fluency

- Integrate cues from meaning, structure, and visual sources

- Monitor for meaning: check to make sure what has been read makes sense, sounds right, and looks right

- Make some analogies from known words to figure out unknown words

- Read increasingly difficult chunks within words

Benchmarks

The following titles are representative of the kinds of books found in this grouping.

The Carrot Seed, Ruth Krauss
Cookie's Week, Cindy Ward
Rosie's Walk, Pat Hutchins
Titch, Pat Hutchins

Assessment

The following titles can be used to determine if a reader is ready to move on to the next grouping. This type of assessment is most effective if the text is unfamiliar to a reader. If these titles will be used as assessment texts, they should *not* be part of the classroom library.

Are You There Bear?, Ron Maris, DRA 10
The House in the Tree, Rigby PM Story Books
Nicky Upstairs and Downstairs, Harriet Ziefert
William's Skateboard, Sunshine, DRA 12

We move a child to Level Five books if that reader can independently use a variety of strategies to work through difficult words or parts of a text. The reader must be reading fluently enough to reread quickly, when necessary, so as to keep the flow of the story going. If a reader is reading very slowly, taking too much time to work through the hard parts, then this reader may not be ready to move on to the longer, more challenging texts in Level Five.

TEXT LEVEL FIVE

This level roughly corresponds to the following levels in other systems:

Reading Recovery© (RR) Levels 13–15
Developmental Reading Assessment (DRA) Level 14

Text Characteristics

- Sentences in Level Five books tend to be longer, more varied, and more complex than they were in previous levels.

- Many of the stories are retold folktales or fantasy-like stories that use literary or story language, such as: "Once upon a time, there once lived, a long, long time ago. . . ."

- Many books may be in a cumulative form in which text is added to each page, requiring the reader to read more and more text as the story unfolds, adding a new line with every page turn.

- The illustrations tend to be a representation of just a slice of what is happening in the text. For example, the text may tell of a long journey that a character has taken over time, but the picture may represent just the character reaching his destination.

- There will be more unfamiliar and sometimes complex vocabulary.

Characteristics of the Reader

Readers in this group will demonstrate most of these behaviors.

- Reread and self-correct regularly

- Read with fluency

- Integrate a balance of cues

- Monitor for meaning: check to make sure what has been read makes sense, sounds right, and looks right

- Demonstrate fluent phrasing of longer passages

- Use a repertoire of graphophonic strategies to problem solve through text

Benchmarks

The following titles are representative of the kinds of books found in this grouping.

George Shrinks, William Joyce
Goodnight Moon, Margaret Wise Brown
Hattie and the Fox, Mem Fox
Little Red Hen, Parkes

Assessment

The following titles can be used to determine if a reader is ready to move on to the next grouping. This type of assessment is most effective if the text is unfamiliar to a reader. If these titles will be used as assessment texts, they should *not* be part of the classroom library.

> *The Old Man's Mitten,* Bookshop, Mondo
> *Who Took the Farmer's Hat?,* Joan Nodset, DRA 14

We move children from Level Five to Level Six texts when they are consistently able to use a multitude of strategies to work through challenges quickly and efficiently. These challenges may be brought on by unfamiliar settings, unfamiliar language structures, unfamiliar words, and increased text length. The amount of text on a page and the length of a book should not be a hindrance to the reader who is moving on to Level Six. The reader who is ready to move on is also adept at consistently choosing appropriate books that will make her a stronger reader.

TEXT LEVEL SIX

This level roughly corresponds to the following levels in other systems:

> Reading Recovery© (RR) Levels 16–18
> Developmental Reading Assessment (DRA) Level 16

Text Characteristics of TC Level Six

- The focus of the book is evident at its start

- Descriptive language is used more frequently than before

- Dialogue often tells a large part of the story

- Texts may include traditional retellings of fairy tales and folktales

- Stories are frequently humorous

- Considerable amount of text is found on each page. A book in this grouping may be a picture book, or a simple chapter book. These books offer extended stretches of text.

- Texts are often simple chapter books, and often have episodic chapters in which each chapter stands as a story on its own

- Texts often center around just two or three main characters who tend to be markedly different from each other (a boy and a girl, a child and a parent)

- There is limited support from the pictures

- Texts includes challenging vocabulary

Characteristics of the Reader

Readers in this group will demonstrate most of these behaviors.

- Reread and self-correct regularly

- Read with fluency

- Integrate a balance of cues

- Demonstrate fluent phrasing of longer passages

- Use a repertoire of graphophonic strategies to problem solve through text

Benchmarks

The following titles are representative of the kinds of books found in this grouping.

Danny and the Dinosaur, Syd Hoff
The Doorbell Rang, Pat Hutchins
Henry and Mudge, Cynthia Rylant
The Very Hungry Caterpillar, Eric Carle

Assessment

The following titles can be used to determine if a reader is ready to move on to the next grouping. This type of assessment is most effective if the text is unfamiliar to a reader. If these titles will be used as assessment texts, they should *not* be part of the classroom library.

Bear Shadow, Frank Asch, DRA 16
Jimmy Lee Did It, Pat Cummings, DRA 18

TEXT LEVEL SEVEN

This level roughly corresponds to the following levels in other systems:

Reading Recovery© (RR) Levels 19–20
Developmental Reading Assessment (DRA) Level 20

Text Characteristics of TC Level Seven

- Dialogue is used frequently to move the story along

- Texts often have 2 to 3 characters. (They tend to have distinctive personalities and usually don't change across a book or series.)

- Texts may include extended description. (The language may set a mood, and may be quite poetic or colorful.)

- Some books have episodic chapters. (In other books, each chapter contributes to the understanding of the entire book and the reader must carry the story line along.)

- There is limited picture support

- Plots are usually linear without large time-gaps

- Texts tend to have larger print and double spacing between lines of print

Characteristics of the Reader

Readers in this group will demonstrate most of these behaviors.

- Reread and self-correct regularly

- Read with fluency, intonation, and phrasing

- Demonstrate the existence of a self-extending (self-improving) system for reading

- Use an increasingly more challenging repertoire of graphophonic strategies to problem solve through text

- Solve unknown words with relative ease

Benchmarks

The following titles are representative of the kinds of books found in this grouping.

A Baby Sister for Frances, Russell Hoban
Meet M&M, Pat Ross
Nate the Great, Marjorie Sharmat
Poppleton, Cynthia Rylant

Asessment

The following titles can be used to determine if a reader is ready to move on to the next grouping. This type of assessment is most effective if the text is unfamiliar to a reader. If these titles will be used as assessment texts, they should *not* be part of the classroom library.

Peter's Pockets, Eve Rice, DRA 20
Uncle Elephant, Arnold Lobel

More Information to Help You Choose the Library That is Best for Your Readers

Library A

Library A is appropriate if your children enter kindergarten in October as very emergent readers with limited experiences hearing books read aloud. Use the following chart to help determine if Library A is about right for your class.

Approximate Distribution of Reading Levels of a Class Matched to Library A		
Benchmark Book	Reading Level	Percentage of the Class Reading at about This Level
The Cat on the Mat, by Wildsmith	TC Level 1	45%
Fox on the Box, by Gregorich	TC Level 2	30%
Mrs. Wishy-Washy, by Cowley	TC Level 3	25%

Library B

Library B is appropriate for a class of children if, in October, they are reading books like *I Went Walking*. Use the following chart to help determine if Library B is about right for your class. (Note to New York City teachers: Many of your students would score a 3 on the ECLAS correlated with titles such as, *Things I Like to Do* and *My Shadow*.)

Approximate Distribution of Reading Levels of a Class Matched to Library B		
Benchmark Book	Reading Level	Percentage of the Class Reading at about This Level
The Cat on the Mat, by Wildsmith	TC Level 1	10%
Fox on the Box, by Gregorich	TC Level 2	10%
Mrs. Wishy-Washy, by Cowley	TC Level 3	30%
The Carrot Seed, by Krauss	TC Level 4	25%
Goodnight Moon, by Brown	TC Level 5	15%
Henry and Mudge, by Rylant	TC Level 6	5%
Nate the Great, by Sharmat	TC Level 7	5%

Library C

Library C is appropriate for a class of children if, in October, many of your students are approaching reading books like *Mrs. Wishy-Washy* and *Bears in the Night*. (Note to New York City teachers: Many of your students would be approaching a 4 on the ECLAS that would be correlated with *Baby Bear's Present* and *No Where and Nothing*.)

Approximate Distribution of Reading Levels of a Class Matched to Library C		
Benchmark Book	*Reading Level*	*Percentage of the Class Reading at about This Level*
Fox on the Box, by Gregorich	TC Level 2	8%
Mrs. Wishy-Washy, by Cowley	TC Level 3	8%
The Carrot Seed, by Krauss	TC Level 4	20%
Goodnight Moon, by Brown	TC Level 5	20%
Henry and Mudge, by Carle	TC Level 6	20%
Nate the Great, by Sharmat	TC Level 7	15%
Pinky and Rex, by Howe	TC Level 8	5%
Ramona Quimby, by Cleary	TC Level 9	2%
James and the Giant Peach, by Dahl	TC Level 10	2%

Library D

Use the following chart to help determine if Library D is right for your class.

Approximate Distribution of Reading Levels of a Class Matched to Library D		
Benchmark Book	*Reading Level*	*Percentage of the Class Reading at about This Level*
Good Night Moon, by Brown	Level 5	8%
Henry and Mudge, by Rylant	Level 6	20%
Nate the Great, by Sharmat	Level 7	25%
Pinky and Rex, by Howe	Level 8	30%
Ramona Quimby, by Cleary	Level 9	10%
James and the Giant Peach, by Dahl	Level 10	2%

Library E

Library E is appropriate for a class of children if, in October, a readers list tends to look approximately like the following chart.

Approximate Distribution of Reading Levels of a Class Matched to Library E		
Benchmark Book	*Reading Level*	*Percentage of the Class Reading at about This Level*
Nate the Great, by Sharmat	Level 7	10%
Pinky and Rex, by Howe	Level 8	25%
Ramona Quimby, by Cleary	Level 9	30%
James and the Giant Peach, by Dahl	Level 10	22%
Shiloh, by Naylor	Level 11	5%
Baby, by MacLachlan	Level 12	5%
Missing May, by Rylant	Level 13	2%
Scorpions, by Myers	Level 14	1%

Library F

Library F is appropriate for a class of children if, in October, a readers list tends to look approximately like the following chart.

Approximate Distribution of Reading Levels of a Class Matched to Library F		
Benchmark Book	*Reading Level*	*Percentage of the Class Reading at about This Level*
Pinky and Rex, by Howe	Level 8	2%
Ramona Quimby, by Cleary	Level 9	20%
James and the Giant Peach, by Dahl	Level 10	25%
Shiloh, by Naylor	Level 11	30%
Baby, by MacLachlan	Level 12	20%
Missing May, by Rylant	Level 13	2%
Scorpions, by Myers	Level 14	1%

Library G

Library G is appropriate for a class of children if, in October, a readers list tends to look approximately like the following chart.

Approximate Distribution of Reading Levels of a Class Matched to Library G		
Benchmark Book	*Reading Level*	*Percentage of the Class Reading at about This Level*
James and the Giant Peach, by Dahl	Level 10	10%
Shiloh, by Naylor	Level 11	10%
Baby, by MacLachlan	Level 12	30%
Missing May, by Rylant	Level 13	30%
Scorpions, by Myer	Level 14	20%

About the Guides

Soon we'd begun not only accumulating titles and honing arrangements for dream libraries, but also writing teaching advice to go with the chosen books. Our advice to the contributors was, "Write a letter from you to others who'll use this book with children. Tell folks what you notice in the book, and advise them on teaching opportunities you see. Think about advice you would give a teacher just coming to know the book." The insights, experience, and folk wisdom poured in and onto the pages of the guides.

A written guide accompanies many of the books in the libraries. These guides are not meant to be prescriptions for how a teacher or child should use a book. Instead they are intended to be resources, and we hope thoughtful teachers will tap into particular sections of a guide when it seems fit to do so. For example, a teaching guide might suggest six possible minilessons a teacher could do with a book. Of course, a teacher would never try to do all six of these! Instead we expect one of these minilessons will seem helpful to the teacher, and another minilesson to another teacher. The teaching guides illustrate the following few principles that are important to us.

Teaching One Text Intensely in Order to Learn About Many Texts

When you take a walk in the woods, it can happen that all the trees look the same, that they are just a monotony of foliage and trunks. It is only when you stop to learn about a particular tree, about its special leaf structure and the odd thickness of its bark, about the creatures that inhabit it and the seeds it lets fall, that you begin to see that particular kind of tree among the thickets. It is when you enter a forest knowing something about kinds of trees that you begin to truly see the multiplicity of trees in a forest and the particular attributes and mysteries of each one. Learning about the particulars of one tree leads you to thinking about all of the trees, each in its individuality, each with its unique deep structure, each with its own offerings.

The same is true of texts. The study of one can reveal not just the hidden intricacies of that story, but also the ways in which truths and puzzles can be structured in other writings as well. When one book holds a message in the way a chapter ends, it gives the reader the idea that any book may hold a message in the structure of its chapter's conclusions. When one book is revealed to make a sense that is unintended by the author, we look for unintended sense in other books we read. Within these guides, then, we hope that readers like you will find truths about the particular books they are written about, but more, we hope that you find pathways into all the books you read. By showing some lengthy thinking and meditations on one book, we hope to offer you paths toward thinking about each and every book that crosses your desk and crosses your mind.

Suggesting Classroom Library Arrangements

Many the attributes of a book, detailed in a guide, can become a category in a classroom library. If a group of students in a class seems particularly energized by the Harry Potter books, for example, the guide can be used to help determine which books could be in a bin in the library marked, "If You Like *Harry Potter*—Try These." The similarity between the *Harry Potter* books and the other books in this group may be not only in difficulty gradient, but also in content, story structure, popularity, or genre. That is, a class of children that like *Harry Potter* might benefit from a bin of books on fantasy, or from a collection of best-selling children's books, or from a bin of "Long-Books-You-Can't-Put-Down," or from stories set in imagined places. As you browse through the guides that accompany the books you have chosen, the connections will pop out at you.

Sometimes, the guides will help you determine a new or more interesting placement for a book. Perhaps you have regarded a book as historical fiction, but now you realize it could alternatively be shelved in a collection of books that offer children examples of "Great Leads to Imitate in Your Own Writing." Or, perhaps the guides will suggest entirely new categories that will appeal to your class in ways you and your students haven't yet imagined. Perhaps the guides will help you imagine a "Books That Make You Want to Change the World" category. Or maybe you'll decide to create a shelf in your library titled, "Books with Odd Techniques That Make You Wonder What the Author Is Trying To Do."

Aiding in Conferring

Teachers' knowledge of what to ask and what to teach a reader who says, "this book is boring" comes not only from their knowledge of particular students but also from their knowledge of the text they are talking about. Does "boring" mean that the book is too easy for the reader? Perhaps it means instead that the beginning few chapters of the book are hard to read—confusing because of a series of flashbacks. A guide might explain that the book under discussion has mostly internal, emotional action, and, if the reader is accustomed to avalanche-and-rattlesnake action in books, she may need some time to warm up to this unfamiliar kind of "quiet" action. The guide can point out the kinds of reactions, or troubles, other readers have had with particular books. With the guides at our fingertips, we can more easily determine which questions to ask students, or which pages to turn to, in order to get to the heart of the conference.

Providing a Resource for Curriculum Planning

One Friday, say, we leave the classroom knowing that our students' writing shows that they are thirsting for deeper, more complicated characters to study and imitate. As we plan lessons, we can page through the guides that correspond with some of the books in our library, finding, or remembering, books that students can study that depict fascinating characters.

On the other hand, perhaps we need a book to read aloud to the class, or perhaps we need to recommend a book to a particular struggling reader.

Maybe a reader has finished a book he loves and has turned to you to help him plan his reading for the next weeks. When designing an author study or an inquiry into punctuation and its effects on meaning, it also helps to have the guides with you to point out books that may be helpful in those areas. In each of these cases, and many more, the guides can be a planning aid for you.

Reminding Us, or Teaching Us, About Particular Book Basics

No teacher can read, let alone recall in detail, every book that every child will pick up in the classroom. Of course, we read many of them and learn about many more from our colleagues, but there are far too many books in the world for us to be knowledgeable about them all. Sometimes, the guides will be a reminder of what you have read many years ago. Sometimes, they will provide a framework for you to question or direct your students more effectively than you could if you knew nothing at all about the book. "Probably, you will have to take some time to understand the setting before you can really get a handle on this book, why don't you turn to the picture atlas?" you might say after consulting the guide, or "Sharlene is reading another book that is similar to this one in so many ways! Why don't you go pair up with her to talk." You might learn to ask, "What do you think of Freddy?" in order to learn if the student is catching on to the tone of the narrator, or you might learn you could hint, "Did you get to chapter three yet? Because I bet you won't be bored any more when you get there. . . ." The guides provide a bit of what time constraints deny us: thoughtful insights about the content or unusual features of a given book.

Showcasing Literary Intricacies in Order to Suggest a Reader's Thinking

Sometimes, when we read a book, our idea of the author's message is in our minds before we even finish the story. Because we are experienced readers, much of our inferring and interpreting, our understanding of symbols and contexts, can come to us effortlessly. In the guides, we have tried to slow down some of that thinking so that we can all see it more easily. We have tried to lay out some of the steps young readers may have to go through in order to come to a cohesive idea of what the story is about, or a clear understanding of why a character behaved the way she did. As experienced readers, we may not even realize that our readers are confused by the unorthodox use of italics to show us who is speaking, for example. We may not remember the days when we were confused by changing narrators, the days when it took us a few chapters to figure out a character wasn't to be believed. In these guides, we have tried to go back to those days when we were more naïve readers, and have tried to fill in those thoughts and processes we are now able to skip over so easily.

By bringing forth the noteworthy features of the text, features experienced readers may not even notice, we are reminded of the thinking that our students need to go through in order to make sense of their reading. It gives us an idea of where to offer pointers, of where readers may have gone off in an unhelpful direction, or of where their thinking may need to go instead of where it has gone. By highlighting literary intricacies, we may remember that every bit about the construction of texts is a navigation point for students, and every bit is something we may be able to help students in learning.

Providing a Community of Readers and Teachers

The guides are also intended to help teachers learn from the community of other teachers and readers who have used particular texts already. They make available some of the stories and experiences other teachers have had, in order that we might stand on their shoulders and take our teaching even higher than they could reach. These guides are intended to give you some thinking to go with the books in your classroom library, thinking you can mix with your own ideas.

In the end, we don't all have a community of other teachers with whom we can talk about children's literature. The guides are meant not to stand in for that community, but instead to provide a taste, an appetizer, of the world of supportive professional communities. We hope that by reading these guides and feeling the companionship, guidance and insight they offer, teachers will be nudged to recreate that experience for the other books that have no guides, and that they will ask their colleagues, librarians, and the parents of their students to talk with them about children's literature and young readers. Then, when teachers are creating these guides for themselves, on paper or in their minds' eyes, we will know this project has done the work for which it was created.

Bibliography

Atwell, Nancie. 1987. *In the Middle: Writing, Reading, and Learning with Adolescents*. Portsmouth, NH: Boynton/Cook.

Calkins, Lucy. 2001. *The Art of Teaching Reading*. New York: Addison-Wesley Educational Publishers, Inc.

Cambourne, Brian. 1993. *The Whole Story: Natural Learning and the Acquisition of Literacy in the Classroom*. Auckland, NZ: Ashton Scholastic.

Krashen, Stephen. 1993. *The Power of Reading: Insights from the Research*. Englewood, CO: Libraries Unlimited.

Meek, Margaret. 1988. *How Texts Teach What Readers Learn*. Thimble Press.

Smith, Frank. 1985. *Reading Without Nonsense*. 2nd ed. New York: TC Press.

A Field Guide to the Classroom Library Ⓖ

A Time of Angels

Karen Hesse

Book Summary

In Boston during WWI, separated from their parents, Hannah and her two younger sisters fight to stay together and survive the influenza epidemic sweeping through the city. After her sisters fall ill, their caretaker Vashti sends Hannah away. With the help of an angel, Hannah ends up in Vermont where she meets a farmer who befriends her and helps her return to the family she loves.

Basic Book Information

A Time of Angels is a 270-page fictional story. There are no pictures in the book and there are thirty chapters grouped into three parts.

Noteworthy Features

A Time of Angels is an evocative, slow-moving, earnest story about faith and hardship. Character, more than plot, moves the story forward. Written in first person from Hannah's point of view, the story contains lyrical descriptive language and gives readers a clear sense of Hannah's personality.

The story does not provide exposition up front (the who, what, when, where, why), but allows details to accumulate over time. The first ten pages of the book tell us little about Hannah, with whom she lives, how old she is, or her family circumstances; this may be confusing for some readers. Deeper into the book, descriptions of Boston and rural Vermont provide a colorful historical backdrop.

A full understanding of the book requires some outside knowledge. Readers unfamiliar with Jewish rituals and holidays, and Yiddish expressions (e.g., "schmatte," "trayf") may need background information to understand those parts of the text completely. Many readers will also benefit from background on the war, the flu epidemic, and the state of medicine in 1918.

The mystical aspects of the book inject an element of fantasy into an otherwise historically-grounded book (e.g., there are several appearances by a violet-eyed angel). Some readers may find this vacillation disconcerting-they may have a hard time understanding how much of the tale is historically accurate and how much is fantasy. For readers who prefer not to mix their genres, and who prefer not to believe in magic, the angels can be seen as products of Hannah's imagination, symbols of her faith.

One theme involves overcoming prejudice. Hannah, who is Jewish, is rescued by an older German-American man in Vermont. Both suffer prejudice. Through Klaus, Hannah comes to feel sympathy for those whom she previously considered the enemy.

Publisher
Hyperion Books for Children, 1995

ISBN
0786806214

TC Level
14

Teaching Ideas

The theme of overcoming prejudice will probably come up as a topic of discussion. Readers can consider the instances of prejudice in the story, and the process by which Hannah comes to recognize her own prejudices and overcome them.

Hannah develops during the story from a girl who sees the world fairly simply, as a place with heroes and villains, to a young woman who can see things from many perspectives. Readers can trace this development by looking at Hannah's attitude toward Klaus, Vashti, and her Boston neighbor Ovadiah. While Hannah is a fairly resourceful person at the start, readers might also track ways in which she becomes more independent.

Genre is another area that more sophisticated readers can examine. What are the elements of realism? In this light, the book could accompany research on WWI and/or the flu epidemic, or could be part of a study of immigration as Hannah and her sisters are recent immigrants from Eastern Europe. In addition, the book could be looked at as a fantasy, with elements of fairy tales-magical events, angelic helpers (the angel and Klaus), and even an unfriendly, potion-making old woman (Vashti).

Genre
Chapter Book; Fantasy

Teaching Uses
Character Study; Independent Reading; Content Area Study

A Field Guide to the Classroom Library, Lucy Calkins and the Teachers College Reading and Writing Project, Heinemann, ©2002 Teachers College, Columbia University; http://www.heinemann.com/fieldguides

A Wrinkle in Time
Madeleine L'Engle

Book Summary

In *A Wrinkle in Time,* Meg, her little brother Charles Wallace and her friend Calvin are guided by three mysterious women on an intergalactic journey through time and space. Taken suddenly from their ordinary suburban existence, they have been sent on a quest to find Meg's father, a famous scientist who disappeared while working on a secret project many years earlier. Before time runs out, the three children must overcome a terrible force that threatens not just their lives, but the fate of the earth.

Basic Book Information

Newbery Medal-winner *A Wrinkle in Time* is a classic science fiction story, an adventure, and a political tale all wrapped up in one. The next books in the quartet are: *A Wind in the Door, A Swiftly Tilting Planet,* and *Many Waters.*

Noteworthy Features

The main characters, Meg, Charles Wallace, and Calvin, are misfits at home. Meg is a poor student who speaks her mind too freely to be liked by her teachers; Charles Wallace is a five-year-old prodigy who reads Genesis for fun and understands complex physics concepts; Calvin is an articulate, well-liked athlete who feels out of place in his coarse unpleasant family. Some readers are likely to sympathize with the more ordinary Calvin and with Meg, whose problems in the arena of day-to-day life turn out to be assets.

While the three children's characters are clearly drawn, the other characters tend to operate as symbols. As in a fairy tale, there are minor characters who help the main characters: these are the mysterious Mrs. Whatsit, Mrs. Who, and Mrs. Which. These otherwordly beings take a variety of shapes and provide the heroes with clues and talismans. The enemy, "It," is a dark force that emanates from a brain. This symbolizes the dark side of intelligence-its aim for perfection-rather than the messy, complex, and creative products of real humanity.

The book touches on physics concepts, such as dimensionality, which will be difficult or impossible for readers to really grasp, but full understanding is not necessary. The concept of a "wrinkle in time," which allows the characters to travel through time and space almost instantly, will strike many as more magical than scientific.

The principal horror of "It" involves perfection, as noted above, and is embodied by the planet Camozatz. There, where the children's father is imprisoned, people play identically, speak identically and fail to think. Only

A Field Guide to the Classroom Library, Lucy Calkins and the Teachers College Reading and Writing Project, Heinemann, ©2002 Teachers College, Columbia University; http://www.heinemann.com/fieldguides

Series
The Time Quartet

Publisher
Bantam Doubleday Dell, 1962

ISBN
0440998050

TC Level
14

by resisting this uniformity-by being imperfectly, beautifully human-can the children escape with their father and their lives.

Teaching Ideas

A Wrinkle in Time is a good choice for reading independently or in small groups.

Readers might do a character study of Meg, Charles Wallace, or Calvin, keeping track of their characteristics and the consequences of those characteristics. For example, Meg's emotionality and expressiveness work both for and against her in different scenes. Through these consequences, the characters learn something about themselves.

Another area of study could be the themes in *A Wrinkle in Time*. One major theme is that intelligence can be used in both good or bad ways. Readers can look at the different uses of intelligence on Earth and on Camozatz.

Another theme is the importance of keeping an open mind, truly thinking things over, rather than making assumptions. Over and over, the main characters find that their fixed ideas are incorrect. For example, the "beasts" of Ixchel are terrifying-looking but helpful, and though they are blind, they perceive more clearly than the humans. In the most striking example, a brilliant "It" is beaten by a powerless young girl. Students might discuss how many characteristics, such as sight, strength, warmth, or anger, turn out to be more or less useful than one would think. This is a topic many book groups eventually come up with when given time to think and talk over the book.

Book Connections

Skilled readers could find similarities between *A Wrinkle in Time* and fairy tales. Both involve young or immature characters that go on a quest, receive help from magical figures, and overcome evil. Parallels might also be drawn between other *A Wrinkle in Time* and journey/adventure stories, such as *My Side of the Mountain*.

The next books in the Time Quartet are: *A Wind in the Door*, *A Swiftly Tilting Planet*, and *Many Waters*.

Genre
Fantasy; Chapter Book

Teaching Uses
Independent Reading; Book Clubs; Interpretation; Character Study

A Field Guide to the Classroom Library, Lucy Calkins and the Teachers College Reading and Writing Project, Heinemann, ©2002 Teachers College, Columbia University; http://www.heinemann.com/fieldguides

Adaline Falling Star

Mary Pope Osborne

Book Summary

This story is fictional, but is based on the real story of eleven-year-old Adaline, the daughter of Kit Carson and his Native American Arapaho wife. Set in St. Louis, Missouri in the 1840s, Adaline is staying with her Uncle Silas, as her father travels west over the Rocky Mountains with "Pathfinder" Lieutenant John C. Fremont. Adaline's mother has died. Adaline lives with her uncle and cousins, and faces prejudice because of her Native American heritage. After many misunderstandings and abuses at home and at school, Adaline strikes out alone, into the surrounding wilderness. Along the way Adaline finds and falls in love with a dog. In doing so, she realizes that it is not only risky, but also wonderful to depend on another being.

Basic Book Information

Mary Pope Osborne is known for her *Magic Tree House* series for younger readers, which is also historical fiction. Osborne has also written several books in the *Dear America* (Scholastic) series. *Adaline Falling Star* is a 170-page historical fiction book. It includes an Author's Note at the very beginning, which helps the reader to understand the author's motivation in writing the story as well the setting. There is a bibliography on the last page of the book entitled "A Note on Sources," which could lead a reader to further investigate Adaline and this time period.

Noteworthy Features

This book is written in Adaline's first person point of view. Dialogue is frequent in this book and rarely referenced with tags such as "he said." Dialogue is indicated unconventionally with long dashes that make the speech stand out from the narrative. Adaline's memories and internal dialogue with her dead mother appear in italics throughout. A teacher might point out, or children may discover, that the italics indicate a change in time and setting, as well as a break in the flow of the story. There are also parts of the dialogue in which Adaline talks to herself. This is indicated with one dashed dialogue line after another. These lines could be considered thought bubbles; readers may need a pointer to help them make sense of them at first.

Osborne does a good job of recreating the language of the time period, which adds to the flavor and dimension of the characters. Throughout the book, there is a western dialect that readers may not be familiar with. For example, Kit Carson calls Adaline his "darter," Native Americans are called "Injuns," and animals are called "critters." Readers will also note the use of an old form of the language. In one place, a dog is described: "He looks

A Field Guide to the Classroom Library, Lucy Calkins and the Teachers College Reading and Writing Project, Heinemann, ©2002 Teachers College, Columbia University; http://www.heinemann.com/fieldguides

Publisher
Scholastic, 2000

ISBN
043905947X

TC Level
13

grieved." As in many cases in this book, the reader can often discern the words' meaning from context and previous experience.

Teaching Ideas

If a teacher observes a child beginning to read this book, it might be helpful for her explain the context of this piece of historical fiction to the child. The teacher might explain that at the time of this book, St. Louis was the west, and it was known as a (western) frontier town. During this time, many of the people in the town were afraid of different cultures and beliefs. The teacher might also explain to the reader that Kit Carson was known to be hostile to the Native Americans cause. Although Kit Carson had two Native American wives (one Arapaho, the other Cheyenne), he joined the U.S. Calvary and was a leader in the systematic extermination of the Navajo. After reading this book, readers may want to start an inquiry into Kit Carson, western explorers, the United States Calvary, or into Arapaho history.

Adaline Falling Star presents several views of Kit Carson. A teacher might want to point these views out to the reader, or raise them through a discussion with the reader. Children may also come to see the various views of the man through a character study. For the most part, Carson is portrayed sympathetically, as a father who returns, as he promised, to his motherless daughter. However, there are many moments at the end of the book, where Adaline doubts her father's sincerity and integrity, as she runs away from white civilization. Adaline believes that she has been abandoned and that Carson exploits Native Americans as well as the American landscape she so loves. These two very different views can be brought to the forefront of a study or discussion, and will contribute well to a study of Westward Expansion.

If the teacher wanted to conduct a mini-lesson on dialect, he could bring together four students, each with copies of the text, and they could study particular pages that show dialect. Students could look at how these words are written. Then, by using available content and context clues, they could assess the meaning of the pages and the words and how they should be read aloud. Dialect is represented phonetically (for example, "darter"), and the teacher and readers can discuss how words sound in relation to what they look like written down. Readers could then search for and attach post-it notes to any interesting uses of dialect they find in their own independent reading books in order to share their discoveries with the group.

Investigation could also be done on the use of punctuation, and especially Pope's use of italics. In *Adaline Falling Star*, Pope uses italics to show a change in the narrator's voice, such as Adaline's mother talking through Adaline's memories. Readers can theorize about why and when the author does this, and then continue to mark examples within the text as they read and explore this book. This use of punctuation and its relation to the story's meaning will probably be referred to often as the reader continues in her small group and independent reading.

Book Connections

There are a number of other books in these libraries that tell of Westward Expansion, and readers may find it beneficial to have discussions about

A Field Guide to the Classroom Library, Lucy Calkins and the Teachers College Reading and Writing Project, Heinemann, ©2002 Teachers College, Columbia University; http://www.heinemann.com/fieldguides

some of these texts. *The Coyote Bead* (Hausman) is also historical fiction and it deals with the Navajo "removal" in the West by the United States Cavalry (where Kit Carson played a major role in the extermination of the Navajo and the resulting "Long Walk" of 1864). *Digger*, a non-fiction book by Jerry Stanley, relates the story of the California Indians and their extermination by Europeans and white Americans. This too would be a helpful book to make connections with since Kit Carson also spent time in California.

Genre
Historical Fiction

Teaching Uses
Independent Reading; Character Study; Critique; Content Area Study; Language Conventions

Afternoon of the Elves

Janet Taylor Lisle

Book Summary

This book tells the story of the friendship that develops between Hillary, who is middle class, and Sara-Kate, who is poor. The story centers around the miniature villages Sara-Kate builds and the community of elves she imagines lives there. The two girls' growing friendship is tested by peers who discourage the mixing of different social classes.

As the girls' friendship grows stronger, Hillary learns that her friend is doing everything in her home from buying all the food to paying the bills. As it turns out, Sara-Kate's mother is sick and the young girl does not want to be taken away from her. Ultimately, Hillary is unable to protect her friend from being taken away, and is left to stand guard over elf village herself.

Basic Book Information

This book has 122 pages, and is divided into 15 chapters. It is realistic fiction. Another book by this author is *Forest*, a fantasy tale about the world of squirrels.

Noteworthy Features

One aspect that could challenge readers is that Sara-Kate speaks of the elf village she builds as if it were real. Readers might mistakenly think that the elves are, in fact, real and miss the more important details about Sara-Kate and Hillary's friendship.

Teaching Ideas

This is a captivating story that moves along quickly. It is the kind of book that helps reluctant readers want to read. Student might use post-its or charts to help them gather evidence about what is real and what is make-believe in the story. Rereading, monitoring for sense, and coming to a part of the text with a question in mind are all strategies teachers can help readers use to get more out of this text.

As this is an early read, conferences might include helping students remember and retell the story well. A teacher might make sure readers use the basic story elements of character, events, setting, movement of time, and change in these retellings.

Readers could challenge each other with questions that push their thinking and force them to support their ideas with evidence from the text. Since this is a book that tends to generate questions in readers easily, various questioning strategies work especially well here. This might also be a time to

Publisher
Scholastic Inc., 1989

ISBN
0590439448

TC Level
12

A Field Guide to the Classroom Library, Lucy Calkins and the Teachers College Reading and Writing Project, Heinemann, ©2002 Teachers College, Columbia University; http://www.heinemann.com/fieldguides

help children learn to integrate and revise their ideas with their partner's ideas in order to understand more completely what is going on in the book.

Teachers could use the book to teach strategies for conversation. For example, it is not enough to come up with a prediction; the reader should find the clues in the chapter that support that prediction, that way, readers can talk and decide which predictions are most accurate. Without such evidence, the conversation tends to just go around in a circle without any overlap, without any weighing of evidence or measuring of opinions.

To assign a set of readers a single chapter a night is one way to focus the conversation on a particular aspect or small chunk of the book. Different focusing possibilities include, but are not limited to: the perspective of each major character; Sara-Kate's relationship to each of the other characters; specific examples of both time and setting in each chapter and how changes in both become apparent through the text; and the developing trust between the two friends.

Book Connections

Books with similar themes include *Crazy Lady* by Connolly, *The Great Gilly Hopkins* by Katherine Paterson, Lois Lowry's *Atta Boy Sam,* Robert Kimmel Smith's *The War with Grandpa* and some of the Jerry Spinelli books, including *Picklemania.* Another book by this author is *Forest,* a fantasy tale about the world of squirrels.

Genre
Fantasy; Chapter Book

Teaching Uses
Independent Reading; Partnerships

A Field Guide to the Classroom Library, Lucy Calkins and the Teachers College Reading and Writing Project, Heinemann, ©2002 Teachers College, Columbia University; http://www.heinemann.com/fieldguides

Alice-by-Accident

Lynne Reid Banks

Book Summary

In two notebooks, one private and one kept for school, nine-year-old Alice writes about life in London with her prickly mother, and how she longs for her absent grandmother Gene. With imagination and piercing directness, Alice manages to sort out her feelings about her move to London, family rifts, and the father she has never met. Along the way, Alice's relationships and the turmoil she weathers help make her into a real writer-one who takes charge of her creations.

Basic Book Information

Lynne Reid Banks is also the author of *The Indian in the Cupboard* series.

Noteworthy Features

Alice-by-Accident is a fictionalized memoir. The book alternates between entries from a private journal and a school journal, the latter of which contains Alice's short stories. The teacher's notes appear on the school journal entries. Each chapter title indicates from which journal the entry is taken. Because the book opens with an (private) autobiography, the basic facts of Alice's life are established early in the text.

Alice-by-Accident is a head-on treatment of complicated and mature topics: Alice's learning that she was an "accident," her father's abandonment of her, her mother's fights with Alice's grandmother Gene, Alice's mother's illness, a babysitter's abuse of the girl, a near-fatal bout of meningitis, and the physical abuse her mother suffers under the hand of Alice's stepfather. Alice expresses worries about being sexually abused and talks about Peony's shoplifting. Younger readers, especially those expecting another book like those in Banks' *Indian in the Cupboard* series, may find this book is too much to handle.

Alice is an engaging, complex character who will appeal to many readers. Grammatical and spelling mistakes establish her age and off-the-cuff personality. Her concerns are ones that certain readers will identify with on some level: a difficult parent, bad babysitters, a strict teacher, and the pain of growing up. The focus of Alice's journals is how she comes to an understanding of these problems and takes control of her life. Over the course of the book, she develops from an uncertain and dependent child into a more savvy and confident one.

Characterizations are thorough and realistic. Because the book is written in the first person, the reader sees others through Alice's eyes. Alice is weary of her mother, and they seem to have very little intimacy-journal entries portray her mother primarily as a self-centered and unhappy woman. Though Alice praises her mother's ambition and independence, most of

A Field Guide to the Classroom Library, Lucy Calkins and the Teachers College Reading and Writing Project, Heinemann, ©2002 Teachers College, Columbia University; http://www.heinemann.com/fieldguides

Alice's warmth is directed toward her paternal grandmother Gene. In contrast to the mother, Gene is warm, dramatic, and was, until a rift in the family developed, highly involved. The portrayal of Peony, a neighborhood friend, is brief but memorable. Alice's teacher, who appears via her comments on Alice's school journal, is someone whose demands of Alice bring out her best.

Readers may occasionally find Alice's misspellings confusing, especially when the misspellings reflect Alice's English pronunciation ("iyon" for iron, and "hornt" for haunt). The many examples of Briticisms add to the book's atmosphere, and should not get in the way of comprehension ("toffee-nosed," "grotty," "child minder").

A principal theme involves writing. A variety of influences help make Alice into both a good writer and a happier person. Her grandmother's love of the arts, her teacher's demands, her friend Peony's dark view of life, and Alice's mother's (perhaps unintended) neglect helps Alice become an imaginative, conscientious, realistic, and independent writer.

As Alice takes control of her writing, she takes control of her life. Against her mother's wishes, she arranges a reunion of her mother and maternal grandmother. She learns to tolerate and then enjoy coming home alone after school. She re-establishes a relationship with Gene. And she becomes sure enough of herself to look past her mother's opposition and make contact with her father and his new wife. One theme is that part of growing up involves making active decisions, rather than suffering passively with the flawed decisions of grown-ups.

Teaching Ideas

The process and purpose of writing is, naturally, a major topic in *Alice-by-Accident*. The story illustrates the range possible in journal writing. Alice's journals contain humorous anecdotes, musings, autobiography, fiction, and fictionalized autobiography. Students can discuss the transformation of fact into fiction and talk about how these forms differ. Students might try their hands at writing factual anecdotes, selecting elements of those anecdotes, and re-using those elements in fiction.

There are various opportunities for character study. The characters of the mother and Gene can be compared, as can Alice and Peony. Students can discuss what each of the characters, including Alice's teacher, contributed to Alice's development and how Alice's views of these characters changed over the course of the book.

Some students may also find this book is a good one to learn how to build personal connections with a text. How does the reader's life help him understand how Alice is feeling about growing up? How does what Alice is going through help the reader understand her own life? The character and the reader might not have ever gone through the exact experience, but teachers can help children see emotional connections that can inform each other.

Book Connections

Another book that involves a character who keeps a journal is *Harriet the Spy* by Louise Fitzhugh. In an effort to make sense of life's absurdities,

A Field Guide to the Classroom Library, Lucy Calkins and the Teachers College Reading and Writing Project, Heinemann, ©2002 Teachers College, Columbia University; http://www.heinemann.com/fieldguides

Harriet literally spies on people and writes about them in her secret diary. Lynne Reid Banks is also the author of the *Indian in the Cupboard* series. Disobeying adult figures is a feature common to many children's stories, from *Rapunzel* to *The Wizard of Oz*. Readers might look for this theme in other stories they have read.

Genre
Chapter book; Memoir

Teaching Uses
Independent Reading; Teaching Writing; Character Study

A Field Guide to the Classroom Library, Lucy Calkins and the Teachers College Reading and Writing Project, Heinemann, ©2002 Teachers College, Columbia University; http://www.heinemann.com/fieldguides

Anastasia Again!

Lois Lowry

Book Summary

In this second installment of the *Anastasia* series, twelve-year-old Anastasia discovers that her artist mother and English professor father are planning to move the family from sophisticated Cambridge to the suburbs. Anastasia is convinced that, in the suburbs, every living room is dominated by a huge television set, all walls are hung with paint-by-number art, and all housewives wear pink hair curlers to the supermarket. To vent her feelings, Anastasia begins to write a mystery story-the title and content of which change in amusing ways over the course of the book. Anastasia's regret over leaving their much-loved apartment and her friends is tempered by her pleasure over the big house her family buys, complete with a tower room for Anastasia.

Anastasia and her little brother Sam meet the next-door neighbor Gertrude Stein, a lonely and grouchy old woman, and Anastasia becomes friends with Steve Harvey, who will be in her seventh grade class. Meanwhile, Anastasia keeps in touch with two classmates from Cambridge, Jenny and Robert. She invites them to visit. Trying to help her lonely neighbor, Anastasia also invites members of the local Senior Citizen Center to come to her house for Kool-Aid, intending to introduce them to Gertrude. Only later does she realize that she invited her old friends and the seniors to come on the same day. The get-together turns out to be a huge success.

Afterward, touring the house, Robert, Jenny, and Anastasia discover a declaration of love for Gertrude Stein written on the wall of Anastasia's tower room many years ago. Gertrude enjoys the note, which recalls the neighbor boy she always loved, even after he married another woman. And so the Krupniks are happy with their new house, Gertrude has broken out of her shell, and Anastasia has made new friends while keeping the old. The book ends with Anastasia winding up her mystery novel, the final title of which is "The Mystery of Saying Good-bye."

Basic Book Information

This book contains 145 pages and twelve chapters. Many chapters are divided into shorter segments, the breaks marked by white space and an asterisk. The book is very humorous.

The book received excellent reviews and was named an American Library Association Notable Book for Children. The book is part of an *Anastasia* series, which has been in print almost twenty years. Lowry has written many books for young readers. She received the Newbery Medal for *Number The Stars* and *The Giver*.

Series
Anastasia

Publisher
Houghton Mifflin, 1981

ISBN
0440400090

TC Level
12

Noteworthy Features

The story is told in third person with Anastasia as the character whose viewpoint we see through. The sequence of events unfolds chronologically during the summer before Anastasia starts seventh grade. Lowry's gift for making ordinary situations funny enhances the lively, engaging plot, and the dialogue between characters is witty. Anastasia lives in a warm, loving household. Her cosmopolitan parents bicker amiably from time to time, sometimes losing patience with Anastasia's exaggerated behavior.

Teaching Ideas

Independent readers or book clubs may choose to embark on a character study of Anastasia. They may end up documenting Anastasia's proclivity to make snap judgements, and seeking evidence to determine whether or not this aspect of her changes throughout the story. Anastasia's father informs her that she is making "premature assumptions" about the suburbs when she tells them she is unwilling to move. The phrase "premature assumptions" recurs throughout the book as Anastasia observes her own attitudes and the behavior of other people and realizes the errors that can result from hasty conclusions. Another line of thinking students may pursue is to seek evidence that supports or discredits Anastasia's stereotypes about the suburbs.

Lowry's inclusion of Gertrude Stein stands out in this story, as most of the *Anastasia* books stick closer to characters Anastasia's age. Students may want to consider why Lowry chose Stein as a character, and what her presence in the book reveals to us about Anastasia. What did the author want Anastasia, and us, to learn from Gertrude? In addition to looking at Gertrude, readers may wish to look at other characters in this text.

Readers may also use post-it notes to mark important places in Anastasia's writing, to discuss the effect of Anastasia's experiences on the mystery book she is writing for catharsis. The title and content of the book change (quite humorously) as Anastasia experiences various emotions in connection with her experiences.

Book Connections

Lois Lowry is a prolific writer for children. Her *Anastasia* series includes *Anastasia Krupnik, Anastasia Ask Your Analyst, Anastasia on Her Own, Anastasia at Your Service, Anastasia Has the Answers, Anastasia's Chosen Career*, and *Anastasia at This Address*. Although Anastasia's age changes as the series progresses, children who like this engaging heroine may take pleasure in exploring both earlier and, later (more challenging) stories about her life.

Genre
Chapter Book

A Field Guide to the Classroom Library, Lucy Calkins and the Teachers College Reading and Writing Project, Heinemann, ©2002 Teachers College, Columbia University; http://www.heinemann.com/fieldguides

Teaching Uses
Independent Reading; Character Study

Anastasia Krupnik

Lois Lowry

Book Summary

Anastasia Krupnik, age 10, has a mother who paints, a professor/poet father, and a teacher she dislikes. She also has a green notebook where she keeps lists of favorite words and important private information. Most significant to the story are the lists of things Anastasia loves and hates, which trace the themes that make up the plot of the book. The story is not action-oriented -- the strongest element of suspense lies in learning what name Anastasia will choose for her new baby brother.

During the nine months before the baby arrives, Anastasia has a crush on a boy, tries to write poetry, considers becoming a Catholic, learns the importance of memories, changes her feelings about her very elderly grandmother, and comes to terms with her mother having a second child. By the end of the book, her grandmother has died, Anastasia's baby brother has arrived, and Anastasia has taken her teacher off her list of "things I hate" after the teacher calls Anastasia to express sympathy over the death of Anastasia's grandmother. Despite the lack of an action-driven plot, the incidents that make up the story are highly engaging, and Anastasia's decisions about a name for her baby brother resolves the book in a satisfying way.

Basic Book Information

This book received strong reviews at publication (The Bulletin of the Center for Children's Books named *Anastasia Krupnik* "A Book of Special Distinction"), and *Anastasia Krupnik* was so popular with readers that it engendered a series and has stayed in print for over twenty years. Lowry has written many books for young readers from lower middle grades, as well as young adult books. She has received the Newbery Medal for *Number The Stars* and *The Giver*.

This middle-grade novel contains eleven chapters, which are each six to eight pages long. Though quietly plotted, the book is written in a lively, humorous style that may appeal to a wide range of readers. Because the book was first published in 1979, some minor details are dated (e.g., Mrs. Westvessel wears stockings with seams up the back), but Anastasia's experiences are so interesting these details don't undercut the story's authenticity.

Noteworthy Features

The story uses third-person point of view with Anastasia as the central character. The plot unfolds chronologically, covering nine months of

Series
Anastasia

Publisher
Houghton Mifflin, 1979

ISBN
055315253X

TC Level
12

A Field Guide to the Classroom Library, Lucy Calkins and the Teachers College Reading and Writing Project, Heinemann, ©2002 Teachers College, Columbia University; http://www.heinemann.com/fieldguides

Anastasia's fourth grade year in school. Lowry's writing style is engaging and accessible. She includes vivid details that create memorable characters. Anastasia has hair the color of Hubbard squash and a pink wart in the middle of her left thumb. Her father has a beard the same color, but not much hair on his head. Her mother paints and smells sometimes of turpentine, sometimes of vanilla and brown sugar, sometimes of Je Reviens perfume. Mrs. Westvessel, Anastasia's teacher, has brown spots on her hands, large, lop-sided bosoms, and a faint moustache. Children may take note of Lowry's style and try it in their own writing.

Each chapter ends with a reproduction of Anastasia's latest list of things she loves and things she hates. The alterations to the lists-items added, deleted, or moved from one column to the other-provide insight into the developing themes of the book and reflect growth and change in Anastasia. Students may well note this in a character study.

Teaching Ideas

Lowry's depiction of the only African American character in the book needs special attention from the teacher. Washburn Cummings, a sixth grader, wears an enormous Afro, wiggles his hips as he bounces an imaginary basketball, listens to music on his transistor radio, and shows up for school in a tee shirt with an obscenity on the front. Anastasia develops a brief crush on him, but no other details are added to move the character beyond the stereotype. Readers will need to critique this stereotypical depiction, with or without help from a teacher.

Anastasia's attitude toward several people changes significantly, especially her grandmother, her teacher, and the owner of the drugstore, Mr. Belden. To understand why and how Anastasia's feelings change, students might make a list of the things Anastasia dislikes about each person and a list of the things that eventually make her feel differently. This list could be compiled as readers move through the book, in order to help them understand the changes as they happen in the story.

Book Connections

Lois Lowry is a prolific writer for children. Her *Anastasia* series includes *Anastasia Krupnik, Anastasia Again!, Ask Your Analyst, Anastasia on Her Own, Anastasia at Your Service, Anastasia Has the Answers, Anastasia's Chosen Career, and Anastasia at This Address*. She's also written the richly layered book *Autumn Street*, which would be an appropriate precursor book to this series.

This is one of many books in which the main character writes. Readers could make a collection of these writing books to see what they can discover. See other Anastasia books, Kimmel Smith's *War With Grandpa*, Moss's *Amelia's Notebook*, MacLaughlan's *Arthur for the Very First Time*, or *Cassie Binegar*.

Genre
Chapter Book

A Field Guide to the Classroom Library, Lucy Calkins and the Teachers College Reading and Writing Project, Heinemann, ©2002 Teachers College, Columbia University; http://www.heinemann.com/fieldguides

Teaching Uses
Independent Reading; Teaching Writing; Character Study

Animal Monsters: The Truth About Scary Creatures

Laurence P. Pringle

Book Summary

This is a collection of informational vignettes about real and imagined monsters that have scared people through the ages. The monsters range from the black widow spider to the Komodo dragon, the vampire bat to sea "serpents." These vignettes usually begin with an anecdote about that animal, perhaps an interaction with a human, but in short order, Pringle tells readers the truth about that particular monster.

Basic Book Information

The book is organized into twenty vignettes, each telling about a monster. It begins with an incredible page-long introduction, "Monsters of the Mind or Real Monsters" that gives readers an overview of how people came to believe some animals were monsters. The introduction ends, "Some animals with such words as 'killer,' 'devil,' or 'monster' as part of their names rarely harm people. However, there are animals that can hurt and even kill humans. . . . You can learn about a few 'monsters' that live only in the wildest habitat on Earth: the human imagination."

Pringle won the Newbery Medal for his beautiful book on Monarch butterflies and he has written a number of science and environmental books. Though Pringle addresses issues that aren't always immediately appealing, he writes well enough that he can draw readers into an engagement with the topic. He seems to resist the temptation to engage readers in the coy and cute ways that are often seen in non-fiction for young readers. He doesn't ask rhetorical questions like, "Have you ever looked a mountain lion in the mouth?" He doesn't sprinkle his text with exotic or gory details. Instead he trusts in the power of lucid, understated, straightforward prose. Everyone's classroom should have at least one non-fiction book by Larry Pringle.

Noteworthy Features

The sections in the book are short, between a page and a page-and-a-half long, and they are always accompanied by a painting or a photograph. The longest section is about the Loch Ness monster. Pringle's style is direct, clear, and engaging.

For the introduction and conclusion, Pringle ties together his separate sections and addresses his larger theme. He argues that a lot of what we "know" about animals has come from books and movies in which harmless creatures are demonized so as to create an effect. At the same time, however,

Publisher
Marshall Cavendish, Inc., 1997

ISBN
0761450033

TC Level
12

he emphasizes that there are indeed animals that can harm humans and he encourages people to use common sense.

Teaching Ideas

One way to bring young readers toward non-fiction is to help them see that the topics of their fictional books are often addressed in non-fiction texts. For example, if a child was reading a fictional story about sharks such as *Jaws* or *Swimming with Sharks*, by Twig C George, the child might learn from juxtaposing that story with the section from this book on the great white shark. Readers could in a similar way think between Will Hobbs *Beardance* and Benchley's section on grizzly bears.

The animals in Pringle's book are often the subjects of newspaper stories. It's not unusual, for example, for there to be controversies over whether or not wolves, bears and bats should be allowed to "encroach upon" inhabited areas. The excerpts from this book could be juxtaposed with any of these articles. The bigger lessons, of course, are not only about animals but also about learning to become critical readers, realizing that one person's story is not the only story that can be told. We can help readers to read with a skeptical eye, asking, "Who is the author and what point of view might he or she bring to this text?"

Teachers will probably want to have this book available, and to wait and watch for the opportunity to use this text to bring home important lessons. These opportunities might arise in the local newspaper, current events, movies, and so on. When the opportunity arises and we do bring out Pringle's text, it's helpful for us to avoid preaching about, for example, the value of a wolf, and to let Pringle's text do this work. Students need to learn to put two texts alongside each other and realize that sometimes the one calls the other into question.

Book Connections

Pringle has written a collection of parallel books which each tell the story of a different scientist: *Bat Man* is about a man who works with bats; *Scorpion Woman* is about a woman who studies scorpions. These are other books in the collection that demonstrate to readers the life and habits of being a scientist.

Genre
Nonfiction; Picture Book

Teaching Uses
Reading and Writing Nonfiction; Critique; Content Area Study

Are You There, God? It's Me, Margaret

Judy Blume

Book Summary

Are You There, God? It's Me, Margaret is a coming-of-age story set in the 1970s. Margaret Simon is a young girl who has recently moved to the unfamiliar New Jersey from her native New York City. The tale narrates her adventures in her new school, and particularly with her friends in the Four PT's club, Nancy, Gretchen, and Janie. Margaret matures as she explores social and religious issues. She cannot wait until she starts to menstruate, grow breasts, or be liked by boys. She, like her friends, believes that these changes will transform her into an adult.

Amidst the pressure to grow and be "normal," she begins a serious religious inquiry. She secretly prays to God, and even attends her friends' various services. She eventually stops praying, however, because of her personal and surrounding pressures, not least coming from her Jewish Grandmother and her non-religious parents. Ultimately, she realizes she does not need to reach a clear conclusion yet, and can take one day at a time because answers will come.

Basic Book Information

The book has been a favorite for girls for years. In a fashion, then, it has become almost a classic among young adult novels. It has become part of the way many adolescent girls address feminine development, friendships, and questions too big to answer immediately. It is also, not surprisingly, become an object of great interest to many young boys who seek the book as a way to learn about a culture that is not their own. The book is most appropriate for young people who are beginning to experience puberty.

Noteworthy Features

Blume wraps the natural and social conditions of adolescence with magic. She helps students look forward to the maturation of mind and responsibility that is attached to menstruation. She also beautifully describes childhood crushes, while not covering up the reality of the indifference and crude comments that can surround them.

Margaret is a keen observer. The book is in first person, and so this character reveals everything she takes in and experiences. Blume's style of writing Margaret's experiences can serve as an interesting model for a writer's notebook, especially since she incorporates much dialogue.

Although the book is about sophisticated topics, the language is relatively simple and direct. The chapters are short. There is also a great deal of

Publisher
Bantam Doubleday Dell, 1970

ISBN
0440404193

TC Level
12

dialogue, which is usually helpful for readers. These factors mean that this intriguing book, about grown-up topics, is not a particularly difficult read for most fifth graders.

Teaching Ideas

If there is one goal above all which most teachers have for their young readers, it is for children to read hungrily and with rapt attention. We want books to ignite conversation, to be passed from child to child, generating a much excitement as baseball cards or comic books. This is a book that can teach youngsters on the cusp of adolescence to love reading. It is a book that can help a child feel less alone in the world; it can help her wrestle with the big questions of her life; it can help her to grow up.

Margaret cannot wait to grow or to menstruate. However, she does not realize all that is implied, in terms of pain, discomfort, and actual biological processes. A reader may feel that the book informs them about the social implications of these biological changes, much more so than any lesson in health class. The social implications of growing up are much more vivid and important for many girls at this stage of development. This book, then, can help these readers feel connected to print in ways they may not have experienced before.

On the other hand, the way Margaret handles growing up is only one way to handle it, and there are many other ways very different from hers. Some readers may feel a distance between themselves and Margaret that only increases their feelings of isolation and turmoil in this difficult stage of life. Teachers could keep *Are You There, God* in a basket of books in the classroom that contains other books about adolescence that represent different experiences of this time of life.

The text may inspire some readers to think about society and social values in new ways. Readers can analyze how family units are formed. Margaret is close to her grandmother from her father's side of the family, but she does not want to see her mother's parents, even though she's never met them, because their visit will interfere with her trip to Florida. She does not care to meet these strangers because she has other plans, but mostly because her parents have prejudiced her views about them. Though the reader may realize that Margaret wants to go on the trip, and may even sympathize with her, many readers will question whether Margaret is right to sideline her family in such a way. These readers may come up with better solutions.

The way the girls gossip in this book is realistic and hurtful. It is so hurtful that Margaret ends up violently insulting Laura, a girl she's jealous of because she has a big chest. The reader will probably want to critique Margaret's motivations and actions and critique the effects of gossip on people in life as well. In this respect, the text helps students to develop the thinking skills necessary to understand a character, and yet to say, "I disagree," or "I hope I would have handled this differently." This sort of reflection can, of course, help readers make moral decisions in their own lives. If this book is the center of small group conversation in a book-club, readers will do a lot of lifework as well as reading work, and in the end this will help them see that books can matter to our lives.

The text may also trigger other conversations and even personal inquiries

A Field Guide to the Classroom Library, Lucy Calkins and the Teachers College Reading and Writing Project, Heinemann, ©2002 Teachers College, Columbia University; http://www.heinemann.com/fieldguides

about religions, just as Margaret's school assignment launched her on an inquiry. Many students do not know about the religions of their peers, or even their own religion, and this book can change that.

Often, readers will want to write about the connections between this text and their lives. Using the text can help them think about their own feelings and experiences, and using their own lives to help them understand what Margaret is going through.

The text would be best for readers who understand and are ready to talk about puberty, since the issues are so intimate and personal.

Book Connections

It may be a good idea for readers to be familiar with Blume's other books at lower levels, which don't have such sophisticated ideas, such as *SuperFudge* and *Freckle Juice*. This way, the student becomes familiar with her style of discussing real, raw everyday child events. A Blume book that is harder than this one, which may interest admirers of the present text, is *Just As Long As We're Together*, which deals with adolescent friendship and coping with divorce. Because Blume writes books at different levels, her books can support all readers in the class.

Genre
Chapter Book

Teaching Uses
Small Group Strategy Instruction; Independent Reading; Character Study; Teaching Writing; Critique

A Field Guide to the Classroom Library, Lucy Calkins and the Teachers College Reading and Writing Project, Heinemann, ©2002 Teachers College, Columbia University; http://www.heinemann.com/fieldguides

Autumn Street

Lois Lowry

Book Summary

While her father is off fighting in World War II, six-year-old Elizabeth lives with her grandparents on Autumn Street in a small town in Pennsylvania. Now an adult looking back on that time, Elizabeth conjures up in luminous detail the people who filled her life: her mother and older sister, her grandparents, the three spinster great-aunts, and-especially-her beloved Tatie, the black cook, and Tatie's young grandson Charles, Elizabeth's best friend. With the world she knew disrupted by war, the imaginative Elizabeth suspects danger everywhere. She worries that her father will never return and that her pregnant mother will die in childbirth. She is terrified by tales she hears of flesh-eating turtles, and a man ground flat by a train.

As the months pass, significant events, both good and bad occur. Elizabeth's mother safely delivers a baby boy. Her grandfather buys Elizabeth an autograph book, but she is dismayed to discover that Tatie doesn't know how to write her name in it. She and Charles ignore the cries of a neighbor boy who is ill because they despise him for his cruelty to animals; when the boy dies, they believe they are to blame. Charles and Elizabeth visit her three great-aunts, who make such a fuss over Charles that Elizabeth, in a fit of jealousy, calls him a nigger. Elizabeth's elegant grandfather suffers an incapacitating stroke, and Elizabeth struggles to make contact with him.

When fall arrives, both Elizabeth and Charles start first grade, but in separate, segregated schools. Elizabeth makes friends with a girl named Louise and encounters the town crazy man, Ferdie Gossett, of whom she has heard many stories. During Thanksgiving dinner at the home of the great-aunts, Elizabeth learns a family secret concerning an engagement between her grandfather and one of the great-aunts. And finally, with chilling inevitability, comes the painful event alluded to in the opening of the book.

Despite a sore throat, Elizabeth goes sledding with Charles, taking him to the local park. Older boys mistreat him and order him off the hill because he is black. Enraged and humiliated, Charles runs off into the woods. Elizabeth, feverish and fearful of some nameless threat, turns back. While Elizabeth lies ill, the police discover Charles in the woods with his throat slit, a victim of Ferdie Gossett. Elizabeth struggles with her illness and with the awful news of the tragedy. On her seventh birthday, her father arrives, using a cane because he has lost part of one leg. "Bad things won't happen any more," he assures Elizabeth and the adult narrator.

Basic Book Information

Seventeen chapters and 188 pages long, this novel looks back at a year in a child's life as seen from adulthood. The main character is only six, but the

Publisher
Dell Yearling, 1986

ISBN
0440403448

TC Level
14

richly nuanced story and sophisticated writing make the novel more appropriate for readers from age nine and up. Although the narrator and central character is a girl, there is also a male character of the same age who figures prominently in the plot. Boys who enjoy challenging themes and high-quality writing will like this complex story. The book received starred reviews from *Booklist* and *School Library Journal*. Lowry has written many books for young readers from lower middle grades up to young adult. She received the Newbery Medal for *Number The Stars* and *The Giver* and won acclaim for *A Summer to Die*.

Noteworthy Features

The first-person story is told in the voice of the adult narrator. The opening and closing sections frame the tale and set the tone for the often painful memories that will be recounted. Characters are strongly developed.

Stylistically, Lowry accomplishes a difficult feat, unifying the adult voice of the narrator with the perceptions and emotions of the child she was at six.

Teaching Ideas

The story is set in a small town in Pennsylvania during World War II, a setting unfamiliar to many young readers. Teachers may find it helpful to readers to provide some orientation to the setting to prepare students for the story.

This book is full of symbolism and deeper meanings for an astute reader who is willing to dig below the surface. It is, therefore, a great book for readers who are learning to do interpretive work. In a conference, a teacher could ask, "Why did the author do this? What do you think she is trying to say?" One challenge, when a reader interprets, is to go from saying something about one part of a text to saying something about the entire text. "Why are the woods portrayed in such a foreboding way, do you think?" a teacher might ask and then respond to *whatever* the child says by asking, "so go from that to saying something about the book as a whole. How do your ideas of the woods, for example, fit with the title?" There are no right and wrong answers but readers need to learn to justify their interpretations with evidence from the text and to try to compose interpretations that account for as many parts of the text as possible.

When helping youngsters to think about the deeper meanings in a book, it is helpful to remind them that nothing in the book is accidental. The way the book opens and closes, the names of the characters, the metaphors Lowry uses etc. are all chosen for deliberate reasons. Lowry could have done all of these things differently. Why might she have made these choices?

The opening section makes it clear that the story will culminate in tragedy, and the description of the murky color the narrator would paint the woods ("the hueless shade that I know from my dreams to be the color of pain") hints that the tragedy will happen there. However, Lowry withholds the exact nature of the painful event and builds suspense by including other elements and incidents that suggest horrifying possibilities, but which don't prove central to the ultimate tragedy. Students can analyze the way she accomplishes this by listing those elements and incidents: the giant flesh-eating turtles Elizabeth believes inhabit the woods; the statement that baby boys are often born during the war to replace fathers killed in conflict; Willard B. Stanton's gruesome death under the wheels of a train; the knife found by Charles; Noah Hoffman's cruelty to animals and to his brother. In the opening section the narrator describes the painting she would make of Autumn Street in a way that suggests a Chagall painting. A reader might briefly research works by Chagall to help imagine the way that painting would look.

Teachers have used selective excerpts from this book as examples of good writing. Children could spend days discussing the passages in which Tatie shows Elizabeth the taste of cinnamon (and she in turn shows her grandfather) or Elizabeth's description of the awful taste of school milk.

Book Connections

Lois Lowry is a prolific writer for children. Her *Anastasia* series includes *Anastasia Krupnik, Anastasia Again!, Ask Your Analyst, Anastasia on Her Own, Anastasia at Your Service, Anastasia Has the Answers, Anastasia's Chosen Career*, and *Anastasia at This Address*. She has also written *Number The Stars* and *The Giver*. A book that takes a similar, but light-hearted, look at two kids staying with their grandmother during the 1924-42 era, is Richard Peck's *A Long Way from Chicago*.

Genre
Chapter Book

Teaching Uses
Independent Reading; Interpretation; Teaching Writing

A Field Guide to the Classroom Library, Lucy Calkins and the Teachers College Reading and Writing Project, Heinemann, ©2002 Teachers College, Columbia University; http://www.heinemann.com/fieldguides

Baby
Patricia MacLachlan

Book Summary

The story begins at summer's end. The tourists have left the island, and Larkin's family returns home to find a baby on their doorstep. A note reads, "This is Sophie. She is almost a year old and she is good. I cannot take care of her now, but I know she will be safe with you." Although it has not yet been revealed to the reader, the family has recently suffered, yet not acknowledged, the loss of their own baby. They are as yet incapable of even mentioning his brief presence in their lives, as the grief is too big for words. Larkin's father warns her against loving Sophie. It will be too painful, he thinks, when her mother returns and removes her from them. What he doesn't yet realize is that by allowing himself to love her, then leave her, he will be able to name and experience his grief. He will be capable of mourning the loss of his son.

The book begins its journey toward resolution when Larkin's teacher, Ms. Minifred tells the story of her own brother William, who has died. She says, "He wanted to be a writer, and he once said to me that words were comforting. Words had power, he told me. There was no way I could accept his death. . . . And then I found a poem among my brother's books. . . . When I read it I felt a strange and powerful comfort-not because it made me feel better, but because it said what I felt." She then recites "Dirge Without Music," by Edna St. Vincent Millay. Although Ms. Minifred will never accept William's death, she can now find the words to name it. The poem provided her with a mirror, through which she can see and ultimately accept the unnamable magnitude of her grief. Through this experience, Larkin is now able to do the same. She names the family baby William. At the conclusion of the story, her family marks his grave with a headstone bearing his name. In naming the baby, they are acknowledging his brief existence in their lives and are ultimately able to mourn his loss.

Basic Book Information

This book has 132 pages, divided into seventeen chapters. The chapters are not titled, and signal new phases in Larkin's family's journey toward naming and accepting their grief. The story is told in four parts: Summer's End, Winter, Spring, and Summer-Ten Years Later. It ends where it begins, yet the characters are not the same, thus reflecting the circular, transformative nature of time. The seasons are also reflective of the characters' experiences of their loss.

An excerpt from "Dirge Without Music," a poem by Edna St. Vincent Millay, precedes the title page, and is cited in its entirety on page eighty-five. MacLachlan uses italics to set poetry, songs, and glimpses into Larkin's thinking apart from the rest of the text. The first chapter, and every second chapter after that, begins with a brief, italicized passage clearly describing a

A Field Guide to the Classroom Library, Lucy Calkins and the Teachers College Reading and Writing Project, Heinemann, ©2002 Teachers College, Columbia University; http://www.heinemann.com/fieldguides

Publisher
Bantam Doubleday Dell, 1993

ISBN
0440411459

TC Level
12

memory. These are Sophie's memories of the family that was for a brief time her family, as told from a future, undisclosed place and time.

Noteworthy Features

The text begins with a stanza from Edna St. Vincent Millay's "Dirge Without Music." MacLachlan clues her readers into the central theme of this story, namely, Larkin's family's inability to face and accept the death of their infant son. Through Larkin's character, it is this poem that provides them with the language to express a feeling for which there are no words.

Students may not understand the poem at the opening of the book. MacLachlan probably intends for her readers to uncover and discover its meanings along with Larkin, who also does not understand the poem when it is first read to her. Teachers can encourage students to use the context of the poem to build their own theories about what it means to be resigned to something. When the poem finds its place in the story, it is probably not necessary to discuss it in its entirety. Instead, readers can look at it through Larkin's eyes, focusing primarily on the two lines she repeats to herself. These are essential to her story.

Along with providing her readers with a deeper understanding of the journey Larkin's family needs to take, MacLachlan creates an outstanding opportunity to discuss the real purpose literature serves in their lives. The characters feel that among other things, books and poems make them feel less alone helping them to hold mirrors up to experiences and feelings, empowering them with the language to talk. As Byrd says to Larkin, "You will have to find your way. Your dream is like a poem, you know. It puts in words what you think about but can't say. Maybe that's what poems do."

The italicized passages that precede every two chapters are also a potential source of difficulty. These are Sophie's memories of Larkin's family, as remembered from a future time and place. They are written from Sophie's point of view. MacLachlan begins, "The memory is this: a blue blanket in a basket that pricks her bare legs, and the world turning over as she tumbles out." While to a more experienced reader it is clear that these are Sophie's future memories of the story that is presently unfolding, MacLachlan's playfulness with both time and point of view will most likely confuse young readers. Teachers can provide students with a moment to develop hypotheses concerning the function of these passages, then explain them. This will probably greatly facilitate their understanding of the text, and free them to focus on the questions that are closer to the heart of the story.

Finally, MacLachlan does not initially reveal the secret that hangs heavy in the air surrounding Larkin's family. Although it will be tempting, teachers should be wary of telling students the story of William's death before the author does. She intends to keep her readers guessing, all the while providing clues toward the development of their own theories. By the time the plot is fully explained, most students will have accurately guessed the specifics of its content.

Teaching Ideas

This book is absolutely perfect for reading aloud and studying closely

A Field Guide to the Classroom Library, Lucy Calkins and the Teachers College Reading and Writing Project, Heinemann, ©2002 Teachers College, Columbia University; http://www.heinemann.com/fieldguides

through daily, whole class book talks. Its subject matter is extremely emotional, and it is filled with metaphors, layers of meanings and themes that less experienced readers may not discern independently. Some teachers have found it helpful to gently guide conversations toward the fact that Larkin's family will not articulate a secret that needs to be articulated, then support readers as they gather evidence toward the resolution of this central tension.

Some teachers have found that after spending time reading aloud and discussing this book, it is worthwhile to encourage children to harvest all their insights into literary essays. Each reader will need to review his or her jottings and notes and scan the pages of the book asking, "What is an insight or an idea about this book that snags my attention, that seems to matter?" Hopefully a class of readers will have a whole array of beginning ideas. One may notice that this is a book about the events that break the circles and patterns and rhythms of life. Another may notice that this is a book about Baby-an unnamed infant-who has the power that all babies have, the power to turn life around. Another may notice that the book is knit from Sophie's memories, and that what she remembers and doesn't remember is significant. Some will see this as the story of a family learning to accept a loss. Yet others will see this as a book about the silences in our lives, about the words that can bridge awful silences, and about families needing to communicate.

Larkin already knows the deafening sounds of silence. When Ms. Minifred moons over the power of words, Larkin thinks, "What about when there are no words?" "Silence can change you too, Ms. Minifred." Over time, Larkin begins to learn that words are powerful as well. A reader could gather evidence of this growing appreciation. After Ms. Minifred shares the experience of her brother's death and use of poetry as catharsis, Larkin runs home to read Millay's poem. She finally becomes equipped with the words to confront her mother. "I never saw the baby!" she said softly. "And you never named him! And you never talked to me about him!" Larkin learns to speak into the silence choking her family.

Book Connections

MacLachlan's *Journey* also addresses the title character's journey toward facing and accepting the truth. As Larkin's family is initially incapable of finding the language to cope with their loss, the boy Journey initially refuses to acknowledge the fact that his mother is never coming back. In both books, the transformative power of relationships and the arts eventually allow characters come to terms with their grief. For Journey, it is photography as introduced by his grandfather. For Larkin it is Sophie, and the poetry that empowers her with words for a previously unnamable loss. *The Monument*, by Gary Paulsen, is also a story of acceptance and change as made possible through Rocky's relationship with Mick and her emerging artistic sensibility.

Genre
Chapter Book

A Field Guide to the Classroom Library, Lucy Calkins and the Teachers College Reading and Writing Project, Heinemann, ©2002 Teachers College, Columbia University; http://www.heinemann.com/fieldguides

Teaching Uses
Read Aloud; Teaching Writing; Book Clubs

A Field Guide to the Classroom Library, Lucy Calkins and the Teachers College Reading and Writing Project, Heinemann, ©2002 Teachers College, Columbia University; http://www.heinemann.com/fieldguides

Baseball in April and Other Stories

Gary Soto

Book Summary

This collection of short stories focuses on the everyday lives of Hispanic children and teens growing up in Fresno, California. Many of the stories revolve around the main character's yearning for something (a guitar, a Barbie doll, a new dress for a dance, a chance to play Little League) and tell how the character goes about trying to achieve that goal.

In "Barbie," Veronica "had wanted a Barbie for as long as she could remember." Her Uncle Rudy does eventually buy her the doll she wants, while at the same time announcing his upcoming wedding, but at the end, Veronica's Barbie's head falls off and is lost.

In "The No-Guitar Blues," Fausto wants a guitar so badly he tells a small lie to gain the money to buy one. Consumed with guilt about his wrongdoing, he puts the money into the church collection. This story ends on a happy note, though, when his mother remembers that his grandfather has an old "guitarron" stored in his garage.

In "Mother and Daughter," Yollie and her mother share a special closeness. Mrs. Moreno is so poor she often can't afford to buy her daughter the clothes she needs, especially a new dress for the upcoming outdoor dance. They dye Yollie's white summer dress black, and for a while the dress is a big hit, until it begins to rain. The dye runs out, leaving Yollie's dress and her mood, gray.

Basic Book Information

This collection of short stories, 134 pages long, was named an ALA Best Book for Young Adults, A Booklist Editors' Choice, and A Horn Book Fanfare Selection. It also won the Beatty Award. Each chapter is a separate story from nine to fifteen pages long. The chapter titles hint at the focus of each story and draw readers in with names like "Broken Chain," "The Karate Kid," and "The No-Guitar Blues." While some figures later reappear as minor characters in other chapters, each story stands on its own. Except for the cover, there are no illustrations. However, Soto, who is also a poet, describes characters with such telling details that he provides readers with strong images. In the first story, young Alfonso keeps trying to push his crooked teeth back into place with his fingers. In a later story, Lupe works so hard to strengthen her thumb (in order to become a marbles champion) that her mother thinks her thumb is broken. There is an appealing simplicity and innocence to the children Soto describes. The stories are funny and ring true to life. Children will enjoy reading them and will probably identify with the characters.

Publisher
Harcourt Brace & Company, 1990

ISBN
015205720X

TC Level
12

Noteworthy Features

"Baseball in April," set in Fresno, California, is rich in details drawn from Hispanic life.

While each chapter stands on its own as an independent story, it is also possible to trace the common themes of growing up, love and friendship, success and failure throughout the anthology. Although the vocabulary and sentence structure are not complex, there is a maturity level to the stories that stems from the fact that some characters are as old as fifteen and also from the adult nature of some of the themes, such as being poor and falling in love for the first time. At times the author uses Spanish words and expressions; however, the characters who use them usually follows up immediately with the English words. There is also a glossary of Spanish words and phrases at the back of the book.

These stories reflect Gary Soto's own experiences growing up in California's Central Valley. Although the incidents in these stories have broad appeal and could have happened to practically any child at any time, there is a rich strain of Latino culture threaded through the narrative. Food plays an important role. One mother is cooking papas and chorizo con huevos. In another story, "a pile of tortillas lay warm under a dishtowel." Although poverty is common among the families in the stories, what stands out is their strong sense of family bonds; their pride, loyalty, and respect; and the way family and friends support each other. An offshoot of this is that these children are polite and respectful. Extended family is highly visible throughout the stories. In "La Bamba," the whole family comes to see Manuel pantomime Ritchie Valens's "La Bamba" in the school talent show. When Lupe shoots her way to victory in the marbles tournament in "The Marble Champ," her brother and father come along to cheer her on. "Growing Up" tells the story of Maria, a tenth grader who considers herself too old to go on the family vacation this year. After a heated argument with her father, she is allowed to stay behind with an aunt, but she winds up missing her family and worrying that something terrible has happened to them.

Teaching Ideas

Gary Soto creates rich characters, placing them in true-to-life situations. These stories could support work with students "putting themselves in their character's shoes," and emotionally empathizing with them. In doing this, they can help to create the world of the story in their minds. Some students may have connections to their own lives that help them in this endeavor. Several of the stories appear to have "unsatisfying" endings, such as "Baseball in April," "Two Dreamers," "Barbie," and "The Karate Kid." It might be useful for readers to consider why he or she thinks Gary Soto ended some stories this way (and not others).

In addition, Soto uses strong, vivid details in his stories, such as Lupe's swollen thumb and Alfonso's crooked teeth, which look like "a pile of wrecked cars." Yollie's mother is portrayed as "a large woman who wore a muumuu and butterfly-shaped glasses." Students who are trying to create the world of the story in their minds may find it useful to visualize these details, making pictures of the world they wish to visit.

The short stories in "Baseball in April" also provide an opportunity for students to look at author choices in crafting a text. Teachers can encourage students to dig for the deeper message in the story, and to think about what Soto is *really* trying to say. Book clubs or partnerships who are experienced with these types of discussions may hold themselves accountable for the author's meaning. While this can be done with each story on its own, students may weave together meanings they discuss for each story and integrate them into a larger statement about the book as a whole.

A teacher may also choose to use these short stories to support story element work, and to encourage broader discussions of how the story elements influence each other. How does the setting, in a Latino neighborhood in Fresno, California, influence the plot? Can we always expect significant change with the passage of time? A related line of thinking some students may wish to pursue is seeking to document subtle, rather than overt, changes in character. For example, in "Barbie," Veronica gets the doll she always wanted, but the doll's head falls off. This may or may not have a profound influence on Veronica's character, but may have more subtle implications.

Book Connections

Students may want to read other books by Gary Soto. In *Taking Sides*, athlete Lincoln Mendoza must deal with conflicting loyalties when the basketball team at his new, suburban school plays the team from his old neighborhood school. In *Pacific Crossing*, a sequel to *Taking Sides*, Lincoln studies karate and travels to Japan.

Genre
Short Story Anthology; Memoir

Teaching Uses
Whole Group Instruction; Small Group Strategy Instruction; Partnerships; Book Clubs

Baseball Saved Us

Ken Mochizuki

Book Summary

This is the story of a Japanese-American boy who was forced, with his family, to live in an internment camp during WWII. The family tries to stay positive and keep their values and beliefs intact in the face of this cruel injustice, but slowly the situation wears down their community. When the boy's older brother is rude to their father, the father knows it's time for drastic measures. They create a baseball team within the camp that helps morale. Even after he is allowed to leave the camp, when the boy faces rudeness and prejudice at school, his skill at the game helps teammates to accept him. Thus, baseball eases hardship for them.

Basic Book Information

This picture book could be classified as either fiction or historical fiction. It is certainly true that the context for this story is based on historical realities, and for this reason, many teachers use the book more as historical fiction than as fiction.

The book is about twenty-five pages long and contains about two paragraphs of mid-sized text on each double page spread. The text is presented as a continuous story, with only an author's note at the story's beginning. This is not a book meant for note-taking or fact gathering like a book with an index and labeled pictures, instead, it is a book intended to describe a reality and to put a personal face on a part of history. For this reason the illustrations aren't scientific, but instead descriptive and emotive.

Noteworthy Features

This book contains an Author's Note at the beginning, rather than at the end of the book. This note is also set to catch attention, in the middle of a white page just after the title page, right where the reader would expect the actual story to begin. Although it is set in a smaller font than the rest of the text, it does call out to be read. Undoubtedly, many students will read it instead of turning directly to the next page on which the story begins. If however a teacher notices in a conference that a reader has bypassed this section, the teacher will want to direct readers to this part. Teachers, too, will want to read this part aloud if they read the book aloud. Although the small note could stand alone, it is likely that readers unfamiliar with this piece of history will have questions about it, and the conversations that ensue may well serve as the best possible introduction to this book.

Illustrator
Dom Lee

Publisher
Scholastic, 1993

ISBN
0590808052

TC Level
12

A Field Guide to the Classroom Library, Lucy Calkins and the Teachers College Reading and Writing Project, Heinemann, ©2002 Teachers College, Columbia University; http://www.heinemann.com/fieldguides

Teaching Ideas

The realistic and careful illustrations in the book will probably help readers picture the setting and the emotions in the story.

Many teachers read this book aloud and support whole-class discussions while working with children on the subjects of racism and discrimination. Some teachers use it at the beginning of the school year, to start discussions about the students building an inclusive community in the classroom. Some move from this book to some sophisticated talk about what would have happened if the little boy hadn't hit a home run, or even if he had struck out. They can talk about what it means that when he wasn't a good baseball player he wasn't accepted, and when he got better, he began to be accepted. Sometimes readers talk also about the anger the boy felt just before he hit the home run at the camp. Where did that anger come from? Was he also feeling anger when he hit the second home run? Was this anger good for him? How does this book lead us to critique society? There are many important issues even on the surface of this book, and teachers can support children in delving into them.

The historical setting of this story is complicated and tragic, and therefore difficult for some readers to grasp. While the author's note and the explanations contained within the text may be enough for readers to understand the book, it may leave them with many questions. Why, for example, did the brother's rudeness to his father mean that the father should build the baseball diamond immediately? Students would have to be able to understand a lot about the camp, life for the family before the camp, and the emotions involved in being there in order to answer that question. Answering the question may get in the way of the reading, or it may further it, if students are ready to try to answer it. Of course, that question is not the only one in the book that requires hard thinking or deep understanding to find an answer. The boy's treatment by his teammates and the spectators at his schools is also hard to understand. Why are they behaving so badly? The characters in the book and their motivations are not at all easy to understand. Even without a full understanding, however, the book can be very powerful.

The text describes and begins to explain an enormous and hard-to-understand subject with fairly simple language and easy-to-grasp details. Readers drawn in to the boy's experience with baseball can begin to feel also his experience being at the internment camp, and being the survivor of cruel discrimination by his schoolmates. By following the boy's sports experience, one with which many children can identify, readers can begin to understand how it would feel to be in an unfamiliar situation. The familiar part of the book can support children in understanding the unfamiliar. This is a unique feature of this book.

Book Connections

The book *Farewell to Manzanar* is a much more difficult book that also deals with the issues of Japanese internment camps. There are many others available to teachers and readers.

A Field Guide to the Classroom Library, Lucy Calkins and the Teachers College Reading and Writing Project, Heinemann, ©2002 Teachers College, Columbia University; http://www.heinemann.com/fieldguides

Genre

Historical Fiction; Picture Book; Memoir

Teaching Uses

Reading and Writing Nonfiction; Content Area Study; Read Aloud; Critique

Ben and Me

Robert Lawson

Book Summary

In this sixty-year-old classic, Amos, Benjamin Franklin's faithful mouse, recounts his exploits with the inventor. According to this clever mouse, many of Franklin's discoveries and inventions were made because of Amos' influence.

Basic Book Information

Robert Lawson, famous for his Newbery award winning *Rabbit Hill*, created this fantastical account of Amos the mouse over sixty years ago. The story is told tongue-in-cheek by Lawson who introduces the book with a letter explaining his discovery of this manuscript. The story is then narrated by Amos the mouse in the first person. From the language of the story, we know Amos is a very learned mouse, with possession of an incredible vocabulary and knowledge of many literary works as well as the happenings of the Colonial times.

Noteworthy Features

Having a mouse tell his own story is very appealing to young readers, however, readers who are too young won't have enough knowledge of the world, literature, and vocabulary to understand much of this book. There are some black and white drawings by Lawson that illustrate particular scenes.

Readers will need to have some knowledge and understanding of Benjamin Franklin and the Colonial period to appreciate most of the humor in this book. For example, when Ben and Amos go to France and experience the Battle of Versailles, readers will benefit enormously, understanding much more of the humor and twists if they already know what this is all about.

Teaching Ideas

Lawson presents history from an interesting perspective and shows life in Colonial times in a way that readers will not have heard from in non-fiction material that they read. Although this is considered a "classic children's story," it really is for sophisticated readers and adults. *Ben and Me* would make a great read aloud, especially selected chapters such as "We Invent the Franklin Stove," and "Electricity." In these chapters the principles behinds

Illustrator

Robert Lawson

Publisher

Little, Brown, 1939

ISBN

0316517305

TC Level

14

the discoveries are explained in an entertaining manner, though some of them may need annotation by the teacher.

Reading *Ben and Me* aloud serves another purpose: introducing the students to the style of Robert Lawson. Lawson's *Rabbit Hill*, long a favorite of children, has fallen out of fashion with modern readers who favor *Redwall* and *Harry Potter*-type fantasy. *Rabbit Hill*, though belongs in this club too, and readers will understand his humor better if they are introduced to Lawson's style with *Ben and Me* first.

This book reads like a joke intended for savvy readers with a sense of history. Amos as a character is not young; rather he is an opinionated bachelor, who indulges his patron Ben Franklin in his eccentricities. Taking on a cultural icon such as Ben Franklin, with such humor may open many possibilities for proficient readers. Humorous historical fiction is not common, probably because it could be seen to incite skepticism among young people. However, it is this skepticism that gives readers a critical lens to view the world.

Upper- grade readers who are learning to discern and read for the author's point of view (not just the character's point of view) need to recognize humor and see how writers use it as a literary device. Readers could use post-it notes to mark all the occasions that Amos pokes fun at Ben Franklin, as well as the times when the author shows the ludicrous nature of Amos himself, his egotism and reticence to experience high-flying adventure (especially in the chapter where Amos goes flying on the kite and is electrocuted!). Lawson includes a letter to the reader on the first page, which explains how he found the manuscript of Amos the mouse. Lawson's tone is self-effacing and understated. If a reader can recognize this, they can begin to see the kind of humor that pervades this book.

Ben and Me can also offer a great introduction to literary criticism. Literary criticism is a study of literature that breaks open the author's intent, through the use of language, the elements of story (plot, character, setting, theme), and the resulting interpretation. Readers learn to ask questions such as: What does the author intend for this piece to mean? How has it been achieved? Has it been achieved? How does the author's view go with reality?

Book Connections

Teachers may also want to read aloud portions of Lawson's *Mr. Revere and I*, which contains a similar story, but centers around Paul Revere.

Readers who enjoy this humorous take on history, may also appreciate the humor in the *Horrible Histories* series.

Another book that features a "historically important" mouse is *She Was Nice to Mice* by Alexandra Elizabeth Sheedy. The main character in this tale is a mouse named Esther Long Whiskers Gray Hair Wallgate who happens to be a friend of Queen Elizabeth I of England.

Genre
Historical Fiction; Chapter Book

A Field Guide to the Classroom Library, Lucy Calkins and the Teachers College Reading and Writing Project, Heinemann, ©2002 Teachers College, Columbia University; http://www.heinemann.com/fieldguides

Teaching Uses
Content Area Study; Independent Reading; Read Aloud; Critique

A Field Guide to the Classroom Library, Lucy Calkins and the Teachers College Reading and Writing Project, Heinemann, ©2002 Teachers College, Columbia University; http://www.heinemann.com/fieldguides

Birthday Surprises
Various, Edited by Johanna Hurwitz

Book Summary

This is a collection of short stories, written by noted children's authors and centering on the theme of receiving an empty box as a present. Each author has taken the idea of the empty box and fashioned a unique story. Writers include Jane Yolen, Richard Peck, James Howe, Karla Kuskin, Ann M. Martin, and David Adler.

Basic Book Information

This is a collection of short stories, ranging in length from ten to fifteen pages. The stories explore the nature of family relationships, friendships, hope, and humor.

All proceeds of this book are generously donated to the Teachers College Reading and Writing Project at Columbia University and to the National Writing Project of the University of California, Berkeley.

Noteworthy Features

At the end of the book there is a selected bibliography of the authors and their works. This information encourages readers to pursue other writing of authors they like. There is also a letter to the reader from Johanna Hurwitz, who has contributed to, as well as edited, this collection. It is interesting to know that these stories were contracted, and not just collected over time. This was a project that Hurwitz conceived of, prompting writers with a theme and seeing what would happen. This is an example of how prompts can work in writing, especially for authors who are experienced at finding their own topic out of their lives. Giving a prompt like this to students may be less advisable.

Teaching Ideas

Birthday Surprises can be used for a study of interpretation. In each story, all of the story elements (plot, character, setting) combine with an empty box to create the story. All of these stories have a major piece that is the same, and yet there are many other pieces that are different.

There is one story, "What the Princess Discarded," by Barbara Ann Porte that has a fairy tale structure. However, the story ends abruptly, with a change in tone of the narrator. Until this part, the narrator had kept a distance from the story, telling it as the third person omniscient (all-knowing) narrator, with an impartial stance. At the very end, the story reads, "And that's a true story." This brings the narrator front and center to

Publisher
Morrow Junior Books, 1995

ISBN
0688131948

TC Level
12

A Field Guide to the Classroom Library, Lucy Calkins and the Teachers College Reading and Writing Project, Heinemann, ©2002 Teachers College, Columbia University; http://www.heinemann.com/fieldguides

the reader as well as unveiling the fairy tale as really a true story. This shift can create some difficulty. Yet none of this was done accidentally, and readers will want to muse over how this form supports the author's meaning. How does the last line in the story change everything that has gone before it? Readers should be encouraged to re-read this story (and others) to see if the subsequent read is different than the first. And if so, how?

Birthday Surprises can also serve as an introduction to some children's authors that are unfamiliar to readers as well as the genre of story collections. The stories are short, and yet provide a rich introduction to the author and his or her style. Some teachers have even used these stories as advertisements for these authors, reading them one at a time between other Read Alouds, to whet the appetite of curious readers.

Short texts such as those in this book are also treasures when we want to teach children to talk, think, and write well about a text. Short stories like these are also perfect to use when the teacher wants to model use of a particular writing tool (like a highlighter) or strategy (like marking the most interesting parts for a discussion).

With permission, teachers can duplicate one of these stories and ask children to read it in preparation for a book talk. Perhaps the talk begins with, "So what are some of the ideas you developed while reading this story?" but after laying out an array of possibilities, the class will probably agree upon a focus for their discussion. The great thing about a short story is that students can re-read it, marking it up, so as to be prepared for a talk which deepens a shared, agreed upon focus.

This book is a treasure chest of short texts, each of which can be used in some depth to demonstrate strategies good readers use when they read. Short stories are precious teaching tools because they allow teachers and children to hold themselves accountable to more of the text. When a child has read a novel, that child can usually say quite a few things about the story and there is *always* so much that by definition *must* be left unsaid that it's hard for a teacher to really see what children delete from their accounts. But when children read a short story that teachers know well, it's much easier to get an accurate glimpse of what any particular reader sees and overlooks in a text. If, for example, a child misses the motivation for the central action, and has no sense of how much time passed over the course of a story, this tends to show up when a teacher and child discuss the story together.

Book Connections

Johanna Hurwitz, the overall editor of this book, is famous for her *Russell* series, as well as many other older books for upper grade readers. Ann M. Martin has written the *Babysitter's Club* as well as the *California Diaries* series that many adolescent readers love. Pam Conrad has written *My Daniel* and *Holding Me Here*. Richard Peck has written many books, most notably the *Soup* series and a follow-up book, *Blossom Culp and the Sleep of Death*. David Adler is the author of the *Cam Jansen* series and the *Andy Russell* books. James Howe may be best known for his *Bunnicula* series. Karla Kuskin is mostly known as a poet and a picture book writer.

A Field Guide to the Classroom Library, Lucy Calkins and the Teachers College Reading and Writing Project, Heinemann, ©2002 Teachers College, Columbia University; http://www.heinemann.com/fieldguides

Genre
Short Story Anthology

Teaching Uses
Whole Group Instruction; Interpretation; Small Group Strategy Instruction

Bluish
Virginia Hamilton

Book Summary

This story, set in an urban classroom, tells of the friendship and hope among three young girls. Natalie, or Bluish as the children call her, is recovering from cancer. She comes to Dreenie and Tuli's classroom in her wheelchair wearing a knitted hat. She is frail and weak, with her blue veins showing through her skin. Despite their fear, Dreenie and Tuli reach out to Bluish and the three make a pact in the end to not let anything happen to her.

In this story the entire class becomes a symbol of hope and acceptance. At first many of the students are too shy to wear the hats that Bluish knit for them. Later, as they are all sitting around the Christmas tree with their teacher, they surprise Bluish by putting on their hats. To this, Bluish says, "We're a field of flowers. We're all the same; we're different, too. Now you all look just like me."

Basic Book Information

Bluish is a 127-page, realistic fiction chapter book. There are seven chapters and five chapter-like journal entries. The chapters are told in third person and the journal entries are told in first person (from Dreenie's perspective). There are no illustrations in the text. The plot is told in chronological order and takes place in December.

Virginia Hamilton is a noted, highly acclaimed, and prolific author of children's literature. Her books often feature African American characters.

Noteworthy Features

Hamilton smoothly incorporates both the third- and first-person point of view in this text. While chapters are told in third person, giving us an unbiased description of the characters, Dreenie's journal is only about Bluish. The journal is interspersed evenly throughout the text, in chronological order, making it easy for students to make the transition to the journal and back again.

Bluish uses simple prosaic descriptions and a more colloquial language, which at times, reads more like poetry: "[Dreenie] described how this girl stood out, or sat out. Outside, after school, in her wheelchair." While most sentences are complete, Hamilton's short fragments may help slow the reader down so that they can better visualize the story. Here's another example: "Snow on her ski jacket. Bluish had on pink mittens. Wore a pink fuzzy hat."

In *Bluish,* Hamilton presents Hanukkah, Kwanzaa, and Christmas in an informative and interesting way. After their teacher introduces the holidays, Bluish brings out her dreidel and explains the Hanukkah game that children

A Field Guide to the Classroom Library, Lucy Calkins and the Teachers College Reading and Writing Project, Heinemann, ©2002 Teachers College, Columbia University; http://www.heinemann.com/fieldguides

Publisher
Scholastic, 1999

ISBN
0590288792

TC Level
14

play with it. Later in the book, Dreenie's parents describe the Kwanzaa celebration and the candle representations in the kinara of the candelabra. This book celebrates and embraces differences between cultures in a refreshingly compassionate way.

Teaching Ideas

Few characters remain flat in this story- they all go through changes. As students read, they can attach post-it notes to places in the text where they see changes or turning points occurring in the characters, especially in their feelings towards Bluish. These notes can be used to discuss why and how the class changes.

An important theme in the text is the idea of community. Hamilton takes great care in describing effective steps for such a project. Students could list the steps Dreenie's class takes in doing their class project and discuss how they would go about taking on a class project of their own.

Readers might also do a character study of the three girls. They could make three columns with Natalie, Dreenie, and Tuli and find and make notes about pages where their character traits are shown. They could then break into small conversations and discuss how the girls are alike and how they are different. How do they change over the course of the story? How can the readers make personal connections to them?

Book Connections

Virginia Hamilton is an award-winning author. She has written many moving and wonderful books for young adults including *The Planet of Junior Brown, Zeely, M. C. Higgins the Great* and many, many others.

Genre
Chapter Book

Teaching Uses
Character Study; Independent Reading

California Diaries #7: Dawn: Diary Two

Ann M. Martin

Book Summary

This book, the second diary of Dawn, reveals how she deals with the loss of her "former" best friend, Sunny, while tending to Sunny's dying mother and Dawn's own pregnant step-mother, all while attending middle school and later preparing to go to Connecticut for the summer. As she says, she feels "lonely. Tense. Sad," because she moved back to California to live with her father's family to console Sunny. However, Sunny is into an older crowd of friends, hangs on older boys, is truant, and ignores Dawn. Dawn tries to seek comfort from her other peers, Maggie, Amalia, and Duck. Dawn leaves for the East Coast at the end of the book with lingering unease over her "break-up" with Sunny, with concern for Maggie's weight issues, and with a longing to stay with her new baby sister.

Basic Book Information

Like a diary, the book has no page numbers. All in all, there are 21 entries, each varying in length from one paragraph to six pages. This may make it difficult for readers who are accustomed to stopping at the end of chapters. This book encourages a reader to pay close attention to where the text may suggest stops, instead of relying on chapter ends. Some entries are from the same day, but most are from different days. Keeping track of the dates of the entries is not as important as keeping track of the reflections and events that take over the text.

Noteworthy Features

This may be a comforting book for students who feel lonely, overwhelmed, and misunderstood. They may feel a connection to Dawn, who though a fictional character, is very realistic and experiences very real problems. Martin wonderfully captures all the confusion and drama of life as a middle school student. She ingeniously leaves the text unsettled and unsettling, just as life is. She presents life as real, ongoing, and complex, appropriate to how her readers may feel in their own lives. Thus, she comforts and supports them, since they know it is common to feel this way.

The text is written like a diary, so there are no chapters, but instead entries, which begin on any part of the page. Since it is a diary, the text primarily consists of Dawn's reflections, anguishes, and her retelling of her life events. She only tells what is necessary to reflect on her emotions, and does not give other information. Thus, the text helps students learn to infer events.

Series
California Diaries

Publisher
Scholastic

ISBN
0590018469

TC Level
12

For the careful writer, the text may serve as an example to follow. Students may want to try the diary genre for themselves.

The problems in this story are left unresolved at the end. The problem of Dawn's relationship with Sunny has not undergone any changes for the better. It has worsened because it has remained stagnant. In fact, she only addresses Sunny twice in the book. The text is a reflection of the narrator's ongoing life. It can influence a reader's life, because it provides support for young people dealing with life's difficulties. It can help readers understand that life's problems are ongoing, and thus teaches them that they must learn how to deal with life's paradoxes and complexities. The story suggests that writing, as Dawn does with her diary, can be a means for dealing with life. Thus, the text can transform students' lives, by offering writing as a strategy for understanding and coping with life issues.

Teaching Ideas

This text can be useful when writing in both the memoir and the diary genre. Dawn both retells and analyzes her own emotions to write in her diary-both techniques students can emulate when they write their own personal essays.

When students read this book within a partnership, readers will probably end up talking about Sunny's presence in the book. She plays a very powerful role, though she actually only appears twice. Although she attracts attention, she would probably not make for a good character study since she does not seem to undergo change and does not present much evidence of herself for readers to sort through.

It may be difficult for some students to understand Dawn's isolation, and extreme feelings of loss; thus, Martin emphasizes it throughout to help the reader understand it from different angles. Dawn feels as if she's not a real part of her father's union with Carol, his pregnant wife. She does not feel as if she has any close friends; she is just getting to know Amalia, and Maggie. She does not say she can use her East Coast family as support; in fact, Dawn refers to them as part of her other world. She, like others her age, is having a difficult time dealing with and not understanding change, particularly in friendships. Teachers can help readers better understand Dawn by thinking about their own lives. In the same way, teachers can help readers understand their own lives by thinking about Dawn. This is the power in making personal connections with books.

Book Connections

This is the seventh book in the series, and the second with Dawn as the protagonist. Martin has developed this series out of the best-selling *Babysitters Club,* which was written for a slightly younger audience, TC levels 10-11. In this series, the girls, including Dawn, have light-hearted babysitting and (middle) school adventures. Readers who grow out of this series may easily grow into *California Diaries,* though the themes differ. Martin has also written the *Little Sisters* series, for TC Level 8.

This is one of a whole batch of books written in diary fashion. Readers may want to compare this structure with that of *Letters from Rifka* (Hesse) which was written for readers of the same age.

Genre
Chapter Book

Teaching Uses
Teaching Writing

A Field Guide to the Classroom Library, Lucy Calkins and the Teachers College Reading and Writing Project, Heinemann, ©2002 Teachers College, Columbia University; http://www.heinemann.com/fieldguides

Call It Courage

Armstrong Perry

Book Summary

When Mafatu was a young boy he almost drowned in the "sea's angry fingers." It was an accident that claimed his mother's life and made him ever fearful of the waters that surrounded his Polynesian island. "Stout Heart," Mafatu's christened name did not seem fit for a boy who could never become a fisherman or warrior of the sea. The Hikeru people believed that, "A man who was afraid" had no place in their midst. So, Mafatu sets out in a lone canoe to prove himself. He conquers his fear of the sea and eventually comes ashore to an island. There, Mafatu is faced with great challenges. He stabs a wild boar, single-handedly kills a shark, and builds a canoe that will take him home. After escaping a group of cannibals that inhabit the island, Mafatu returns to his island a hero. As the ship sets shore his father cannot believe his eyes-"Here is my son come home from the sea. Mafatu, Stout Heart. A brave name for a brave boy!"

Basic Book Information

Call It Courage is a Newbery Award-winning book by Armstrong Perry. It is a fictional chapter book. Illustrations by Dom Lupo are on approximately every tenth page.

Noteworthy Features

The year that the story is set is not firmly established. The story opens, "It happened many years ago, before the traders and missionaries first came into the South Seas. . . ." Young readers may not know just how many years ago this was. Readers will probably get the sense that these are primitive times, but they may fall into the trap of thinking that life on a Polynesian island is still this way.

There are places in the book that have non-English phrases, usually without translation. Oftentimes, Mafatu will make an exclamation ("Aia, Ma'o!") or sing a song the reader cannot understand. Deciphering the exact meaning of the phrases is not essential to understanding the story. Most times, the author lets readers know the sentiment behind the statement.

The sentences in *Call It Courage* tend to be very short. They create a staccato rhythm. Oftentimes, the text borders on poetic with vivid descriptions of nature. "The sea was sparking and benign. The sun's rays were unbroken in their violence." Mafatu, while living on the island, is living in tune with nature. The narrator reflects the same astute observations of natural surroundings that Mafatu himself might make.

Mafatu is alone for the majority of the book. Stranded on the island, he learns the self-reliance that will eventually make him a hero. There are however other characters on the deserted island-animals and elements of

Illustrator
Dom Lupo

Publisher
Scholastic, Inc., 1940

ISBN
0590406116

TC Level
14

A Field Guide to the Classroom Library, Lucy Calkins and the Teachers College Reading and Writing Project, Heinemann, ©2002 Teachers College, Columbia University; http://www.heinemann.com/fieldguides

nature. His animals Uri and Kivi are his companions. And, the sea, a tiger shark and wild boar are enemies with whom Mafatu must contend.

Teaching Ideas

If a teacher pulls alongside a child who is reading this book, the teacher may want to chat a bit about the setting for this story. Readers may interpret "It happened many years ago" in different ways, and ". . . before the traders and missionaries came into the South Seas" will not provide a great deal of further clarification. It is important to dispel the misconception that life in the South Pacific is savage with tribes of "eaters-of-men" who make "terrible sacrifices."

Readers may notice the use of ellipses (. .). Throughout the book Perry uses ellipses when Mafatu is contemplating something (i.e., "The sea muttered its eternal threat to the reef. The sea...And a terrible trembling seized the boy's limbs."). The punctuation mark shows an intentional omission of words. Readers may want to note what events cause Mafatu's thoughts to trail off to gain a better understanding of the character's mind frame.

In *Call It Courage*, there are references to gods who control the forces of nature. Some readers may be unfamiliar with polytheistic cultures. So, references to "Moana, the Sea God" and "Maui, the God of the Fisherman" may be intriguing for these readers.

The treatment that Mafatu endures on his island will be alarming for readers. After the angry sea kills his mother and leaves him "too weak to even cry," Mafatu is fearful of it. Many readers will be empathetic to his terror. They may be shocked that even Mafatu's own stepbrothers mock, "Moana, the Sea God, thunders on the reef. He is angry with us all because Mafatu is afraid!" Obviously, this will create an opportunity for readers to read critically, thinking, "I'll disagree with the way Mafatu is treated in this book." The deep shame that Mafatu experiences makes him risk his life on the waters. The first few pages of the story set the circumstances for such extreme events-"There was only courage. A man who was afraid-what place had he is[ED: should be "in" instead of "is"?] their midst? And the boy Mafatu-son of Tavena Nui, the Great Chief of Hikueru-always had been afraid." Readers may need to reread the opening pages to better understand the context of the situation.

At the end of the book, Mafatu returns to his island a hero, ". . . a necklace of boar's teeth shone upon his chest; a splendid spear flashed in his hand." When his father meets him at the shore, Mafatu sways and says "My father, I..." His father catches him as he falls. Mafatu's death is only alluded to. Some readers may argue that Mafatu is merely overcome with fatigue from his battle with the sea. Readers individually or in partnerships may want to cite evidence for their argument.

The closing of *Call It Courage* is a full-circle ending-text is directly repeated from the opening-"It happened many years ago, before the traders and the missionaries first came into the South Seas, while the Polynesians were still great in number and fierce of heart." The ending then goes on to say that even today "the people of Hikeru sing this story in their chants and tell it over the evening fires." Understanding that the story of Mafatu has been told over generations may lead to a reinterpretation of the text. In *Call*

A Field Guide to the Classroom Library, Lucy Calkins and the Teachers College Reading and Writing Project, Heinemann, ©2002 Teachers College, Columbia University; http://www.heinemann.com/fieldguides

It Courage, Mafatu kills a wild boar, octopus, and tiger-shark with a knife. These seem like impossible feats. Understanding that this is a "story" and may be completely fictional or an exaggerated account may change reader's perspective on the events of the books.

Book Connections

Some readers may enjoy the book *Island of the Blue Dolphins,* which has the similar topic of survival. Jean Craighead George writes many books that feature people on their own in challenging natural settings as well.

Genre
Chapter Book

Teaching Uses
Independent Reading; Book Clubs; Partnerships

A Field Guide to the Classroom Library, Lucy Calkins and the Teachers College Reading and Writing Project, Heinemann, ©2002 Teachers College, Columbia University; http://www.heinemann.com/fieldguides

Chocolate-Covered Ants

Stephen Manes

Book Summary

After Max's little brother Adam gets an ant farm for his birthday, Max figures he can make a lot of money betting Adam that people really do eat chocolate-covered ants. Max's sneaky attempts to prove his point and his brother's skepticism lead to some humorous and unappetizing incidents. Even though Max himself eats quite a few ants, he still comes out the loser.

Basic Book Information

Chocolate-Covered Ants has 103 pages and is divided into eleven untitled chapters. There are no illustrations.

Noteworthy Features

This light, entertaining book has simple characters and straightforward plot development. It is one of a mini-genre of books with mostly male characters and an emphasis on mildly disgusting humor.

Max, Adam, and the mother are generic. Few details are available about their personalities, and all the reader knows of Max is that he is the older brother and finds his younger brother annoying. The mother is stereotypically squeamish about insects and pops up in the book mostly to enforce rules when things have gotten out of hand.

The writing is clear and the vocabulary is simple. Dialogue tags make it clear who is speaking.

While the setting appears to be suburban and at least middle-class, there is not much of a sense of place. Ages are unspecific as well, though the description of Max's school schedule implies that he is in middle school.

Max's character is not changed by his experiences. Though he is reprimanded for trying to take advantage of his brother, he continues to feel cheerfully competitive toward him. He jokes at the end that he wants an exterminator kit for his birthday-one that works "on little brothers."

Teaching Ideas

This book is appropriate for independent reading. While entertaining to readers who enjoy this style of humor, *Chocolate-Covered Ants* does not have well-developed characters or themes. One lightly-handled theme is sibling rivalry. Readers might consider rivalry in their own families and how it compares to Max and Adam's. Students may also want to discuss the bet Max made, and bets in general, and whether or how they lead to trouble.

Publisher
Scholastic, 1990

ISBN
0590409611

TC Level
10

Book Connections

In *How to Eat Fried Worms* by Thomas Rockwell, 10-year-old Billy faces the most revolting bet of his life. He must eat 15 worms in 15 days-but the reward will be worth it: $50 for a shiny new mini-bike.

Genre
Chapter Book

Teaching Uses
Independent Reading

A Field Guide to the Classroom Library, Lucy Calkins and the Teachers College Reading and Writing Project, Heinemann, ©2002 Teachers College, Columbia University; http://www.heinemann.com/fieldguides

Chuck Close Up Close

Jan Greenberg and Sandra Jordan

Book Summary

This is an incredible, visually intriguing book about one of the most famous American artists alive today, Chuck Close. He is handicapped and has a learning disability which is brought out at the start of the book. Chapter one tells about Chuck's difficulties in school. No one expected Chuck would amount to much-and of course, this has an important message for any child who doesn't feel valued. Chuck began his career as a somewhat traditional artist, living in Soho, New York, painting portraits. Now he takes photographs and divides them into squares on a grid and paints these squares onto giant 7' by 9' canvasses, like a mosaic. These are featured in museums including the Metropolitan Museum of Art and the Whitney Museum in New York.

Within the five chapters of this book, the authors tell the story of Close's life, his evolution as a painter, and his efforts to deal with his condition. As a young adult, he had a spinal artery collapse which left him partially paralyzed and in a wheelchair.

Basic Book Information

This biography is a mixture of a sophisticated book and a Nonfiction chapter book. Based on extensive interviews, the book is laced with quotes from Close and anecdotes told by him. It is filled with photographs, mostly showing his art.

The book begins with Close's childhood, tells about his development as an artist, and concludes with what the authors seem to regard as the final chapter, a chapter on his disease. The book doesn't end there, however, because this final chapter is followed by an informative three-page piece entitled, "What is a portrait?" which talks about the history of portraiture in both art and photography. This final piece contextualizes the art of Chuck Close.

Noteworthy Features

There are many reasons for the appeal of this book. First, the subject himself is intriguing. Close's art and his story appeal to kids. Some of that appeal is probably from the fact that he was an underdog surmounting all obstacles and reaching the top of his field. The book's appeal comes also from the way in which it is written. The authors juxtapose scenes from Close's life with information about him. The first paragraph, for example, begins, "Slip into Chuck Close's studio. You find yourself in a long white room with a thirteen-foot-high ceiling. . . ."

Written in italics, this is set against a paragraph which begins, "Do the people who knew Chuck Close when he was growing up in Tacoma,

A Field Guide to the Classroom Library, Lucy Calkins and the Teachers College Reading and Writing Project, Heinemann, ©2002 Teachers College, Columbia University; http://www.heinemann.com/fieldguides

Publisher
Dorling Publishers, 1998

ISBN
0789426587

Washington, still remember him?" If his teachers came across his name . . . do they recognize this celebrated artist as the uncoordinated kid in their classes with the Coke-bottle eyeglasses ... ?"

Teaching Ideas

Children would profit from having this book read aloud to them. In three sittings, a teacher could read the text aloud and pause to invite children to talk in pairs about their response to the text. Later, pulling the whole group together, a teacher might help children develop a shared, whole-class conversation around this text.

If a teacher pauses so that children can talk in pairs toward the end of the first chapter, at the picture of Close as an adult, some children will look closely at the picture and notice Close's handicap, asking "What's the matter with him?" They may ask questions which lead to a whole set of theorizing as the story of his life and his illness unfolds.

Often, children's conversations will begin with reactions to Close's art, and if this happens, teachers may want to help children extend that observation into something that is said in the text. If, for example, a child comments, "That's a weird way of painting," we might respond by asking that child and the class, "What have we learned about Close's life that can help us figure out why he paints in this way? What can the story teach us about what we are thinking?"

The book also invites readers to do some thinking about character. Most readers will be familiar with the idea of thinking about characters in fictional stories. The interesting thing is that when reading fiction, children may be used to thinking about the character's personality and motivations but often, when reading Nonfiction, readers are more apt to collect facts. If the personality and motivations of a character are present in a Nonfiction text, it is often explicitly defined rather than revealed. That is, often in biographies, the author takes the work of getting to know a character's personality and motivations out of the readers' hands. In this book, however, readers are given enough raw data-or story-about the character that it's easy and inviting to think about this true character as one might think about a character in a novel. Because this book juxtaposes the work and the life of Close, it almost sets us up to do rich inferring work between the two.

Genre
Nonfiction; Biography; Chapter Book

Teaching Uses
Reading and Writing Nonfiction; Read Aloud; Whole Group Instruction; Content Area Study

Clockwork: or All Wound Up
Philip Pullman

Book Summary

On a biting, snowy winter evening the night before the unveiling of a new animated figure for Glockenheim's clock, the townsfolk gather in the White Horse Tavern to listen to a young storyteller, Fritz, spin his latest yarn. Fritz, however, has no ending to his story, and Karl, the apprentice clockmaker, has been lazy and is the first apprentice in hundreds of years to produce-nothing. Both are desperate, and both have sworn their souls to the Devil for solutions to their problems.

Fritz begins his story about a local aristocrat, Prince Otto, and Otto's young son, Prince Florian. The two went out together on a hunting trip. None knew exactly what happened, but when they returned Otto was dead, and a clockwork mechanism replaced the space in Otto's chest where his heart should have been. It was rumored that Otto was so desperate to have an heir that he *created* a son using the mechanics of a clock. Now that Florian has gotten older, his mechanisms are beginning to slow down.

Just as storyteller Fritz is about to introduce Dr. Kalmenius, a fictitious devil, into the story, the doors of the inn open and Dr. Kalmenius himself steps inside. Pullman writes, "Oh the silence as he stepped inside! Every single person in the parlor was gaping, mouth open, eyes wide, and when they saw what the stranger was pulling behind him-a little sledge with something wrapped in canvas-more than one crossed themselves and stood up in fear."

While Karl and Fritz have sold their souls, Gretyl, an innocent barmaid, is able to give her heart to poor Prince Florian, but she manages to keep it at the same time, and ultimately shows that goodness can triumph over evil.

Basic Book Information

Clockwork: or All Wound Up is a 107-page fantasy book. This book is divided into 3 parts and given an introduction in, "A Note about Clocks." This note gives the reader some clues to the structure and reason for the structure of this book. There is a table of contents that documents Part 1, Part 2, and Part 3, and figuring out why there are 3 parts can be supportive to the reader. These are not chapters, but instead parts without titles. Illustrations by Leonid Gore are black and white drawings that have a dream-like quality. All illustrations are captioned and are supportive to the text.

Noteworthy Features

There are 3 parts to this book and there are 3 parts of a clock. The book explains these parts as a few gears and pins, a little balance wheel oscillating

Illustrator
Leonid Gore

Publisher
Scholastic, 1999

ISBN
0590129988

TC Level
13

to and fro or a pendulum swinging from side to side, and the strength of the spring and the power of the weight.

The difficulties of this text include spiraling story lines of Fritz's story and the "real" story; the characters of both stories start to merge into one. The challenge lies in keeping each strand straight, and in seeing how they fit together. Because the story moves so quickly, readers can easily become lost. Vocabulary is very sophisticated throughout the text, but often there are contextual clues. The use of German words like "Burgomaster" and names like Fritz, Gretyl, and Prince Otto lends to the fairy tale tone of the story, as do the illustrations. Readers who are familiar with the general fairy tale structure will find this to be helpful, as this is structured a bit like a fairy tale.

Music notations are used in the text as well. However, not knowing how to read music won't hinder the reader. There are literary references to Marlowe's *Dr. Faustus* on the page preceding the table of contents. These references will be meaningless unless the reader knows those stories. The name of Dr. Kalmenius may need some interpretation, but knowledge of language and root words can help. "Kal" is the "Cal" of "calamity," "disaster." Going by the sound of the name "Kalmenius," sounds like "mean," and these clues can help the reader get at his evil importance. Everything in this book is heavily laden with symbolism, some of which is bound to be missed by some readers. This won't affect their understanding, although they will miss out on some of the fun of the reading.

Teaching Ideas

Overt use of symbolism makes this a great book to study when readers are trying to develop their skills at interpretation. The overt symbolism also makes this a less than perfect read for a child to encounter during independent reading. The book deserves to be the center of a book-club study group so that the single reader gets the benefit of a group full of thoughts. Because it has a fairy tale quality, the story is attractive to readers who like fantasy. It also moves along quickly which propels the reader on so she can find out what will happen next and what it all means.

This book is sophisticated, with plot, character, setting, language, and themes that are all complex, dynamic, and intermingled. It would be good for read aloud and discussion, and followed up with independent reading within book clubs, small discussion groups, or in written response to literature. Children who like fantasy and fairy tales will love this book, but it also appeals to a broader readership, pulling readers into the genre.

Book Connections

Students may wish to follow this book with *Grimm's Fairy Tales*, *Dr. Faustus*, or Shelley's *Frankenstein*. Since *Dr. Faustus* and *Frankenstein* are more fantastical than this book, *Grimm's Fairy Tales* would be better for readers in grades 5 and 6. Some other fantasy chapter books include: *M. L'Eugle*, *The Dark Is Rising* series, *Harry Potter*, and *Skellig*. Students could also follow with an author study and read the *Golden Compass*.

A Field Guide to the Classroom Library, Lucy Calkins and the Teachers College Reading and Writing Project, Heinemann, ©2002 Teachers College, Columbia University; http://www.heinemann.com/fieldguides

Genre
Fantasy

Teaching Uses
Interpretation; Book Clubs; Partnerships; Read Aloud

Conestoga Wagons
Richard Ammon

Book Summary

Conestoga wagons were the tractor-trailers of colonial America. Built in Lancaster County, Pennsylvania, they were named after the Conestoga Valley, which lies in the heart of Pennsylvania Dutch country. These sturdy wagons transported goods from state to state between 1750 and 1850.

Basic Book Information

Bill Farnsworth depicts these massive wagons and the historical period they thrived in through beautiful paintings that both support and enhance the text (e.g., An enlarged painting of a wheel lies on the page opposite the one where the wheels are described). A map of Pennsylvania and its surrounding states is found at the beginning of the book. This helps children to see the routes the wagons traveled.

Noteworthy Features

The author helps the reader understand the colonial period by making comparisons to the familiar. He points out that these rugged wagons could haul up to 5 tons of supplies or as the author points out-"the weight of about 160 fourth graders." Horses, the author says, weigh 1800 pounds-or the same as 29 fourth graders. Richard Ammon states that Conestoga wagons were not built in factories as today's cars are, but were made by hand. The author does this throughout the book, which makes things more concrete for children and gives them a frame of reference.

The author describes how the teamsters would stop at taverns to rest. Whenever these men ordered beer, the innkeeper would keep a tab on a slate: P = pint; Q = quart. If the tab started to mount, the innkeeper would remind the wagoneers "to mind his P's and Q's." Ammon goes on to tell the reader that today this expression is a reminder to mind our manners. This example illustrates how the author, whenever possible, connects the past with the present to help the reader.

Conestoga Wagons is full of information about the massive wagons. A specific topic is addressed on each page or double pages. Some of the topics covered include: Conestoga wheels, Conestoga brakes, Conestoga features of horses, and teamsters. Surprisingly, there are no headings to tell the reader what he or she will be reading about. In addition, there is no index for easy reference for the reader who is interested in finding out specifically about any of the topics covered in the text. As mentioned, this is an informative text. It is not a book that takes the reader on a journey and does not necessarily have to be read from beginning to end. If the book had headings and/or and index, the reader would have the freedom to choose to read what interested him or her.

Illustrator
Bill Farnsworth

Publisher
Holiday House, 2000

ISBN
0823414752

TC Level
9; 10; 11

A Field Guide to the Classroom Library, Lucy Calkins and the Teachers College Reading and Writing Project, Heinemann, ©2002 Teachers College, Columbia University; http://www.heinemann.com/fieldguides

Teaching Ideas

This informative text describes the Conestoga wagons and the vital role they played in American history. Obviously, it can be used for researching transportation during the colonial period. Additionally, the text generates questions that can lead to an inquiry into colonial ports, colonial craftsmen, American locomotives, or the Pennsylvania Dutch country.

If students have been reading other Nonfiction books which have sub-headings that tell them how the text can be divided into sections and what the key concept in each section is, it would be interesting for them to notice that this book lacks sub-headings and to see if they could read, using captioned post-it notes to create their own sub-headings. This, of course would take students one step toward learning to take notes. If a teacher wanted to go a few steps farther with teaching students to take notes, he or she could suggest that students record their sub-headings on paper, and then jot down some of the main things the author wants them to know that fit under these sub-headings. Then, in order for students to understand the purpose for note-taking, it would be important to ask students to use their notes as a scaffold while they retell what they've read to a partner.

Of course, the system just described for taking notes assumes that students are trying to use their notes to outline and eventually reconstruct the main gist of what they have read. This sort of outlining should not be an every day practice for readers of Nonfiction, but when a text seems especially interesting as this one is, this sort of outlining will help readers "hold onto a text" and will meanwhile teach them to pay attention to the structure of a Nonfiction text and to the author's main ideas.

Book Connections

Other books that relate to Westward Expansion include: The Coyote Bead *(Hausman) and* Adaline Falling Star *(Osbourne).*

Genre
Nonfiction

Teaching Uses
Reading and Writing Nonfiction; Content Area Study

A Field Guide to the Classroom Library, Lucy Calkins and the Teachers College Reading and Writing Project, Heinemann, ©2002 Teachers College, Columbia University; http://www.heinemann.com/fieldguides

Cracker Jackson

Betsy Byars

Book Summary

Eleven-year-old Jackson Hunter (called "Cracker" by his former babysitter, Alma) lives with his mom in an apartment 1,000 miles from his father. Cracker suspects that Alma and her baby daughter, Nicole, are being abused by Alma's husband, Billy Ray. When his fears are confirmed, he tries to help but is unsuccessful. Cracker eventually enlists the help of his mom, who finally resolves the situation.

Basic Book Information

Betsy Byars, an ALA Newbery Award winner, has written numerous books for young readers. She is noted for her easy-to-read, well-constructed stories with vibrant characters.

The front cover is illustrated by Diane de Groat and perfectly captures the mood of the story. It depicts a boy crouching beside a bicycle, which glows with Day-Glo paint, as he searches the bushes outside a tattered house. A young woman holding a baby stands on a wraparound porch in the background.

Noteworthy Features

Cracker Jackson is set in the South and the setting is subtly rendered by its speech pattern such as, "None," "Cracker," and names like, "Bubba," or "Billy Ray." Many readers won't know the context of these words and how they are used and may not pick up on the setting-teachers will need to decide whether or not to fill readers in on this bit of information if they have missed it.

There are many issues explored in this book, the most prominent being divorce, single parenthood, and spousal abuse. This book perpetuates some stereotypes of Southerners, especially in the Southern man Billy Ray who has a python tattoo on his arms, works his blue-collar job, and beats up his wife. Teachers have a responsibility to help readers see beyond this damaging stereotype of a Southern man.

Byars portrays her characters as complicated, real people, which is recognized by most readers. Some students will find Cracker's memories of school and his friend Goat's gags are portrayed realistically. Cracker Jackson's mom seems real in her frustrations over her ex-husband's inability to be serious, her fears about perception, and her insistence of Cracker's safety. Almost all of us know mothers who portray some or all of these character traits. This sense of reality engages readers in the story and can help readers create a bond with the characters of Cracker and Alma that can help them overcome the difficulties posed by the story's structure.

Publisher
Puffin, 1985

ISBN
014031881

TC Level
12

A Field Guide to the Classroom Library, Lucy Calkins and the Teachers College Reading and Writing Project, Heinemann, ©2002 Teachers College, Columbia University; http://www.heinemann.com/fieldguides

The plot structure consists of many flashbacks (memories) embedded in chronological order. The flashbacks can be confusing. Early on in the book this structure appears with a memory of when Cracker was in first grade receiving his first anonymous letter. This memory begins in past perfect tense to clue in the reader. "His first had been left on his desk." Then the verb tense in the memory switches to regular past tense, "he fumbled." Another helpful clue is that when the memory ends the reader is signaled back to chronological time by a double space between the lines. The reader should be aware of the flashbacks if he uses the verbs and spaces as indicators. [Ed: ok?]

The vocabulary in the text is generally routine, although there is some use of commercial products that kids today may not know such as: Cracker Jacks, Day-Glo, Serta Perfect Sleeper, Sourdough from San Francisco, and Stride Rite orthopedic shoes.

There is humor in this book, for example when Cracker spit in preschool (in the chapter called, "Thpitting"). It is funny because it is a memory with toddler rationales, accompanied by lisping ("th"), and a sideways look at overprotective parents and traditional schools. Kids generally like to laugh over these parts with a partner.

The author uses italics and capitalized words to create emphasis in language. Students might puzzle over the intent and meaning of this form of punctuation.

Teaching Ideas

There are some books in our library that seem too intense, rich and complex to simply sit on the shelves, waiting for an individual child to open its cover and begin to read. This is such a book. It is an intense book about intense issues-abuse, sexism, divorce, friendship-and the book deserves to be discussed. In some upper-elementary and middle school classrooms, groups of children who can read similar books take on a social issue and then search for and read several novels which address that issue. Students would benefit from using this book in such a context.

Another avenue into the heart of this book might be a character study. Cracker and Anna both deserve close, empathetic attention. What does Anna want? What gets in her way? What supports her? What kind of person is she and how does this influence the events which happen to her and her response to those events? How do others relate to her? How does she change? What are the turning points? (The same questions could be asked of Cracker or of *any* character in any novel, and it is important for readers to be able to generate these questions or others like them.)

Finally, the book could be revisited in order to talk and think about how authors control time, moving forward and backward. Readers as well as writers need to be aware of how authors do this so we can follow these crucial junctures in another person's text and create them in our own.

Book Connections

Many of Jerry Spinelli's books tackle real-life issues such as these, and may interest readers who have been engaged with this one.

A Field Guide to the Classroom Library, Lucy Calkins and the Teachers College Reading and Writing Project, Heinemann, ©2002 Teachers College, Columbia University; http://www.heinemann.com/fieldguides

Genre
Chapter Book

Teaching Uses
Language Conventions; Character Study; Partnerships; Teaching Writing

Crash

Jerry Spinelli

Book Summary

This book is about a seventh grader named John Patrick Coogan, nicknamed "Crash." The story is of how Crash lives up to his nickname and then how he undergoes change. Crash lives in Pennsylvania with his mother, father, and younger sister, Abby. The story begins with Crash looking back seven years when he first encountered a new neighbor named Penn Webb. Crash learns that Penn's family is Quaker, vegetarians, and live in a small garage-like house. This gives Crash reason to tease Penn unmercifully. Despite Crash's teasing, Penn remains friendly and good-natured. But, Crash continuously rejects Penn's attempt at friendship. At the beginning of sixth grade, Crash meets a new boy named Mike Deluca. They find that they have a lot in common. Crash and Mike play many pranks on Penn.

Crash experiences disappointment when his parents don't attend his football games or do many things as a family. Then, Crash's much-loved grandfather, Scooter, comes to live with the Coogans. Now that Scooter has moved in, he attends Crash's games and is there when Crash breaks the school's touchdown record. Right before Christmas, Scooter suffers a stroke. This dramatic change in his family begins to cause change in Crash and his relationships. Crash also experiences a shift in his family dynamic as his mother cuts back her work to spend more time with the family. Crash then moves toward undoing two of Mike's nasty pranks on Penn. As time goes on, the name Crash doesn't seem to fit him anymore; he has changed.

The final change in Crash comes when he gives the ultimate gift-letting Penn win a race-off to qualify for the Penn Relays. The story ends with significant changes in the way Crash's life works. His final statement is "Penn Webb is my best friend."

Basic Book Information

The story is told in the first person narrative, from Crash's point of view.

Jerry Spinelli has written numerous young adult novels. In 1991, Spinelli won the Newbery Award for *Maniac Magee,* and in 1998, *Wringer* was named a Newbery Honor book. Whenever students ask him where he gets his ideas, he replies, "From you. You're the funny ones."

Noteworthy Features

The illustration on the cover of the book provides for a good talk. There are no other illustrations, but students tend to think hard about the cover illustration and how it could be different.

A Field Guide to the Classroom Library, Lucy Calkins and the Teachers College Reading and Writing Project, Heinemann, ©2002 Teachers College, Columbia University; http://www.heinemann.com/fieldguides

Publisher
Alfred A. Knopf, Inc., 1996

ISBN
0679879579

This book provides a good character study. It gives strong evidence for Crash's metamorphosis. The reader can track how Crash undergoes change as he moves through the story. One way is to follow his involvement with Penn from when they first meet to the book's closing that announces that they are best friends. Different situations that involve Penn have an impact on Crash. They allow the reader to see one of the ways that Crash's strange-bad feelings change to strange-good feelings, as they did when Crash sacrifices winning the race as a gift to Penn and his great-grandfather. Crash's behavior also changes as a result of Scooter's stroke, when he faces Scooter's survival and recovery.

Students should re-read any passages that contribute to the significant changes that Crash undergoes. They can talk and write about these passages and carry them over into texts where character study is also possible.

Teaching Ideas

Students can learn about Crash from the other characters in this story. The beginning of the book sees Crash living up to his nickname by not allowing anyone to stand in his way. Students can see how the different characters react to Crash. Readers can learn about Crash from his family members. Crash has strong feelings about his parents' commitment to their work and leaving little time for him. Seeing Crash and his relationship with his sister Abby and becoming part of her world is significant. Also seeing how Crash connects with Scooter is a noteworthy study. Students can relate this family dynamic with their own.

Crash can also be viewed by his relationship with his friend Mike and how he breaks away from things that had bonded them. Readers also get a glimpse of Crash and his interest in the new girl, Jane Forbes. An investigation into how Jane sees Crash as a person and then how things turn around with an invitation to her Fourth of July party is noteworthy.

Reading and writing about Penn's effect on Crash gives students a good grasp on what's going on inside of Crash. It becomes evident that Crash begins to see the things in his life that are most important. As the story unfolds around Crash, his shell begins to crack allowing him to see things in a different light.

The different ways in which the author tells the reader about Crash make this book an excellent choice for a character study.

Book Connections

Jerry Spinelli has written numerous books for young readers on various topics and of various levels. Most of them have young boys as the protagonists.

Genre
Chapter Book

A Field Guide to the Classroom Library, Lucy Calkins and the Teachers College Reading and Writing Project, Heinemann, ©2002 Teachers College, Columbia University; http://www.heinemann.com/fieldguides

Teaching Uses
Character Study

Crazy Weekend

Gary Soto

Book Summary

This is the story of two Latino teenagers, Hector and Mordo, who go to visit one of their bachelor uncles for the weekend. Uncle Julio is a freelance photographer who takes farm pictures. During the weekend visit, Uncle Julio and the two boys are in the midst of photographing a family farm when they inadvertently take pictures of an armored-car robbery. They hear on the radio that a reward has been offered, develop the pictures, and a search for the robbers ensues. The boys' pictures are published in the newspaper and soon the rotten, bumbling robbers are looking for the boys, while the boys, in turn, are looking for them. The story ends with a slapstick sequence of events as the boys capture the bad guys and save the day.

Basic Book Information

This is a lively, chronological, and accessible story that resembles the old-time television shows. The humor is not unlike "I Love Lucy" or "Family Ties" and meanwhile, the story is held together by an obvious and entertaining storyline.

Noteworthy Features

The heroes of this story are Latino teenagers and Spanish words are sprinkled through the text. The entire story, however, is not tailored specifically to a Latino culture. Latino youngsters live their variation of the universal American story. That is, this is not an immigration tale, or the tale of grocer who surmounts prejudice. It is, instead, the story of two teenagers who surf, go to dinner, are interviewed for the newspaper, hang out with their uncle, fly in a rickety plane-and end up in a scrape.

Teaching Ideas

This book might not fare particularly well as the subject of deep book talks, but young people who sometimes feel alienated from books are often drawn to this text. The storyline is familiar. Just as in *Little Red Riding Hood* and *The Gingerbread Boy*, the teenagers outsmart the big bad crooks. In *Crazy Weekend*, these young heroes also scrape together whatever they can to catch the thieves.

Although this book isn't heavy or deeply symbolic, students who find it difficult to talk about texts may find it easy to make predictions while reading this book, and then ground these predictions in evidence from the text. They may also find it easy to compare this book with other stories they've read, noticing similarities and differences.

Students love to talk over this book in partnerships, as it has the

Publisher
Scholastic, 1995

ISBN
0590470760

TC Level
10

 A Field Guide to the Classroom Library, Lucy Calkins and the Teachers College Reading and Writing Project, Heinemann, ©2002 Teachers College, Columbia University; http://www.heinemann.com/fieldguides

adventure and quick action of a television show embedded in it. It is an easy one to make "cool" because of its fast, butnot-too-fast pace. It is also easy book for a reader to find fun. For these reasons, it might be especially good for a struggling or unengaged reader.

Genre
Chapter Book

Teaching Uses
Partnerships; Independent Reading

A Field Guide to the Classroom Library, Lucy Calkins and the Teachers College Reading and Writing Project, Heinemann, ©2002 Teachers College, Columbia University; http://www.heinemann.com/fieldguides

Deenie
Judy Blume

Book Summary

Deenie's mom tells her "God gave you a beautiful face. Now he wouldn't have done that if he hadn't intended for you to put it to a good use." It angers her mother that every modeling agency recognizes Deenie's pretty face, but ultimately rejects her because she walks funny. A school nurse notices Deenie's bad posture when she is at cheerleading tryouts. After being seen by a host of doctors, it's determined that Deenie has scoliosis. She has to wear an unattractive and restricting brace for four whole years. All of a sudden, the school knockout has something in common with Old Lady Murray who has a "big bump on her back," Barbara Curtis with "creepy crud," and Gena Courtney who rides the "special bus." This humbling experience makes Deenie realize that her life must become about more that her attractiveness. Ultimately she puts aside her mother's constant pressure on her to be a "pretty face" and comes to terms with her scoliosis. I'm not just a face!" Deenie finally shouts to her mother . . . "I'm a person, too."

Basic Book Information

Judy Blume is the author of *Deenie*, as well as, many other books for children. This prolific writer of young adult books has written such books as *Blubber*, *Are You There God? It's Me, Margaret* , *Tiger Eyes*, *It's Not the End of the World*, and *Superfudge*.

Noteworthy Features

Deenie is a young adult book and contains some sexual content. There are a few portions of the text that deal with the topic of masturbation. Deenie is a thirteen-year old girl who touches her "special place" several times throughout the story, wondering if what she is doing is normal. Later, when she is in a sex education class in school a teacher gives an informative explanation of masturbation in response to Deenie's anonymous question, "Do normal people touch their bodies before they go to sleep and is it all right to do that?" In addition, there are a few scenes that contain some sexual content between Deenie and Buddy, i.e. " . . .moving one hand down from my shoulder to my chest. I knew he was trying to feel me. . . ."

Deenie is written in first-person narration and contains a lot of dialogue. Readers must have a good ear for dialogue in order to pick up nuances from the speech. There are places in the dialogue where certain words are emphasized, "Modeling *is* hard work." Also, there are places in the text where the speaker's words trail-off, i.e. "Oh well. . . ;" or, contain gaps, "Please Ma . . . please believe me . . . I didn't do it on purpose."

There are many changes in setting. Deenie goes to different doctor's offices, out with her friends, stays at home, and goes to school. Her active

Publisher
Bantam Doubleday Dell, 1973

ISBN
0440932599

TC Level
14

thirteen-year old life may be hard for some readers to keep track of. In addition, jumps in time sometimes have to be inferred.

Teaching Ideas

Because of it's sexual content *Deenie* would not make an ideal read aloud. Children will most likely be reading this book individually or in partnerships. If children are reading this book with a partner it may provide a good introduction for some discussions about the adolescent issues that both Deenie and themselves may be facing but are too embarrassed to talk about, including their sexuality, parental expectations, and social relationships.

If the readers are adolescent girls, their own experiences may help them to relate to thirteen-year old Deenie and give them insight into her problems. Deenie's character may help them to see that other adolescents are faced with dilemmas similar to their own. They may relate to such adolescent issues as the embarrassment of changing in gym class and wearing an undershirt instead of a bra. The value of a book that deals openly with adolescent issues can't be underestimated since it's a time when many young adults are experiencing many changes and often feel alone.

Many readers may see Deenie's mother as the villain of the story. The mother initially blames Deenie for her scoliosis. She also makes the experience of wearing a brace for Deenie much harder by crying every time she looks at the brace and blaming the scoliosis on her husband's side of the family. Some readers may make the realization that there are two sides to Deenie's mother. In a climatic scene, Deenie's mother says, "I wanted better for you," she said. "Better than what I had myself. That's what I've always planned for my girls . . .is that so wrong?" Realizing where Deenie's mothers's unrealistic expectations of her children are stemming from may help readers to see that there are multi-dimensions to her character. This understanding can extend to other books. Children may begin to notice that a character is not always as they appear. Sometimes they act contradictory to their initial impressions.

There are many characters and events that contribute to Deenie's eventual peace with scoliosis. Readers may want to note these places in the text with post-its to keep track of their development. One of the prevailing factors is tough love. Deenie's father makes her go to school with her brace, a teacher gives her a zero for an incomplete assignment, and the school nurse does not excuse her from gym. All of these instances seem harsh, but eventually are the very thing that helps Deenie overcome her initial anger and withdrawal from society. They force normalcy on Deenie at a time when she is " . . . sitting around the house and feeling sorry for herself."

Deenie is truly the *main* character of this book and much of the story revolves around her thoughts and reactions to scoliosis. All of the characters can be seen in direct relation to Deenie. For instance, Buddy is Deenie's boyfriend and Janet is Deenie's friend. This strategy can help readers keep track of the many characters throughout the book.

The teacher could make the reader aware that the setting and scenes often change throughout the book to signal that a significant event will occur. Understanding that the author has a purpose in changing the setting will draw readers' attention to these changes and may help them keep focused

A Field Guide to the Classroom Library, Lucy Calkins and the Teachers College Reading and Writing Project, Heinemann, ©2002 Teachers College, Columbia University; http://www.heinemann.com/fieldguides

on the unfolding events. Readers may also come to this conclusion themselves in the course of a setting or plot study.

Book Connections

Judy Blume is the author of many books for young adults, primarily adolescent girls. Readers who enjoy *Deenie* may want to read other books by Judy Blume including *Are You There Go? It's Me, Margaret*, *Tiger Eyes* and *It's Not the End of the World*. These books are similar in content and structure and may be grouped together in a classroom library.

Genre
Chapter Book

Teaching Uses
Partnerships; Independent Reading

A Field Guide to the Classroom Library, Lucy Calkins and the Teachers College Reading and Writing Project, Heinemann, ©2002 Teachers College, Columbia University; http://www.heinemann.com/fieldguides

Dicey's Song
Cynthia Voigt

Book Summary

Dicey's Song is a story about settling-in. "When first unto this country, a stranger I came," the song Dicey hums throughout the book becomes the motif or theme. The four Tillerman children, worn out from their long trek from Provincetown described in the first book in this series, *Homecoming*, finally have a home. But now they must learn how to live with a grandmother whom they have never known, and most people in Chrisfield think is crazy. Dicey, matured beyond her thirteen years, now must learn how to relinquish the role of shepherd and learn to be a teenager. The story of her learning unfolds gradually. The boy Jeff who waits for her after school, her schoolmate Wilhelmina, who pursues her as a friend, even Millie Tydings, whose store Dicey cleans, all contribute to that story. But Gram, with her short, clipped remarks, her bare feet and long skirts, her matter-of-fact, day-by-day battle with life, moves that learning forward more than anyone else. And as we follow along to the end of that taleand watch Dicey learn how to reach out to others and how to let go what she cannot hold on to, we grow in admiration of her and of her surprising grandmother.

The six books in this series begin with the journey Dicey and her three siblings are forced to make when their mother, mentally ill, deserts them. *Dicey's Song* focuses on Dicey and the adjustments she faces learning to live in Chrisfield. In the subsequent books, Voigt focuses on other characters: Dicey's friend Mina; Bullet, the uncle after whom Sammy is named; Jeff; Sammy and James who search for their father and Dicey, now a woman. While each story stands independent of the others, the whole is greater than its parts.

Basic Book Information

Dicey's Song, a Newbery Medal winner is 211 pages long and is the second in a series of six books about the Tillerman family. The story is told in twelve chapters. Some are only four pages long; others, like chapter one, need as many as twenty-one pages to tell their part of the story. Each chapter begins, untitled, marked only with a number.

Noteworthy Features

The story moves through time with references to the past but without flashbacks. The sentence structure and vocabulary of this book are not necessarily difficult for a strong fifth, sixth, or seventh grade reader, but the books are long for children who do not read quickly or often. The challenge lies in the subtle manner that Voigt tells the story. The text alternates

Series
Dicey Tillerman

Publisher
Fawcett Books

ISBN
0449702766

TC Level
14

between dialogue, actions (sometimes fast but more often lazily slow), and carefully laid out descriptions. It is peppered with cryptic half-messages, particularly between Dicey and her grandmother, that leave the reader puzzling over meaning. Sometimes the reader can infer the answer but at other times, the intent is only revealed later in the text. Voigt sometimes holds back information-what happened to Bullet, Gram's son, for instance. His story will be told in a later book in the series. For all these reasons, the complex story, more a study in character development then a tense tale with problem and resolution clearly defined, will capture the attention of strong readers but will prove a challenge to the less experienced reader.

Teaching Ideas

The Tillerman children, particularly Dicey, often act older than their age. The responsibilities Dicey has had to shoulder have matured her. If a teacher notices that a child or a partnership are about to start reading this book, the teacher might want to talk a bit with the readers about the fact that often if we see a person who acts in surprisingly mature ways, that person has lived through experiences-often hard ones-which have matured him or her. That discussion can lead the teacher to briefly summarize the first book in the series, *Homecoming*. Dicey and the three younger siblings were abandoned in the car at the shopping mall. Alone, with little money and no one to turn to, they had to rely on themselves-an experience that has matured them. As students read and discuss this book, one topic they will probably follow is that of how the actions of the Tillerman children show us their maturity. Dicey, for example, seeks out a job on her own so that she can bring in money and she plans to share her earnings with the other children. Sammy helps James with his paper route.

The setting of the story, the rural Chesapeake Bay area in Maryland, explains in part why Gram and the Tillerman children can live the informal lives they do. Readers may also discuss how the lives of people without TV, with limited means of transportation, and with few if any near neighbors differ from the busier lives of a city family.

Each of the Tillerman children has a personality that makes him or her different from the others. Students may decide to note these differences in their notebooks as they read. While following this topic of inquiry, children may pause after each chapter to reflect on what they learned about each of the four children. After they have gathered enough evidence about each one (which will probably be around chapter 8), students reflect on which character they each believe they are most like. It would be helpful to nudge them to use examples from their own experiences that match those described in the book to support their claims.

Gram is another strong character in this book. If readers keep tabs on their views of Gram, they will probably find this yields interesting material because over the course of the book, most readers-like Dicey-go through a journey that includes rejecting Gram, and ends in a very different place. It's worth asking why Voigt wrote the book in such a way. The author seems to want us, her readers, to judge Gram and reject her, and then she wants us to begin to see her differently. Is there a larger message here? Then, too,

A Field Guide to the Classroom Library, Lucy Calkins and the Teachers College Reading and Writing Project, Heinemann, ©2002 Teachers College, Columbia University; http://www.heinemann.com/fieldguides

readers can consider why Gram is the way she is and perhaps learn to walk-a-mile-in-her-moccasins. It is easy to empathize with Dicey, but a strong reader learns to fall for many of the characters in a book, not just the lead character. Events in the story force Gram to change, to "take from others." Applying for welfare will probably be one of those changes that readers cite. Students may discuss those events that "force" Gram to look at life differently.

Voigt often raises questions that are only answered in subsequent chapters. In a conference, teachers might encourage students to jot questions they have about certain events that are not explained in their notebooks, answering these when they later come upon an explanation. Sammy suddenly begins to fight again, for example, but we do not learn why until we read the story about the marbles.

Mr. Lingerle, Maybeth's music teacher, appears at first as a minor character. Yet, the significance of his role in the story becomes clear as he appears more and more frequently. This is a good reminder to readers that it is important to notice "minor" characters. The author puts them there for a reason. Teachers might nudge students to follow some of the minor characters, steering them toward this one.

Dicey's relationship with Jeff takes a turn when he asks her to the dance. Students will probably discuss whether they agree with Dicey's decision to refuse the invitation. They will want to consider the fact that her friend Mina, admits that she will attend the dance. It would be worthwhile for readers to predict whether they think that relationship will continue in subsequent books.

At the end of the book, Mama's life comes to a close. It is worth noting how Gram, Dicey, and the others honor Mama. Students might reflect on the facts: Mama was a person who had abandoned them and yet they grieved for her and made her burial so special. Why? As part of that discussion student may also want to discuss Gram's decision to bring down the albums of photos and how that act related to the death of Mama.

Book Connections

The *Homecoming* series adopts a theme that is extraordinarily common in young adult literature. In countless books, children are abandoned and need to use their own ingenuity and resourcefulness in order to create a world for themselves. This is the underlying theme to George's *My Side of the Mountain*, Paulson's *Hatchet*, Wyss' *Swiss Family Robinson* and Taylor's *The Cay*. In these books, the main character struggles mostly alone, and the struggle is all about survival in the wilderness. In the *Homecoming* series, these children struggle as a family unit, and much of the story involves what happens within the family. Their struggle has less to do with physical survival and more to do with survival in a social world. In MacLachlin's *Journey*, the struggle is similarly socially situated.

Reading *Dicey's Song* will prompt many students to read the other books in the series. In addition to *Homecoming*, the first in the series, other titles include: *A Solitary Blue, The Runner, Come a Stranger, Sons from Afar,* and *Seventeen Against the Dealer*.

A Field Guide to the Classroom Library, Lucy Calkins and the Teachers College Reading and Writing Project, Heinemann, ©2002 Teachers College, Columbia University; http://www.heinemann.com/fieldguides

Genre
Chapter Book

Digging for Bird-Dinosaurs: An Expedition to Madagascar

Nic Bishop

Book Summary

This is the story of a woman paleontologist as she works on a dig in Madagascar. She is looking for fossils that will help her study of bird evolution, and her story educates the reader both about ancient birds, dinosaurs, and excavation techniques. There is some cultural and geographical information about Madagascar as well.

Basic Book Information

This Nonfiction picture book has about 50 pages. Although there is no table of contents, the book is divided into chapters or sections of about four pages each. Each one is marked clearly with a large, bold sub-heading that is often a tantalizing lead for the section, more than a summary or a label for the information found within. There is a lot of text, perhaps the equivalent of one full page for every double-page spread. The book is illustrated with large, clear professional photographs, one or two per page, of the people and places and techniques in the book. The captions are in smaller, lighter font, but they are easy to read and easily distinguishable from the text of the narrative. The main text is a continuous story. Each section builds on the past ones and refers back to them. The captions under the photographs do make some sense without the text of the story, and can be read separately if students are merely browsing the book.

At the end of the book there is a two-paragraph postscript that brings the findings of the dig up to date. There are also some diagrams that further illustrate the link between dinosaurs and modern birds. These diagrams are followed by a short list of recommended reading and a short plea for donations for the villagers in the village in which the dig was taking place. Finally, there is a one-page, fairly comprehensive index to some of the topics in the text. All of these pages are written in the same text font with the same attention to graphics and illustration as the rest of the story. The inside back flap of the jacket has some interesting data about the author that children, who enjoyed the book, will probably enjoy.

Noteworthy Features

This is the kind of book that will make some readers want to go on a dig themselves. Since the processes are so thoroughly explained, they feel very accessible. Since the whole expedition is told mainly through the experience of the one leader, Cathy Forster, the dig is also personalized in a way that makes many children able to picture themselves there. At the very least, the

Illustrator
Nic Bishop

Publisher
Houghton Mifflin, 2000

ISBN
0395960568

TC Level
12; 13; 14

book will probably trigger readers to take out atlases and maps to find Madagascar and to take out other books about scientists working on dinosaurs. The book may even prompt a trip or several calls to a museum of natural history. The photographs in this book are of especially good quality and make the book attractive to most readers.

Teaching Ideas

Some readers find themselves a little confused by the different characters (people) in the dig. Since there are several, and some are only referred to briefly, it can be hard to hold onto exactly who is who. On the other hand, this is not central to the text, and even if all the characters outside of Cathy are smeared together a bit, the excitement, processes, and information explained about the dig won't be diminished. Readers might benefit from this advice.

There is quite a lot of information offered within a short amount of text and reading time. Readers who are trying to hold onto every last piece will probably be discouraged. These readers could be encouraged to find information relevant to a particular topic or question and keep track of that, and that alone. Or, readers could take notes as they read, or use post-its to mark particularly dense or interesting parts to go back to and try to retain and understand them further.

As mentioned above, the book has a lot of information in it. For this reason, it would be a perfect book for a partnership or small groups to read together. The members can discuss the significance of the information with each other and help one another to understand and remember important parts. The excitement of the discoveries always tends to be amplified in small groups as well.

Since the book is quite long, it probably would not be an ideal read aloud, unless teachers wished to model for readers the ways to gather and hold onto and make sense of information in Nonfiction reading. Even with this particular goal, the book is probably too long to fulfill it well. The suspense of each section would probably not hold readers over the amount of time needed to read it aloud. Perhaps teachers could consider reading just sections of the book, if it seems perfect for a read aloud in other ways.

Genre
Picture Book; Nonfiction

Teaching Uses
Reading and Writing Nonfiction; Content Area Study

A Field Guide to the Classroom Library, Lucy Calkins and the Teachers College Reading and Writing Project, Heinemann, ©2002 Teachers College, Columbia University; http://www.heinemann.com/fieldguides

Dive

Adele Griffin

Book Summary

This first-person narrative is told by eleven-year-old Ben as he works through his relationships with his mother, who has abandoned him, his stepfather, Lyle, who has provided the only home Ben has ever known, and his troubled older stepbrother, Dustin.

Basic Book Information

Dive is a realistic fiction novel of 155 pages. The chapters are short, ranging from two to eight pages, with an average length of five pages. This is a deceptively complex novel, which looks rather short and innocent with fairly large type. It is written in an unidentified first-person voice; all the stories are presented from an "I" character to a "you" character and information about all characters is revealed only over the course of the novel. The chapters alternate between stories of the past and the story of the present in the life of the narrator, Ben, and his complicated family. The book deals with complex family issues as well as suicide. The word suicide is never used; again all the work of inferring is left to the reader.

Adele Griffin often uses large jumps in time (flashbacks, daydreams, etc.) in her novels (*Split Just Right*, *The Other Shepards*, *Sons of Liberty*), but *Dive* is her most complex work. She leaves a lot of work to the reader to follow the stories, piece together the character history, and infer what really is happening from what the narrator tells the reader. Because of this, the book can be extremely satisfying, but also confusing, and it is recommended for very proficient 6th, 7th, and 8th grade readers and above.

Noteworthy Features

The chapters in *Dive* alternate between the present and stories of the past; this is worth pointing out explicitly to readers because it makes it easier to go back and look up events, but also because it prepares the reader to better negotiate the difficulties of the plot. It is written in an unidentified first-person voice; all the stories are presented from an "I" character to a "you" character and information about all characters is revealed only in stories over the course of the novel. This requires the reader to not only trust the author, but also to pay close attention, registering new information in the character puzzle as it appears. It doesn't become clear that "you" and the Dustin referred to in stories are the same person until page 24, for example. It could be additionally confusing that the narrator talks about his mom, but lives with his stepdad, Lyle, while Lyle's son (Ben's stepbrother)

A Field Guide to the Classroom Library, Lucy Calkins and the Teachers College Reading and Writing Project, Heinemann, ©2002 Teachers College, Columbia University; http://www.heinemann.com/fieldguides

Publisher
Hyperion, 1999

ISBN
0786804408

TC Level
13

lives with the narrator's mother. Again, this is not explained explicitly, but left for the reader to puzzle out through stories and conversations.

Teaching Ideas

Because of this book's complexity, a teacher may want to give a reader a brief introduction to it. One teacher prepared a student to read it by saying, "*Dive* is a fascinating book about a very complex family. The narrator is a boy named Ben, but the story is in the first person (I) and he doesn't explain much to the reader-you have to figure it out as you read. He's writing to a 'you,' who turns out to be another character in the book. This kind of narrator perspective requires that you pay a lot of attention to the subtle ways that the author, Adele Griffin, lets you know about the characters. You could read the back of the book or the book flap to help you, but it's also fun to figure it out yourself. The chapters alternate; in the first one, the narrator tells the story of the present in the book, in the second chapter, he tells a story of the past, and so on. I'd recommend a character list on a post-it note or something, at least until you get them all straight in your head."

This is an excellent book to study in middle school when revisiting the story elements. If the class as a whole is very aware of the story elements and their group conversation could support such a complex book, it could be used toward the end of the 6th grade year or in the 7th grade year as a read aloud. Conversation and lessons about retelling and accumulating, inference, perspective and voice, interpretation, and writing craft would be important. It could be a good book for writers to revisit and think about how Adele Griffin reveals information about characters through flashback, conversation, and description.

Book Connections

Like this book, *The View from Saturday* by E.L. Konigsburg and *Seedfolks* by Paul Fleischman are both told in third person, but require the reader to negotiate multiple stories and perspectives. *Bull Run* by Paul Fleischman and *Bat 6* by Virginia Eewer Woolf are more similar to *Dive* in that they are written in first person, but contain several perspectives and narrators.

Whirligig by Paul Fleischman (grades 7 and up) is also very complex and deals with mature subject matter. *Whirligig* has five plot lines and is written in third person, but leaves much of the piecing together of the story to the reader.

When She Hollers by Cythia Voigt is similar to *Dive* in that it is written in first person from sister to sister and leaves much inference work to the reader.

Genre
Chapter Book

Teaching Uses
Independent Reading; Book Clubs

A Field Guide to the Classroom Library, Lucy Calkins and the Teachers College Reading and Writing Project, Heinemann, ©2002 Teachers College, Columbia University; http://www.heinemann.com/fieldguides

Eagle Song
Joseph Bruchac

Book Summary

Danny Bigtree is a young Iroquois boy who has recently moved to Brooklyn. He is subject to alienation and taunts like "Hey Chief, going home to your teepee?" For the first time in his life, Danny is made to feel ashamed of his Native American heritage. He does not want to end up like his Native American friend who has joined a gang. When Danny's father, Richard, comes home from his job, he tells him the story of Aionwahta "to give Richard strength." Together, they decide that Richard should tell Danny's class this Native American tale about how people "can use their energy to do good instead of bad."

The story does not seem to change the way the children treat Danny. The very next day, he is hit square in the face with a basketball. When it seems like things cannot get any worse, Danny's father has an accident on the job. Luckily, he survives. Danny, relieved, returns to school to find out that being hit in the face was an accident. Danny's classmates *had* heard Danny's message of peace. The new friends shake hands and give one another the Mohawk greeting, "She: kon."

Basic Book Information

The book was well received by the School Library Journal. There are beautiful pencil illustrations in each chapter that offer some textual support and help to create the mood.

Noteworthy Features

The book is primarily told in third person, except for when Richard Bigtree tells the story of Aionwahta. This change in voice is clearly marked. It may be confusing, however, when the story changes back to third person, since readers must infer the switch.

There are not many characters or setting changes throughout the book, with exception to Danny's father's story. This story within a story contains a lot of fantastical characters like a man with snakes growing from his heads. It recounts many strange events like a turtle dancing. This tale is a major departure from the rest of the text. Otherwise, *Eagle Song* doesn't present special challenges.

In the story, there is a flashback to "long ago." Otherwise, it shifts along chronologically and is usually only marked with the time on Danny's alarm clock-such as "It was only 6:05 in the morning." Readers may infer that only one night has gone by, but others may feel that it could be any morning.

Illustrator
Dan Andreasen

Publisher
Penguin Group, 1997

ISBN
0141301694

TC Level
11

A Field Guide to the Classroom Library, Lucy Calkins and the Teachers College Reading and Writing Project, Heinemann, ©2002 Teachers College, Columbia University; http://www.heinemann.com/fieldguides

The book uses many Native American names and terms. Often, the meanings can be inferred from the passage. In addition, a glossary is provided at the back of the book.

Teaching Ideas

Readers may notice how the tale of Aionwahta connects with Danny's life. In the story, a dream foretells an event. Danny, also, has a premonition about his father's accident in a dream. In the tale, the main character spreads the word of peace just like Danny and his father had at school. In the end, both Adodarhonh (the villain of the tale) and Danny's classmates learn that they "can use their energy to do good instead of bad." Readers may attach post-it notes to parts of Danny's life that seem to parallel Aionwahta's.

The tale of Aionwahta may be more challenging for readers who are unfamiliar with Native American tales. There are a host of mythical creatures and monsters, and the otherworldly events are deeply embedded with meaning. In addition, characters, such as the Creator and the Peacemaker are introduced into the text with little explanation. Frequent retells during this tale may help readers get a clearer image about the unfolding of the strange events. If *Eagle Song* is read in conjunction with some traditional Native American stories readers may develop an ear for this kind of story.

Eagle Song contains many terms and names from several Native American tribes. In a writing workshop, it may be interesting to study how to incorporate terms from another language into pieces. Bruchac uses Native American terms. He relays meaning in English by using a glossary. Often, he gives a direct translation in the proceeding sentence. Writers may find it may enable them to create characters that speak their native tongue. Some children may find that this will allow them to write characters like themselves who switch between English and other languages.

In a read aloud, it may be useful to reflect on how a single event in a story can tell readers so much about character relationships. In Chapter 1, when Richard Bigtree comes home from his job, Danny's mother pushes him to the ground and starts tickling him. Danny then, jumps in and winds up being tickled, too. The narrator recounts, "Then, when he had laughed so much it started to hurt, the three of them just stayed there on the floor, their arms around each other." Readers may notice how this single event demonstrates a tightly bound and fun-loving family.

In a writing workshop, children may want to look at how *Eagle Song* tells a story within a story. Young readers may want to experiment with a similar idea. They may want to use a character in their writing that acts as a storyteller. The tale that the storyteller tells could move their plot further along (e.g., the story about peace and life enlightens Danny's classmates). Writers may also want to include a story within their pieces that gives their readers different ways of seeing the events in the story.

Genre
Chapter Book

A Field Guide to the Classroom Library, Lucy Calkins and the Teachers College Reading and Writing Project, Heinemann, ©2002 Teachers College, Columbia University; http://www.heinemann.com/fieldguides

Teaching Uses
Read Aloud; Teaching Writing; Independent Reading

Ella Enchanted
Gail Carson Levine

Book Summary

Ella is a young girl who receives the dubious gift of obedience from a well-wishing, but errant fairy. Ella grows up and meets ogres, fairies, and Prince Charmant at her mother's funeral. The familiar story of a father remarrying a wealthy but mean woman, with two wicked daughters, emerges later in the book. Before the remarriage of her father, Ella develops into an interesting, clumsy, intelligent, and contrary girl.

Basic Book Information

This book has won many awards, most notably the Newbery Honor in 1997, the ALA's Notable Children's Book of 1998 and its 1998 Best Books for Young Adults. Both *Publishers Weekly* and the *School Library Journal* named it one of their "Best Books of 1997." *Ella Enchanted* is Levine's version of the Cinderella fairy tale, updated with added characterization and information for today's readers.

This 232-page book has twenty-nine chapters with an epilogue at the end. Chapters are long, but are broken up by triple spacing showing an elapse of time or a change in the setting. A reader lacking stamina for the long chapters could easily break the reading up into shorter sittings.

This book is a combination of fantasy and fairy tale, weaving the two genres together. Knowledge of the Cinderella fairy tale would be helpful, but not absolutely necessary for enjoyment. In fact, the realization that this is the Cinderella story could be put off until the last third of the book when her father remarries the evil stepmother.

Noteworthy Features

This story, told from the first-person point of view of Ella, immediately sweeps the reader into the story of her life, beginning at birth. Initially it is hard to pinpoint the setting of the story, as Ella speaks to the reader in such a nonchalant way, about that "fool of a fairy Lucinda," and that she didn't even know her fairy godmother. The tone combined with the generic profession of her father, "away on a trading expedition as usual," can set the reader up to expect the setting to be more modern than it is. Even Ella's relationship with Prince Charmant, so unguarded at their first meeting, so silly and very casual, can add to this sense of timelessness of the setting. Not until Ella runs away from her finishing school (which only sounds as ancient as the 1950s!) and runs into ogres, knights and giants, does the setting of a fairy tale emerge completely.

Publisher
Harper Trophy Newbery, 1997

ISBN
0064407055

TC Level
13

There are parts of this book that use fictional languages that may be confusing to readers. Ella has a gift for languages, and she knows elfish, ogrese, and other languages of mythical creatures. Ella's ability to communicate with anyone she encounters makes her a friendly and sympathetic character, yet her frequent diversion into Ayorthian or elf languages can leave a reader's head spinning. Readers need to know that they don't need to crack the code of the language, it is always translated for the reader. The author's choice of language and dialogue in this fashion is interesting and could lead readers to ponder the intent of the author, especially regarding the audience of the book.

Teaching Ideas

One fifth grade book club compared this text to the Cinderella tale and discovered, "Ella in *Ella Enchanted* is fuller as a character. We know more about her than about Cinderella. In the fairy tale we read, we didn't know very much about Cinderella except for the fact that she was unlucky and had to work all the time. In *Ella Enchanted*, we know that Ella is smart, but she doesn't like to do what she's told. She likes to be asked," said one club member. "Yes, and we know that Ella is a good friend and that she likes to make jokes," said another student.

A third club member added, "We talked about how Ella in *Ella Enchanted* is a three dimensional character. We know what she looks like, we can hear her talk, and we can also know what she thinks. Cinderella, well she is a flat character. We don't know what she thinks, really. It's just a story that some old guy tells us. We've decided that the fairy tale is something good for a beginning. Gail Carson Levine makes this story so kids like us can like it. We want to read her other books now."

Ella is fifteen years old as she begins her tale, which often contains banter and flirtation. The end of the book details her inevitable marriage to Prince Charmant. Younger readers (younger than fourth grade) may not appreciate the humor or the playful sarcasm of Ella and the double entendres of Prince Charmant.

Book Connections

The Search for Delicious as well as *Tuck Everlasting* (both written by Natalie Babbitt) incorporate elements of fairy tale to their fantasy and would make for a great study of how the two authors accomplish their purpose. Katherine Paterson's *The King's Equal* is another fairy tale that has been embellished and given new life with added characterization.

Gail Carson Levine's current book, *Cinderellis and the Glass Slipper* would make an interesting author study as well as theme study.

Genre

Fantasy; Fairy and Folk Tale; Chapter Book

A Field Guide to the Classroom Library, Lucy Calkins and the Teachers College Reading and Writing Project, Heinemann, ©2002 Teachers College, Columbia University; http://www.heinemann.com/fieldguides

Teaching Uses
Independent Reading; Book Clubs; Character Study

Ereth's Birthday

Avi

Book Summary

This story is set solely in Dimwood Forest and involves Ereth the porcupine, feeling insecure and sorry for himself, on his birthday. He runs off and has an adventure he would never seek out on his own. He becomes the surrogate parent of three fox kits.

Ereth's Birthday is the fourth and final book in the *Tales of Dimwood Forest* stories that begin with *Poppy*. Like the other three books, the characters are animals. This story centers around Ereth the porcupine who plays important roles in *Poppy* and *Poppy and Rye*. Poppy appears only at the end of *Ereth's Birthday*, but she is referred to often. A reader could enjoy *Ereth's Birthday* on its own, but for full appreciation the entire series should be read in the order that Avi wrote them: *Poppy*, *Poppy and Rye*, *Ragweed*, and *Ereth's Birthday*. It is possible to read *Ragweed* last because that book is a flashback and is the story of Rye before he met Poppy.

Basic Book Information

There are 180 pages with 27 chapters (all the Dimwood Forest books have 27 chapters). The chapter titles are supportive of the text; for example, "The Return of Bounder" or "Traps." Chapters are five to nine pages in length with the exception of Chapter 1, "Traps," is thirteen pages long. There is an illustrated map in front for reference.

Noteworthy Features

As with the other *Tales of Dimwood Forest*, Avi uses a shifting point of view, which usually changes from chapter to chapter. Point of view shifts from Ereth to his predator, Marty the Fisher. Avi does this in each of his books, bringing the reader in to understand the point of view of the two opposing characters. Avi also brings in elements of animal interdependence and their importance to the environment.

Colloquial language is used repeatedly in *Ereth's Birthday*. Ereth speaks very colorfully, with hyperbole and with his own set of curse words. Students love his vitality and real speech patterns, which quickly engage a reader into the intricacies of the story.

Although students are attracted to Ereth's blustery language and style, it can be difficult to understand his terms. Not all students will know what a "smidgen of slipper slobber" is. Ereth frequently speaks using assonance and alliteration, combining and presenting a very funny mouthful.

Teaching Ideas

If a teacher pulls his or her chair alongside a child who is reading this book,

A Field Guide to the Classroom Library, Lucy Calkins and the Teachers College Reading and Writing Project, Heinemann, ©2002 Teachers College, Columbia University; http://www.heinemann.com/fieldguides

Series
Tales of Dimwood Forest

Publisher
Harper Collins, 2000

ISBN
0380977346

TC Level
12

one obvious and fruitful line of inquiry will be to discuss ways in which this book is like and unlike other books in the series. A teacher might listen to a child explain how this book is the story of a porcupine who was not the main character in *Poppy* or *Poppy and Rye* (and Poppy appears only at the end of this book) and the teacher might then suggest the reader could think about all the series books he or she knows. Have others been written in a similar fashion? For most readers, the answer will be no. In *Frog and Toad*, *George and Martha*, *Nate the Great*, *Marvin Redpost*, *Commander Toad*, *The Box Car Children*, and so on, the series are held together by the fact that the same people are the main characters throughout the series. Children may be interested to know that this will change as they read more complex books. *The Wizard of Oz* books and the *Redwall* series are more similar to Avi's series.

The point of view is a very strong feature of the text. Readers could study how Avi writes from Ereth's and then Marty's point of view. How is the shift accomplished? There are four chapters entitled "Marty the Fisher," and each one is in Marty's point of view. Chapter 3 is a good one to focus on, as Avi directs the reader, like a film director, into the eyes of Marty: ". . . he [Ereth] had no notion that two dark eyes were looking down at him. The eyes belonged to Marty the Fisher."

Marty appears in other chapters. It is interesting to note that the point of view is seen through Marty's eyes. "From his lookout on the aspen tree branch," Avi overtly shows the shifting point of view by using eyes as his medium. By studying point of view with Avi, the reader will be better able to understand more sophisticated books that are less overtly laid out.

There are opportunities throughout the book to stop and research the various animal characters. Marty, a kingfisher, is an endangered animal. Once readers know more about his endangered status and role in the forest, a reader can understand Marty's anger, frustration, and violence. The text provides many opportunities for character analysis, non-fiction reading, and role-playing in this story. Some other teaching ideas could be:

Point of view study in read alouds, centers and book club

Point of view study for writing, especially locating the medium to show point of view

Language study of Ereth, the old salt

Character study of Ereth, the old salt. Are there characters like him anywhere else?

Author study: Avi has also written 2 *Amanda* books, where the central characters are animals. *Amanda* books are a level 6 book and much easier to read

Genre study: animal books (fantasy)

Context clues can indicate to readers that he is talking nonsense, but at the same time he is angry and that these are also his curse words. Much of the vocabulary can be figured out with context clues. We suggest that the vocabulary be decoded through context clues, and also by looking up some of the words when necessary. Perhaps students could collect odd and unusual word sayings as a result of this language study.

Book Connections

The Wizard of Oz books and the *Redwall* series.

A Field Guide to the Classroom Library, Lucy Calkins and the Teachers College Reading and Writing Project, Heinemann, ©2002 Teachers College, Columbia University; http://www.heinemann.com/fieldguides

Genre
Chapter Book

Teaching Uses
Independent Reading

Esio Trot

Roald Dahl

Book Summary

Shy Mr. Hoppy is in love with Mrs. Silver, the widow who lives in the apartment below. However, Mrs. Silver doesn't seem to notice him and instead showers all of her attention and affection on her pet turtle, Alfie. One day as the two characters are out on their balconies, Mrs. Silver comments on Alfie, "I do so wish he would grow a little faster" so Mr. Hoppy devises a plan.

He gives Mrs. Silver a piece of paper with some magical words that she must whisper to Alfie three times a day in order to make him grow. He then buys 140 turtles from the pet store and as Mrs. Silver is away each afternoon at her job, inch by inch, Mr. Hoppy replaces Alfie with slightly bigger turtles each week until "Alfie" no longer fits in his little turtle house. When "Alfie" is too big, Mr. Hoppy gives Mrs. Silver some new magic words to make him a bit smaller. In the end, Mr. Hoppy's plan works, Mrs. Silver is forever grateful and the two get married and live happily ever.

Basic Book Information

This 62-page book has no chapters. Illustrations on every page carefully compliment the text. An author's note at the beginning the book explains that during the time of this story, there was a glut of tortoises. The dialogue comes infrequently and is easy to follow as there are only two main characters. The progression of time in this text though rapid (within two pages, seven weeks pass) ought not be a source of confusion for too many students.

The author, Roald Dahl, is as prolific as he is imaginative. His stories are most always full of fantasy, and if not fantasy, at least some sort of silliness to smile about. It is that kind of energy which can turn a love story between two older people-a type of story that would have little to no appeal into one that really engages children.

Noteworthy Features

This plot is rather straightforward and simple to understand. There are only two main characters, both of whom can be studied for their predictable actions and reactions. The plot will be easy to relate to for children who live in urban areas. Most of the story takes place in a high rise apartment building, a place where typically enough neighbors make polite conversation but may not invite each other over for dinner.

Another interesting aspect of the text that draws readers in is the "magic words" that Mr. Hoppy gives to Mrs. Silver to make Alfie grow. The first time children read these words, they may want to stop and try to decode them before Dahl does it for them on the next page.

Publisher
Penguin, 1990

ISBN
0140360999

TC Level
11

A teacher may wish to highlight the fact that the story takes place in England. This can be deciphered from the author's note as well as the British English used throughout: the author uses "flat" in place of apartment, he spells color with a "u," and has characters who eat tea and biscuits.

Teaching Ideas

Esio Trot could be an excellent text for character study. Students could write both main characters on a sheet of paper and list their character traits along with textual support for their opinions. For example, a student may write that he thought Mr. Hoppy was a very patient man. The textual support could be as follows: "He had loved her from his balcony for many years, but he was a very shy man and he had never been able to bring himself to give her even the smallest hint of his love." If Mr. Hoppy wasn't patient he may have given up on his love years earlier.

Dahl presents some interesting non-fiction information on turtles throughout the text. The reader learns where turtles originate from, what they eat, and that they hibernate in the winter. A teacher might use this as a springboard to get students more involved in non-fiction. Using outside reference materials, students could work to substantiate, disprove, or further the claims made about turtles.

Book Connections

Any of Roald Dahl's books would be a great follow up to this one such as *Matilda*, *James and the Giant Peach*, or *George's Marvelous Medicine*. There are a number of different points on which one could make a comparison, starting with, but not limited to: the presence of fantasy, or how characters change.

Genre
Chapter Book; Fantasy

Teaching Uses
Independent Reading; Character Study

A Field Guide to the Classroom Library, Lucy Calkins and the Teachers College Reading and Writing Project, Heinemann, ©2002 Teachers College, Columbia University; http://www.heinemann.com/fieldguides

Exploding Ants: Amazing Facts about How Animals Adapt

Joanne Settel

Book Summary

This book is full of short vignettes that convey interesting and disgusting information about what animals do to adapt in order to survive. For example, readers will learn that swallowtail butterfly larva mimic the appearance of bird droppings and in this way, avoid being eaten by predators. Soldier Ants are designed to explode in order to defend their colony from invaders. When they explode, they spray a glue that holds their opponents in place.

At a glance, this resembles a picture book but it's actually closer to a Nonfiction chapter book. But, rather than reading vast expanses of text, readers can quickly glean the author's content. The sections are several pages long and each contains several smaller vignettes. In this way, the text is structured a bit like the memoir *Childtimes* by Eloise Greenfield or *The House on Mango Street* by Sandra Cisneros.

Basic Book Information

The book is well written. The author sometimes uses technical vocabulary such as "regurgitate" but she quickly follows this word with the more accessible term, "throw-up." The author is a biology professor and writes with that voice. For example, she begins one vignette by saying, "When a male deep-sea angler fish finds a female, he gets really attached." The book contains a glossary and an index and has a scattering of small color photographs.

Noteworthy Features

Kathy Doyle, a teacher renowned for her work with Nonfiction reading and writing, says, "If I could choose one book to give kids a feeling for how interesting and compelling Nonfiction can be; this would be the book. Just reading aloud the introduction, 'Why Animals Do Gross Things,' will captivate children who have not yet learned to love Nonfiction."

Teaching Ideas

This book deserves to be read aloud. If it was to simply be shelved in a Nonfiction shelf, children may be apt to overlook it. But, once a section of the book has been read aloud, children will be clamoring to read it themselves.

After oohing and ahhing and sharing the required "yuck" responses, a

Publisher
Simon & Schuster

ISBN
0689817398

TC Level
11; 12; 13

teacher might decide to use this book as a way to teach children that when you are the kind of person who knows things about the world, it's fun to drop these facts into conversations and see what happens. "At lunch today," a teacher might say, "Try turning to someone from a different classroom and saying, 'Did you know that . . .' Bring their reactions back to our class and let's talk about them."

Teachers can also encourage kids to fact-drop at home. "When parents ask, 'What did you learn today?' try telling them that male fireflies that flash in search of friendly females risk being eaten if they flash at the wrong species." Over time, students can become more sophisticated at fact-dropping. They can learn how to listen to what's being said so as to insert information when it fits. They can learn, also that the point of all of this is not merely to show-off or to raise eyebrows but that, in fact, it's thrilling and fascinating to live the life of a person intoxicated by ideas and information. One bizarre fact can lead to big, thoughtful conversations.

This book also serves well within the writing workshop. Because the vignettes are short, full of both voice and interesting information, children benefit from using sections of this book as models for their own Nonfiction writing.

Genre
Picture Book; Nonfiction; Chapter Book

Teaching Uses
Reading and Writing Nonfiction; Content Area Study; Read Aloud; Partnerships; Book Clubs

Flight: The Journey of Charles Lindberg

Robert Burleigh

Book Summary

This Nonfiction book is the story of Charles Lindberg's first flight across the Atlantic. It tells the story from the moment just before he gets into the plane until he finally falls asleep after his arrival. The amazing thing about this beautiful picture book is the author's style and voice. The book is beautifully written. It begins, "It is 1927." The book incorporates Lindberg's actual words from the diary he kept as he crossed the Atlantic.

Basic Book Information

The book deserves to be categorized as a sophisticated biographical picture book. It has full-page paintings that capture the mood and make us feel as if we are standing in the world of the story.

The print is set rather like a poem without stanzas and it may be that the author intends for this to be read not only as a biography but also a romantic poem.

Noteworthy Features

This book is an extraordinary read-aloud text. The words, written with lyrical lilt and intimacy, create a mood and draw readers into a drama. The language is heart-shaping. The pictures are breathtaking. Meanwhile, every bit of the text is informational: "Lindberg is nearly as tall as the plane itself."

Burleigh gives us the precise time, down to the minute, throughout the text (e.g., 7:52, 12:08), so that we can sense how slowly time passes during this 33-hour flight. We are there with him looking at his watch.

Teaching Ideas

This book could be one of several texts that weave its way across the entire school year, serving as a mentor text to teach children countless lessons about the craft of good writing. For the text to work as a mentor text, however, children must first fall in love with it. This is sure to happen if a teacher rises to the occasion of reading it aloud. Practice reading it. Read it slowly. Read it with your mind fully attuned to what the book is saying, pausing with the line breaks, "Across the Atlantic / Alone."

The line break requires that we pause-pause and think about making a flight clear across that wide, wide sea. Then we add the word "alone," a word that says it all.

This is probably not a book that provides stopping points for mid-way

Illustrator
Mike Wimmer

Publisher
Putnam Publishing, 1991

ISBN
0399222723

TC Level
12

conversations. Read it in one long luxurious read. And then be silent. On another day, re-read it and invite kids to re-read their favorite pages to feel this text in their mouths. Invite them to find the lines they love most and to write them in their writer's notebook.

Later, return to sections to study the craft. Your writers will notice the repetition, which at times is almost like an echo. "Later, they will call him" (1). There is other more subtle repetition such as the repetition of the time and date. The end then circles back to the beginning. Because this is a true Nonfiction biography, this is surprising.

Burleigh uses the craft that one might expect in a pretty fictional picture book, but there aren't many true Nonfiction books that are written with these craft elements. Burleigh chooses simple but powerful words, often selecting particularly precise verbs. He savors detail. Burleigh balances short and long sentences. He makes readers read quickly, then slowly, then pause. His punctuation is worth noting, and young readers could profit from discussion about why he chose a dash instead of a comma, or why he chose a fragment instead of a whole sentence.

This text could teach fluent readers a great deal about how to read with phrasing and intonation. "Find a page you love and practice reading it aloud so, so well." We could also ask children to do the same with a page of their own writing. This may make them want to revise their own text.

Book Connections

This book could initiate independent studies of the complex character of Charles Lindberg. Readers may want to read James Cross Giblin's marvelous book, *Charles A. Lindberg: A Human Hero*.

Burleigh is the author of other books, and all deserve to be studied and admired. He's written *Black Whiteness* about Admiral Perry in the Antarctic and *Home Run* about Babe Ruth, where again, he chooses individuals who are independent.

Genre
Nonfiction; Biography; Picture Book; Poetry

Teaching Uses
Read Aloud; Independent Reading; Teaching Writing; Language Conventions

A Field Guide to the Classroom Library, Lucy Calkins and the Teachers College Reading and Writing Project, Heinemann, ©2002 Teachers College, Columbia University; http://www.heinemann.com/fieldguides

Flip-Flop Girl
Katherine Paterson

Book Summary

Flip-Flop Girl is the story of a nine-year old girl named Lavinia, Vinnie for short, who moves from Washington, DC, to her grandmother's town in Virginia after her father dies. Her five-year old brother stops talking after her father's funeral and, because of this, gets much more attention from her mother and grandmother than Vinnie does. Vinnie has a hard time adjusting to her new school-she loves her teacher, but doesn't have any close friends. Lupe, another girl in her class who always wears flip-flops, is kind of mysterious and strange, but Vinnie starts to become friends with her. A strong feature of this book is the character, Vinnie, who acts like a real person. She is someone who gets mad and says mean things and is confused about stuff sometimes.

Basic Book Information

Flip-Flop Girl is a realistic fiction book of 120 pages with 14 chapters. The chapters have an average length of eight pages.

Noteworthy Features

The book moves chronologically through time, with no flashbacks, which makes it fairly easy for readers to follow. It's written in third person, but told from Vinnie's perspective. The reader gets to hear her thoughts about events and people in the book. Any major jumps in time or scene are done at chapter breaks.

Most of the dialogue in this book is straightforward, but some dialogue contains tricky parts. Sometimes it is unattributed; sentences are spoken but the reader has to know that the characters are alternating lines. There are also places where the reader has to pay very strict attention to quotation marks because there is internal monologue interspersed with dialogue.

"He's got to be somewhere!"

"I've looked everywhere. . . I've never known him to just up and disappear."

"I told him to go away-that I never wanted to see him again as long as I lived. If he could stop talking, he might disappear as well."

"Do you have any ideas? I hate to call Grace. She'll be frantic, and I'm sure he's right here under out noses."

Here, the first paragraph is Vinnie speaking, the second and fourth are her grandmother speaking, and the third is Vinnie's thoughts.

Because the story is told from Vinnie's perspective, a teacher may want to remind readers that it is necessary for them to sometimes doubt her story. For example, Vinnie often thinks and talks about how stupid her little brother is-but the reader should be able to figure out that she's jealous of the

Publisher
Puffin Books, 1994

ISBN
0525674802

TC Level
12

attention he gets and guilty about the part she played in his not talking even though she never says this explicitly.

Teaching Ideas

Flip-Flop Girl could be an independent reading book or a read aloud in 4th or 5th grade. It provides wonderful opportunities to talk about character development and change. It deals with moral issues of right and wrong and also with social issues of isolation and friendship that all students can identify with on some level. Readers feel that Vinnie is a real person, who gets mad and yells and has a hard time being sorry because she's hurting so much herself. She doesn't always do the right thing at the right time.

Book Connections

The Great Gilly Hopkins is another book by Katherine Paterson that has a strong and sometimes dislikable girl as protagonist. Both books deal with fitting in in new places and issues of friendship and family. Both Gilly and Vinnie do bad things that they need to come to terms with during the story.

There are of course many books that deal with the anger and confusion that accompany the death of a parent, sibling, or close friend: *Fig Pudding* by Ralph Fletcher, *Sort of Forever* by Sally Warner, *Mick Harte Was Here* by Barbara Park, and *Bridge to Terebithia* by Katherine Paterson. *Missing May* by Cynthia Rylant or *Sun and Spoon* by Kevin Henkes would be good books to look at in conjunction with *Flip-Flop Girl* because they deal primarily with the story of coping with the absence of a family member who has passed away.

Genre
Chapter Book

Teaching Uses
Character Study; Independent Reading; Read Aloud

A Field Guide to the Classroom Library, Lucy Calkins and the Teachers College Reading and Writing Project, Heinemann, ©2002 Teachers College, Columbia University; http://www.heinemann.com/fieldguides

From the Mixed-up Files of Mrs. Basil E. Frankweiler

E.L.Konigsburg

Book Summary

E.L. Konigsburg tells the story of Claudia and Jamie Kincaid, two elementary school children from a Connecticut suburb that run away from home to the Metropolitan Museum of Art in New York City. Claudia feels unappreciated at home. Her parents don't realize that she does more chores than anyone else, like taking care of her baby brother (even though she claims he's a pain). She is also better behaved than her siblings. Claudia decides that it's time for everyone to realize how important she is, so she and her brother, Jamie, take off for the Big Apple. Hiding out in the Metropolitan may seem like a difficult challenge, but with Claudia's brains and Jamie's money these two make it happen.

During the day the kids explore the museum and the city and right before closing they return to the museum and hide in the bathrooms. When no one is left in the museum, Claudia and Jamie have full reign of the place. They sleep in the beds of historical figures like Marie Antoinette, and they take baths in a huge fountain by the café. During one of their daily romps, Claudia and Jamie stumble upon a sculpture that is under scrutiny by the museum curators. Many argue that this little sculpture of an angel is the work of the famous Michelangelo. Skeptics believe that it is nothing more than a fake. Claudia and Jamie decide to do some researching on their own. They discover that the key to solving this mystery is to contact its previous owner, one Mrs. Basil E. Frankweiler. Mrs. Frankweiler used to live in Manhattan, but she now lives in upstate Connecticut, so the kids say goodbye to the museum and head to Farmington, home of the mysterious and wealthy woman.

Claudia and Jamie's bravery and intelligence are challenged in Mrs. Frankweiler's home. The children are asked to look inside themselves to figure out how to solve this sculpture mystery. Claudia and Jamie prove to Mrs. Frankweiler and to themselves that their insightful ways and courageous risk-taking can lead them to the answer. Mrs. Frankweiler shares her mystery with the children: indeed, the sculpture is Michelangelo's! Impressed by the children, Mrs. Frankweiler promises the two that she shall leave them in her will the one article of proof that can authorize the sculpture's authenticity as a Michelangelo work. The children will only receive this artifact (a note written by Michelangelo describing the work) if they promise not to say anything until after Mrs. Frankweiler dies. Claudia returns home with a new outlook on her life. She didn't need to run away to do something amazing, and heroine-like, she already is a hero! The story closes with Mrs. Frankweiler (who happens to narrate the entire story to her lawyer named Saxonberg) sharing with the reader that while the children

A Field Guide to the Classroom Library, Lucy Calkins and the Teachers College Reading and Writing Project, Heinemann, ©2002 Teachers College, Columbia University; http://www.heinemann.com/fieldguides

Publisher
Dell Yearling, 1967

ISBN
0440431808

TC Level
12

believe their grandparents to be deceased, Saxonberg is really their grandfather.

Basic Book Information

This book is broken into ten untitled chapters. Periodically there are sketches in the book that correlate to what is going on in the story. Narrator Mrs. Basil E. Frankweiler tells the story chronologically.

The Mixed-up Files of Mrs. Basil E. Frankweiler won the Newbery Award, and has already been hailed as a classic.

Noteworthy Features

As stated above, the reader may wonder, "Who is Mrs. Frankweiler?" She enters the story as a character about three-quarters of the way through. The book begins with a letter from Mrs. Frankweiler to her lawyer, Saxonberg. In this letter, which may confuse first-time readers of the book, Mrs. Frankweiler writes that she wants her will to be updated with particular changes that are mentioned in her attached file. The story of Claudia and Jamie begins in that file in Chapter 1. Teachers may want to refrain from explaining all that they know about Mrs. Frankweiler since the author clearly wanted her identity and importance to be revealed later in the story. If readers can hold onto the mystery until they are properly introduced to the character, they may be even more curious about the story.

Both Claudia and Jamie seem well advanced for their years. Some readers may have a difficult time with their accelerated vocabulary.

Teaching Ideas

Teachers could do a character study mini-lesson. Students could team-up with partners and pick one of the three main characters (Claudia, Jamie, or Mrs. Frankweiler) to research. Then, students could discuss who they think these people are and why they made the decisions they did in the story, supporting their ideas from the text. Students could use post-it notes to mark passages that describe, for example, Claudia's determined spirit, Jamie's miserly ways, and Mrs. Frankweiler's insightful being. The students could present their evidence to the class and discuss with their peers why they like/dislike particular characters' traits. This activity will help the children see the characters in a more three-dimensional way.

Another mini-lesson to introduce could focus on problem solving. The teacher could have a short discussion with the class about the obstacles the main characters face. The teacher could then chart the students' answers on chart paper and ask the class to pair up. Each pair could pick a problem and go back to the book and find details that describe how Claudia and Jamie use their minds to problem solve. When the teacher calls the pairs back to the whole group, each pair can share which obstacle they picked and give examples from the text to show how the characters overcame them. The class can discuss: What are some good strategies to try to solve problems?

As mentioned above, the character of Mrs. Frankweiler is mentioned before she is introduced. Teachers may want to talk with children about ways to hang on to a mystery as you read, looking for clues and looking for answers. Teachers can explain that sometimes an author doesn't tell you everything you want to know all at once, but instead the author tells you little by little, when he or she wants you to know it. Children may want to discuss other books in which the writer has done this, and they may want to try it in their own writing. The important thing to communicate to students is that they are not at fault for not understanding exactly what is going on in the story right from the beginning, they are not wrongly confused-that unknowing is part of the mystery and excitement of the book.

Book Connections

Konigsburg has also penned other children's books such as: *The Second Mrs. Giaconda*; *Father's Arcane Daughter*; and *Jennifer, Hecate, Macbeth, William McKinley, and Me, Elizabeth* which was a runner-up for the Newbery Award.

Genre
Chapter Book

Teaching Uses
Character Study; Independent Reading; Partnerships; Teaching Writing

A Field Guide to the Classroom Library, Lucy Calkins and the Teachers College Reading and Writing Project, Heinemann, ©2002 Teachers College, Columbia University; http://www.heinemann.com/fieldguides

Gathering Blue

Lois Lowry

Book Summary

Set in a post-apocalyptic world, most of civilization has collapsed. In one secluded village Kira, the daughter of a master weaver, is born with a twisted leg which keeps her from running, or doing much in the way of work. Kira's father disappears just before she is born. Suddenly, Kira's mother dies of a mysterious disease and their home is burned to keep the disease from spreading.

Almost immediately a crowd of townspeople gather, and decide that they want Kira taken from the village, and left in the forest to die, as she has no use to the village. So she is sent before the all-powerful Guardians, the rulers of the village, to plead her case before them. Suddenly she finds herself innocent, and living in the Guardian's mansion, with the Master Weaver who repairs the cloak that contains the world's history. As she takes up this position she learns to make every color, except blue. She also discovers what happened to her father when he returns from the dead, and what her "protectors" plan to do with her.

Basic Book Information

Gathering Blue is one of Lois Lowry's newest books, and another book that follows the pattern of *The Giver*, in which a young person is chosen for a position of great importance, but great isolation from the rest of the community, and breaks free, and in doing so discovers another world, outside of his or her home. The culture in *Gathering Blue* is very rigid and feudalistic. This book is interesting in that it takes a slightly different spin on the usual post-apocalyptic world, with its complete lack of technology, but its careful record keeping.

Noteworthy Features

Gathering Blue can be viewed as a mystery, but it is primarily fantasy. There are two very different cultures in this book-the town folk, and the swamp (Fen) folk. The Fen Folk talk with a slight accent that some students might find slightly difficult to read at first.

Students who have some experience with fantasy may have an easier time with the book, as it jumps right into the unusual world without set up or explanation. Readers will have to pick up what is going on as they go, without a narrator translating or explaining the new culture to them. Some students read books like this and find themselves confused and unsure of what is going on without knowing that that is how it is for every reader. These readers may give up the book prematurely, not realizing that they are comprehending the book perfectly well, and not waiting for the mysteries and complexities to be explained.

Publisher
Walter Lorraine Books, 2000

ISBN
0618055819

TC Level
13

A Field Guide to the Classroom Library, Lucy Calkins and the Teachers College Reading and Writing Project, Heinemann, ©2002 Teachers College, Columbia University; http://www.heinemann.com/fieldguides

Teaching Ideas

Students may love to discuss this book in partnerships or book groups. There is a lot going on, and most of it is strange and begs to be interpreted, guessed at, pondered over, and theorized about. Once again, Lowry has created a wonder of a book, with food for thought, hard questions, and vivid images.

One very interesting possibility for this book is to compare it to other books. It compares in interesting ways to Lois Lowry's *The Giver*, and/or to Gary Paulson's *The Monument*. The link to *The Monument* is more physical than *The Giver*. Rocky, the main character in *The Monument* has a bad leg, and is an orphan adopted by a small family that runs a small Kansas farm's Grain Elevator. Kira also has a bad leg is an orphan, and is adopted by people that are vital to her community.

Students might decide to follow a character's development. One of the best characters for this is Jamison. He appears suddenly on the Council of Guardians, a man that Kira did not know well. He then goes on to defend her and it seems that he is the voice that lets her live, and gives her a place in the Council Edifice, the Guardian's mansion. He seems to be friendly and kind, but as the book progresses readers discover his darker side. He forces them to work. Then in the final pages we discover that he is the one who tried to kill Kira's father. Another interesting character to study might be Matt. In the book's beginning, Matt seems to be a very petty young child, trying to go on a hunt, but as the reader reads further into the book we discover the awesome depths of his friendship and love for Kira.

Book Connections

This book has some similarities to *The Giver* and *The Monument*. It is not part of a series. Lois Lowry often writes about young children in dire straits, and about children who are somehow different from their peers. *The Giver* and *Gathering Blue* fit into this mold, as does her award-winning book *Number The Stars*. Both *Number The Stars* and *The Giver* have won the Newbery Medal.

Genre
Chapter Book; Fantasy

Teaching Uses
Independent Reading; Partnerships; Character Study

Girl Reporter Snags Crush

Linda Ellerbee

Book Summary

In *Girl Reporter Snags Crush*, 11-year-old Casey Smith describes her journalistic campaign against corporate advertising in school during the weeks leading up to a (gasp!) middle-school dance. Casey's no-nonsense approach is perfect for investigative reporting, but is not so useful when it comes to the sometimes embarrassing, sometimes thrilling, and sometimes inane world of middle-school crushes. Determined to find out the truth about Crush Cola's proposed sponsorship, Casey investigates the deal, as well as some mysterious anti-Crush vandalism. By the time the dance arrives, the case is solved, the article is written, and Casey can even enjoy herself on the dance floor.

Each of the books in the *Get Real* series involves the journalistic and personal adventures of sixth grader Casey Smith. Serious political, educational, and social topics are addressed through the articles Casey researches and writes, but the topics are grounded in events that many students will find familiar.

Basic Book Information

In each installment of the *Get Real* series, Casey Smith investigates a timely, relevant issue and navigates-with humor-the social complexities of middle school.

Noteworthy Features

Girl Reporter Snags Crush involves mostly sunny descriptions of 11- to 13-year-olds and middle school social life. Set in a small town in western Massachusetts, the book has a fast-moving plot and a clearly-drawn cast of characters.

Casey, the narrator, is a self-possessed 11-year-old who is confident enough to stand up for her beliefs, wears what she likes despite others' comments, and manages happily at home despite having parents who travel much of the time. Her closest friends are boys, though she has girl friends as well. Casey's character is well-developed through the narration, which includes the use of melodramatic headlines such as "Parents Protest Barfaroni Hot Lunch" and "Editorial Staff Overcome By Toxic Dance Fumes." Casey's character does not evolve over the course of the book (or the series), though she emerges from each book having learned new journalistic and personal lessons.

Series
Get Real

Publisher
Harper Collins, 2000

ISBN
0060282487

TC Level
11

A Field Guide to the Classroom Library, Lucy Calkins and the Teachers College Reading and Writing Project, Heinemann, ©2002 Teachers College, Columbia University; http://www.heinemann.com/fieldguides

In her parents' absence, Casey lives with her dynamic grandmother. The grandmother is a role model, a reporter who spent her career working on Capitol Hill. An anti-stereotype, the grandmother hates to cook and is writing her memoirs.

Other characters include stock characters, such as the ultra-feminine editor of the paper, nicknamed "The Princess of Pink," and the sports-crazed sports reporter. On the other hand, Casey's best friend is a tie-dye-wearing boy who is the school's only male cheerleader. The methods Casey uses to investigate events are well-illustrated. Casey takes notes, does interviews, discusses questions with friends, takes surveys, and does background research before writing her articles. She pursues answers even when her peers and the administration fault her.

The book raises the thought-provoking question of whether schools should accept school sponsorship, and what they stand to lose or gain if they do. The book details the two sides of the question but comes down squarely against such corporate involvement. The book also brings up freedom of speech, and how much freedom the writers of a school newspaper actually have.

Teaching Ideas

This book is a good one to offer as a selection for beginning book clubs or partnerships as it doesn't present any unique difficulties to most readers, and it offers topics for discussion that come up without much probing by readers.

Corporate sponsorship of schools is a possible discussion topic. Students might follow up discussions with editorials (like Casey's) either for or against such involvement. What "freedom of speech" means in general, and to children in particular, can be discussed or researched. The book can be a part of a discussion about politics or history, the Bill of Rights, and student newspapers' rights in terms of freedom of speech.

Girl Reporter Snags Crush also, of course, deals with crushes, dances, and other social issues. Students will probably want to talk about social pressure to act or dress in certain ways, and how they or others deal with those pressures.

This book can also be referred back to in the teaching of writing. As students re-read, they can collect information on how Casey researches and writes news articles. After discussion of each of those steps, students might select topics for investigation and indicate how they, too, might employ Casey's techniques and write articles.

Book Connections

If students enjoy this book, there are the others in the series to turn to.

Genre
Chapter Book

A Field Guide to the Classroom Library, Lucy Calkins and the Teachers College Reading and Writing Project, Heinemann, ©2002 Teachers College, Columbia University; http://www.heinemann.com/fieldguides

Teaching Uses
Small Group Strategy Instruction; Teaching Writing; Content Area Study

Gorilla Walk

Ted Lewin; Betsy Lewin

Book Summary

Gorilla Walk is a Nonfiction story written by the husband and wife team Ted and Betsy Lewin. They take the reader with them on their journey to the continent of Africa. We join them in the Impenetrable Forest of Uganda where they venture to see the elusive mountain gorilla. The well-crafted narrative text and gorgeous watercolor illustrations bring the story to life.

Basic Book Information

The 46-page book has three sections: an introduction, the story, and Mountain Gorilla facts. The three-age introduction is written very differently than the story. It is densely packed with historical information about the Mountain Gorilla, the Congo, Uganda and the continent of Africa and could be difficult to understand for many readers. A map of Africa with a zoom-in map of the Congo is included.

The introduction does not have to be read prior to reading the story. There is a quote on a page between the end of the introduction and the beginning of the story. This shift can be confusing to the reader. However, the strong storytelling voice of the authors recounting their adventure pulls the reader right into the story. The book includes illustrations around the perimeter of the pages, which both support and extend the text. Vocabulary that is particular to this subject is well supported by context clues within the text.

This book is a combination of expository text (the introduction and gorilla facts) and story/narrative. Therefore, it lends itself to being used in many different ways in the Reading Workshop. The teachers reviewing this text felt it had many possible uses in classrooms across grade levels.

Noteworthy Features

Gorilla Walk could be chosen by students for many reasons. In some cases, readers may want to browse through the book, enjoying the pictures and reading snippets of information here and there as they snag the eye. Some readers may come to the book with questions about gorillas, and they will want to read the book with pencil and paper in hand, ready to jot down information they come across that is relevant to their inquiry. Others may read the book for the story that unfolds of the gorilla walk itself.

Teaching Ideas

Gorilla Walk can be used as a read aloud. Once the text is being read aloud over time (several days to two weeks depending on the amount of time

Illustrators
Ted Lewin; Betsy Lewin

Publisher
Harper Collins, 1999

ISBN
0688165095

TC Level
11; 12; 13

available), the teacher needs to stop and talk frequently to support understanding of the story and particular vocabulary by letting children talk about what they are understanding so far. The stop and talk can be done with the whole group, in partnerships, or in small groups. The teacher can demonstrate how to talk about the text with the students. The conversation can continue and grow throughout the reading of the book, as questions are answered and confusions cleared up.

We recommend reading the introduction at the end of the story or perhaps after about half of the story in order to create a context for the information. It is recommended that this text be used after the students have had experience with sustaining conversation on a topic, not when they are initially learning about how to have a book conversation.

Gorilla Walk could be used in a study of interpretation. It lends itself to looking at a story and what it is really about within a particular context. Although this story can stand alone and be understood, it is situated within an historical and political context that has an impact on the story. Taking an historical/political angle to interpret the story can get students to think more deeply. This study may require additional research, which can be supported by small groups working together and gathering more information about the history of the region, and so on. Once the information is gathered, and the book read and talked about, the students can develop theories about what the text is really about and support their theories, using evidence from the text and the information about the history/politics of the region. This could promote thinking beyond the literal level. It can also lead students to realize that they can consider more information than what is just presented in a story to form an interpretation. In turn, this interpretive work can prompt students to take social action.

Gorilla Walk can be used to model active reading and processing of expository text. The introduction could be put on an overhead transparency and projected so the whole class can see the text as the teacher reads and models active meanings (as it is being read). The teacher can model strategies like questioning the text; restating what was just read in the students' own words; underlining parts that are important; jotting notes in margins or on post-its about new information being learned; stopping and talking about the text, or stopping and writing. It is sometimes necessary to show students how to do this active reading with expository text. Shared reading of the introduction is appropriate for this work.

Book Connections

Other texts that can be used in similar ways are *Through My Eyes* by Ruby Bridges and *Koko's Kitten* by Francine Patterson and Ronald H. Cohn.

Genre

Nonfiction; Picture Book

A Field Guide to the Classroom Library, Lucy Calkins and the Teachers College Reading and Writing Project, Heinemann, ©2002 Teachers College, Columbia University; http://www.heinemann.com/fieldguides

Teaching Uses
Reading and Writing Nonfiction; Content Area Study; Independent
Reading; Read Aloud; Interpretation; Small Group Strategy Instruction

A Field Guide to the Classroom Library, Lucy Calkins and the Teachers College Reading and Writing Project, Heinemann, ©2002 Teachers
College, Columbia University; http://www.heinemann.com/fieldguides

Granny the Pag

Nina Bowder

Book Summary

This is the story of Catriana, a little girl who lives with her eccentric grandmother. Her grandmother is a retired psychiatrist who has nine cats and four dogs, rides a motorcycle, and makes home-visits to people who are strange. Catriana lives with her grandmother because her parents are actors and have other priorities. *Granny the Pag* chronicles the unusual relationship between Catriana and her eccentric grandmother.

Catriana's parents decide, when she is twelve, that they want her back. Catriana is now caught in a tug-of-war. She ends up being forced to live with her parents, but the ensuing court battle for joint custody allows Catriana to at least visit her grandmother and realize that the things that once seemed strange about her grandmother now seem perfectly delightful.

Basic Book Information

At a glance, *Granny the Pag* seems to be an easy and accessible chapter book. It's only 184 pages long and the story moves along quickly. It doesn't focus on the heaviest of topics. It's written in the first-person voice of twelve-year-old Catriana. Despite the outward appearance of being an easy read, the book has complexities that could derail readers and make the book worthy of being discussed either within a small group or as a whole class read aloud.

The section breaks in the text (signified by the row of diamonds) may or may not signify discontinuities in the text. At times, these section breaks seem almost superfluous, and at other times they suggest a gigantic turn in the setting, topic, or point of view. This feature may make the book merit more attention than it would otherwise seem to call for.

Noteworthy Features

The title comes from the beginning of the story after Catriana is sent to live with her grandmother and angrily writes a note "Grandma is a Pag." She leaves it for her grandmother to discover. The only problem is that she has misspelled the word "pig," on the note. "Grandma is a Pag"-becomes a source of fun between the two of them.

Teaching Ideas

The text is perfect for a character study. Readers' first instinct might be to collect information about the weird and wonderful character of the grandmother, but this will be fairly straightforward work. The more challenging and fun project for readers may be to gather insights about

Publisher
Penguin Putnam, 1997

ISBN
0140384472

TC Level
12

A Field Guide to the Classroom Library, Lucy Calkins and the Teachers College Reading and Writing Project, Heinemann, ©2002 Teachers College, Columbia University; http://www.heinemann.com/fieldguides

Catriana herself. Readers may want to chart her turmoil as she struggles between two worlds. As the custody issue gathers momentum, readers could imagine how the arguments for and against giving custody to the grandmother might go and could even try their hand at some debate using evidence from the text to build an argument for one side or the other.

Readers will also want to talk about how it must feel for this girl to be in the midst of a battle over her own life and yet to be so helpless in that battle. Young readers may have their own parallel stories to tell with ways in which their stories are like and are unlike this one.

Book Connections

This story is built around the archetype of a character who is torn between two worlds. It is similar to the story of Mila in Hesse's *Music of the Dolphins,* who is torn between the world of humans and that of dolphins. It is also similar to the story of Dean in Alfordo's *I Can't Believe I Have to Do This,* who is torn between the worlds of alcohol and joyrides and that of school and family. Neither Mila nor Dean, however, are as powerless as Catriana. But Catriana, too, has the power to make peace with her life.

Genre
Nonfiction; Chapter Book

Teaching Uses
Partnerships; Book Clubs; Independent Reading; Read Aloud; Character Study

Graven Images
Paul Fleischman

Book Summary

Graven Images is a collection of three short stories about people whose lives are affected by statues. In the first story, *The Binnacle Boy,* a statue is the only surviving relic of a mysterious ship disaster. Since the statue is considered to have guarded the secret of the disaster, the townspeople begin to entrust their secrets to the Binnacle Boy. When a wealthy woman hires a partially deaf cleaning woman, it becomes sport to read the lips of the townspeople as they disclose their secrets. Little does the wealthy woman know that the cleaning woman would discover her own secret . . . that she was the one who poisoned the crew. In the second story, a shoemaker's apprentice follows a broken weathervane of St. Crispin and finds love. In the third story, *The Man of Influence,* a ghost commissions an out of work sculptor to the wealthy to render his likeness in stone. Desperate for money, the sculptor agrees to create a sculpture of this grotesque man. Eventually, the arrogant sculptor learns that wealth and power do not make a great man.

Basic Book Information

Graven Images is a Newbery Award winner written by Paul Fleischman. The book contains three short stories: *The Binnacle Boy, St. Crispin's Follower,* and *The Man of Influence.* These stories are outlined in a table of contents and are further divided into chapters.

Noteworthy Features

The three stories each take place in a different part of the world. *The Binnacle Boy* takes place in New Bethany, Maine. *St. Crispin's Follower* takes place in "Charleston, capital of the colony of South Carolina." And *The Man of Influence* takes place in Genoa. Readers will most likely know where the first two locations are but may be unaware that Genoa is part of Italy.

The story setting must be inferred in each of the stories contained in *Graven Images.* In *The Binnacle Boy,* there are references to ships, scurvy, spinning, and hearth fires. *St. Crispin's Follower* is about a shoemaker's apprentice who works on "jackboots and brocade slippers." And, finally in the third story the king rides through the marketplace on horseback. A reader must pick up on clues such as these to realize that the stories most likely happened about 200 years ago. The stories contain elements of fantasy and read like fairy tales. Therefore, exact identification of the time these stories took place is not a prerequisite.

All of the dialogue in *Graven Images* is antiquated and formal. Children may be confused by some of the dated terminology and references. The shoemaker Mister Quince says things like "Aye, and I'll wager you'll serve it

Illustrator
Andrew Glass

Publisher
Harper & Row Publishers, Inc., 1982

ISBN
0060219068

A Field Guide to the Classroom Library, Lucy Calkins and the Teachers College Reading and Writing Project, Heinemann, ©2002 Teachers College, Columbia University; http://www.heinemann.com/fieldguides

well." And, in the first story the women says lines such as, "All boys be apprenticed to the devil." While the antiquated speech can help to transport readers to another time in history, such language could also make it hard for children to fully comprehend the story.

Children can read the stories independently and out of sequential order. Therefore, they do not have to retain a long, continuous story in their heads. However, the stories are undeniably related and by reading them together readers may begin to get deeper meaning from them.

The book design may be confusing. The pages are numbered chronologically throughout the course of the book. However, the chapters begin again at "one" at the start of each story.

Teaching Ideas

Graven Images would be a wonderful selection for a read aloud. The stories are no greater than 25 pages in length and do not have to be read in order. The stories contain a number of references that readers may be unfamiliar with and could be explained when they are encountered. Children who are listening to the read aloud may derive meaning from context and voice intonation.

Readers who are reading this book by themselves or with a partner will most likely encounter unfamiliar terms. If a child comes upon a word that is interfering with their comprehension of the story, then a child may need to know that this is a good time to call on a partner for help. "What could this mean?" They can work together. However, if a reader is constantly stymied by words from the story, that is a good sign that the book is too difficult.

In a conference, a teacher might nudge children who are reading *Graven Images* to begin to speculate over how the three stories are connected. In each of the tales, the main character is led to a revelation with the help of a statue. In the first story, the cleaning lady discovers the horrible truth about the ship disaster with the help of *The Binnacle Boy*. In *St. Crispin's Follower*, a boy follows the path that a broken weathervane points to and finds love at the end. In the third, through sculpting a specter Zorelli learns that power and influence are not the only characteristics that should define greatness. The three stories provide a wonderful opportunity for readers to draw connections. Readers independently or in partnerships might want to attach post-it notes to common elements of the stories. Finding the threads that weave together the stories may lead readers to a more thorough understanding of the stories.

Readers may notice that Paul Fleischman does not tell readers exactly when the story is taking place. As readers progress through the book they may find that many clues are provided that point to a historical era. Gathering evidence to support the setting of the stories will help readers begin to picture the events of the story in another time frame.

In a writing workshop, young authors may want to look at *Graven Images* as an example of the short story genre. All of the stories are complete onto themselves, with their own set of characters, setting, time and plot. Yet, children may notice that the author, Paul Fleischman, uses related stories in his collection. All of the stories are set in the past. They are about a serious or "graven" issue related to a statue. The title "Graven Images" could be used as a title for all of the entries in his book, therefore it is an element that helps ties together the stories. Children may want to embark on a project that lets them write short stories on a shared topic for a collection.

It could be conceivable that the entire class is asked to read from a collection of anthologies (these could all be short anthologies or could include poetry anthologies) and to speculate about why these texts are combined under a single title. What do they have in common? Why would the editor/author put them in this particular sequence? One teacher pointed out to her students that one or two of the anthologies contained a beautifully written foreword in which the editor spoke of the common themes in that anthology. We recommend *Birthday Surprises* (Hurwitz) and *The House on Mango Street* (Cisneros) be included in this work.

Book Connections

An interested child might find it fascinating to see all the texts that Paul Fleischman and his son Sid Fleischman have written. Each writes in an extraordinary range of genre and uses a wide diversity of settings.

Genre
Fantasy; Short Story Anthology

Teaching Uses
Whole Group Instruction; Small Group Strategy Instruction; Partnerships; Teaching Writing; Read Aloud

Greenwitch

Susan Cooper

Book Summary

The *Dark Is Rising* saga continues with *Greenwitch*, the third book, in the sequence. The segment brings together the Drew children and Will Stanton. The Trewissick Grail, which the children discovered in the first book, has been stolen and the children must retrieve it. Getting it back entails a series of adventures for the Drew children as well as for Will.

The Greenwitch, the title character in the story, is a symbolic figure, constructed of limbs of trees and local greenery by the women of the village as a spring rite. Once made, the men of the village toss the icon into the sea. But tradition dictates that, before this happens, the women touch the image and make a wish. Jane joins in, saying, "I wish she [the Greenwitch] could be happy." Because of Jane's unselfish wish, the Greenwitch visits her in a dream and reveals the fate of the tube that was dropped into the sea in the first book.

The character who represents The Dark in this book is a sinister looking artist who casts spells in an attempt to recover the lost tube. Through a series of adventures that include Merriman and Will's visit with Tethys in the depths of the sea, in addition to spells and Jane's apparition of the Greenwitch, the children manage to recapture the lost tube despite the machinations of the artist gypsy. Using the recovered manuscript, the Old Ones read the message carved on the grail. Then Merriman destroys the manuscript that can translate it. The cryptic message, now known only to the Old Ones, sets the scene for the continuance of the story in the next volume in the sequence, *The Grey King*.

This is the third of the five-book sequence. Merriman Lyon not only acts as mentor in this story but plays the role of warrior against the forces of the Dark. Will Stanton is united with the three Drew children in this book. As in *The Dark Is Rising*, this volume, too, follows the pattern of "high" fantasy, containing all the elements that are characteristic of that genre. The sense of journey or quest is combined with other high fantasy elements-moving across thresholds into different worlds-this time underneath the sea, the sense of the marvelous, and the timelessness of characters.

Basic Book Information

This is the third in the award-winning *Dark Is Rising* sequence. *The Grey King*, the next book, received the Newbery Award and *The Dark Is Rising*, the previous book was a Newbery Honor book. Containing only 131 pages, this book is shorter than the first two books in the sequel. It nevertheless presents a challenge to the reader. It would be difficult to follow the plot of this sequel without having read the first two books, since there are many references made, particularly to the first of the books, *Over Sea, Under Stone*. The sentence length varies, ranging from seven to thirty-seven words

Series
The Dark Is Rising

Publisher
Macmillan Publishing, 1974

ISBN
0689710887

TC Level
14

with the average length being around twenty. It is this sentence length, combined with the complex syntax-clauses strung together with semi-colons and structures such as: "this alien element in which by enchantment they briefly breathed and swam." The chapters are numbered but not titled. Cooper, at times, uses flashbacks, first describing a scene with several of the characters, then returning to the same block of time and describing a second scene with the simultaneous actions of other of the characters.

Noteworthy Features

Each chapter of this book takes us through one episode in the plot. Many of the chapters end with a puzzling event whose meaning is revealed in the next chapter. The story is told in third person and frequently changes point of view. At times, we watch the action through Jane's eyes, then we are inside Will's mind, then Barnaby's. Unlike the first two books, this one includes many long descriptive paragraphs that are, at times, difficult to follow. There are many more references to Cornish folklore than were in the first two books as well. Some of the longer sentences contain so much detail that the reader will find it necessary to re-read it. The greatest challenge, however, will be to visualize the long descriptions, particularly for those readers who have not experienced such terrain as one finds in Cornwall, England. The plot demands much from the reader, for Cooper often implies meaning, uses foreshadowing and includes information explained in one of the books that precede this one. There is some dialogue in Cornish dialect but it should not present a problem. Also, having read the first two books, students by this time should be used to British spelling of words like "colour" and "tyre."

Teaching Ideas

Teachers may want students to read and discuss this book chapter by chapter, since the plot is more complicated and the text is more difficult than the first two books of this sequence. Readers can compare the plot lines and events of either or both of the first two books, *Over Sea, Under Stone* and *The Dark Is Rising*, keeping notes on events in *Greenwitch* that remind them of an event and/or character in either of the other two books. At appropriate points in the reading, teachers might invite students to discuss the connections they made and how making that connection assisted comprehension.

Cooper uses descriptive passages frequently in this book. In Chapter 1, the three Drew children are in the museum, looking at the case where the grail had been displayed. The teacher might select other equally descriptive passages and ask students to draw a picture of what those words describe. At the beginning of Chapter 2, Jane stands at the end of Kemare Head at sunset. Depicting the scene will help students focus on the details, thus better comprehending the passage.

Aside from the action that describes the continuing struggle between the Light and the Dark, this book contrasts the four young characters in the saga. Each plays a specific role in the story. Barnaby continues to have a sense of Arthurian legend. It is his drawing that is stolen, and he who, in a

A Field Guide to the Classroom Library, Lucy Calkins and the Teachers College Reading and Writing Project, Heinemann, ©2002 Teachers College, Columbia University; http://www.heinemann.com/fieldguides

trance, is used as a spokesperson for the Dark. Jane's intuitive sense is even stronger in this book than in book one of the series. Simon seems not to have any of the special abilities of his siblings. He provides support and follows along with the ideas of the other two. And Will, having assumed his role as an Old One, appears much older and wiser than the others. Students might choose one of these four young characters and keep a notebook of events that happen to that character and how they react to those events as an exercise in character development.

Students should raise many questions as they read this book. Drawing on what they have learned from the previous books, they might make a list of questions before they begin to read the text. Such questions can continue as they read each chapter. At the end of each chapter, or at appropriate points, teachers might ask students about the questions they raised and discuss possible answers for those questions. When the answers have not yet been revealed, students can be encouraged to make predictions before reading further.

Book Connections

It would be difficult to grasp the significance of the events in this book without having read at least one of the first two books in the sequence, preferably both. Students will enjoy continuing reading of the struggle between the Dark and the Light in the next two books, *The Grey King* and *Silver on the Tree*.

Genre
Fantasy; Chapter Book

Teaching Uses
Independent Reading; Small Group Strategy Instruction

A Field Guide to the Classroom Library, Lucy Calkins and the Teachers College Reading and Writing Project, Heinemann, ©2002 Teachers College, Columbia University; http://www.heinemann.com/fieldguides

Harry Potter and the Sorcerer's Stone

J.K. Rowling

Book Summary

Harry Potter and the Sorcerer's Stone tells the story of a supposedly ordinary boy who suddenly finds himself part of a magical world of wizards, monsters, and heroic exploits. Orphaned as a baby, Harry Potter lives with his wholly unpleasant aunt and uncle in a suburb of London until a letter (delivered by owl) informs him that he is, in fact, a wizard, and due to leave for Hogwarts, the wizard boarding school. There, Harry meets Ron and Hermione, and the trio embarks on both humorous and hair-raising adventures: surviving nasty classmates, learning wizardry, and battling the forces of evil. Harry's first year in boarding school concludes with a narrow escape from a powerful enemy, and the promise of future escapades.

Basic Book Information

Harry Potter and the Sorcerer's Stone is a plot-driven adventure story about the struggle between good and evil.

The *Harry Potter* series is projected to include seven books, one for each of Harry's years at Hogwarts. Each combines humor, clever settings and props, compelling characters, and life-or-death struggles with a series of antagonists Harry must outwit.

Noteworthy Features

Inventiveness and adventure are key attractions in *Harry Potter*. The structure and subject matter are fairly simple. The chronological narrative unfolds in detailed settings, and changes of scene are clearly established. While the language is moderately challenging, the short paragraphs and simple syntax of the book make it manageable for younger readers.

Characters are fairly straightforward and easy to keep track of. Harry is brave, athletic, and quick-thinking, but possesses a certain humility and fear of failure; Ron, who is from a poor family, is Harry's faithful companion; Hermione, born of a normal ("muggle") family, is a brain; Draco Malfoy, Harry's chief rival, is rich, nasty, and deceitful. Readers looking for something other than a richly imagined fairy tale should look elsewhere.

Rowling's inventiveness with the elements, settings, and accessories of the wizard world is one of the book's main delights. Most readers should enjoy the dramatic settings. Hogwarts, the boarding school, is a vast castle equipped with mysterious stairways and doors guarded by ghosts. A magic sorting hat, placed on incoming students' heads, decides to which of the four houses a student will belong. The students play a game on broomsticks

Series
Harry Potter

Publisher
Scholastic, 1997

ISBN
059035342X

TC Level
13

A Field Guide to the Classroom Library, Lucy Calkins and the Teachers College Reading and Writing Project, Heinemann, ©2002 Teachers College, Columbia University; http://www.heinemann.com/fieldguides

with a self-propelled golden ball. It may be in these fanciful details that may make *Harry Potter* so enjoyed by so many young people.

Though in some circles *Harry Potter* represents an immoral kind of children's literature with its references to witchcraft (and a few parents may express this concern), a case could be made that the *Harry Potter* books affirms basic humanist values. The character of Harry Potter possesses honesty, loyalty to his friends, charity for the less fortunate, duty to his elders, and humility. In fact, *Harry Potter* is the latest in a long line of stories, in which religion plays a role, and which portray life as the struggle between good and evil.

In the end, *Harry Potter* is a fairy tale. Raised as a commoner, Harry Potter is in fact of royal birth (by wizard standards-his parents were beloved and powerful wizards). His skills are repeatedly tested by evil characters, and like King Arthur, for example, he has a magical mentor, Professor Dumbledore, who assists and instructs him in times of need.

Teaching Ideas

Because the characters are static, character studies will be straightforward. Students can examine how Rowling economically clues readers in to the character's inclinations. But just because the characters can be tagged with a handful of defining characteristics does not make imitating the author any easier. Students reading *Harry Potter* with an eye toward writing similar stuff might do well to pay attention to how seemingly inconsequential details can speak volumes about a character. One of the antagonists goes by the name of Draco Malfoy. He is introduced as a boy with a "pale, pointed face." Right off, he tells Harry of his plan to smuggle in contraband to school. The name (with its hint of dragons and malfeasance), the physical description, and the brief dialogue make it clear that he is bad news.

For students with limited experience keeping track of characters, *Harry Potter* is a good place to start. It may be worth the time to have such students record the names of characters as well as their physical description, defining characteristics and their introductory dialogue. After interpreting those features, readers can go on to test the accuracy of their interpretations against the characters' future actions.

Once characters have been established, it may be worthwhile to have students examine which virtues and values are being advocated. If indeed *Harry Potter* is a fairy tale, what is the moral? Certainly the book was written to entertain, but what message does it contain? What about this message do some people find objectionable? Sophisticated readers might want to research the opposition to *Harry Potter* and explore the validity of such concerns.

One matter that may be worth discussing is *Harry* Potter's allusion to matters of racism. Hogwart's students who are from non-wizard families are scorned by some adults and students. Hermione, in particular, experiences this prejudice in several of the *Harry Potter* books. The prejudiced characters are invariably evil ones. Some readers may note and be bothered by the absence of strong female characters. While Hermione is the smartest character, she is neither brave nor influential, some readers feel, and most other female characters are inconsequential.

A Field Guide to the Classroom Library, Lucy Calkins and the Teachers College Reading and Writing Project, Heinemann, ©2002 Teachers College, Columbia University; http://www.heinemann.com/fieldguides

Book Connections

Harry Potter draws from a rich tradition of mythical beings and beasts. The warlocks, vampires, unicorns, and witches are almost too many to count. Students who develop an affinity for *Harry Potter* might enjoy learning more about these beings. They also might enjoy reading more fantasy. Antoine de Saint-Exupéry's *The Little Prince* and C.S. Lewis' series *The Chronicles of Narnia* are both excellent and will offer readers roughly the same level of difficulty.

Genre
Fantasy; Chapter Book; Fairy and Folk Tale

Teaching Uses
Character Study; Interpretation; Independent Reading; Book Clubs

A Field Guide to the Classroom Library, Lucy Calkins and the Teachers College Reading and Writing Project, Heinemann, ©2002 Teachers College, Columbia University; http://www.heinemann.com/fieldguides

Heaven

Angela Johnson

Book Summary

Fourteen-year-old Marley has lived in Heaven, Ohio, a small quiet unchanging town for so long that she knows there are "1,627 steps from my house to Western Union." Momma, Pops, Butchy, and Marley live a quiet life only interrupted by the letters Marley gets regularly from her Pops' twin brother, Uncle Jack. Shoogy Maple sees shadow ghosts and has been kicked out of every school she'd gone to before her family moved across the playground from Marley. The reason they become and stay friends is that Shoogy isn't like anyone in her family.

Heaven is structured into four parts. Rich details of Marley's happy small town life are the basis of Part two. This part ends with a letter from the deacon of the burned Alabama church requesting an original copy of Marley's baptismal certificate. This is the way the Marley finds out that her Uncle Jack is really her father, and that her real mother, Christine, died in an accident. She is adopted. Part three is dedicated to the coming to terms with the lies and the realities in both friends' lives. Angela Johnson weaves together the lives of each of her characters in the concluding fourth part of this book.

Basic Book Information

Angela Johnson's 138 page novel is divided into four parts. The short chapters in each part have intriguing titles: burning dark, storm, time, more shadow ghosts, armed, dreams. The book begins with a letter from Uncle Jack and Boy. The author won the Coretta Scott King Award for this book, and for an earlier book, *Toning the Sweep*. She is the author of six books for younger readers. One of these, *When I Am Old With You* is a Coretta Scott King Honor Book.

Noteworthy Features

Heaven is written in the first person in narrative form. Interestingly, as Marley's story unfolds, she is trying to discover her own identity. The characters, the setting, and the story are revealed through her eyes. Integral to the story is Marley's close friend Shoogy's story. Shoogy wants more to be a part of Marley's family than her own. The constant parallel between these two stories serves as an important balance in the telling.

The story is told in four parts, but within each part, the chapters are separated carefully among the characters. The italicized letters are also carefully positioned in the story to allow the author to slowly unravel the important details. The letters are often ambiguous. It would be important to

Publisher
Scholastic, 1998

ISBN
0439142652

TC Level
13

share this with readers as they might have to return to re-read these letters after they have read more into the chapter. There is a lot of dialogue in this story that may be colloquial or unfamiliar. Also, various historical references, such as the church burnings, could be explained and discussed. This may lead to further investigation in the reading.

Teaching Ideas

Angela Johnson's *Heaven* is a book that might be most effectively used as a read aloud. The opening letter from Uncle Jack and Boy leaves the reader with so many questions. We are unsure of what the dreams mean. The foreshadowing in this letter might be an interesting place to start, returning to it after the children have begun to understand who all the characters are in the book.

There are four communications from Uncle Jack in the first part of the book-all italicized. It might be interesting to watch how Angela Johnson uses internal thinking after each of these letters to help the reader understand Marley. This technique is particularly intriguing, as the rest of the story is simple and direct. Angela Johnson shares Marley's thinking through the use of dialogue and scene. Juxtaposing these two techniques helps the reader to understand how the author invites them into the character's thinking. This might lead to a study of interpretation. How does an author assist the reader in understanding the subtle connections and meanings she is trying to make? Which relationships, which connections are the most essential?

As mentioned earlier, Angela Johnson uses interesting language systems. All of her chapter titles are short, often one or two words, and all lower case. They focus the reader on a single concept in each chapter. It might be interesting to study the patterns and the intentions of the author. Teaching here might focus on theory building. As a read aloud, a teacher might try to help children hold onto different parts of the texts and use the accumulation of these parts to develop larger ideas that make connections to their own lives or to try to place this story in a larger world context. Readers could study this book as one that answers the essential question: How does this book affect the way we view the world? To do this we might embark on a study of this author's work. A teacher might also encourage outside connections to their newspaper readingwhat's happening in the world today that connects to this story?

Book Connections

Books that have strong protagonists faced with difficulties might be one set of connections. *Guests* by Michael Dorris, Katherine Paterson's *The Great Gilly Hopkins*, Kimberly Willis Holt's *When Zachary Beaver Comes to Town*, Cindy Dawson Boyd's *Chevrolet Saturdays* are a few that come to mind. An author study of Angela Johnson's books is another approach. This might also be a time to introduce African American authors, particularly using realistic fiction. Some of the ones already named might be combined with Christopher Paul Curtis's *The Watsons Go To Birmingham*, Jacqueline Woodson's *Miracle Boys*, and Sharon Bell Mathis' *Teacup Full of Roses*.

A Field Guide to the Classroom Library, Lucy Calkins and the Teachers College Reading and Writing Project, Heinemann, ©2002 Teachers College, Columbia University; http://www.heinemann.com/fieldguides

Genre
Short Chapter Book

Teaching Uses
Read Aloud; Independent Reading; Interpretation; Author Study

Hiroshima

Laurence Yep

Book Summary

In *Hiroshima*, Laurence Yep interweaves the story of two sisters on the day of the atom bombing with historical detail. It includes an account of the bombers, statistics, scientific information, and information on the spread of nuclear weapons. The result is a concise, lyrical text that will involve, inform, and move readers. Some students will undoubtedly find this book upsetting. Though the topic is wrenching, the treatment is not graphic. The emphasis is not on horror, but on the importance of understanding history, and acting on that knowledge.

Basic Book Information

This text contains 56 pages with nine titled chapters. The chapters range in length from three to eight pages. There are no illustrations.

Noteworthy Features

History is brought to life in this book with the use of present tense ("It is only seven o'clock in the morning . . .") and with well-chosen images of daily life. We read of trolleys, of children hurrying to school, and all of this brings the time and place to life.

This book is a hybrid of historical fiction, Nonfiction, and political writing. Readers who are leery of Nonfiction may be drawn into this genre.

The detailed settings, clear explanations, and concise background information make the large amount of material in this book easy for readers to absorb. In early chapters, the book cuts back and forth between the story of the bomb and the sisters' story. This *could* be confusing, but Yep handles the transitions with great clarity, establishing the new setting each time with tags such as, "In the meantime, down in Hiroshima . . ." or "On the Enola Gay. . . ." Clear, factual information is unobtrusively woven into the main narrative about the sisters. The last few chapters are more straightforwardly Nonfictional.

The writing is not only rich in information, explanation, and story, but it is also poetic, with similes such as, "the seven rivers shine like ribbons" and "she feels as if she has fallen into boiling oil." Woven throughout the book is the recurring image of a Japanese colonel on a white horse, symbolizing the military, and, perhaps, its formal, old-fashioned sense of honor. There are also occasions of symbolism, such as in the mention of a child's white glove. The Afterword explains the author's attempts to portray the facts accurately.

Publisher
Scholastic, 1995

ISBN
0590208330

TC Level
13

The subsequent chapter of sources underlies the importance of depicting the truth, and will provide opportunities for further research.

Teaching Ideas

There are some books that are so rich, complex, and significant that it's hard to imagine an individual reader simply stumbling upon the book on a library shelf, and reading it without the context of conversation. This is one such book. Its subject is so wrenching and its treatment of the subject so novel and skillful, that the book begs out to be a whole-class read aloud or perhaps the subject of a book-club study group. Perhaps a teacher will want to read this book aloud as part of some whole-class work on the fact that books can change those of us who read them. Sometimes in schools, children are led to believe that the goal in reading is to be able to retell a book skillfully, or to develop and defend ideas about a book. But many of us read because reading can change us, just as the most searing and powerful moments of our lives can change us. Perhaps a teacher will want to tell the story of a book or two in his or her life, which altered one's world view, which shaped one's destiny, which left a mark. "I'm going to read a book aloud now that is meant to shake us up, to stop us in our tracks, to make us think and talk differently," the teacher might say.

Perhaps the class will want to think together about the ways to use time and community so that this book *does* make a difference. Should I read, and then when I pause, should we stop and write? Should we be silent for a bit and then turn and talk? Should we deliberately talk less or read more, saving up the talk for later? Should a book like this be read intensely, several times in a day, instead of being read in the usual way?

If the class talks, writes, and thinks in response to this book, the result may be for the class to do more related reading, either together or as individuals. The result may be a new concern for world news. The result may be an involvement in social action.

When children read historical Nonfiction, this provides teachers an opportunity to coach them toward reading-as-a-historian. These are some of the skills and strategies we may want to teach:

The reader's challenge includes devising a course of study for oneself. In real life, no one says, "Read these four texts in this order." Instead the reader needs to devise a plan to make wise decisions. For example, one might first read an easy overview of a topic and then dig deeper.

The reader looks between sources asking, "Can facts be questioned? Can something one person sees as a fact, not be seen as a fact by another?"

The reader tries to understand the point of view of the author and asks, "How does the point of view influence this text?" Often the point of view isn't stated. Sometimes a reader can infer the point of view by learning about the author's job. As part of this line of thinking, the reader also asks, "What bias might this author show?"

The reader might study the historian's treatment of quotes. Usually a historian won't have characters saying what they think because the historian would need to fictionalize to do this. A historian may take what a character has written in diaries or letters and act as if it is speech.

Readers of history may be wise to bring the knowledge of geography to whatever they read. It's helpful to look between a text and a map.

A Field Guide to the Classroom Library, Lucy Calkins and the Teachers College Reading and Writing Project, Heinemann, ©2002 Teachers College, Columbia University; http://www.heinemann.com/fieldguides

Genre

Nonfiction; Chapter Book; Historical Fiction

Teaching Uses

Book Clubs; Read Aloud; Content Area Study; Reading and Writing Nonfiction; Critique

Holes

Louis Sachar

Book Summary

Stanley Yelnats is in the wrong place at the wrong time and is convicted of stealing a pair of sneakers. Stanley is sent to Camp Green Lake, a barren stretch of land with neither a lake nor a shred of green in view. A facility for delinquent boys, yes. A boys' sleep-away camp, hardly. Stanley, along with the other boys, digs a hole a day, five feet deep and five feet round in the blazing sun. Suspense builds as Stanley gradually figures out why they are digging these holes, goes looking for his run-away friend, Zero and finally, exonerates himself and his family of the curse laid on his ancestor.

Basic Book Information

Louis Sachar's jigsaw puzzle of a novel won both the Newbery Award and the National Book Award (young people category). A prolific author, Sachar has also written *Sideways Stories from Wayside School*, *There's a Boy in the Girl's Bathroom*, and *Dogs Don't Tell Jokes*, books popular among middle school students. While the vocabulary of *Holes* may not be challenging for average middle-school students, they may need assistance in understanding Sachar's use of flashbacks and irony. Fifth and sixth graders may enjoy the humor in this book; early-teens may grasp its sophisticated undertone. The 233-page, 50-chapter book is divided into three parts: part 1, You are entering Camp Green Lake; part 2, The last hole; part 3, Filling in the holes.

Noteworthy Features

Irony is at the core of the tale Sachar weaves in *Holes*. From the first sentence: "There is no lake at Camp Green Lake" to the final page, the story unfolds with example after example of simple twists of fate, circumstances that change the lives of the characters. The humor of the story emerges from these ironic curves. There are flashbacks to events that occurred generations ago and yet have a significant bearing on Stanley's experience at Camp Green Lake and the connections between him and characters like Zero and the Warden. The chapters are short but deep, a factor that may escape one who reads for surface details only.

Holes is an excellent selection for a close study of the elements of a novel. The characters are well developed and the setting varies from urban to rural, from lush to stark, from Europe to America, and from century to century. The plot is captivating, particularly as the ensemble of the three stories leaves the reader in suspense as each tale unfolds. The changes in characters and settings create great material for discussion while the movement through time provides an excellent example of how varied the passing of time can be within one novel. While the central theme seems clear initially,

A Field Guide to the Classroom Library, Lucy Calkins and the Teachers College Reading and Writing Project, Heinemann, ©2002 Teachers College, Columbia University; http://www.heinemann.com/fieldguides

Publisher
Scholastic, Inc., 1998

ISBN
0439128455

TC Level
14

a closer look will produce other morals, messages, and main ideas for discussion and debate.

Some readers will identify with the characters and if not personally relating to all of them, they might recognize traits of the dictator-like warden, the corrupt Mr. Sir, the bully X-Ray, the sympathetic parents, and the loyal Zero, Stanley's only friend. Furthermore, while readers may quickly detect a theme of good versus evil, they may also sympathize with Stanley's wrongful accusation, the poor treatment of children or powerless groups, and the desire to overcome wrongdoing, and return valiant and vindicated. While readers may initially question Stanley's original acceptance of his plight, they will most likely, grow to appreciate Stanley's endurance, creativity, generosity, and skill as he steers his course around this difficult situation.

Teaching Ideas

Teachers may well choose to use this book as a read aloud to guide students' understanding of Sachar's use of irony. As an alternative, groups of students might read and discuss the book together, figuring out Sachar's use of irony on their own.

The first several chapters of the book lay the foundation that Sachar uses later in significant ways. In Chapter 1, for example, we learn of the deadly yellow-spotted lizard, it is scary in this chapter and critical in Chapter 45. For this reason, teachers might want students to write down their reflections on the events of each chapter or groups of chapters in a two-column format. The first column can be headed: What I read; the second column: What I thought about. In the left-hand column, students could record happenings that they feel are significant, that they wonder about, that they question. In the right-hand column they can write their reflections, the "why" of these events. Later, these notes can be used in group discussions.

Students might also explain ironic twists in the story. The teacher might, as an example, point out the irony that, in court, where one is supposed innocent until proven guilty, no one would believe that Stanley didn't steal the sneakers; while at camp, where everyone is supposed guilty, none of the boys believed that he did!

One story within a story, in Chapter 7, explains why Stanley's father blamed bad luck on "my dirty-rotten-pig-stealing-great-grandfather." The teacher may want to call students' attention to this technique of embedding one story within another and point out how a longer space between paragraphs sometimes is the only indication that there is a change of scene. Students could discuss how the vignette of Stanley's ancestor bringing a curse down on himself and his descendents, ties in with the present day Stanley. The teacher may want to discuss the question: Do we have control over the circumstances in our lives?

Understanding the second story within a story-that of Katherine Barlow and her friend Sam-has significance because it deals with the results of an interracial relationship. The act, despicable at any time, would be even worse today when we are, supposedly, enlightened. Teachers might also want to ensure that students see how the outcome may well have driven Kate Barlow to become the "kissing bandit." While the story seems a simple

A Field Guide to the Classroom Library, Lucy Calkins and the Teachers College Reading and Writing Project, Heinemann, ©2002 Teachers College, Columbia University; http://www.heinemann.com/fieldguides

sidebar, its significance is critical to the plot development as all of these factors meet like streams that lead to a river later.

Stanley changes significantly during the development of the story. Teachers might ask students to contrast the character-in terms of physical appearance as well as personality-before and after his experience at Camp Green Lake. One technique might be to draw two outlines of a head that represents Stanley. Inside the first head, they can print words that describe Stanley as he arrives at camp, inside the other head, words that describe Stanley at the end of the book.

There are significant changes in the lives of Zero and the Warden as well. Teachers might ask students to write a script and act out one of these characters as they appear before a judge, justifying the time spent at Camp Green Lake and what they learned there.

A popular author among middle school students, Sachar offers a variety of teaching possibilities in *Holes*. As previously mentioned, *Holes* is an excellent tool for developing a firm understanding of the elements of a novel and how they interact with and affect each other. The story is not only plot-driven, but also offers appreciable and realistic characters and a setting that is clearly imaginable through Sachar's word choice and use of language. Astute students will observe that when Sachar's setting is sparse and barren, such as the desert surrounding Camp Green Lake, his words reflect that environment and create images of the desolate and inescapable landscape surrounding Stanley's prison. When the warden appears, her fingernails are described as red claws, her clothes as black and studded with turquoise. Her appearance causes the hair to stand up on the back of Stanley's neck, and possibly that of the reader, too.

The movement through time can be challenging to some students who may find the braiding together of the three stories difficult to sort out. Additionally, students may struggle to understand the passage of time as each tale takes place in a different time and features members of different generations. Thus, students may find it worthwhile to chart the events of each story separately while reading the book. Doing so can not only clarify comprehension but also support theories or clues to determining the actual outcome.

The variety of themes prevalent in the story also produce a number of worthy investigations. Students can discuss, debate, and write about the various themes observed in *Holes*. While *Holes* is a story of the forces of good and evil, other themes include honesty, loyalty, ingenuity, family, and friendship. In addition to examining the various themes, readers may want to examine *Holes* in conjunction with current events. Although the first read may indicate that *Holes* could only be fictitious, a closer read may produce a striking resemblance to present day life. Stanley is sent to a prison-like "camp" where "inmates" are subjected to brutal labor under horrific conditions. Students could investigate where and why children today might be subjected to such conditions. For example, bullies remain ever present, leadership and authority are corrupted by power and privilege, youth can be tried and punished as adults, and children in middle and far eastern countries are forced to work for hours a day with few or no rights or rewards. Students may want to explore the perseverance and existence of such situations and even campaign against such injustices.

A Field Guide to the Classroom Library, Lucy Calkins and the Teachers College Reading and Writing Project, Heinemann, ©2002 Teachers College, Columbia University; http://www.heinemann.com/fieldguides

Book Connections

In *Holes*, we encounter individuals who surprise themselves with qualities of courage, strength, and cleverness that the characters themselves may never have even detected until forced to face adversity. Readers who have enjoyed *Holes* could explore other works by Louis Sachar as well as novels written by Robert Newton Peck, Gary Paulsen, J.K. Rowling, or Katherine Paterson where positive forces eventually conquer evil powers with creativity, wit, and sagacity.

Genre
Chapter Book

Teaching Uses
Read Aloud; Partnerships; Independent Reading; Interpretation; Character Study

A Field Guide to the Classroom Library, Lucy Calkins and the Teachers College Reading and Writing Project, Heinemann, ©2002 Teachers College, Columbia University; http://www.heinemann.com/fieldguides

Homeless Bird
Gloria Whelan

Book Summary

Like many other thirteen-year-old girls in India, Koly is getting married. The marriage "is considered a good one," since the bridegroom is a sixteen-year-old boy from "a decent family." Koly quickly realizes her family has been lied to. The groom is a young boy who is suffering from a fatal case of tuberculosis. The family had arranged the marriage to gain dowry money that would pay for their trip to the miraculous waters of the Ganges River. The waters fail to save Koly's husband, Hari, and the thirteen-year-old widow is subject to the abuses of her cruel mother-in-law. Koly takes solace in her friendship with Hari's sister, Chandra, her secret reading instruction from Hari's father, and in the process of making quilts.

When Chandra is married off and Hari's father dies, Koly is abandoned by her mother-in-law in a strange city filled with widows in white saris. When she resolves to join the crowd of faceless, abandoned widows, her fate takes a turn for the better. A young rickshaw driver takes her to a "widow's house" funded by a wealthy patron, where Koly meets girls who have faced a similar fate. There she finds a job, shelter, and friendship. And, eventually, Koly's artistry in making quilts is discovered by the wealthy patron. She is given her dream job-decorating saris with designs from her mind. Koly also finds love with the young rickshaw driver who turns her life around.

Basic Book Information

Homeless Bird is a 212-page chapter book. Whelan is the author of *Once On This Island*, *Farewell to the Island*, *The Indian School*, and *Miranda's Last Stand*. The book contains Author Notes at the closing, which explain some of the Hindi words used in the book.

Noteworthy Features

Gloria Whelan never specifies in what year this story takes place. Koly is an illiterate thirteen-year-old bride who travels by wagon. She lives a rural life with no electricity or running water. Some readers may believe that such a story must be taking place far in the past. They may find it confusing when Chandra's bridegroom says, "my husband is bringing home a computer from his workplace," more than halfway through the book.

The setting and Indian customs may also be challenging (and important) for readers to picture. Koly lives in a house with mud-brick walls, held together with manure spread. The other major setting is the city of Vrindavan, a city filled with temples and young widows in white saris. Koly looks forward to attending a Holy Feast where a "special red powder mixed with cow's dung and urine is thrown at everyone." The book challenges

Publisher
Harper Collins, 2000

ISBN
0060284544

TC Level
14

readers to envision places and customs they may have had no experience with, either directly or through the media.

Koly is the narrator of the story. She provides simple descriptions of the events in her life. Often, Koly quotes dialogue from herself and other characters.

There are terms in the book that are commonly used in India, such as "monsoons" and "fasts." Words like these may be new and interesting to some readers. But the most interesting words may be the Hindi words used throughout the book. Koly calls her parents Maa (mother) and Baap (father). The foreign words are translated at the end of the book in the Author's Notes. Some readers may benefit from this reference tool. Unfortunately, since there is no table of contents, readers may not know that there are definitions for these foreign terms until they reach the end of the book.

Teaching Ideas

Whenever we read a fictional text, we are called upon to build (in our mind's eye) the world of the story, and to enter into that dream world as if it was real. When students read books such as this one, which are set in worlds, in some cases, utterly unlike their own, it is especially important that they pause to envision the scene, the place, and the life. Early on when reading this text, students may simply pause at the end of every few pages to say, "I'm picturing. . . ." It may also be important for them to read, identifying with Koly. "If I was her," they might say, "I'd be thinking . . ." "I'd be feeling . . ." "I'd be wanting to say. . . ."

Readers may have a hard time picturing such a harsh and grown-up life led by a character so close in age to themselves. Koly is a widow by thirteen. She is also abandoned and robbed by her mother-in-law. The events may seem very foreign to many readers and therefore it's all the more important to encourage readers "to walk a mile in the moccasins of this character."

Koly is a character with tremendous strength. Despite the utter harshness of her life, she survives and finds happiness. Koly takes solace in her embroidery; she is an artist, who weaves periods of her life into quilts and saris. She also learns how to read and delights in the poems of Tagore. Readers may see these pursuits as Koly's survival mechanisms. Even when Koly has no chance of physically escaping her predicament, she escapes in her mind.

Koly often uses comparisons of nature to explain how she feels. She says things such as, "She was a great boulder, shutting me into a cave," and "I felt as if I was a small fly in the web of a cunning spider." Lines like these create vivid imagery. This book can offer readers a rich experience with metaphor.

Readers in partnerships or independently may want to attach post-it notes to all the metaphors Koly uses. They'll soon notice that throughout the course of the book, Koly often compares herself to animals. Readers may not notice that Koly is, in fact, weaving images of nature into her sense of herself, just as she weaves these images of nature into the quilts and saris that represent her life. It may be interesting for readers to notice that when Koly meets her young husband at the beginning of the book, she notices his fascination with pinned butterflies and says, " . . . I wouldn't want to stick butterflies to the wall." Later, when Koly finds true love in a man and a profession, she decides however, that she will weave "a homeless bird, flying at last to its home" into a sari border. Readers may find it interesting to follow Koly's life through metaphors-from the pinned butterfly to the homeless bird, flying home.

Tagore becomes Koly's favorite poet. The poet writes about "a flock of birds flying day and night through the skies. Among them was one homeless bird, always flying on to somewhere else." For readers who understand that Koly is that homeless bird, they will be able to frame Koly's experience in a poetic way. When Koly finds happiness at the end of the story, her first thought is to embroider the picture of the homeless bird, flying home. Readers who grasp the metaphor will smile at the thought of Koly flying free to a home, because she has lived in many houses, but has never been truly home.

Genre
Chapter Book

Teaching Uses
Independent Reading; Book Clubs; Character Study; Language Conventions

A Field Guide to the Classroom Library, Lucy Calkins and the Teachers College Reading and Writing Project, Heinemann, ©2002 Teachers College, Columbia University; http://www.heinemann.com/fieldguides

House on Mango Street
Sandra Cisneros

Book Summary

This book consists of a series of vignettes of Esperanza Cordero, a young MexicanAmerican girl coming of age in the Hispanic quarter of Chicago. For her, Mango Street is a barren landscape consisting of concrete and dilapidated tenements. It is here that she discovers life's most trying realities: the chains of class, gender, and racial hatred.

The house in which the Corderos live is falling apart physically. Esperanza describes it as "the house I belong but do not belong to." She desires a house she takes pride in. At the end of the book, she vows not to let her sad memories prevent her from living in a way that will result in her personal satisfaction.

Basic Book Information

Sandra Cisneros was born in Chicago in 1954. Acclaimed internationally for her poems and non-fiction, as well as the recipient of many awards, she has also written *Woman Hollering Creek and Other Stories* and two collections of poetry, *My Wicked, Wicked Ways* and *Loose Woman*.

This is a novel written from the point of view of an adolescent, Esperanza Cordero but teachers and children often rely upon this as an example of memoir writing at its best. Each vignette is approximately one page long and can stand on its own as an example of how writers can make literature out of the fine detail of their lives. One of these vignettes, "Hairs" has been printed in English and Spanish as a self-standing picture book.

Noteworthy Features

One important aspect of this text is Cisneros' use of carefully chosen, spare prose. She succeeds in creating unforgettable characters. One example of such a character is Minerva who is "only a little bit older than (Esperanza) but already she has two kids and a husband who left... Minerva cries because her luck is unlucky. Every night and every day. And prays. But when the kids are asleep after she's fed them pancake dinner, she writes poems on little pieces of paper that she folds over and over and holds in her hands a long time, little pieces of paper that smell like a dime."

Along with creating characters who will remain indelible on the mind of the reader, her use of words also endears the reader to Esperanza's plight. Esperanza desperately wants "a house. A real house. One that I could point to. But this isn't it. The house on Mango Street isn't it. For the time being, Mama says. Temporary, says Papa. But I know how those things go." Ultimately, Esperanza succeeds in realizing for herself, if only in her mind, "a house all of [her] own...quiet as snow, a space for [herself] to go," despite the restrictive nature of her surroundings.

Publisher
Random House, 1991

ISBN
0679734775

TC Level
11

A Field Guide to the Classroom Library, Lucy Calkins and the Teachers College Reading and Writing Project, Heinemann, ©2002 Teachers College, Columbia University; http://www.heinemann.com/fieldguides

Cisneros also presents the craft of writing as liberating. It is the poetry that allows Minerva to escape her plight as a struggling single mother. Similarly, it is when Esperanza puts her story down on paper that Mango Street sets her free. She vows one day to leave with books and paper to "come back. For the ones [she] left behind. For the ones who cannot out."

Teaching Ideas

Though this book was not written for young children, it can be used selectively in all classrooms. Many of the short vignettes are both the length and the tone of the writing that students can do in elementary school. Pieces (such as "Hairs") are simple enough and short enough to be read aloud and again re-read independently by students in grades two or three and above. Teachers may not want to put this book on the shelves of their classroom library (unless they are in middle school) because for most classrooms of children this will be a teaching resource more than a good independent read.

This book contains many injustices that the discerning reader will recognize. These include issues such as racism, discrimination based on class and gender, and roles in families based on cultural beliefs. One example of this racism is Cathy, Queen of Cats, who moves a little father away north from Mango Street every time "people like [the Corderos] move in." If the piece is at the center of a book clubs discussion, children often notice and begin to discuss this issue.

This text would work well as a text for children to imitate in their own writing. Cisneros writes in a very controlled manner, sometimes with very sparse, almost staccato sentences and other times with fabulous description, in long word-filled sentences. Children can try this in their own writing, often with extraordinary results.

"Those Who Don't" is an extraordinary statement about the world and teachers have often used it as a short text when they want to begin a unit of study focusing on improving the quality of their book talks. It invites students to say something about home, and family and fear and prejudice.

Many teachers pull together "Laughter," "Hairs," "My Name," "The House on Mango Street," "Bums in the Attic," "Smart Cookie," "A House of My Own," and "Mango Says Good-bye Sometimes" so that together they provide an example of memoir in vignette form. The beginning of this text and the ending are so closely matched that they help us teach that the beginnings and endings of memoir often fold back on each other.

We also use this book in a study of the list as a structure for writing. Although some of the vignettes are stories, they combine in a list-like way. Teachers show students that these episodes are not arranged chronologically, though some of them individually may be stories.

Many teachers of writing have put selected pages from this book on overheads and projected them for the class to see, to study, and to emulate. "Papa wakes up tired in the dark," for example retells five minutes in time, and yet within these five minutes the narrator does a lot of internal thinking, enriching the story. Children benefit from seeing that they can retell a tiny vignette and weave memories into it. (i.e., "I stood at the edge of the sea, my toes dug into the sand. Nearby I saw a shell. I picked it up and remember a stormy August morning two years ago when. ..." "Papa who

A Field Guide to the Classroom Library, Lucy Calkins and the Teachers College Reading and Writing Project, Heinemann, ©2002 Teachers College, Columbia University; http://www.heinemann.com/fieldguides

wakes up tired..." is worth studying.) Cisneros collects tiny detail to bring her characters to life, and she reveals one character through the point of view of another (e.g., Her papa "crumples like a coat and cries").

Book Connections

List books for the older, more sophisticated writer would include: this text, *Childtimes* by Eloise Greenfield, *Flora and Tiger* by Eric Carle, and *Walking the Log* by Bessie Nickens. The study of these more sophisticated books would come after studies of simpler list books such as *When I Was Young In the Mountains* by Cynthia Rylant and *Uptown* by Bryan Collier.

Genre
Short Chapter Book; Memoir

Teaching Uses
Teaching Writing; Partnerships; Read Aloud; Book Clubs

A Field Guide to the Classroom Library, Lucy Calkins and the Teachers College Reading and Writing Project, Heinemann, ©2002 Teachers College, Columbia University; http://www.heinemann.com/fieldguides

Hurricanes: Earth's Mightiest Storms

Patricia Lauber

Book Summary

The first section of the book describes the great hurricane of 1938 and the devastation it wrought on towns, cities, people, and homes in the northeastern United States. The next section describes the natural forces that come together to create hurricanes. Next, the reader learns about how people are improving their understanding of hurricanes. After that, a section describes another huge hurricane, this one in 1992 in the Bahamas and Florida, and the destruction of the wildlife and habitats it left in its wake. Finally, the book explores patterns in hurricane existence and predictions about the future of the storms.

Basic Book Information

This Nonfiction picture book is about 60 pages long. It is about half text and half maps, diagrams, and photographs. The table of contents shows that the book is divided into five sections of about ten pages each. These sections are followed by an extensive small-font index and a list of recommended further reading, with a special notation to indicate books for advanced readers. Within each section, the text relates a story of a violent hurricane, presents a scientific explanation for the laws of nature that make hurricanes happen, or describes the technology of weather that helps us to understand those laws. There are occasional boxes in the text giving details about a topic related, but not central to the topic at hand.

Noteworthy Features

The footage of these storms printed on these pages is real and powerful. The devastation these storms can bring is apparent and provides a compelling reason to read about them. Although the book is not particularly good for browsing alone since the text is not divided into small chunks, a browse could get a reader convinced the book is worth reading in its entirety.

As usual, Patricia Lauber's style of writing is clear and scientific when called for, but not overly so. She does not talk down to the reader, but instead relies on clarity of organization, style, and presentation to bring her point across. As always, her books show a concern for the environmental balance between humans and nature-one brought out in this book in her chapter revealing the environmental hazards brought by hurricanes on land that has been tampered with by humans. Many teachers appreciate her evenhanded concern and awareness of the environment in even apparently non-environmental issues.

The index is particularly helpful for readers looking for specific information. The table of contents, however, has titles of sections that are meant to interest the reader rather than to describe the information the

Publisher
Random House, 1996

ISBN
0590474065

TC Level
11

sections contain. Readers won't be able to use the table of contents to locate bits of information.

Teaching Ideas

This book is considered by most to be a high quality piece of Nonfiction for young readers. For this reason, teachers often use this book when they are teaching any aspect of reading Nonfiction, from how to use an index, how to read technical diagrams, how to make the jumps in style from the narration of an event to the description of natural forces in the weather, to how to make personal connections from Nonfiction. Teachers often use this text to help children practice note-taking, since it is so predictably structured. The text can also serve as a model to students in ways to construct Nonfiction they may be writing, from the tone of its sentences to the format of its pages.

It is difficult to use this book to help children learn to read with a critical eye because so few readers will disagree with anything presented in the text. Lauber chooses her words carefully and makes her book carefully objective wherever possible. For these reasons, the messages and text to be critiqued remain particularly invisible for readers, and particularly unfruitful for those with an eye to critique.

Many teachers find this book especially valuable not only in units about the weather, but when a storm has struck in the news. Often, when a catastrophic storm hits a faraway land, it is hard for people to understand what has really happened to those people affected by the storm. While this book may not help people explain the emotional aspects of the devastation, it will certainly make the storms seem real and immediate. In these cases, teachers sometimes read sections of the book aloud and leave the book available to readers who want to continue.

This book deserves close study on many fronts. It demonstrates that Nonfiction writing can be full of drama and narrative suspense. A teacher needs only to read aloud the first few pages of the book to make this point. The text is also noteworthy because Lauber has written a cohesive book, in which one part of the text builds and develops into the next section. Whereas some Nonfiction texts contain little bits of information, strung together, other Nonfiction texts create a coherent, multi-faceted structure. This text falls into the latter category.

Chances are likely that over the course of a school year, children will live through some extreme weather. This book can contextualize the storms as class experiences, helping people to realize that a storm is not only a local occurrence; storms always have paths through geographic terrain, and in this way they bind people together.

Book Connections

Patricia Lauber has written several other high-quality Nonfiction books for young readers.

Genre
Nonfiction; Picture Book

A Field Guide to the Classroom Library, Lucy Calkins and the Teachers College Reading and Writing Project, Heinemann, ©2002 Teachers College, Columbia University; http://www.heinemann.com/fieldguides

Teaching Uses

Reading and Writing Nonfiction; Content Area Study

I Can't Believe I Have to Do This

Jan Alford

FIELD GUIDE

Book Summary

The story begins with the main character, 12-year-old Dean Matthews, getting a journal as a birthday present. He is not pleased. He has no plans to write in it, but nevertheless, finds himself writing in it. *I Can't Believe I Have To Do This* is a weave of his journal entries and his reflections on them. For example, he writes an eight-line italicized entry, "My name is Dean Matthews . . . I'm short. I weight sixty-eight pounds, have blonde hair and blue eyes. I live in Fillmore."

Then, for the next page, Dean seems to put down the journal and to speak directly to his reader. "Actually, where we live is pretty cool," he says and goes on to describe Fillmore. During the course of the book, we journey with Dean as he wrestles with the difficulties of being a somewhat unpopular junior high school boy whose mother is pregnant and whose friend who runs with a bad crowd. Dean wants to be cool-with an earring, a weird haircut, and a bit of alcohol, but he is wary of the road his friend has chosen. Nevertheless, Dean is drawn into this bad crowd and ends up in the police station.

In the end, Dean watches his friend make wrong choices, but Dean makes the hard choice and turns the other way.

Basic Book Information

This book is one of a line of books in which the author uses journal entries of a fictional character to carry the main plot. Like *Mostly Michael* by Robert K. Smith, *Strider* by Beverly Cleary, and *Hey World, Here I Am* by Beverly Cleary, this story is built primarily out of journal entries, buttressed by a discussion of them. The understory in the book is that of a boy coming to feel at home with writing; the entries become longer and more full of voice and the discussions of those entries carry less and less of the story as they read farther. There is another understory; this is the familiar tale of a teenager boy's struggles to come of age.

Noteworthy Features

Dean gets his journal on his twelfth birthday and this book chronicles his year, ending with Dean's thirteenth birthday. This time, he takes his birthday money and buys himself a journal for the year ahead.

Teaching Ideas

This is a book that merits being read aloud for fifth or sixth graders who feel as they are on the brink of adulthood. It is also a book that youngsters will enjoy without support from a teacher. It's written in the voice of a teenager

Publisher
Penguin Putnam, 1999

ISBN
0698117859

TC Level
12

A Field Guide to the Classroom Library, Lucy Calkins and the Teachers College Reading and Writing Project, Heinemann, ©2002 Teachers College, Columbia University; http://www.heinemann.com/fieldguides

wanting to sound cool and it is full of real-world difficulties that young people encounter. Dean wrestles with alcohol, alienation from his parents, difficulties at school, and resistance to writing. He ultimately comes out of all this just fine. Because the story is not heavy-handed and moralistic, young teenagers are more likely to feel understood than chided by the author.

If students are reading this in a partnership and need to talk about the unfolding text, they may follow the ups and downs of Dean's relationship with his parents. This study might lead youngsters to realize that although Dean resists his parents, in the end it is his relationship with them which saves him. What do his parents do well? Not so well? Readers may find it interesting to infer the whole journey that Dean's parents travel over the course of the year. What might the turning point be for Dean? For his parents?

Then, too, readers may want to chart or mark (with post-it notes) the pages indicating Dean's struggle to find his place between different worlds. What draws him toward academics, drinking, shoplifting and joy-riding?

If readers are keeping their own journals, it will be important to think and talk about how Dean finally made his journal into a survival tool.

Book Connections

Mostly Michael by Robert K. Smith, *Strider* by Beverly Cleary, and *Hey World, Here I Am* by Beverly Cleary.

Genre
Chapter Book

Teaching Uses
Read Aloud; Partnerships; Independent Reading

A Field Guide to the Classroom Library, Lucy Calkins and the Teachers College Reading and Writing Project, Heinemann, ©2002 Teachers College, Columbia University; http://www.heinemann.com/fieldguides

I Hadn't Meant to Tell You This

Jacqueline Woodson

Book Summary

Marie and Lena become the best of friends, drawn together by the loss of their mothers. They are in their own little world, and no one can steer them away from each other. But Lena has a secret, a secret that eventually makes her leave, a secret that Marie can't tell another living soul. This poetic memoir-like piece deals with racism, class prejudice, and sexual abuse.

Basic Book Information

I Hadn't Meant to Tell You This, which won the Coretta Scott King Honor, is a 115-page memoir-like chapter book. There are 28 chapters, which range from one to eight pages in length. Dialogue is not always referenced but there are usually only two people speaking at one time so it is not difficult to follow. The story is told in first-person from Marie's point of view.

Noteworthy Features

Postcards are incorporated into the text in their own chapters or in the beginning of other chapters. They all are in the form of a poem, a thought, or a moment that Marie's mother, who has abandoned her, is going through. "In the beginning I had been frustrated, reading each one over and over again with the hopes of getting something more from them. But there were no real messages between the lines, at least nothing I could decipher."

I Hadn't Meant to Tell You This lends itself to being a memoir piece because of the reflection and thought we continuously see from Marie as she tells the story. She is dealing with the loss of her mother. She is choosing her friends. She is becoming independent and we see this transition in her actions and more especially in her thoughts. Eventually Marie realizes that no matter what happens she just has to get through it, "A postcard from my mother said, 'You never wake up any morning sure of your life's interaction with the day.' Before I leave the house, I write her a note, 'No, Mama, you don't. But so what? You get through it, if you're strong enough-and move on!' then crawl into the back of my closet to add it to the stack of letters there."

The language and description in the text is very poetic. Woodson creates pictures in our minds and draws us in with description, "Lena's eyes seemed to hold on to that sadness as though any minute she'd start crying and no one in the world, not even God, could stop the tears. ...Behind the sadness in her eyes there was something-like a thin layer of steel. And no matter how hard you looked, you couldn't see past it." Woodson isn't telling the reader "Lena is sad," she's showing how, and slowly telling us why until her pain is almost visibly palpable.

Publisher
Bantam Doubleday Dell, 1994

ISBN
0440219604

TC Level
14

A Field Guide to the Classroom Library, Lucy Calkins and the Teachers College Reading and Writing Project, Heinemann, ©2002 Teachers College, Columbia University; http://www.heinemann.com/fieldguides

Teaching Ideas

This book would lend itself well to a character study of Marie, who changes throughout the book. As students read, they can mark sections that show Marie's character traits. Marie must deal with the loss of both her mother and Lena. What remains constant about Marie through all of this and what changes?

Poetry and poetic language are key elements incorporated in the text. The postcards from Marie's mother are all in the form of poems. Readers could write the poems down on paper. They could then break up into small conversations and discuss what the poems may have meant. Marie was constantly struggling to figure out if the poems had any hidden meaning. A teacher might discuss the difference between figurative and literal meaning in poetry and students could decide if these poems had a deeper meaning or were simply literal reflections of Marie's mother's moments.

Lena loved to draw. She uses her drawing to escape the pain in her life, "When I'm drawing, it's like I go into another world or something. Nobody can't bother me. Guess that's why I draw those kinds of pictures all full of trees and water and sunshine." Lena uses drawing as an outlet for her feelings.

Friendship is an important theme in this text. Before Lena arrives, Marie is in the "popular group" with Sherry being her "best friend." After Lena arrives things are different, "Lena refused to click with the other white kids at school, and Sherry made sure the black kids stayed far away from her." And once Marie befriends Lena she realizes, "I hadn't known until that moment, that I was sick and tired of her [Sherry]." In befriending Lena she has automatically lost all of her old "friends," Sherry even teases her and accuses her of "kissing Lena's butt."

The relationship between Marie and her father is another important theme to examine in this book. After her mother leaves, her father is all she has left. But in the beginning, her father has nothing left to give to Marie. "I wanted to learn how to grieve and how to walk through the world feeling whole when half of me had walked away. So I listened to my father and realized that you cry at night when you think no one is listening. You cry with the water running behind a closed door where you can wash your face and pat the red from your eyes. You cry hard and you cry alone." Readers could examine and discuss the different ways Marie and her father deal with her mother's leaving. Marie's father also doesn't approve of her friendship with Lena. He doesn't understand it, mostly because of their different skin color. But then he says, "You're old enough to make your own decisions Marie.... Be careful." Readers could discuss how they think the relationship between Marie and her father changes by the end of the book using text to support their opinions.

One of the most important themes in the book is that of touching. Lena's father touches her too much, beyond the boundaries of a father's love. Marie's father won't touch her at all, not a hug or a pat or anything. At first Marie is afraid to touch Lena, but then is surprised at the softness of her skin. Readers could write down the moments in the book that deal with the theme of touch and discuss how touch affects the lives of the characters, and how touch affects them in their daily lives.

A Field Guide to the Classroom Library, Lucy Calkins and the Teachers College Reading and Writing Project, Heinemann, ©2002 Teachers College, Columbia University; http://www.heinemann.com/fieldguides

Genre
Memoir; Chapter Book

Teaching Uses
Independent Reading; Book Clubs

I Have Heard of a Land

Joyce Carol Thomas

Book Summary

This poem/story is an account from an African American woman who went West, to the frontier, to accept free land and grueling hardship in order to feel the freedom and self-ownership the new place offered.

Basic Book Information

This historical fiction picture book has about thirty pages. The text is set in bold, so it is easy to read, despite being set on top of the illustrations. On each page there are from three to ten lines of text, written in the form and style of a poem. Some readers might say the text *is* a poem. Certainly, the book follows the format of a fictional picture book, or of a poem put to pictures, more than any other format despite being historical fiction. Of course, there is no table of contents, index, chapter headings, or subtitles.

At the end of the book, there is a note from the author that is made up of two pages of dense, smallish text. In this text, the author explains the facts behind the text and the historical inspiration for the story. She also adds to the adventures of the pioneer voyage in the book by telling another short story from those times.

Noteworthy Features

While the pictures in this book are softly beautiful and enticing to the story, they don't do a lot of work in helping the reader understand either the story or the visual imagery. They do represent the events of the text, but without visual references for many of the poems images. Therefore, readers who tend to rely heavily on pictures when they are having comprehension trouble will be at a bit of a loss in this text.

However, the very first illustration in the text, the picture opposite the dedication, does contain some information that may help the reader understand the story. Many readers may skip over this picture, since it appears before the story begins, and it does not at first seem to contain anything of particular significance. The sign in the picture, however, reads "Free Land!" and if readers see that, it may clue them into the historical context of the story, and may help them realize what the narrator is talking about. Teachers will have to decide whether or not to point out that detail.

Some of the poetic language, when coupled with the little known historical facts, is very difficult to understand. If readers don't know that the offer was made for people to take all the land they could run across for free, those poetic lines could baffle them, at least at first. This type of difficult reading is sprinkled throughout the story.

Illustrator
Floyd Cooper

Publisher
Harper Trophy, 1998

ISBN
0064436179

TC Level
9; 10; 11

Teaching Ideas

Some teachers will want to read the text of the author's note at the end of the book for themselves, before reading or summarizing it for the readers. Other teachers will want children to discover for themselves what the book is about and whom it honors and why. In all likelihood, however, many children will not read the author's note at the end of the story, and may leave the book uncertain about some of the facts if the teacher does not introduce or close the book for them.

Teachers may also want to inform the reader that the book is written almost as if it is poetry, and for that reason, should probably be read through several times in order to understand it. Like poetry, trying to understand line by line and word by word without understanding the whole story first may be nearly impossible, and is almost certainly counter-productive. Teachers can therefore remind kids that this is probably the kind of book where you don't stop and try to figure something out slowly, first you read to the end and see if it makes sense, and then you come back to parts you want to think about further.

Often, the pioneer phase of American history is taught as though the only people who traveled West were white men. This book offers the point of view of a black woman, a voice too seldom heard from in the teaching about the American West. This book is an excellent resource for children who need to learn of a wide range of experiences in the opening of the new frontier in America.

Some teachers like to add to this book accounts of the hardships that the pioneers suffered, both on their journey and once they were settled. Of course, life was very difficult and not all dreamy as the book suggests, or as the dreamers at first thought. Of course, these hardships do not negate the beauties of the adventure and the life, or the importance of the freedoms achieved. These accounts would only serve to broaden the picture of the life of the pioneer.

In a writing workshop, young children often have a hard time finding a genre for their Nonfiction writing. This book is an example of a nearly fictional, nearly poetic form for Nonfiction. As an example for young writers, this text can be invaluable.

Genre
Historical Fiction; Picture Book; Poetry

Teaching Uses
Reading and Writing Nonfiction; Partnerships; Content Area Study; Teaching Writing

A Field Guide to the Classroom Library, Lucy Calkins and the Teachers College Reading and Writing Project, Heinemann, ©2002 Teachers College, Columbia University; http://www.heinemann.com/fieldguides

Immigrant Kids

Russell Freedman

Book Summary

This book, about the immigrant experience of the youngsters in America in the late 1800s and early 1900s, is divided into five sections: coming over, at home, at school, at work, and at play. In each section there are stark and revealing photographs of the conditions, places, and types of families discussed. Each section also has at least one extended quotation from a primary source, from people who lived in those places during those times. Sometimes these excerpts are spoken memories, sometimes journal entries, and sometimes parts taken from literature. The book tells details of daily life from the perspective of a young newcomer to the country.

Basic Book Information

This Nonfiction book is about seventy pages long. Every two-page spread has at least one clear, powerful black and white photograph from the times, and from three to six paragraphs of text. These pictures each have captions that describe their contents as well as crediting the renowned photographer who took them. There is both a table of contents and an extensive index. There are no maps, diagrams, or sidebars. Rather, the book is arranged like a chapter book with photographs.

Noteworthy Features

This book is perfect for helping children realize that history is real and involved real people, real children, like themselves. The photographs, though they are clearly old and different from photographs today and in that sense distancing, are so realistic that children cannot fail to see the children's faces as faces that could have been their own. The author has chosen photographs that reveal faces and personal details of the immigrant children especially well. The pictures and captions alone are worth reading.

The categories of the book are also inviting to children. It is easy to look at the table of contents and find yourself asking questions-how did immigrant children play back then? What does that mean, "work?" and so forth. The categories are ones that children can easily grasp hold of, as opposed to dates in time, or ethnic groups being the organizer of the chapters.

The vocabulary is not technical, but it is aimed at experienced readers. The sentences are sometimes long or somewhat complicated by extended clauses, and the vocabulary is precise. Words and phrases like "peddler," or "hawked wares," or "voyage was an ordeal" are representative of the specificity of the diction.

Publisher
Scholastic, 1980

ISBN
0590465651

TC Level
12; 13; 14

This book is unique and valuable in that it presents a child's view of immigration to children without being in any way childish or cute. The text and photographs are simple and direct.

Teaching Ideas

Because this book is a high-quality book of Nonfiction, teachers often turn to it to assist in the teaching the reading Nonfiction. With this book, children can learn to skim for specific information, to find a fact from an index reference, to read history without losing sight of individuals, to make sense of the subjective nature of most primary sources and so on,

Teachers often use this book in areas of the curriculum outside of reading or writing, usually history or social studies. The chapters on different areas of life can stand alone-for example, some teachers like to read the section about "coming over' if they are studying Ellis Island.

Book Connections

Although the format is very different, the content of this book is similar to the *How Would You Survive as an Ancient Greek* series, and readers who love the content of those books might enjoy this one as well.

Genre
Nonfiction; Chapter Book

Teaching Uses
Reading and Writing Nonfiction; Content Area Study; Book Clubs

A Field Guide to the Classroom Library, Lucy Calkins and the Teachers College Reading and Writing Project, Heinemann, ©2002 Teachers College, Columbia University; http://www.heinemann.com/fieldguides

Indian in the Cupboard

Lynne Reid Banks

Book Summary

Omri, the youngest of three brothers in an ordinary English household, receives a cupboard for his birthday that can magically turn miniature plastic figures into miniature live ones. When Omri becomes friends with the Native American named Little Bear and the cowboy Boone, he learns to respect different ways of life, and finds out how difficult and important it is to keep the secret of the cupboard.

The Indian in the Cupboard is the first of three books about Omri, Little Bear, Boone, and the magic cupboard.

Basic Book Information

This text is 181 pages in length. There are 16 titled chapters, which vary in length from seven to fifteen pages. There are also illustrations by Brock Cole.

Noteworthy Features

This classic narrative is an adventure/fantasy story that is well grounded enough to be almost believable. The details of Omri's life-his school experiences, hurried breakfasts, fights with his brothers-take the story beyond simple fantasy. As in other stories of the genre, such as Edith Nesbit's books or *Peter Pan*, the power of a child's imagination transforms ordinary materials into something marvelous-something beyond the reach or understanding of adults.

Omri and the magical figures of Little Bear and Boone have distinct personalities and undergo changes during the course of the book. Omri finds out that his "toys" are as feeling and real as he is, and learns, in a sense, how to be a parent to them. He finds a way to get Little Bear and Boone to become friends, and he helps heal their wounds, sympathize with their feelings, and worry about their future.

The characterizations of Little Bear and Boone dispel the cowboy and Indian stereotypes. Through these characters, Banks provides detailed information about the Iroquois, the French and Indian War, and the West in the late 1800s. Paragraphs are fairly long and descriptive, but the lively pace keeps the story moving. Teachers should be aware that at first Omri thinks of these characters only as the stereotypes he knows, and readers who give up the book before its end may have these ideas reinforced in their minds. Teachers should also be aware that the name "Indian" instead of "Native American" is generally considered offensive. Little Bear's speech patterns are also oddly stereotypical, in direct conflict with Banks' apparent goal of challenging stereotypes.

Series
Indian in the Cupboard

Illustrator
Brock Cole

Publisher
Avon, 1980

ISBN
0380600129

TC Level
11

Vocabulary throughout is varied and quite challenging (e.g. "foreboding," "gesticulating," and "tousled"). Some English vocabulary may be unfamiliar, such as the word "marrow" for "squash." Boone uses cowboy colloquialisms such as "varmint" and makes slangy statements like "Ah'm plumb full o' vittles." Some of the vocabulary is clear from context, but much is not, as in the line, "He gazed back imperiously at Patrick." The many delights of the book may make some struggling worthwhile for less accomplished readers.

Themes students may decide to explore include the power of the imagination, the pains and joys of responsibility, and the value of life, regardless of the form it takes.

Teaching Ideas

The Indian in the Cupboard is a good independent read for versatile readers. It also works as a read aloud for students who might have trouble making their way through the vocabulary. In either case, the rich detail, plot twists, and suspense will engage many readers' attention.

Students can take notes on the historical information. Omri begins by seeing Little Bear as his inferior not just in size, but in other ways. Students can discuss how Omri alters his views after he learns about Little Bear's culture.

The Indian in the Cupboard might be viewed as a book about overcoming cultural divides. Banks presents more than three very different cultures-Omri's, Little Bear's, Boone's and a handful of others-and shows how the differences in cultures can cause misunderstandings and conflict. Students might take notes on how those conflicts are resolved and apply them to their own lives. Does learning about other cultures or circumstances help people get along better?

Students can trace Omri's development as a character, comparing his behavior and his attitude toward the Indian in the first few chapters with his behavior and attitudes at the end of the book.

Book Connections

There are two other *Indian in the Cupboard* books that follow this one.

Genre
Fantasy; Chapter Book

Teaching Uses
Independent Reading; Read Aloud; Book Clubs

Island of the Blue Dolphins

Scott O'Dell

Book Summary

When she is still quite young, Karana, a Pacific Islander girl living with her people on an island far off the coast of California, watches as her father, the chief of their tribe, is killed by invaders who have come to their island to hunt otter. The new chief decides that his people are no longer safe on their island (called the Island of the Blue Dolphins because of the dolphins who swim nearby) and arranges to have his people transported by ship to California. Once the ship has sailed, Karana realizes her younger brother, Ramo, is still on shore, and she dives into the ocean and swims back to him. The ship does not return for them, and Karana and Ramo are left alone on the island. Soon after that, Ramo is attacked and killed by wild dogs and Karana is left completely alone. She waits for the ship to return but in the meantime she must learn to survive. Karana builds a shelter and the weapons she needs to protect herself. She fishes, cooks, makes clothes for herself, and ultimately befriends the animals of the island, including the wild dogs. Karana spends eighteen years alone on the island until a ship finally comes to take her away.

Basic Book Information

Island of the Blue Dolphins is a Newbery Award winner and a winner of the Hans Christian Andersen Medal. *Island of the Blue Dolphins* has 189 pages, broken into 29 untitled chapters. An author's note is included at the end.

Noteworthy Features

The book is narrated by Karana and takes place over the course of eighteen years. Because she is alone on the island for much of the story, there is little dialogue. Instead, after the first few chapters, readers will engage almost exclusively with Karana. Her resourcefulness and her apparent fearlessness are themes in the book.

The language of this book attempts to be true to the way in which Karara would have understood the world. For example, time passes in suns and moons; a teacher may want to check to be sure that a reader grasps the meaning. Vocabulary might be new to the readers: Aleut, brush, kelp, cove, ravine, parley, mesa, league, pelt.

There is very little mention of Karana's feelings throughout the story. Students could be encouraged to speculate on what those feelings might have been and why they are not mentioned more in the story. They might surmise that Karana was too busy to feel lonely or that the animals kept her company, but it would be worth exploring this more deeply so that the students' could really get a full sense of the experience.

Publisher
Dell Publishing, 1960

ISBN
044094000

TC Level
14

O'Dell includes an author's note at the end of the book which explains that the story is based on fact. This will be of interest to the readers.

Teaching Ideas

A teacher may find that readers need a bit of assistance in order to become captivated by this fascinating and beautifully written story. The book is something of a classic and merits readers' attention, but its opening chapter asks quite a lot of readers and sometimes puts them off. Ideally, a teacher might read a chapter or two aloud to a child or to the class as part of a book promotion talk, and help readers to become acclimated to the selling of the island, the names of characters, and the language of the text.

In the first few pages of the story, Karana uses metaphors and similes to describe the ship she sees approaching. Her brother also uses a metaphor to describe the sea, but Karana argues that Ramo's description is not accurate. If a child is reading or listening to this section of the text, a teacher may want to call attention to these metaphors. It is interesting to realize that when a character creates a metaphor to describe something, the metaphor reveals the thing but also reveals the character because the metaphor comes from the life and mind and moods of the character. Readers may want to imagine how they might have seen and described the ship, or they could do this for the sea, which Ramo describes as "a flat stone without any scratches." Why did Karana not find this description appropriate? What does this show about her?

In the second chapter, Karana guesses at how the island got its name. Again, if a teacher is close by while a reader reads this section, it might be worthwhile to pause and talk with the reader about the significance of names in stories. Literary critics often take notes of the names an author chooses for characters and places, and it is important for young readers to grasp that every name was created for the occasion of the book. O'Dell has his character doing the same sort of thinking that a skilled reader does. We may learn why O'Dell named his island as he did. He most likely named it as he did to give Karana the opportunity to contextualize the island in history and place. Why is Karana named as she is? Ramo? This conversation would benefit from going to other books. Why did MacLachlan name her characters in *Baby* after birds? Why is there Bird, the grandmother, and Larkin, the boy? What does Journey's name have to do with the theme of the book *Journey*? Why is the pig in Orwell's *Animal Farm* named Napoleon? Could the donkey, Benjamin, have a relationship to the biblical Benjamin?

The Aleuts came to the *Island of the Blue Dolphins* to hunt otter. Readers could be asked to attach post-it notes to bits of the book that interest them and to discuss these with a partner during partnership conversations at the end of silent reading time. A teacher may say to a reader or a group, "When you continue reading, you may want to keep an eye on an aspect of the book that you have found interesting, for example,.the role animals play in this book."

There are many opportunities in this book to discuss the treatment of animals. Later in the book, Karana kills some of the wild dogs. She kills fish for food and even for lamps; she uses birds' feathers to make a skirt for herself, and so on. After some years, Karana decides she does not want to harm any more animals. However, she still must eat and continues to fish.

A Field Guide to the Classroom Library, Lucy Calkins and the Teachers College Reading and Writing Project, Heinemann, ©2002 Teachers College, Columbia University; http://www.heinemann.com/fieldguides

Hopefully, the reader would see the complexity of the issue-although people don't want to mistreat animals, Karana needs to hunt or fish to survive. Readers, too, probably eat meat and fish. Karana has a great knowledge of fish, animals, and nature.

There are no titles given to the chapters. When reading this book or any book without chapter titles, a student or partnership of readers might want to assign an appropriate title to each chapter as they read it as a way to synthesize what they have read. This might help a reader to step back from the drama and details of a chapter and to ask, "What stands out for me in this bit of the story?" Readers could leave a post-it in the book with their invented chapter titles for the next reader to discover.

Probably if a reader attaches post-it notes to interesting details in this story and meets with a partner to talk more about the details, and themes that thread through the text, the reader will probably find themself commenting on Karana's resourcefulness in the struggle to survive. In talking and thinking more about this, a reader may end up thinking about *why* she was able to survive alone on the island. Clearly she survived in part because she already knew how to fish and cook. She had seen and helped in the building of shelters; she was familiar with the island and the animals of the island, i.e., she had skills and knowledge that aided her. Her lifestyle which may seem very primitive to the readers was the thing that saved her.

By making a weapon, Karana breaks one of the laws of her tribe. A reader may want to think more about why the tribe may have forbade the making of weapons by women and why breaking the laws was such a difficult decision for Karana. This discussion could lead into an examination of in the roles of men and women this book and society. The conversation could steer towards a discussion of superstitions, as it is possible that the tribe believed weapons made by women would be ineffective.

The *Island of the Blue Dolphins* is based on a true story, and a reader may want to research the real Karana who was known as Lost Woman of San Nicolas. A reader may want to speculate what became of Karana after she was rescued.

Once in California, Karana discovers that no one speaks her language. It will probably be important for a reader to speculate on why that would be and what the implications of that might be (no one of her heritage is left alive, no one but Karana will remember the culture of her people).

Book Connections

This book is quite special in the way in which it fits alongside other texts. Today's readers may think immediately of the current show *Survivor*, but there are also a host of books that are build around the theme of "child, alone in wilderness, is resourceful enough to survive against all odds." Most of the other lone survivors are boys, so this book is a welcome addition to a list which includes George's *My Side of the Mountain*, Paulson's *Hatchet*, Taylor's *The Cay*, DeFoe's *Robinson Crusoe*, and many more.

Genre
Chapter Book

A Field Guide to the Classroom Library, Lucy Calkins and the Teachers College Reading and Writing Project, Heinemann, ©2002 Teachers College, Columbia University; http://www.heinemann.com/fieldguides

Teaching Uses
Read Aloud; Independent Reading

It's Not the End of the World

Judy Blume

Book Summary

This book centers on the conflict inside of a suburban family. The conflict between the parents gets to a point where the family structure has to change with a divorce. The main character, Karen, goes through an internal journey from denial and scheming to get her parents back together to an ultimate realization that the divorce is the best thing for everyone in the family and that it really isn't "the end of the world."

Basic Book Information

Judy Blume is a well-known author of books for young readers. Her books cover a variety of topics that are relevant to upper elementary school readers, as well as anyone who enjoys a good book. This book is 169 pages long, and is broken into 31 chapters. Italics are used to set written commentary, like letters, notes, and journal entries, apart from the rest of the text. Italics are also used for sound effects, like the clicking of the cat's claws, as well as extra emphasis in speech. The story is told in the first-person narrative, from Karen's point of view. There are no pictures in the book, the plot line is straightforward and the movement of time is basically in a linear fashion.

Noteworthy Features

This book provides a clear line of Karen's thought and how she goes from denial to acceptance of the impending divorce. There is strong evidence of both Karen's denial and ultimate acceptance of the divorce, allowing students to clearly follow and document this central theme. Also, each character in the book copes with the changes in a different way. Amy withdraws, Jeff becomes angry, and Karen tries to stop it from happening.

Gossip plays an important role in the book. Karen plans to tell her best friend Debbie about the divorce one day after school, but she is distracted by a bad grade from her teacher Mrs. Singer. While they are walking home, Debbie says, "I heard about your parents ... and I'm sorry." "Heard what?" I asked, biting my lip. "You know." The use of gossip allows for the situation to be more realistic, and it allows the reader to gain more insight into Karen's thinking, since she always has an internal reaction whenever she is confronted by gossip.

This book also introduces students to journal writing, something they may do themselves or be inspired to start after completing the book. Karen uses her journal to explore and state her true feelings, those that she doesn't feel comfortable sharing with anyone else.

It's Not the End of the World also provides information about divorce itself, helping to explain things like alimony and other terms that would be

Publisher
Bradbury Press, 1972

ISBN
0878880429

TC Level
12

A Field Guide to the Classroom Library, Lucy Calkins and the Teachers College Reading and Writing Project, Heinemann, ©2002 Teachers College, Columbia University; http://www.heinemann.com/fieldguides

unfamiliar to some children. While Karen has a very pessimistic attitude toward marriage, it may be important to make it clear to students that arguments are not necessarily a sign of an impending divorce. Otherwise, they may be alarmed when comparing their own families to Karen's.

Teaching Ideas

A character study of Karen is another way to help student get to the heart of the book. If students pay close attention to Karen's character, they will see her eventual change and her eventual acceptance of the situation. To do this, students might take notes on parts of the text that contribute to their understanding of her motivations and emotions. They might also try to understand her by making personal connections with the experiences she is undergoing and exploring that personal connection in order to understand her, and perhaps themselves, better.

Even though the book centers on Karen's struggle with acceptance, students might trace the routes that Jeff and Amy take to deal with the impending change in their family and their eventual acceptance. Each child in the family, as well as Garfa, their grandfather, has a different path to acceptance which, though not as easy to track as Karen's, and can provide a path from denial to acceptance for students to follow.

Book Connections

In *Baby* and *Journey*, both by Patricia McLachlan, the protagonists are forced to cope with loss and go through a journey from denial to acceptance, much like Karen. In *Blubber* by Judy Blume, the hurtful nature of gossip can be seen and how the main character must go on an internal journey to become accepting of others.

Genre
Chapter Book

A Field Guide to the Classroom Library, Lucy Calkins and the Teachers College Reading and Writing Project, Heinemann, ©2002 Teachers College, Columbia University; http://www.heinemann.com/fieldguides

Jackie Robinson and the Story of All-Black Baseball

Jim O'Conner

Book Summary

Despite the title, this book is mainly about the history of African Americans in baseball. The books opens with a chapter about Jackie Robinson at the plate, and a chapter near the end tells much more about his career, but the rest of the book is devoted to the history of black men playing the sport. It describes barnstorming and racism that black players had to undergo in order to play the sport, then tells the story of manager Rube Foster, and the amazing pitcher Satchel Paige. The reader then hears of the man who signed Jackie Robinson, Branch Rickey and his strategies to make Jackie a success in an all-white league. The book ends with a quick sketch of Jackie's amazing talent and endurance for the unfair treatment he received and a tribute to the players who came before him who only recently have received the recognition they deserve.

Basic Book Information

This is an illustrated, early chapter book. Each page has from one to five paragraphs on it, and on most of the double-page spreads there is at least one illustration. Sometimes the illustrations are drawings, sometimes they are photographs. There is no table of contents or index to this book. Like other books in Random House's Step Into Reading series, it opens with a note to parents about the different levels of which the series is composed. Most of the photographs have captions.

Noteworthy Features

The majority of the text is written in a chronological order. The opening however, is not chronological. Instead, it is a scene in which Jackie Robinson is about to come up to the plate. The next chapter moves back in time to the beginning of "all-black" baseball, and the following chapters gradually take the reader up to the time when the first chapter occurred, and then go past it to the end of the book. This time leap and progression may be a bit tricky for some readers.

The text is written with short, simple sentences for the most part, and although there is not an illustration on every page, the text is broken up enough so that most readers will find the parts to be digestible.

Readers unfamiliar with baseball may be a bit confused by the organization of the various leagues and groups, and they may be confused by the roles various people have-manager, coach, owner, and so on. The book also uses baseball terms without definitions. In a few cases, such as

Illustrator
Jim Butcher

Publisher
Random House, 1989

ISBN
0394824563

TC Level
11; 12; 13

with Rube Foster, it is unclear from the text whether the person being described is black or white.

Of course, the story of African Americans in baseball is intermixed with the story of all African Americans in the nation, and the painful story of racism and prejudice. Readers will need to understand the larger picture of this racism before they can fully understand this book.

Teaching Ideas

Without reference structures, it would be hard to use this book to find particular pieces of information. Readers can however, take notes as they go along in the text, if it is for particular information they are looking.

Reading this book will probably make readers angry at the way these athletes were treated. Teachers can help students channel this anger into productive social or political action-perhaps advocating the inclusion of other deserving black athletes into the various halls of fame. Perhaps writing their own stories to help spread the knowledge of what these sports heroes accomplished for the people of the United States. Perhaps the readers will think of their own projects that can help to address the wrongs that have been committed.

Genre
Nonfiction; Short Chapter Book

Teaching Uses
Reading and Writing Nonfiction; Independent Reading

A Field Guide to the Classroom Library, Lucy Calkins and the Teachers College Reading and Writing Project, Heinemann, ©2002 Teachers College, Columbia University; http://www.heinemann.com/fieldguides

Jaguar

Roland Smith

Book Summary

This is a realistic fiction book that really could be thought of as an eco-adventure. The setting changes from suburban America to the rainforest of Manaus, Brazil, and these changes are flagged by the chapter titles. Although there are jaguars in the story, they aren't as central to the story as the title might suggest. More than anything, this is a story about Jake, his family, remarriage issues, and growing up. This is told by way of a jaguar preserve adventure that includes murder and greed.

The story is told in first-person point of view with Jake as the narrator. This way, Jake's internal story can be told, which is the major story here. There is some reference to geography and an assumption that the reader knows where Brazil and Kenya are located.

Basic Book Information

This book has 247 pages, with a "Before" which serves as a prologue and an "After" that is an epilogue. There are four chapters aside from the Before and After that basically state the setting, "The Home," "Mandus," "The River," and "The Preserve."

Noteworthy Features

Jaguar brings the conflict of the rainforest to light and life. This book is richly reliant upon its setting, and Smith does a great job painting the picture, lacing together history and description to do so. He writes, for example, "In 1839 Charles Goodyear discovered a way to turn the sap from rubber trees into rubber tires . . ." and "The first thing that surprised me about Manaus was the terrible air pollution. A visible haze of wood smoke and diesel fumes hung like fog in the humid air. My eyes watered. . . ." The strength of this book lies in the way it weaves together history, geography, economics, ecology, and people. This tapestry helps the reader understand the sheer complexity of the problems in the Brazilian rainforest.

Readers of the book will benefit if they have prior knowledge of basic geography, world history, and botany. This knowledge is packed into a more readily familiar character of Jake, an honest kid who is adventurous but also has family issues like an absentee dad and a deceased mother. Jake does well in school. He lives with his grandfather in an old age home and has no apparent social life with his peers. Jake is an accessible character and some readers may empathize with his worries about his father and his memories of his mother. But he is also precocious in intellectual ways and does not engage in many of the usual concerns of young people.

Jake is a teenage boy without any academic or adolescent problems. However, he doesn't trust his father as much as he loves him.

A Field Guide to the Classroom Library, Lucy Calkins and the Teachers College Reading and Writing Project, Heinemann, ©2002 Teachers College, Columbia University; http://www.heinemann.com/fieldguides

Publisher
Hyperion, 1997

ISBN
0786813121

TC Level
14

Teaching Ideas

This is an adventure story and it has enough action and intrigue to keep readers engaged. The most notable feature of the book is its setting, and a teacher might encourage a reader to find Kenya and Brazil on a map, and to keep these places in mind as he or she reads. The book contains some specialized vocabulary words, and readers can be encouraged to generate synonyms that might work as substitutes based on the context. For example, the text says, "The first thing you're going to do is to take this thing apart," Buzz said. "Every wire, nut, bolt, and cotter pin." Most readers will not know what a cotter pin is or does. A reader should, however, be able to decide what is important about the terms to the meaning of the text, and to read on, undeterred.

It might be interesting for a reader to do some work studying and explaining the character of Jake. The reader will probably realize that Jake is not as well developed as other characters in other stories, and recognizing this might make the reader a more discerning critic of literature. Alternatively, instead of hoping that a reader notices that Jake is presented as a somewhat stereotypical and flat character, a teacher may want to tell readers that some people have this assessment of the book. "Do you agree?" the teacher could ask, which might launch an interesting exploration.

Genre
Chapter Book

Teaching Uses
Character Study; Independent Reading

A Field Guide to the Classroom Library, Lucy Calkins and the Teachers College Reading and Writing Project, Heinemann, ©2002 Teachers College, Columbia University; http://www.heinemann.com/fieldguides

Jericho

Janet Hickman

Book Summary

Twelve-year-old Angela shivers as she listens to her GranMin ask "Who did you say you were?" There is something about being unrecognized, unnamed, and that bothers her beyond words. Angela's job this summer is to keep her wheelchair bound GranMin occupied, while her grandparents, and her parents and brother, Brian, paint the old house in Gatesville. What started out as a two-week "vacation" turns into a summer when Grandma Kate sprains her ankle. Bored and lonely in this small town, once called Jericho, with no mall, no video store, and no other twelve year old, Angela slowly learns to understand Grandma's confusion. Within each chapter the author carefully weaves the story of GranMin's past, filled with all the people and places of long ago Jericho. Angela's simple daily adventures, a grocery trip to New Liberty with her mother, her family history search through the cemetery where Tom works, give a neat balance to the protagonists in this story. Angela gives an inside view of her family's history and her family's strength. Before "going home," both Angela and GranMin have made a rich connection that will forever be part of each of them.

Basic Book Information

The dedication of this book, "for my mother," and the opening, tell the story of strong women in the author's life immediately. Janet Hickman writes about Jericho, "I started writing shortly after my Grandmother died, in an attempt to explain to myself the kind of person she was. But in the process, the story took over, and the character became Arminda, a fictional person with a life of her own." Ms. Hickman has written several picture books and this is her first novel. Jericho has 135 pages and is 12 chapters long. There is an epilogue that seems to return the characters to a realistic fiction setting giving closure to the book.

Noteworthy Features

It is important to note that within most chapters there are two stories. Many of the chapters are separated into two parts, physically using both white space and a line. The first part of these chapters tells the story of present day Angela and her coming to terms with the strong women in her life and her own strength. It is told from Angela's perspective. Often in this part of the story, the author moves from conversation using dialogue into the character's thinking. The second part tells the story of Arminda, her GranMin, and of her life in that same small town generations ago. In this part of the story, the author moves back in time. The read shifts from realistic fiction almost to historical fiction. Set in the same place, it might take the reader a few chapters to make the connection that GranMin and

Publisher
Greenwillow Books, 1994

ISBN
06881333983

TC Level
13

Arminda are the same person. The setting of this book is particularly important. The parallels of small town life peopled with strong family characters across generations are interesting. Readers should be made aware of this structure as it will help them focus on how the two pieces fit together.

Teaching Ideas

There are many levels of teaching that this book affords. The complexities of *Jericho* include the structure of two stories occurring simultaneously, the rich development of each of the protagonists, and the effect of setting. If in retellings of the story, it is clear that readers are having trouble understanding the story, teachers can try teaching some simple strategies, such as re-reading or making sociograms to separate and make sense of the characters

Janet Hickman has done an extraordinary job of developing Angela's character. In the very first chapter, Hickman presents the reader with opposing characteristics. Angela is bored and lonely and she just wants to go home. Yet when Angela realizes that GranMin wants to go home to the place where she grew up and be with the people that she grew up with and that she can't because they are all gone, Angela escapes into the bathroom to cry. One conversation teachers could have with a small group of readers might be to have them re-read that opening chapter and to have them locate evidence of "both" Angelas. It might lead to an interesting study around how the author uses all of her characters to show the many sides of Angela. Further study can be imagined as soon as readers take these rich characterizations into writing workshop, looking closely at setting or dialogue or simple observations about the physical character to inform their own writing.

Another reading project that might erupt from a study of this text could be the parallels between the two stories. Groups of children could create story lines for each of the stories. This is a kind of a timeline of the story that incorporates not just the plot changes, but each of the major story elements of setting, time movement, characters and change. It might be interesting for readers to set these two protagonist's stories right next to each other to uncover the strengths of the generation.

If this were a read aloud book, visual and artistic readers might draw the details of each of these two settings, carefully lifting lines of text to support their work. Ultimately, conversation around these projects would be in discovering what the artistic process taught the reader about the book and its meanings.

Book Connections

Jericho is a book about family across generations, and it is about strong women. It can easily be placed in a set with Kimberly Willis Holt's *My Louisiana Sky* and Angela Johnson's *Toning the Sweep* and even *The Watsons Go To Birmingham* by Christopher Paul Curtis. The author's writing style allows her to be placed in the category of Patricia MacLauglin's *Journey* and *Sarah Plain and Tall,* or Gary Paulsen's *The Monument.* Connections among these strong characters could easily be used in a study.

Genre
Chapter Book

Teaching Uses
Independent Reading; Character Study

A Field Guide to the Classroom Library, Lucy Calkins and the Teachers College Reading and Writing Project, Heinemann, ©2002 Teachers College, Columbia University; http://www.heinemann.com/fieldguides

Julie of the Wolves

Jean Craighead George

Book Summary

Thirteen-year-old Julie runs away from her village after her man-child husband tries to rape her and she gets lost without food somewhere on the North Slope of Alaska. In order to survive, she must remember what her father Kapugen has taught her about living as an Eskimo in the wilderness. She builds a camp near a wolf den and eventually is accepted by the pack. As winter comes she begins her migration towards civilization and the pack follows her. Eventually Julie, known as Miyax, must make an important decision whether to embrace or abandon her Eskimo heritage.

Basic Book Information

This Newbery Honor text is 170 pages in length and is divided into three parts: Amaroq, the wolf, Miyax, the girl, and Kapugen, the hunter. The story is told in first person from the point of view of Julie, a thirteen-year-old Eskimo girl. The text is chronological, with the exception of the second part which is a flashback, giving the reader a background sketch of Julie's life before she is lost. The dialogue is referenced throughout the text. Illustrations support the reader but appear on the page after the description of the scene being illustrated.

Noteworthy Features

Julie of the Wolves gives a realistic account of Eskimo cultures and traditions. Through the main character, we learn first hand what it takes to survive in the Alaskan wilderness. The ongoing struggle of civilization and tradition is ever-present. As the white man or gussak, begins to take over the land, Eskimo families are finding themselves more and more abandoning their culture and taking on the white man's ways.

The vocabulary in the text may present some difficulty as there are many Eskimo and Alaskan wilderness terms with which readers may not be familiar. However, most vocabulary is followed by a clear description to aid the reader in comprehension. For example, when Julie speaks of "lemming" the reader gets the description immediately following that lemming are "mice-like rodents."

The author leaves out no detail too small, creating a complete and detailed snapshot of Eskimo life. At one point Julie must eat the regurgitated food of a wolf to survive. At another time she tries to suckle a mother wolf for nourishment. Julie cuts open the belly of a caribou and eats the warm liver, the "candy" of her people. And she uses animal dung to fuel her fires.

Teachers should be aware that the book has a brief rape scene in its second part. Readers may need or want a partner or a previous reader to talk

Illustrator
John Schoenherr

Publisher
HarperTrophy, 1972

ISBN
0064400581

TC Level
13

A Field Guide to the Classroom Library, Lucy Calkins and the Teachers College Reading and Writing Project, Heinemann, ©2002 Teachers College, Columbia University; http://www.heinemann.com/fieldguides

to to help them process this and other scenes. There is also a scene where hunters in the sky gun down her beloved Amaroq. Both events can be deeply emotional experiences for the reader, and teachers may want to make sure there is some social support for readers in understanding these parts.

The abrupt ending may present some difficulty for the reader. Julie finds her father, Kapugen in the village of Kangik. But then she leaves him and the village to head back to the wilderness after she learns that he has become Americanized. "Kapugen, after all, was dead to her." Then once her Tornait bird dies in the Arctic cold, she points her boots back toward her father. If students read and understand the song on the last page, they will know that she has finally chosen civilization over wilderness.

Teaching Ideas

Julie of the Wolves is an excellent text for a culture study. Students could attach post-it notes to places in the text where they learn things about Eskimo culture, for example, the Eskimo language, arctic animals, what the houses are made of, clothing, food, and so on. They could then choose an aspect of this culture and do an outside report using other reference guides. Because the fiction and non-fiction elements are so subtly and effectively intertwined in this text, it would be a good introductory book for students who continuously choose one genre over another.

Students often enjoy and learn much from a character study of Julie and a careful look at the decision that she confronts. Some readers even decide to study the characters of the wolves she works with and befriends. They each take on their own distinct personalities. Some students find that these wolf personalities parallel those of the people in her life. Amaroq is like her father and provider until he dies/disappears. Silver, the mother and caretaker is like her Aunt Martha after her own mother dies. Jello is the menacing jealous one, much like her husband Daniel who she runs away from. And Kapu is like her close friend Amy in San Francisco, inviting her to join in the fun. Julie grows through these relationships with the wolves like a coming of age.

This entire story takes place almost entirely in Julie's mind. There is a great deal of internal monologue as Julie is working through the struggle to survive. The wolves are her only friends. She watches them and learns how to become a part of them. She is a stronger person because of them. And when she finally decides to return to civilization, she does so with the memory of her Eskimo heritage strong in her heart. Some students choose to talk about how her learning about the wolves is bound to effect her learning how to integrate herself into the new culture she enters.

Book Connections

Two other books that follow this one in this loose series [ED: enter series name above and here] by Jean Craighead George are *Julie*, and *Julie's Wolf Pack*.

Genre
Chapter Book

A Field Guide to the Classroom Library, Lucy Calkins and the Teachers College Reading and Writing Project, Heinemann, ©2002 Teachers College, Columbia University; http://www.heinemann.com/fieldguides

Teaching Uses
Small Group Strategy Instruction; Independent Reading; Book Clubs;
Content Area Study

Just Us Women

Jeannette Caines

Book Summary

A young girl and her favorite aunt share the excitement of planning a very special car trip for just the two of them. The girl is happily anticipating various scenarios she expects to encounter while driving to North Carolina with Aunt Martha.

Basic Book Information

Just Us Women is a picture book with one to three sentences on each page. Occasionally it may seem as though the characters' activities are happening in the present, but the whole book is the girl's anticipation of what will happen on the trip. The book is nevertheless a memoir.

Every page has pictures on it, some pages having nothing but a large, colorful illustration. Some pictures are symbolic of what is in the text, not necessarily a direct representation of the text. The illustrations are generally large, colorful and interesting and add details to the story that are not in the text.

Noteworthy Features

This timeless book is one of the few African American picture books written during the 1980s that is still in print. Though older now, it is still very much a vital example of a book that brings to life a family relationship. It is a story rich in the traditions of African Americans and life during the late sixties and early seventies. This was a time when old shoe boxes were used to pack lunches, people took long car trips South, and stopping to eat at a fancy restaurant was a grand and exciting thing to do.

The calm, slow rhythm of the text matches the plot's unhurried pace. The trip these characters will take will be a relaxed and slow one. The pictures reinforce this pace by inviting the reader to take his or her time to look over the details before reading further.

As the title indicates, there is an emphasis that the trip is just for women only. Aunt Martha specifically points out that no boys or men will be there. The girl and her aunt are women of color but this is only evident through the illustrations. There is no mention of race in the text.

Teaching Ideas

Just Us Women is one of many picture books which can be read, re-read, studied, and studied again. There are many learning opportunities within these few pages.

Publisher
Harper Trophy, 1984

ISBN
006020941

TC Level
4

Just Us Women can be used as a touchstone text within the writer's workshop, and it can be used to nudge readers to read more thoughtfully within the reading workshop.

Children (and teachers) may wonder at first why this is considered a memoir because it is written in the future tense. This might confuse students who know that a memoir is based on a memory. It is true that this book tells about the *future* trip but the future trip is based on the past trip. The future will be the same as the past. This is something upper grade students could try in their own writing. They could choose an event that has happened and that will happen again and instead of telling us about the past tell us about the future, but base it on the past (e.g., "She picked up two road maps just in case. Last year she forgot the maps and our lunch on the kitchen table.").

When *Just Us Women* is woven into a unit of study on memoir, we might put the beginning of this book (this memoir) on an overhead (alone with the beginning of another memoir) and talk about different ways to begin a memoir and a story. *Just Us Women* begins right in the plot. From the first line of the first page, we know what this story will be about. We know what is to happen. The author also lays her lens or her "angle" out clearly (e.g., "No boys and no men, just us women.").

As a story, it is a great text to study character development. The plot doesn't stop while the author develops the characters, it is carefully woven into the movement of the story.

Just Us Women is a story that can be used to teach the story elements. That is, children can listen to the story and read it, looking for the characters (what do we know of them), the setting (which includes time as well as place), the plot (and this may be structured as a problem and a solution or may not be), the movement in time, and the change that's central to the plot and characters.

Time is especially complex in this story, with the author moving skillfully between now and back to other trips, taken during Aunt Martha's childhood. As with many good memoir, the ending (which begins on page 30) and the beginning (which ends on page 7) hook together as if there were no story in between. A teacher could create a collection of books that do this, by placing the endings and beginnings of several memoirs on one page. Then she could challenge students to try writing just the beginnings and endings of their memoir like this as examples. We've seen teachers do this work with second grade students.

Readers may take note of places in the text (using post-it notes) where they have questions and then develop theories. Some children have read this story asking why the characters are driving to North Carolina. Others will have traced the route on a map, finding the states through which the characters will travel. Some may speculate on how long the trip might take.

The teacher may want to nudge students to consider why the aunt wants to travel with "just us women" and not the boys or men. What might be the benefits? Drawbacks? This can lead to internal personal connections.

Genre
Picture Book; Memoir

A Field Guide to the Classroom Library, Lucy Calkins and the Teachers College Reading and Writing Project, Heinemann, ©2002 Teachers College, Columbia University; http://www.heinemann.com/fieldguides

Teaching Uses
Teaching Writing; Read Aloud; Character Study; Independent Reading

Kissing Doorknobs

Terry Spencer Hesser

Book Summary

Kissing Doorknobs is about Tara, a girl who has undiagnosed obsessive-compulsive disorder (OCD) and can't stop herself from doing things that her family thinks are crazy, such as praying every time someone swears, or counting sidewalk cracks from her house to school. These habits start out as little quirks, but get more serious and greatly disturb her family. She can't control the obsessive-compulsive behavior, and the author helps readers understand how serious this can be. The novel covers several years of her life and shows the destructive influence the disorder has on her family. Her family is afraid she may be crazy and that it might be their fault. She eventually gets treatment and meets a boy with OCD who helps her feel less alone. The book includes an author's afterward about OCD and a list of resources for support and information about this disorder.

Basic Book Information

There are 23 very short chapters in this 149 page-long realistic fiction novel. Written in the first person, the book moves chronologically through time and usually includes very clear transitions at the beginning of chapters (i.e., "By the winter of seventh grade. . . ." "Between March and June. . . .").

Noteworthy Features

This is the story of Tara, a girl who has undiagnosed obsessive-compulsive disorder. She goes through many phases in the book and Hesser does an admirable job of putting the reader inside Tara's head. Tara can't control herself, and we hear her reasoning and questioning herself, her family, and her school life. Tara has a strong voice in the book and her stories are very engaging. The book works hard to help the reader understand what Tara is thinking and going through.

Teaching Ideas

If a teacher wanted to give a book introduction she might say, "*Kissing Doorknobs* is about a girl who can't stop herself from doing things that her family thinks are crazy, like praying every time someone swears, or counting sidewalk cracks from her house to school. These habits start out as kind of little quirks but get more serious and disturb her family a lot. One thing I think is so amazing about this book is that this unreasonable behavior that she really can't control-doesn't it seem kind of weird to you? It's hard to imagine that she really can't stop herself, but the author helps you understand how and why this is true."

Publisher
Delacorte Press, 1998

ISBN
0385323298

TC Level
14

The wonderful thing about reading fiction is that stories allow us to live in worlds other than our own. Through reading, those of us who grew up in cities can wake up on a farm, and can gallop bareback across a meadow with the long grasses swishing against our feet. When we read, however, we are not only invited to live in other worlds, we're also invited to live inside the skin of other people, to see through the eyes of someone other than ourselves. To read this book deeply and well, a reader must come to understand what it is to think like a person with an obsessive-compulsive disorder. Readers who do this will probably find others treating Tara unfairly, and may need to be encouraged to walk in the shoes of other characters as well.

This book is a good book to have out early in the year when students are trying to work on thinking and talking about books. It could be used in a partnership or a book club and is particularly good since there is much in the book to think about. Tara is misunderstood by her family. Students can move beyond "what her mom said was unfair" to talk about perspective and back up their interpretations with evidence from the text.

Book Connections

Multiple Choice by Janet Tashjian is also the story of a girl who doesn't realize she has OCD and has to deal with the consequences of behavior that she feels compelled to do, but isn't really logical or even safe.

Genre
Short Chapter Book

Teaching Uses
Partnerships; Book Clubs; Independent Reading

Lena

Jacqueline Woodson

Book Summary

After the death of their mother, thirteen-year-old Lena and her younger sister Dion run away from an abusive father, hitchhiking from town to town while Lena tries to keep them out of danger. They find refuge with an observant and caring black woman and, finally, a home where they least expected it.

Basic Book Information

This 115-page book has 18 titled chapters of three to fifteen pages. There are no illustrations. *I Hadn't Meant to Tell You This* also by Jacqueline Woodson could be read as a precursor to this book.

Noteworthy Features

Written in first person, *Lena* portrays the thirteen-year-old subject as being unusually mature and thoughtful. She is able to physically navigate a complex and hazardous world, while mentally navigating the complexities of her family situation, racism, honesty, and friendship. While readers may not identify with Lena, they will probably admire her nuances and her deeply considered opinions.

Lena's language contains colloquialisms and non-standard grammar, but is easily understood by most readers at this level.

Teaching Ideas

Lena deals with the subject of sexual abuse and its effects and although the mention is not graphic, students need to be mature enough to handle the topic. Readers may need reassurance about how victims of sexual abuse can get help. In *Lena*, running away turns out to be a solution to Lena's problems in that she encounters no great dangers and finds help. It should be impressed upon readers that this is unrealistic, and that there are other, safer alternatives to difficulty at home. As a practical consideration, readers may want to discuss whether Lena had an alternative to running away, and what they would advise someone in that position.

Characters, other than Lena's, are not extensively developed. The previous book, *I Hadn't Meant to Tell You This*, provides more character development for Marie and her father, as well as for Lena. *Lena* does not contain much plot, as much of the book is devoted to Lena's thoughts and recollections about her life with her father and mother. Students who have not read Woodson's earlier book *I Hadn't Meant To Tell You This* will be able to follow along, but may not find the book as compelling on its own. *Lena* ties up the loose ends of the earlier book in a way that some readers

Publisher
Delacorte, 1999

ISBN
0385323085

TC Level
14

may find unbelievable, though just as many may find the happy ending comforting.

Lena's thoughts and the complexity of her situation are very well developed, and will most likely bring about discussion of the meaning and themes in the text. One major theme is that one must recognize both the necessity of rejecting dependence, and the necessity of trusting others. Lena must leave her father's house for her own sake, and for her sister's sake, but later, she must learn to rely on others. This theme should be meaningful for many late-elementary readers who are wavering between dependence and independence.

Another theme, which continues where *I Hadn't Meant to Tell You This* left off, is that one should not judge others based on skin color. Lena and Dion, who are white, are rescued by Miz Lily, a kind and observant black woman who gives them a ride, a meal and a place to sleep. In the end, Lena's black schoolmate's father overcomes his own racism and invites Lena and her sister to live with him and his daughter. In a discussion about the construct of race, readers might discuss Lena's and Dion's attitudes toward race, and how, or if, they change over the course of the book. Students may also connect with this book through a discussion of the stereotypes related to race, gender or class, and how we can overcome them. They may also be interested in the notion of reverse stereotyping. Are the black characters in the book more heroic? Are the white characters more likely to be evil, flawed, or inconsequential?

Lena is appropriate for independent reading, as long as readers have the maturity to read about sexual abuse.

Book Connections

I Hadn't Meant to Tell You This also by Jacqueline Woodson could be read as a precursor to this book.

Genre
Chapter Book

Teaching Uses
Independent Reading; Critique; Interpretation

A Field Guide to the Classroom Library, Lucy Calkins and the Teachers College Reading and Writing Project, Heinemann, ©2002 Teachers College, Columbia University; http://www.heinemann.com/fieldguides

Letters from Rifka

Karen Hesse

Book Summary

Rifka, a 12-year-old girl, escapes from Russia with her family only to face a series of difficulties, often life-threatening, that interfere with her immigration to America. Rifka records the story of her journey in letters she writes to her cousin Tovah, who is still in Russia. In the first letter, Rifka expresses a doubt that Tovah will ever read the letters but in the final letter, vows to write a "real" letter and send it along with the Pushkin book whose pages hold the other letters.

Basic Book Information

Letters from Rifka, as the name suggests, is written in letter form although these letters are never answered in the book. *Letters from Rifka* has received nine awards, including the National Jewish Book Award and The Christopher Award. It is also listed as an ALA Notable book.

This 148-page book is made up of twenty-one of Rifka's letters. Although there are some references to Jewish customs-such as Yiddish , a mizvah, and tallis, readers should be able to infer the meaning from the context. There are some sensitive portions that teachers may wish to prepare students for, such as when the women are strip-searched by Polish guards.

Noteworthy Features

Although the text we read is in standard format, Hesse has the character Rifka reveal that she writes the letters on blank pages and in the margins of a book of Pushkin's poetry. Hesse also uses lines from Pushkin's poems to introduce each letter. Hesse has chosen the lines carefully and each quote connects in meaning with the events that are described in the letter that follows.

The thirteen letters range in length from three to fifteen pages, with most of them quite short. The first and last letter in the book (thirteen and fifteen pages respectively) are longest in length. The dated letters, arranged in chronological order, span the period of time from September 2, 1919 to October 22, 1920. There are lapses of time, sometimes as long as several months, between many of the letters-a strategy which moves the action quickly from one significant episode to the next.

Hesse includes an author's note in which she attributes many of the events in the book to those experienced by her own great-aunt. She also includes historical notes at the end of the book. These provide background information about the social upheaval in 1919 in Russia, and the conditions that led to the persecutions described in the book.

Publisher
Puffin Books, 1992

ISBN
0140363912

TC Level
14

A Field Guide to the Classroom Library, Lucy Calkins and the Teachers College Reading and Writing Project, Heinemann, ©2002 Teachers College, Columbia University; http://www.heinemann.com/fieldguides

Teaching Ideas

To prepare for reading *Letters from Rifka*, students can read and discuss the historical notes at the end of the book. Of course, students can also dive right into the text, turning to the notes at the end when they feel the need for some more historical grounding.

Students are apt to overlook the connection between the Pushkin quote and the details in the letter, but if they keep a chart in their notebooks, they will be able to make inferences that the two. They can divide a page into three columns. In the first column, they could record their thoughts about the lines. In the second column they can list some of their thoughts about Rifka's letter. In the third column, students can reflect on how the the two might be connected and how the two texts enhance each other or enhance a readers understanding of the story.

Rifka's letters actually fall into a series of categories, chronicling significant events in her journey. For example, the letters dated 9/2 and 9/3 describe the family's escape to Poland while the letters written on 10/5 and 11/3 describe the family's bout with typhus. Students may be interested in forming groups that find and name these internal categories. In addition to all the hardships she describes, Rifka also tells us of pleasant memories she has of her journey, like the kindness of Sister Katrina or the attachment Ilya had for her. Once students have finished reading the book, they can identify these happier events. The students, along with the teacher, might make a two-column chart listing the positive events in one column, and what Rifka might have learned from each experience in the other.

Genre
Chapter Book

Teaching Uses
Independent Reading; Content Area Study; Book Clubs; Partnerships

A Field Guide to the Classroom Library, Lucy Calkins and the Teachers College Reading and Writing Project, Heinemann, ©2002 Teachers College, Columbia University; http://www.heinemann.com/fieldguides

Little Women

Louisa M. Alcott

Book Summary

Jo, Meg, Beth and Amy are the four March sisters who experience the tragedies and joys of growing up in the middle of the 19th century, as the civil war rages. The book begins one dreary Christmas, with their father off at war, and ends about ten years later, in the fall, with the addition of several family members and loss of a dear one. In between, they learn to become morally good with each passing day and challenge. Meg, determined to be sensible, must bear being a governess to rich children but later meets a noble man, her future husband and father to her children. Beth, who is very timid, toils away at the daily housework until she can no longer work due to a debilitating illness from which she dies a slow, painful death. Amy, determined to be a true gentlewoman, goes to school and endures girls' ridicule, until she has the opportunity to go to Europe with her Aunt Carrol to test her artistic talent; here, she encounters her true love and marries. Jo, the protagonist, postpones matrimony as she grows from being a tomboy and playing with their good friend, Laurie, to becoming a serious writer. She does eventually marry, making the circle of happiness complete.

Basic Book Information

Generation after generation of girls, and boys too, have suffered and rejoiced with the trials and triumphs of the March girls, and have been influenced by their manners and lessons. This book is a classic children's novel, which has served as the inspiration for future writers and readers.

Because of the novel's popularity, there have been many movie versions. Some stay close to the text as much as possible within the two-hour limit. The movies may supply more of a sense of the time period and setting through the visuals, dress, and so on, though the book is highly descriptive on this point.

It is important to note that there are several abridged versions to the text, some only containing part one (Modern Promotions), while others contain both parts, but leave out some information (Scholastic Book Services), to attract younger readers and/or to modernize it by leaving out details, dialogue, and/or examples of Jo's writing. As a result, some big ideas and reinforcement of character development and of other big ideas suffer. The original two parts total 500 pages, which requires stamina in readers.

Noteworthy Features

Since the book develops characters in depth, it draws out strong emotions, such as sorrow and joy, from the reader at various points. Some readers cannot help but feel as if they have left some friends behind when they finish, perhaps because the book ends on a happy but nostalgic note.

Publisher
Penguin

ISBN
0140390693

TC Level
13

A Field Guide to the Classroom Library, Lucy Calkins and the Teachers College Reading and Writing Project, Heinemann, ©2002 Teachers College, Columbia University; http://www.heinemann.com/fieldguides

Some editions may include some outdated grammar uses, especially the use of "don't" for "doesn't." It also includes some French words, and thus the book suggests the different speech practices of a bygone era. Readers may take this opportunity to expand their vocabulary by researching the definitions of the words in French.

The book seems to encourage traditional gender roles, especially for women. Today's readers may readily disagree and question these roles. What do these lessons say about the time period in which the book was published? Readers should not feel that they must be influenced by or accept these roles, but they should be able to understand their background. Partnerships may encourage this critical questioning, as can the teacher.

Teaching Ideas

Since the genre of the text is mixed, there are many teachable points. The teacher could select various passages and have the reader identify the different genres that are playing a role in that text. Some of the genres they may identify include: semiautobiography, memoire, story-telling, and sermons. Recognizing the role of genres mixing together may help a writer use a specific genre in their own writing. The reader may also notice the different genres that Jo uses in her writing. What is the purpose of using each genre? How can the reader experiment in these genres in her notebook?

The story serves as a wonderful and simple example of how to develop characters while focusing in on their characteristics, actions, and hobbies. This in turn reveals their interests and motivations.

Readers may naturally feel the fervor to write as Jo does. They may learn that writing keeps improving with practice, and more importantly, that it is a process of writing, editing, and revising, as they watch Jo work on her manuscripts. Readers may also adopt Jo's highly descriptive style, as write in their notebooks. Alcott serves as a wonderful example of how writers stretch a moment by giving appropriate details, and thus making one able to see the image in the mind's eye. Readers may want to ask themselves which details she includes, after reading a small section, and why she includes them. How do these details affect the mood and ideas?

Alcott also uses a mentor text, *Pilgrim's Progress*, as does Jo. Partners can engage in lengthy discussions about the different roles of mentor and touchtone texts. Does a writer write about them, or mold the style into her writing? What can she take from the texts: morals, lessons, the opening or ending style, the twist of story, plot structure, and/or character development? How? A reader can try using a mentor or touchtone text in her notebook to experiment using a traditional writer's practice. Partners can also discuss why one writer would want to imitate another writer. Does it have to do with following a tradition in order to serve a particular big idea, or is it to follow a model to then develop her own style?

Before addressing these questions, readers can identify ways that Alcott and Jo go about using *Pilgrim's Progress*. How do they use it? A teacher might challenge more advanced readers to search for ways that are not very obvious. Does the use of *Pilgrim's Progress* affect the overall style, or big ideas, and how?

Readers may notice the narrator's role in this book. She is intrusive but only names herself as "I" on a few occasions. Readers may want to discuss the general role of a persona in narrative by discussing what the role of the persona is in Little Women. When does she label herself: is it at a crucial point in the story? What does she say in relation to the plot, characters, and so on? Why would Alcott make this story only a semi-autobiography if it has to do with her childhood? Does this affect the big ideas or plot? Why do writers take a step back from their writing? Readers may want to experiment in their notebooks by writing semi-autobiographically. They may want to consider their purposes and goals for the piece, and what kind of piece they would want to write in this way.

The book is from the middle of the 19th century, and many of the values and lessons portrayed in the book reflect that time period. Readers can learn to question the validity of these values and lessons for them and/or for our present society, and can discuss why these values were encouraged then. The values are related to spirituality, though there is no reference to religion. Other lessons deal with gender roles, which are not prevalent today. This book offers a great chance for readers to learn how to respect values presented in books as societal products of the time, and thus can better understand how American society has evolved.

The reader who really enjoys this classic and would like to develop a study of literature surrounding it may want to read an abridged version of the text and compare and contrast it to the full text, or vice versa. Then, she can see the extent of characterization and of enforcing big ideas in the original.

Book Connections

Alcott wrote many other books at the same level, which further develop this original story, such as *Little Men* and *Jo's Boys*. She also wrote other tales, such as *The Inheritance*, which are receiving growing attention.

Genre
Chapter Book

Teaching Uses
Independent Reading; Book Clubs; Critique; Teaching Writing

A Field Guide to the Classroom Library, Lucy Calkins and the Teachers College Reading and Writing Project, Heinemann, ©2002 Teachers College, Columbia University; http://www.heinemann.com/fieldguides

Lives of the Athletes: Thrills, Spills (and what the neighbors thought)

Kathleen Krull

Book Summary

This text acts as a resource for learning about athletes' lives. A reader is introduced to a number of athletes including Jim Thorpe, Duke Kahanamuku, Babe Ruth, Red Grange, Johnny Weissmuller, Getrude Ederle, Babe Didrikson Zaharias, Sonja Henie, Jessie Owens, Jackie Robinson, Sir Edumund Hillary, Maurice Richard, Maureen Connolly, Roberto Clemente, Wilma Rudolph, Arthur Ashe, Pete Maravich, Bruce Lee, Pele, and Flo Hyman.

This book gives a view into each athlete's professional life and also creates a picture of his or her personal life, struggles to become an athlete, and the path he or she has followed to reach this level of fame.

Basic Book Information

Lives of the Athletes is part of a series of research texts. The other texts are entitled, *Lives of the Artists, Lives of the Musicians,* and *Lives of the Writers.*

This particular text is 96 pages in length and each writer is given a section of the text, about three to five pages in length. Within the section on each individual, the reader is given the birth and death dates, further reading and listening to engage in if interested in the particular individual, a section entitled "Athleticisms" that gives relevant pieces of information, and an illustration of the athlete. The text begins with an index of the athletes that are mentioned within the book.

Noteworthy Features

Each vignette about the athlete offers interesting facts and outlines the larger experiences that these particular authors had. The "Athleticisms" section of the biography permits the reader to learn even more about the athlete through the information that is delivered. Another helpful feature of the book is that it offers the portraits of each athlete that allow the reader to place a face with a name.

Teaching Ideas

These texts are perfect for browsing. They also work well to entice students with an interest in sports into reading. Children who are particularly interested in a special athlete will easily be drawn into this book. Because the athletes depicted are from many different racial and ethnic backgrounds, the

Series
"Lives of . . ."

Illustrator
Kathryn Hewitt

Publisher
Harcourt Brace and Company

ISBN
0152008063

TC Level
11; 12; 13

book offers role models and inspiring stories for children of many different backgrounds.

Sometimes, children read this book in partnerships, choosing favorite people and events, and retelling them to their partner.

Book Connections

This text is part of a series and, if a student enjoys the format of *Lives of the Athletes*, they might enjoy *Lives of the Artists*, *Lives of the Writers*, and *Lives of the Musicians*.

Genre
Nonfiction; Picture Book

Teaching Uses
Reading and Writing Nonfiction; Content Area Study

A Field Guide to the Classroom Library, Lucy Calkins and the Teachers College Reading and Writing Project, Heinemann, ©2002 Teachers College, Columbia University; http://www.heinemann.com/fieldguides

Maniac Magee

Jerry Spinelli

Book Summary

Because Maniac Magee's parents were killed on a bridge when he was three years old, he goes to live with an unhappily married aunt and uncle, who will not divorce because they are Catholic. Frustrated, he runs away, and is from then on known only as Maniac. It is the birth of a legend in which Maniac runs to the town of Two Mills, where he continues to run, from one place to the next, in search of a home to call his own. Maniac does the unthinkable when he crosses the boundary between the East and West ends of town, which is strictly divided along racial lines. Ultimately, through a series of truly heroic feats, he brings the two sides together, opening the lines of communication between Blacks and Whites.

Basic Book Information

This 184-page book is divided into three parts and forty-six chapters. The chapters are not titled; they are episodic, and vary in length from two to seven pages. The parts also are not titled but are labeled with roman numerals and separated by a blank page.

Each part addresses a different phase of Maniac's journey. In part one he runs away. Part two tells the story of his relationship with Grayson. In part three, the tensions central to the plot are ultimately resolved. A short passage entitled "Before the Story" precedes part one, and contains a jump rope rhyme that is set apart from the rest of the text with line breaks.

In this third-person narrative, the author frequently uses italics to emphasize certain words and to provide the reader with a glimpse into Maniac's thinking. Jerry Spinelli's writing voice is deliberately crafted to sound as if he is speaking aloud, in a casual way, and his narrative is replete with the kind of incomplete sentences that speakers' really use. It creates the impression that, as readers, we are listening to the story of a local resident of Two Mills, as told on a street corner one lazy summer afternoon.

Noteworthy Features

This book taps into more than one literary theme, as students in a book club will undoubtedly discover. Maniac helps resolve tension between Blacks and Whites while continually searching for home. When he develops a relationship with Grayson, a retired baseball player responsible for the upkeep of the local fields, Maniac teaches Grayson how to read, and Grayson tells Maniac the story of how he almost-but-not-quite-made-it to the major leagues. Together they create a sense of family and Maniac finally feels that he has found his address, but then Grayson dies and he is again without a home. Maniac continually runs from his problems instead of

Publisher
Little, Brown, and Company, 1990

ISBN
0316807222

TC Level
12

facing them, remaining in constant motion to avoid facing the difficult truth of his aloneness.

It is solely his desire to reach out and help Russell and Piper McNab, two runaway kids, that prevents Maniac from following through with his death wish. He convinces them to remain in Two Mills and to continue going to school through a series of bribes, living in the McNab's roach-infested apartment in the West End. Maniac is perhaps the most selfless character to be found in a work of childrens' literature. He is a hero in the classical sense-an issue some children return to again and again in their conversations

This book provides its readers with plenty of incidents that involve the central themes. With support, students may easily follow and document the figurative bridge Maniac constructs between the East and West sides of town. If they do not invent this metaphor themselves, it may be useful to empower students with the image of the bridge. Teachers could point out that Maniac was born in Bridgeport, and that his parents were killed on a bridge. It is ultimately this very bridge that is responsible for the final reconciliation between Blacks and Whites.

The beginning of the book is deliberately crafted to spark readers' curiosity. It has been written "after the fact," and is meant to be returned to again and again, continually becoming more meaningful as the story unfolds. There are several other opportunities to point out Spinelli's craft: his use of the colon, his unique writing voice, and his exceptional ability to bring characters' voices to life.

Until the story has reached its conclusion, the "Before the Story" cannot be understood. The author makes shorthand reference to unknown events, circumstances and characters, but with encouragement, students will learn to continually return to the beginning as events unfold. If they re-read frequently, students will delight in uncovering the "clues" that enable them to make sense of this passage. The clues are interspersed throughout the book.

Teaching Ideas

Maniac Magee works well as a daily read aloud, as it is rich with literary themes and teacher support can help do justice to its significance. Whether reading the book in large/small groups or independently, students may be encouraged to document moments where Maniac is "building the bridge" between Blacks and Whites. It all begins on page ten, when Maniac first encounters Amanda Beale. She thinks, "Who was this stranger kid? What was he doing in the East End, where almost all the kids were black. ...Back in those days the town was pretty much divided. The East End was blacks, the West End was white."

There are many sections of the book that are worthy of a closer look. On page 70, Maniac takes on Amanda's challenge to untie the infamous knot at the Cobble's Corner grocery store, conveniently located on Hector Street. Hector Street marks the boundary between the East and West ends of Two Mills. This wasn't just any knot. "Here and there a loop stuck out . . .pitiful testimony to the challengers who had tried and failed." Maniac is famous for, among other things, his ability to untie the most stubborn of knots.

On page 72, Spinelli writes, "Not only white kids, but grown-ups, too, black and white, because Cobble's Corner was on Hector, and word was racing through the neighborhood on both the east and west sides of the street." Then, "a huge roar went up, a volcano of cheers. Cobble's Knot was dead. It was nothing but string." This is one of several metaphors for Maniac's singular ability to unravel the tension between Whites and Blacks. Students in partnerships or book clubs may be interested in documenting and discussing these metaphors.

On page 171, Maniac begins running alongside Mars Bar Thomson, who is the toughest and fastest kid on the East End. He also happens to be Black. "Morning after morning it happened this way-the two of them dovetailing at an intersection and without the slightest hitch in stride, cruising off together." The book climaxes and the "bridge" is finally complete on page 173, when Russell and Piper are trapped on the very bridge responsible for the death of Maniac's parents. Maniac is running with Mars Bar, and he keeps running. Mars Bar, the toughest kid on the East End, is left with no choice but to rescue the McNab brothers, who hail from the toughest family on the West End. Children will enjoy recognizing how the book has come full circle, and the tensions are resolved exactly where they began.

Students may be encouraged to follow and document not only the resolving tension between Blacks and Whites, but also the ways in which Maniac runs from his problems, and the absolute heroism of his acts. There exists ample evidence to support each strand of thought.

Another difficulty is presented by the content of the story. A teacher can explain to students that the prejudiced attitudes of its characters are due to their ignorance, that if they only knew each other, this irrational, unfounded hatred would most likely not exist. Also, the Grayson's death is nothing short of heartbreaking, as is Maniac's subsequent desire to end his own life. If the book is being read aloud, the teacher will need to take time to discuss these sensitive issues.

Book Connections

The Great Gilly Hopkins, by Katherine Paterson, is also a story of the search for home, family, and acceptance. In Patricia MacLachlan's *Journey*, the title character, like Maniac, refuses to face the truth. Karen Hesse's *The Music of Dolphins* centers around Mila's resolution of the tension between the human and dolphin sides of herself, while Maniac's resolution of the tension between Blacks and Whites is what empowers him to become whole. Much can be learned from reading these books alongside each other.

Genre
Chapter Book

Teaching Uses
Book Clubs; Read Aloud; Interpretation; Critique; Language Conventions

A Field Guide to the Classroom Library, Lucy Calkins and the Teachers College Reading and Writing Project, Heinemann, ©2002 Teachers College, Columbia University; http://www.heinemann.com/fieldguides

Mary Poppins
P.L Travers

Book Summary

When haughty Mary Poppins becomes nanny at the home of the Banks, strange and wonderful things begin to happen. Jane and Michael have tea while floating in the air, they hear the surprising thoughts of the very manicured dog next door, try out a magic compass and, in general, see the world from an unlikely new perspective. Mary Poppins never admits to the magic, however, but only answers their questions with a critical sniff. She leaves when the wind changes, though the children beg her to stay, but the family is left happier and more unified than before.

Basic Book Information

Mary Poppins is one of four books by P.L. Travers about the adventures of Mary Poppins and the Banks children.

Noteworthy Features

Mary Poppins is a light, humorous book that entertains while offering lessons about seeing things from others' perspectives. The main characters-Jane, Michael, and Mary Poppins-have a series of adventures that involve more minor characters, such as the neighbors and servants. Most readers will enjoy the idea that magical things can happen in even the most normal of houses; they may feel as if these peculiar and delightful events could even happen to them.

The characterization in *Mary Poppins* is straightforward. The children are like all children: curious, argumentative, and giddy, sometimes kind, and sometimes badlybehaved. Many readers can imagine themselves in the children's shoes. Mary Poppins is an intriguing character, much less sugar-coated than the usual fairy godmother type. (She is less sweet than in the movie version of the book.) One of her attractions is that neither the characters nor the reader can predict how she'll behave next.

Mary Poppins concerns a family, like that in *Peter Pan* or other English books of the same era, which is significantly more mild and unproblematic than the families of more current literature. Some readers may find this too unrealistic, while others may enjoy varying their reading of contemporary books with more escapist ones like this.

The outside world is at a distance from the domestic scene, and the children's lives seem to consist mainly of walks in the park and tame afternoons at home. The setting is a comfortable but supposedly not rich household in London in the early 1900s. Readers may find it hard to believe that the Banks have four servants but consider themselves hard up for money.

The vocabulary can be moderately challenging, with words such as

Series
Mary Poppins

Illustrator
Mary Shepard

Publisher
Bantam Doubleday Dell, 1934

ISBN
0440404061

A Field Guide to the Classroom Library, Lucy Calkins and the Teachers College Reading and Writing Project, Heinemann, ©2002 Teachers College, Columbia University; http://www.heinemann.com/fieldguides

"gallivanting" and "sedate." There are occasional Britishisms. Compared to other books read by this age group, *Mary Poppins* has longer sentences and more complex diction, which may slow down some readers. An example is the following sentence: "Mary Poppins and the children waited in the Lane outside Miss Lark's gate, Miss Lark and her two maids leant over the fence, Robertson Ay, resting from his labours, propped himself up with a broom handle, and all of them watched in silence the return of Andrew."

Teaching Ideas

Mary Poppins-vain, attentive, haughty, beloved, critical, and loving-could make an interesting subject for a character study. If a teacher pulls a chair alongside a reader and wants to engage the reader in a great book talk, it'd be fruitful to ask about Mary Poppins herself. "What's she like?" the teacher could ask, and soon the teacher could say back the child's words. "So your theory is that she's. . . ." Before long, the child could have resumed reading, this time noticing passages that reveal more about Mary Poppins. The child could be coached to think, "How is she like/unlike other somewhat similar characters in literature? How is she like Maria, the singing governess in *The Sound of Music*? And how is she like the babysitter in *Harriet the Spy*?" (who has some similarities to Mary Poppins).

Within the discussion of this book or of another book, a teacher might also point out to the readers that they might want to look beyond the main characters in a story. They may want to focus on some of the minor characters, too. In this book, for example, a child could be encouraged to develop a theory about the parents or specifically the father.

As in much literature for children, the parents are kind and distracted, unaware of what is really going on with the children. For example, Mrs. Banks, who doesn't seem to have understood how much the children disliked their former nanny, walks up the stairs obliviously while Mary Poppins slides up the banister.

Students can start a study of theme by examining each chapter, and asking themselves, "What is this *really* about?" The chapter "Laughing Gas" stresses the importance of laughter, while "Bad Tuesday" shows how behaving badly can have frightening consequences, but that one can also be forgiven. Magic is used in both circumstances to heighten the message; for example, the consequences of Michael's bad behavior include being threatened by a polar bear.

Genre
Chapter Book

Teaching Uses
Independent Reading; Character Study; Book Clubs; Interpretation

Miracle's Boys

Jacqueline Woodson

Book Summary

Lafayette mourns the loss of his mother, and more recently the change in one of his brothers, Charlie, whom Lafayette now calls, "Newcharlie." A little before his mother dies, Charlie steals from a local liquor store and was sent to Rahway Correctional Facility. Lafayette, a thirteen-year-old, seeks guidance, comfort, and support from his eldest brother, Ty'ree. Ty'ree helps Lafayette discover the good in Charlie, and they continue to be a close-knit family.

Basic Book Information

This book won the Coretta Scott King award in 2001 for "Excellence in African-American literature." Though the issues dealt with in the book-including death and violence-may be most suitable for an older audience, the language in the book is surprisingly simple and easy to read.

Noteworthy Features

The plot of this book, like the lives of too many children, includes gangs, violence, and crime. The book does not deal head-on with the issues, nor is it preachy. Instead, it shows the effects of these acts and groups, respectively, through the characters' emotional reactions and the changes they must face as a consequence. Another powerful theme that the book addresses is punishment even for good intentions; readers at this level may be prepared to consider the grayness of morality, and that happiness does not always come out of goodness, but that instead, good or well-intentioned acts can have negative effects.

The language of the text is the first thing to notice: it is written largely in Black English. The author expands the conservative reader's mental realm of what constitutes "good" and proper literature.

Teaching Ideas

The first thing the reader may notice is the use of ebonics. By using this form of English, the author opens up the world of writing to young writers who may feel the truth is more easily told, the story more easily told, in that form of English. Some young writers may never have considered this before seeing a published work written in this form of English.

The text does a beautiful job of blending the genres of narrative and memoir, and the novel has a circular plot structure. In partnerships, readers

184 *A Field Guide to the Classroom Library,* Lucy Calkins and the Teachers College Reading and Writing Project, Heinemann, ©2002 Teachers College, Columbia University; http://www.heinemann.com/fieldguides

Publisher
G. P. Putnam's Sons, 2000

ISBN
0399231137

TC Level
16

can ask themselves many questions about the genres and plot structure: Why would the author choose to write in flashbacks, instead of traditional prose? What effect does she seek? Does the plot structure, and/or genre mixing, relate to the big ideas? To better answer these questions, readers may want to experiment writing memoir with simple circular plots. Does writing memoir lend itself easily to a circular plot structure? What kinds of stories seem to get the most dramatic effect by being written this way?

The actual plot only lasts two days and a night. The author is able to tell the whole story within this short time frame through inserting flashbacks, and thus she plays with traditional narrative form. The author almost applies a stream-of-consciousness structure in the flashbacks, though the memories themselves are well-organized thoughts. Students may well want to study the structure of the writing after they have finished the book, or as they are reading, in order to help them better understand what is happening.

Charlie, "Newcharlie," to the displeasure of Ty'ree. In partnerships, readers may want to think about the names used in this text. Are names symbolic? Have readers read other texts where the names mattered, and if so, how?

Readers can also address other literary techniques Woodson has used, including metaphor. Readers may want to consider whether *they* write in metaphors in their notebooks. What is the purpose of the metaphor, and why would a writer use one? Which of Woodson's metaphors seem especially effective?

There is also an allusion in the book to Judgment Day. Readers may want to discuss the purpose of allusions; hopefully, they'll remember that allusions involve pointing to something outside the text. Why would an author want to refer to an outside source? In this case, what is the source and why is it important? What is the author suggesting? Readers may discover that books transcend time and space when they reach readers through establishing a shared point of reference.

Also, the novel gently addresses the idea of stewardship of animals and the natural earth. The reader may ask herself how the author gets this theme across so forcefully. Big ideas about nature have and will continually pop up in literature because of man's innate connection with the earth. Viewing the earth from the perspective of this book will give readers a frame of mind when they address the same theme in other works from different places and times.

Book Connections

Woodson also wrote *From the Notebooks of Melanin Sun* and *If You Come Softly*, which similarly deal with complex social situations in young adult books. Like *Miracle's Boys*, this novel also addresses sophisticated themes well.

Genre
Chapter Book; Memoir

Teaching Uses
Independent Reading; Teaching Writing; Book Clubs

Mirandy and Brother Wind

Patricia C. McKissack

Illustrator
Jerry Pinkey

Publisher
Alfred A. Knopf, 1988

ISBN
0440840732

TC Level
11

Book Summary

Young Mirandy is determined to have the wind as her partner in her first cakewalk. She asks her neighbors how to catch him and tries many things, reporting her failures to her clumsy friend Ezel each time. Finally, she catches Brother Wind in the barn, and, at the last moment, asks him not just to dance with her, but to help her and Ezel dance together. Weeks later, people still talk about how the two of them won the cakewalk-dancing with the wind.

Basic Book Information

This is a Caldecott Honor book, and the illustrations are beautiful, just as they are in *The Talking Eggs*, and *New Shoes for Silvia* and Pinkey's other works.

Noteworthy Features

If readers skip over the Author's Note at the story's beginning, which is easy to do since it bears no illustration or special place in the text, they may find the story a bit more confusing than they would otherwise. Although it is possible to figure out what a cakewalk is from the context, the Author's Note explains it outright. It is of course also possible to figure out what Mirandy means when she says she wants to catch Brother Wind, but again, the Author's Note sets the stage for understanding that part of the story by explaining a bit more about capturing the wind for a dance. If the book is a teacher's read aloud, the Author's Note is probably a good place to start. Children will probably want to stop and discuss it after hearing or reading it.

Some children will find this book especially easy since it is written in the dialect of Black English. The more closely the written word matches the way a child speaks, the easier it can be for them to read. This is not always true, however, since some children may have become very familiar with the disjuncture between their own spoken English and the very different, Queen's English in which many books are written. These children may need a bit of the story read aloud to them in order that they hear the type of English a bit and then can stop expecting it to conform to the rules of other dialects, reading it for what it is.

Teaching Ideas

Other children, those who are not familiar with Black English, may find the dialect a bit of a challenge. Besides the addition of some words they may be unfamiliar with ("conjure woman," "cakewalk," etc.), the particular grammatical structures and tenses may confuse them initially. For most children unfamiliar with it, however, the dialect merely makes the read slower, not more confusing. Children often discuss why the book was written in this style and not in another. We can fuel these discussions by offering other books written in Black English or other pronounced dialects of English to help children make decisions about why authors make the choices they do about the dialects in which they write.

The personification of the wind can be a bit hard to grasp for some children who are not used to thinking of forces of nature as alive, or as people. Is the wind the same wind they already know, or is this wind something they have never seen or encountered, like fairies? How do they think about it and picture him? Instead of answering this question for children, it is usually most helpful to let children discuss these questions in their clubs or with partners so that they hear a wide variety of reading techniques for this situation.

Mirandy's relationship with Ezel is another complicated and rich aspect of this story. It is not at all clear from the initial encounters Mirandy has with Ezel that the two are friends. Students will need to infer this by the fact that Mirandy keeps seeking him out, despite the fact that she keeps calling him clumsy and noticing his awkwardness. Ezel teases Mirandy by telling her he is asking another girl to be his partner, and Mirandy pretends she doesn't care. This aspect of the story also can be confusing if students read it literally only, not seeing the emotions under the words of each. If readers do seem to have fallen into that trap and think the two don't care for each other, it might be best for them to re-read the story in the light of the ending. For, at the end, Mirandy stands up for her friend and even asks him to dance, so that the earlier scenes, which may seem hostile, can be reinterpreted. Re-seeing a part of a text in the light of understanding the whole is a technique that can help readers through many kinds of trouble spots in their reading.

The structure of the story is a bit unusual in that the peak event of the plot, the cakewalk dance itself, is skipped over. Instead of a firsthand account, it is told of in the past tense, when people weeks later are still talking about how it went. A few readers will undoubtedly think they skipped a page, since they didn't read about the cakewalk the way we read of all Mirandy's other exploits. That anomaly in the story's structure may be the start of a fruitful discussion about writing choices the author has made.

Genre
Picture Book; Fairy and Folk Tale

Teaching Uses
Independent Reading; Book Clubs; Language Conventions

A Field Guide to the Classroom Library, Lucy Calkins and the Teachers College Reading and Writing Project, Heinemann, ©2002 Teachers College, Columbia University; http://www.heinemann.com/fieldguides

Missing May
Cynthia Rylant

Book Summary

Aunt May has died and Summer and her Uncle Ob try to make sense of the world without May. Both Ob and Summer are depressed in their own ways, but with the help of their friend Cletus Underwood, they go in search of some sign that May is still with them. This is a realistic, yet hopeful portrayal of grief and how two people go through it together.

Basic Book Information

Missing May won the 1993 Newbery Award. This 89-page chapter book is made up of twelve untitled chapters that are divided into two parts, which are named, "Still as Night," and "Set Free." The story in narrated in the first person by Summer. There is a dream sequence that occurs in part two, which moves time back and forth from past to the present. The rest of the story moves chronologically through Summer's grief, interspersed with memories of her Aunt May.

Noteworthy Features

Summer's memories of her Aunt May are interspersed throughout the book and can create difficulty in understanding the time and the setting in this book. These memories take on the feel of the present, as they are extended and just as vividly rendered as the present in the book.

Ob experiences what he calls encounters with the spiritual world and is convinced that May is trying to get in touch with them from the other side. Some readers have difficulty relating to this.

The characters may seem outlandish to readers not from the South, as Rylant paints her characters in the colors of Appalachia and they seem similar to the characters of *When the Relatives Came* and *When I Was Young in the Mountains.*

This book is about grief and grieving. The theme is strong and some readers, especially if they are young, may need support in comprehending the emotional weight of this subject. Older readers and readers familiar with the hard terrain of life will probably not need support in this area.

Teaching Ideas

Since the echoes of her other writings are so strong, *Missing May* could easily be a part of an author study of Cynthia Rylant.

The themes in this book are weighty, and it is recommended that this book be read aloud to readers younger than fifth grade. *Missing May* would make an appropriate independent read with older students, and discussions of it tend to flourish because of the serious content.

Publisher
Dell, 1992

ISBN
0440408652

TC Level
12

Many teachers enjoy reading *Missing May* aloud since it tends to make rapt listeners out of even the rowdiest bunch. The writing is also careful, beautiful, and spare.

Book Connections

Other books by Cynthia Rylant have similar flavor, like *When I Was Young in the Mountains* which is set in the Appalachians, as is *Appalachia*. *The Islander*, also by Cynthia Rylant, carries many of the same themes (grief, imagination, the power of love), and would be a good book to read subsequent to *Missing May*. Other books carrying similar themes to *Missing May* are *A Taste of Blackberries* by D.B. Smith and *Bridge to Terebithia* by Katherine Paterson. *The Library Card* by Jerry Spinelli has some characters that could be from Rylant's world, and so this too would be a good book to read after *Missing May*.

Genre
Chapter Book

Teaching Uses
Read Aloud; Independent Reading; Partnerships; Teaching Writing

A Field Guide to the Classroom Library, Lucy Calkins and the Teachers College Reading and Writing Project, Heinemann, ©2002 Teachers College, Columbia University; http://www.heinemann.com/fieldguides

Monarchs
Kathryn Lasky

Book Summary

The text starts with a butterfly egg. Each chapter takes the butterfly a step farther in its development, and each chapter also has at least one living human character who is admiring and studying the butterflies at this stage of their life. Sometimes these characters are the same as those in earlier chapters, sometimes they are not. The setting of each chapter depends on where the butterflies are in the world-from Maine to Mexico to California. The tone of the book, while it imparts enormous quantities of information about the monarch, is not strictly scientific, but rather reverential and protective of the butterfly and its habitat. Figurative language abounds in the text, creating a mood of admiration for these beautiful and fragile creatures. The author also includes personal details about the lives of the people working with and for the butterflies, adding to the immediacy of the book's tone.

Basic Book Information

This Nonfiction book is a well-illustrated chapter book. It has no table of contents or index, but chapters are clearly defined with headings and often a changed story location or story character. The chapter titles are literary and interest-catching rather than informative about the subject of the chapter.

There are one or two large, clear photographs on every two-page spread. There are five to ten paragraphs of text per two pages. The photographs don't have captions or labels and there are no diagrams. Instead, the photographs serve to illustrate the story of the butterflies' migration-understanding the pictures' content comes from reading the whole text.

Noteworthy Features

Although each chapter is clearly separated from the one before it, it takes some reading concentration to make the changes between characters and settings in the narrative. These elements of the story are not central to the text and are therefore imbedded within it, not stated outright necessarily, making the work of setting them straight a bit more challenging for the reader.

There is quite a lot of information to process, but it is not presented raw. There is usually some comparison and processing done for the reader. For example, "If a six-pound human baby grew as fast as a caterpillar, it would weigh eight tons in twelve days." At other times the information is made easier to retain by having the implications of it affect the course of action taken by the people in the story. This makes understanding and retaining the information easier that it otherwise would be. The photographs are vivid

Illustrator
Christopher G. Knight

Publisher
Harcourt Brace & Company, 1993

ISBN
0152552960

TC Level
11; 12; 13

and make for interesting browsing, although there are no captions or short chunks of text to explain them.

Teaching Ideas

Because of its literary quality, and its migration-driven plot line, this book is as suitable for a read aloud (probably only a few sections would be read, or perhaps the entire book) as it is for independent reading or group discussion.

Because the text has two structures to aid in its use as a reference book, children who are looking for specific bits of information may want to be ready with pencil and notebook in hand during the first read through. Otherwise, the entire text may have to be re-read to glean the information.

Many readers prefer Nonfiction reading to fiction reading, and it can be important for all readers to balance their reading with information books. This book, then, could simply be one among many on the library shelf.

If a teacher sees that the class as a whole tends to select fiction books only during independent reading, the teacher may institute some rituals that steer children toward Nonfiction. The least intrusive might simply be to do promotional book-talks in which one "sells" Nonfiction books. It's possible to go a step further and to suggest that for a time, all children might read only Nonfiction texts during independent reading.

Teachers might want to do minilessons about the strategies of skilled Nonfiction reading. One minilesson may teach children that Nonfiction readers sometimes read like magnets, looking for intriguing details that they pull from a text. One teacher told her students that highly literate people then fact-drop these little bits of information into conversations, sharing in passing whatever they've been learning. The reader of this book could be full of such facts.

Another minilesson might show children that if, for example, a person read this book and loved it, the logical thing to do would be to collect other texts on the same topic. Information can vary from one book to another, sometimes it will develop and other times it will contradict.

Genre
Nonfiction; Chapter Book; Picture Book

Teaching Uses
Reading and Writing Nonfiction; Content Area Study; Book Clubs

A Field Guide to the Classroom Library, Lucy Calkins and the Teachers College Reading and Writing Project, Heinemann, ©2002 Teachers College, Columbia University; http://www.heinemann.com/fieldguides

Monkey Island

Paula Fox

Book Summary

Forced to live on the streets of New York after his mother disappeared from their hotel room, eleven-year-old Clay Garrity first meets Calvin Bosker and Buddy Meadowsweet on the streets of October. Part of New York's "homeless," these two old men become Clay's family.

Calvin's father left the family when he lost his job. His mother disappeared from the welfare hotel that had been their shelter, leaving him only $28. He is afraid to leave these streets because he might never be able to find his parents again. As the weather gets worse, Clay finds that the need to rely more and more on his new friends increases, learning how to understand the "different neighborhoods for the homeless."

He meets Garard, the coffee and doughnut man, who feeds them each morning at 6:00AM. Clay begins to tell his story and builds a trusting relationship with the men. As he loses faith in his mother's return, he slowly becomes a part of the homeless community known as Monkey Island. Reality takes over. The police clean up the place where they live and they are forced to move on. Calvin is hospitalized, and eventually dies of pneumonia. When all looks bleak, Clay's mother returns with his new baby sister.

Basic Book Information

This book is 150 pages long and has ten chapters. Each chapter has a title that helps the reader know what the chapter will be about. Although the issue of homelessness in New York is a difficult one, the story has a fairy tale quality to it. Things work out, despite the death of a good friend. It is a straightforward story, with in-depth characterization.

Noteworthy Features

The concepts in the book are the most difficult part of the read. The dialogue is simple and direct. The characters are well-developed and easy to care about.

Teaching Ideas

Monkey Island by Paula Fox can be a good book to help children talk about possible reading projects. It is a book that might be used to help children explore new topics and make connections with their outside interests. This might motivate some to consider how they might use this text or similar ones to take some form of social action. This might connect to a non-fiction reading study using magazines or newspapers. After or during the reading of this text, some children might be challenged to take up an inquiry about

Publisher
Orchard Books, 1991

ISBN
0531059626

TC Level
12

A Field Guide to the Classroom Library, Lucy Calkins and the Teachers College Reading and Writing Project, Heinemann, ©2002 Teachers College, Columbia University; http://www.heinemann.com/fieldguides

homelessness or some aspect of city living. Conferences with groups of students trying to come up with reading projects could be about ways that they can push themselves in their reading. This might incorporate different kinds of texts, new authors, writing projects, or social action.

Another possible direction of reading work for *Monkey Island* would be to use in reading clubs. Reading a range of books that have strong protagonists might lead to a character work study. Students could create ideas about strong characters using Clay, and Gilly from *The Great Gilly Hopkins,* and Sara-Kate Connolly from *Afternoon of the Elves*, and Roald from *Crazy Lady* and, of course, many more. The students might find ways that these protagonists managed to survive against difficult odds. Another possibility might be to focus on comparing and contrasting these characters.

Toward the end of the school year, this book might be one of many that children read in a study of one essential question. Books impact the way we view the world. How does reading *Monkey Island* affect the way we view the world? Another essential question might be to ask of this book, as of every book, "whose story is being told and whose is left out?" Along the same lines, teachers might ask "is this story fair?". And "How different are people allowed to be in this story?" These questions are designed to help children think about social justice and tolerance in the world.

Book Connections

The Great Gilly Hopkins by Katherine Paterson, *Afternoon of the Elves* by Janet Taylor Lisle, and *Crazy Lady* by Jane Connolly are possibilities for comparisons of main characters.

Genre
Chapter Book

Teaching Uses
Small Group Strategy Instruction; Character Study; Independent Reading; Critique

Monster

Walter Dean Myers

Book Summary

In *Monster*, a sixteen-year-old named Steve Harmon narrates the moral and physical ordeal of standing trial for murder. In the form of a script and a few interspersed journal entries, Steve covers the events surrounding nights at the New York City jail where he is being held, the courtroom proceedings, and the trial's outcome. In flashbacks within the script, he provides scenes from his life in Harlem that help explain what part he took in the crime.

Basic Book Information

This 181-page book is separated into 16 short, titled chapters (seven to fifteen pages each).

Noteworthy Features

Some media- and video-savvy readers will appreciate the innovative format, which combines script and journal entries, but the format may pose some challenges. Scripts, by nature, are more like blueprints than buildings-readers must literally fill in the pictures and flesh out descriptions. In addition, readers may need advance preparation for reading and understanding camera directions such as "zooms," "angles," and "cut-aways."

Monster requires some knowledge about the criminal justice system. Readers accustomed to watching cop shows may know what a courtroom and holding cell look like, what stenographers do in court, what a district attorney does, and what Rikers Island is, but readers without this experience will need background, as the book itself provides very little information.

Also, Steve is said to be a student at "Stuyvesant," but the school is not identified as the elite public high school that it is, nor is Steve identified as a particularly accomplished student. The boy also has a highly sophisticated, dramatic style that may strike some readers as sounding older than 16.

The description of Harlem is brief and stereotypical, and should be balanced with other readings about the neighborhood.

Monster contains subject matter inappropriate for some readers. Steve (the narrator) refers to prison stabbings, beatings, and sexual assaults, and explores a world of vicious young men whose lives consist of imprisonments and who seem to be unable to imagine anything more. Characterization in *Monster* is, with the exception of Steve Harmon, thin. The parents are well-meaning but remain at a distance. The thugs are simply thuggish. The attorneys are generically slick.

Illustrator
Brock Cole

Publisher
Avon, 1980

ISBN
0064407314

TC Level
14

Teaching Ideas

Monster is appropriate for independent reading, and, because it is a script, for reading aloud in small groups. Before beginning the book, students could consider what work goes into reading a script: imagining the appearance of speakers, their speech, settings, and noticing the stage or camera directions. It might be interesting to examine how different students fill in this information differently.

The major questions in *Monster* revolve around the character of Steve Harmon. Because Steve supposedly created the script and provided the journal entries, the reader cannot know whether what he says is true or not. How much of what he says is calculated? Is he using the script and journal to hide from the truth? Does he feel responsible for what his role in the robbery/murder was? Steve (or Myers) offers only snippets of information about his life before the trial, making it difficult to draw conclusions about motivation, actions, or feelings. The ambiguity can be perceived as provocative or frustrating, depending on readers' expectations and points of view.

As a tale of crime and punishment, *Monster* provides many topics of discussion. For example, students can collect evidence of Steve's guilt or innocence and try to determine what motivated his actions. Students may also want to consider why Meyers wrote the book in the structure and form he did-a question readers can ask of any book they read. In this case: Why a television script and journal entries?

Genre
Short Chapter Book

Teaching Uses
Independent Reading; Book Clubs; Partnerships

A Field Guide to the Classroom Library, Lucy Calkins and the Teachers College Reading and Writing Project, Heinemann, ©2002 Teachers College, Columbia University; http://www.heinemann.com/fieldguides

Moonflute

Audre Wood

Book Summary

Firen, a little girl, can't sleep. The moon seems to be calling her outside. Into the mystical summer night she steps, and when she asks the moon to give her sleep back to her, it gives her a flute instead. The music seems to transport her through the clouds and over the countryside to help her look for her sleep.

She visits some frolicking humpback whales who don't have her sleep. She sees some monkeys in the depths of the jungle, but they too don't have her sleep. As the monkeys comfort their baby, she thinks of her own parents. The flute takes her back to her own bed, faster than a shooting star. Her parents pat her head, and she wants to show them the flute, but it is gone. As she finally closes her eyes, she thanks the moon for giving her sleep and promises to find the flute the next night.

Basic Book Information

The haunting, dreamy, magical pictures match the story's tone exactly, and readers who choose the book because of its illustrations won't be disappointed. Though the pictures are captivating, they don't exactly help readers figure out what is going on, but they do offer some support.

Noteworthy Features

This story is a magical, lyrical dream fantasy. With it comes the challenges inherent in this genre. Children need to suspend their common sense and use their imagination when they are thinking through what they have read. No longer can they think "Does that make sense?" after they read, because the things that happen couldn't happen in the real world. Their answer will likely be "no," even when they have read correctly.

Teaching Ideas

In this genre, some children will take things quite literally. They will believe that the trees become old men and the moon has a voice. It is fine for children to take the text literally, as perhaps it is intended, but it will take imaginative work. It may make the envisionment process more complicated and require a slower reading pace.

Some teachers refer to *Moonflute* in the writing workshop when they are discussing mood. There, some students can see how the language is crafted to create the magical mood, and some may even emulate this in their own writing.

Some children like to talk about the what's and why's of the story. Why did the moon show her the whales and the monkeys? Was it to remind her

A Field Guide to the Classroom Library, Lucy Calkins and the Teachers College Reading and Writing Project, Heinemann, ©2002 Teachers College, Columbia University; http://www.heinemann.com/fieldguides

Illustrator
Don Wood

Publisher
Harcourt Brace Jovanovitch, 1986

ISBN
0152553371

TC Level
10

of her fun and her family as nice images to sleep to? Why did the bell-ringer wake the people up to see a shooting star? Was it because it was so beautiful? Was Firen really asleep and dreaming and only awoke when the bells rang? Is there a message in the book or is it written simply to give us beautiful images to think about (like the moon gave Firen)? Generating questions like this about a text can help children sharpen their thinking. Giving them these questions, on the other hand, is of dubious value.

Book Connections

Another book with this magical, nighttime feel is *When the Moon is Like Lace* illustrated by Barbara Cooney. Some books by Barbara Berger, *Grandfather Twilight* and *When the Sun Rose* have this feel as well. These are both much easier to read than *Moonflute*, yet capture the same tone. It might be interesting for children to see how such a similar tone can be captured with fewer words.

Genre
Picture Book; Fantasy

Teaching Uses
Independent Reading; Book Clubs; Teaching Writing

A Field Guide to the Classroom Library, Lucy Calkins and the Teachers College Reading and Writing Project, Heinemann, ©2002 Teachers College, Columbia University; http://www.heinemann.com/fieldguides

Mrs. Katz and Tush
Patricia Polacco

Book Summary

This book tells the story of how Mrs. Katz and a boy named Larnel become very good friends. Larnel visits Mrs. Katz each day and slowly their friendship grows. Mrs. Katz recounts stories of why she came to this country, when she came, where she came from, and how she met Myron, her husband. She wants Larnel to know what her life was like in her old country. Larnel begins to reveal to Mrs. Katz memories of his family as well.

Everyday she has a fresh baked kugel and a glass of milk set out for Larnel's visits. One day, Larnel stops by Mrs. Katz' house with a little ugly unwanted kitten. Larnel asks if Mrs. Katz will keep the kitten. She has sympathy for the kitten, as it reminds her of her husband's unattractive infancy and she decides to keep it.

Tush, the ugly kitten, slowly transforms into a beautiful, wonderful cat. However, one afternoon, when Mrs. Katz invites Larnel to the cemetary to visit Myron's tomb, they return home to find Tush gone. Mrs. Katz is very upset. Larnel prays to "God" to bring the little cat back to Mrs. Katz. Soon after, Larnel's father and two more neighbors knock on Mrs. Katz's door with the little bubeleh (Tush) in their arms.

Larnel asks Mrs. Katz to allow him to spend Passover dinner with her. He and his family have a feast with Mrs. Katz. They drink red wine and water. They eat bitter herbs, lamb, chicken, and gefilte fish. They eat special matzoh bread. And, the next morning Tush gives birth to four wonderful little kittens!

Basic Book Information

Patricia Polacco has written and illustrated over 30 award winning children's books including, *Chicken Sunday*, *Thank You Mr. Falkner*, *Pink and Say,* and *Thunder Cake.*

Mrs. Katz and Tush received the Jane Adams Peace Association Honor Award in 1993. It has thirty pages. The illustrations provide a wonderful, brilliant, vivid image of Mrs. Katz's world. The story is told from Mrs. Katz's point of view in the form of a narrative. It also includes dialogue between the two main characters.

Noteworthy Features

This book is based on a story of friendship among people of different races. The author, Patricia Polacco, knows how important it is for children to learn and understand cultural differences among people. She's also reminding readers that we cannot judge a book by its cover. The kitten was an unwanted ugly cat, but she soon grew up to be an enchanted beauty.

The bright illustrations from this text can empower students with a new

Illustrator
Patricia Polacco

Publisher
Dell

ISBN
0440409365

language to relate similar things from their own experiences. This book can lure early readers into their own idiosyncrasies. Children will often question their identity and where they belong in our society. In addition, pupils will also question themselves about relationships they have with people of different races.

Even though the two families in this book were different in social, religious, and ethnic background they came together as one to honor the observed holiday of the Jewish religion and heritage.

Teaching Ideas

This picture book provides concrete evidence that "the hatred sometimes engendered by racial and religious differences is overpowered by the love of people who recognize their common humanity."

This book can be used to explore the relationship between the elderly and the young. Larnel learned so much from Mrs. Katz. She was a wonderful storyteller and she told him many stories about her country and her Jewish heritage. He, in turn, gave his companionship and love to the very lonely Mrs. Katz.

Genre
Picture Book

Teaching Uses
Read Aloud; Independent Reading; Book Clubs; Critique

Mufaro's Beautiful Daughters: An African Tale

John Steptoe

Book Summary

In this Caldecott award-winner, two sisters, one mean-spirited and the other kind-hearted, go before the king to see if he will take either one as his wife. The king has magical powers and has seen the cruelty of the first sister and the generosity of the second, so he chooses her the second sister who becomes queen, while the other sister becomes a servant.

Basic Book Information

This large-format book is about thirty pages long, and at most, there are four paragraphs on each page.

Noteworthy Features

The gorgeous and haunting pictures draw children to it everywhere that it is showcased. Usually no other enticement is necessary.

The basic pattern of this tale is like many fairy tales from around the world, and without a doubt, those who have read many tales may find this one easier to understand than those readers who haven't. Predictably, there is good sister and a bad one. The good one works hard, is thoughtful and is self-sacrificing, while the bad one is ambitious, self-serving, and two-faced. In the end, the good one marries the king while the bad one must serve her. Readers who know this pattern will be able to mentally cheer and boo for the characters while reading, and can feel the suspense building as the bad sister disobeys the warnings given to her by magic creatures. What horrible fate will befall her?

Teaching Ideas

For readers unfamiliar to them, the three African names, Mufaro, Nyasha, and Manyara can be a bit confusing, and some readers get the two sisters a bit mixed-up in the beginning. If readers stop to check if the behavior they read about matches the "bad" sister or "good" sister, they can self-correct. Before reading the book, it may also be useful for students to see what the names mean in the Shona language (before title page); the meanings should help kids keep the names straight. Of course there are many other ways to keep characters straight from note-taking to re-reading.

Illustrator
John Steptoe

Publisher
Lorthop, Lee & Shepard Books, 1987

ISBN
0688040454

TC Level
11

One part of the book that gives some readers difficulty is when the father tells the two girls that he wishes them to offer themselves to the king, and Manyara deviously tries to be the only one to offer herself. She speaks sweetly about why it would make Nyasha happier not to go, but undoubtedly she is scheming to have less competition before the king. Some children don't see her deceit, and instead think that she has had a change of heart and is trying to be nice. In a read aloud, the teacher can make the sister's deceit more clear with tone and expression or even stopping to talk about it. If reading independently, some children may only realize this at the end of the book, when the pattern doesn't feel right, and then they will need to re-read the book. Was Manyara intending to get ahead of her sister by appearing to be nice, or was she really trying to be nice? Readers will have to decide.

Was Manyara deceitful to her sister in every case? When Manyara goes in to present herself to the king, she comes out screaming and begging her sister not to enter as there is a terrible beast within. When Nyasha does enter, she sees only her gentle, garden snake. Did Manyara see this same small snake and lie to keep her sister from seeing the king since she herself was rejected, or did the king take on a different more frightening form to punish the cruel Manyara? Children interested in that question can gather textual evidence to support their opinions on that, or other, topics. If children center on it themselves, this question's ambiguity may make it better for discussion, either in a book club or among partners.

As always, children may go on from purely enjoying the story to analyzing and interpreting it. What messages does the story contain? Most readers may end up deciding that the main message of the story is that you will reap what you sow: if you are good you will be rewarded, if you are bad, you will be thwarted. Some readers, however, look beyond this message and ask, is it really a reward to be married off to a man you hardly know? And is it really a punishment to serve someone good and true? Readers may ask further questions of the book. What kind of a father is Mufaro, that he doesn't even know the true nature of his daughters, doesn't consult them about whether they wish to be married, and takes such pride in their beauty, despite the fact that one of them is unkind? Is it right that he should remain un-judged in the story? Children invariably have many things to discuss and analyze in this beautiful book.

Book Connections

Putting this book alongside other fairy tales usually makes for a good foundation for a conversation. John Steptoe has written numerous other books for young readers and putting a selection of these together would also make for an interesting study.

Genre

Fairy and Folk Tale; Picture Book

A Field Guide to the Classroom Library, Lucy Calkins and the Teachers College Reading and Writing Project, Heinemann, ©2002 Teachers College, Columbia University; http://www.heinemann.com/fieldguides

Teaching Uses
Independent Reading; Read Aloud; Small Group Strategy Instruction; Critique

My Louisiana Sky

Kimberly Willis Holt

Book Summary

This book is historical fiction and is set in the 1950s in rural Louisiana. Tiger's mother and father are deemed simple by all the people in Saitter and as Tiger enters the summer between sixth and seventh grade, she starts to feel shame and the stigma of her parents. Tiger wants to be normal and to fit in with all the other kids. When Tiger's granny dies, life is turned upside down and Tiger thinks she wants to move away to live with her sophisticated aunt in Baton Rouge. This is a book about identity, finding it, and accepting it, and even celebrating it. How do you fit in with your peers while at the same time remain your parents' child?

Basic Book Information

This is Kimberly Willis Holt's first book, and is recommended by the *Boston Globe*, Home Book Honor, and Top 10 American Library Association Best Books for Young Readers. *My Louisiana Sky* contains 20 chapters without titles, and 200 pages.

Noteworthy Features

The book's setting in rural Louisiana in the 1950s dramatically shapes the plotline and characters in this story. In that historical setting, some people were marginalized, as is evident from passages such as this one: "I guess that in some ways Momma and Daddy were like Otis and Magnolia and even that colored boy outside the drugstore. They were just too different to some folks."

The author emphasizes the discrimination that occurs against the mentally impaired, as well as the racism that was present in 1950s Louisiana. It is written about in a matter-of-fact way that may make readers sit up and protest against the norms and beliefs of the story's characters.

Teaching Ideas

There is much use in the text of 1950s culture and culture icons like Elvis, Audrey Hepburn, and TV. Students will benefit from knowing a bit about these cultural landmarks, but a teacher might help them think how their own cultural icons could easily fit into these pieces.

Tiger's name is different from the norm and so is she. Many readers will be drawn to her because she is within their reach. She is dissatisfied with her looks because she has red hair and is skinny. Tiger is also dissatisfied with her family because they don't have money and she has to wear handmade clothes. She has suddenly become an adolescent and is very confused. Tiger

Publisher
Dell Yearling, 1998

ISBN
0440415705

TC Level
13

A Field Guide to the Classroom Library, Lucy Calkins and the Teachers College Reading and Writing Project, Heinemann, ©2002 Teachers College, Columbia University; http://www.heinemann.com/fieldguides

is an articulate adolescent, and therefore some adolescent readers will find that her voice appropriately echoes their own.

The author's intent is to represent the pervasive and permissive racism of the South, and clearly, to initiate protests in readers. Teachers might encourage the readers to pick up on this throughout the story. If a reader doesn't seem to be noticing the racism of the era, a teacher might want to draw that reader's attention to Otis and Minnie, saying, "we're probably going to the colored school to meet the book mobile there," or to mention Otis and his family standing at the back of the church during Granny's funeral. Likewise, a teacher will want to call a reader's attention to the scene in which Magnolia can't come inside the beauty shop and also the one in which she must sit at the back of the Greyhound bus. There is even some depiction of sexism when Shorty says, "I'll be darned if I'm going to take orders from an idiot or a woman."

This book would also be good for character study, especially of female adolescent characters.

Genre
Historical Fiction; Chapter Book

Teaching Uses
Independent Reading; Book Clubs; Read Aloud; Critique

A Field Guide to the Classroom Library, Lucy Calkins and the Teachers College Reading and Writing Project, Heinemann, ©2002 Teachers College, Columbia University; http://www.heinemann.com/fieldguides

My Side of the Mountain

Jean Craighead George

Book Summary

Tired of living in a crowded apartment with eight brothers and sisters in New York City, Sam Gribley runs away to live off the land in the Catskill Mountains. *My Side of the Mountain* tells the story of how Sam survives on his own in the wilderness. With great courage and ingenuity, Sam learns how to trap and fish, build a fire with flint and steel, and forage for edible plants and nuts. For a home, Sam hollows out a giant hemlock tree. When his city clothes wear out, he sews himself a deerskin suit, lined with rabbit fur.

After a few months on his own, Sam captures a baby falcon that he names Frightful. Sam raises Frightful and trains her to catch prey. More than a source of food, though, Frightful serves as Sam's companion. As time passes, Sam also comes to know the animals who live in the forest around him, like the weasel he names The Baron and a pack of noisy chickadees.

Except for occasional hikers and campers and hunters during hunting season, Sam rarely sees anyone in the forest. One day he comes across a man sleeping near his tree home. Lonely for human companionship at this point, Sam befriends the man, who he calls Bando because he at first thought the man was a college professor. Bando spends several days with Sam and comes back at Christmas to visit him. Also at Christmas, Sam's father comes to visit, the first time the reader meets any of Sam's family.

The following spring, nearly a year after Sam first entered the wilderness, his father shows up again, this time with the entire family in tow, coming to stay for good. As Sam's mother puts it, "If he doesn't want to come home, then we will bring home to him."

Basic Book Information

My Side of the Mountain is a Newbery honor book, an ALA Notable Book, and winner of the Hans Christian Andersen International Award. The Horn Book calls it "An extraordinary book . . . it will be read year after year." *My Side of the Mountain*, 177 pages long, is told through Sam's journal entries. Each chapter is given a specific and detailed title that tells exactly what it will be about. For example, "I Hole Up in a Snowstorm," "I Find Many Useful Plants," "Frightful Learns Her ABC's." Chapter one begins in December, with the first snowstorm of the year. After that, the story jumps back to May, when Sam first ran away and then continues in chronological fashion. Throughout the book, there are rough sketches by the author, illustrating the story. There are also some sketches, presumably done by Sam, that demonstrate something he has made, like his bed or Frightful's perch.

Illustrator
Jean Craighead George

Publisher
Puffin Books, 1959

ISBN
0140348107

TC Level
13

Noteworthy Features

Because the story is told through Sam's journal, it is in first person. While the sentence structure is not difficult to follow, the vocabulary is full of descriptions of plants, trees, and animals and Sam's methods of finding and cooking them, such as the following description. "The inner bark of the poplar tree tasted like wheat kernels, and so I dried as much as I could and powdered it into flour." The author has a profound knowledge of nature, which is exhibited throughout the book. Although an excellent opportunity for children to learn much about the great outdoors and how to survive in it, some children may find the many descriptions tedious, especially when compared to today's fast-paced videos and computer games.

Although Sam's recounting of his adventures is fairly straightforward, his dry sense of humor does shine through, along with his sense of wonder at all that surrounds him. Consider his description of a winter day. "With these (acorn pancakes) as a bracer for the day, Frightful and I would stamp out into the snow and reel down the mountain."

Teaching Ideas

One aspect of the book that some readers might find troublesome is that Sam's parents allow him to run away and don't come after him until seven months have passed. Students could discuss why the author would allow that to happen and whether such a thing is likely to occur in real life.

For a child who loves the outdoors or who has a rich fantasy life, this book is full of hints and tips for surviving in the wilderness, and for creating one's own nook in the woods. Many readers have been inspired by Sam's story, and have made lists and notes from this book of all they, too, might try. The directions for corn pancakes, traps, snares, fishing rods, and home-sewn clothes are all here, and the best response to this book is to set it down and head outdoors.

Some children, of course, do not have ready access to the woods, but this book can feed a child's fantasy just as a story of medieval knights would. Sam is a great student of the woods, and a reader of this book may want to follow his footsteps, studying edible plants and medicinal herbs. Many of the most compelling points of the story, however, are centered around Frightful, the peregrine falcon, and some students may be prompted to research these magnificent and endangered birds.

There is a movie of this book, and a reader may want to watch it to compare and contrast the book and the movie.

Book Connections

This book is one of many boy-alone-in-the-wilderness stories, including Paulsen's *Hatchet* (and also *The Haymeadow*), Mowat's *Lost in the Barrens*, Defoe's *Robinson Crusoe*, and Taylor's *The Cay*. Readers will enjoy thinking between these beloved texts and may, also, pause to wonder why this is such a popular theme.

A Field Guide to the Classroom Library, Lucy Calkins and the Teachers College Reading and Writing Project, Heinemann, ©2002 Teachers College, Columbia University; http://www.heinemann.com/fieldguides

Genre
Chapter Book

Teaching Uses
Independent Reading; Book Clubs

Nightjohn

Gary Paulsen

Book Summary

In this short and intense novel, Sarny, a 12-year-old girl slave, tells the story of *Nightjohn*. Sarny meets Nightjohn when he is brought to the Waller plantation. At the plantation, Nightjohn secretly teaches Sarny how to read. When the Wallers find out, they whip him badly and soon thereafter, he escapes, returning only at the end of the story-to finish teaching Sarny and the others (who are still on the plantation) to read.

Sarney, A Life Remembered is a sequel to *Nightjohn*, and is less graphic and more accessible for children reading on their own.

Basic Book Information

This is a first-person fictional narrative written in dialect. It is very short with eight very short chapters (each less than nine brief pages). The chapters are untitled, except for "The Cast," which is titled in words and is written in Sarny's handwriting. The first seven chapters are written in present tense; the final chapter is only a page long and reads almost like an epilogue or a reflection.

The book is graphic. The slaves are described as eating out of troughs, sleeping in pallets. Two brutal beatings are described in *Nightjohn*.

In some places, Paulsen includes curse words and derogatory words used at that time to describe African Americans. For example, one slave is described as being "good for breeding." Often, slaves are referred to as "niggers." In reading this aloud, some teachers don't want to say words like "nigger" and "hell" that appear in the book. You might want to pause and say to children, "Back in these times, this is how Whites spoke to Blacks. Though this is not respectful language, it is a part of America's history and the writer is using it to help you understand what the earliest African Americans went through."

Noteworthy Features

A teacher we respect spoke to Gary Paulsen recently, telling him, "In my opinion, this is the best book ever written about slavery." Paulsen responded by telling this teacher that the book is based on true slave narratives.

It would be hard to write a book like this without basing it on true historical documents. The truth of what slaves endured is beyond anyone's imagination and this book brings the truth home in a way which leaves us silent.

A Field Guide to the Classroom Library, Lucy Calkins and the Teachers College Reading and Writing Project, Heinemann, ©2002 Teachers College, Columbia University; http://www.heinemann.com/fieldguides

Publisher
Dell Publishing

ISBN
0440219361

TC Level
13

Disney has made a movie of *Nightjohn*, but it is absolutely different (and not as good as) the book.

Teaching Ideas

Mortimer Adler once said, "Some people think a great book is one you can't put down, but me, I think a good book is one you must put down-to muse over, to question, to reflect on." This is the sort of book that deserves to be read aloud and this asks of teachers, who are willing, to put the book down and to talk. Teachers will need to pause to discuss the graphic, painful sections such as this description of a typical day for the slaves on Waller's plantation:

"Two times a day at the wooden trough-that's how we eat. Mornings they pour buttermilk down the trough and we dip cornbread in it and sometimes pieces of pork fat. We take turns on a calabash gourd for a dipper to get all the milk out except the little ones don't always get much of a turn and have to lick the bottom of the trough when it's done. For midday meal the field hands-men and women both, 'less a woman is a breeder in her last month, then she can work the yard-each carry a piece of cornbread and pork fat or meat with them. When the sun is high overhead they stop long enough to stand and eat the bread and fat. They don't get to sit or rest. Even do they have to do their business they dig a hole with their hoe and do it standing and cover it with dirt and get back to work." (29-30)

Teachers may also want to put down the book and talk about the extraordinary struggle these characters made in order to learn to read. Some readers feel that the point of the book is summed up on pages 57 and 58 when Paulsen helps all of us reflect on the power and poignancy of reading:

"Why does it matter? Mammy leaned against the wall. She had one hand on the logs, one on her cheek. Tired. "Why do that to these young ones? To Sarny here. If they learn to read-"

"And write."

"And write, it's just grief for them. Longtime grief. They find what they don't have, can't have. It ain't good to know that. It eats at you then-to know it and not have it."

"They have to be able to write," John said. Voice pushing. He stood and reached out one hand with long fingers and touched mammy on the forehead. It was almost like he be kissing her with his fingers. Soft. Touch like black cotton in the dark. "They have to read and write. We all have to read and write so we can write about this-what they doing to us. It has to be written."

Mammy she turned and went back to her mat on the floor. Moving quiet, not looking back. She settled next to the young ones and John he turned to me and he say:

"Next is *C*."

So, why does Nightjohn come back to the plantation? Because "it has to be written."

Genre
Short Chapter Book

A Field Guide to the Classroom Library, Lucy Calkins and the Teachers College Reading and Writing Project, Heinemann, ©2002 Teachers College, Columbia University; http://www.heinemann.com/fieldguides

Teaching Uses
Read Aloud; Book Clubs; Content Area Study

Otherwise Known as Sheila the Great

Judy Blume

Book Summary

When city slicker Sheila Tubman learns that she will be spending the summer in the suburbs, she is not sure if she likes the idea. Although it would be nice to live in a house for a while, the particular house Sheila's family is planning to stay in comes with a dog and Sheila is petrified of dogs. Her parents also tell her that she has to take swimming lessons and pass a big swim test by the end of the summer. Sheila's problem is that she's deathly afraid of swimming.

Sheila reluctantly goes to Tarrytown, New York, with her family and she meets her new neighbor, a girl her age named Mouse Ellis. Mouse quickly becomes Sheila's new best friend and the two of them enroll in summer camp. Sheila and Mouse do everything together, but Sheila doesn't have the courage to tell her friend how scared she is of dogs and swimming. Sheila is nervous to confide to her friend because Sheila has a reputation to uphold of being a smart, witty, and fearless fifth grader. Sheila also meets other friends through Mouse and together they spend the summer playing and having sleep-overs.

Some of Sheila's friends find Sheila to be bossy and they are turned off with how perfect Sheila makes herself out to be. But inside, Sheila is just as nervous as any of her friends would be about their fears. Sheila's problem is that she doesn't open up to her friends and admit to them when she is scared about something. One example of this is Sheila's idea to run a camp newspaper. Sheila has wonderful ideas for her Update, but she wants to do this all on her own-that way, she'll get all credit. Sheila learns the hard way that it would be much easier and more fun if she collaborated with her friends. She ends up spending one whole week at camp driving herself crazy with all of the aspects of running a newsletter. After instances like this, Sheila learns that she has the strength to face her fears, whether it is asking for help, learning to swim, or learning to like dogs. By the end of the summer, Sheila has made some wonderful friendships and learned a lot about who she is as a person.

Basic Book Information

This book has sixteen chapters with approximately four to five pages per chapter. *Otherwise Known as Sheila the Great* is narrated in the first person by Sheila Tubman. The book is a traditional narrative as it moves chronologically along without any flashbacks or time changes in the story. This book predominately takes place in a white upper/middle class suburban town. Though *Sheila* was written in 1972, the language and

Publisher
Yearling, 1972

ISBN
0440467012

TC Level
10

expressions do not seem dated, save for a reference to a mimeograph and a slam book, but the author explains both terms.

Noteworthy Features

Sheila confides her fears to the reader often, and this helps the reader to understand where she is coming from when she does such things as trying to run a newsletter on her own. Though Sheila acts cocky at times, the reader understands and forgives her because Sheila does these things out of fear. Sheila is a great narrator because she is good at details, and keeps the reader informed of everything they should know about her family, Mouse, and other friends. Sheila's experience as the new kid in town is something many readers can relate to as there are times when most of us have felt like an outsider. This book teaches the importance of facing our fears and suggests it can be a great adventure to meet new people, and go to new places.

Teaching Ideas

As teachers, we need to consider what growth in reading entails once children can read. In part, our children become stronger readers as they read more and more difficult books with relative ease and comprehension. But growth in reading can also develop a more complex, layered, and nuanced understanding of texts. Interestingly enough, as children develop more complex ways to think about the characters and events in texts, they learn to think in more complex ways about the characters and events in their lives.

For example, a less mature reader (and friend) sees a character (or a friend) doing something and responds, "I would *never* do that." A *more* sophisticated reader (and friend) might, instead, see the same actions and think, "She must really have been hurt in order to act like that," or "I wouldn't act that way but then, I've never been in her situation. I wonder if I *had*, would I act similarly?" Then, too, a less mature reader might see characters (and people) as all good or all bad; a more sophisticated reader could understand there are problems in the best of us, and sterling qualities in people others see as all-bad.

This book can provide teachers with an opportunity to coach readers to try to understand why characters sometimes act in problematic ways. Sheila *is* bossy and cocky, but the reader who has the imagination and generosity to walk a bit in Sheila's shoes will understand that Sheila acts as she does out of fears and insecurities.

This book can also remind readers that in books, as in life, *all* people have stories to tell. So often readers attend only to the main character's comings and goings. In this story, readers only glimpse the neighbor, Peter Hatcher, who becomes the lead character in Blume's other books. This is a lesson. What other characters have we, as readers, ignored? What might *their* stories say?

Book Connections

Sheila is a minor character in some of Blume's other books, including *Tales of a Fourth Grade Nothing, SuperFudge,* and *Fudge-A-Mania.* Readers who liked Sheila's story might enjoy reading some of Blume's other books, including *Are You There, God? It's Me, Margaret, Blubber, Freckle Juice, Starring Sally J. Freedman as Herself,* and *Iggie's House.*

Genre
Chapter Book

Teaching Uses
Character Study; Independent Reading

A Field Guide to the Classroom Library, Lucy Calkins and the Teachers College Reading and Writing Project, Heinemann, ©2002 Teachers College, Columbia University; http://www.heinemann.com/fieldguides

Over Sea, Under Stone

Susan Cooper

Book Summary

The first volume in Cooper's *Dark Is Rising* series, *Over Sea, Under Stone* is actually a mystery with links to the marvelous-the defining characteristic of high fantasy. The story, a contemporary one, takes place in Cornwall, a maritime county in the extreme southwestern part of England. This particular corner of England is one in which many artifacts of early inhabitants have been discovered, a fact that allows Cooper to introduce a sense of mystery and myth. The three Drew children discover an old manuscript in the attic of the house in which their family is vacationing. Helped by Merriman Lyon and their Great Uncle Merry, the children must unlock the mystery of the manuscript and find the treasure it speaks of, a chalice or grail that once belonged to King Arthur and his knights.

Throughout their adventure they are pursued by sinister characters who also seek the chalice. Great Uncle Merry, or Gumerry as the children call him, can protect them but cannot provide answers to the puzzles they face; that is the children's role-to solve the mystery and find the grail. The children are successful in finding the grail. To save it from capture by The Dark, they toss it to Merriman who awaits them in a boat off shore. He catches the chalice but a tube that rested inside it falls into the water. This accident allows Cooper to link the action in this volume with that of the third one of the series, *Greenwitch*.

Basic Book Information

The books in this series are challenging for readers. *Over Sea, Under Stone* is 243 pages long. The story is divided into fourteen chapters and a short epilogue. Most of the chapters are made up of more than seventeen pages although several have only ten or eleven pages. Each untitled chapter ends with the promise of something ahead-something that makes the reader want to continue reading.

This book is the introduction to an award-winning series. Cooper inserts reminders of King Arthur and his knights throughout the series. She also uses the time-honored fantasy theme of the "quest" but in *Over Sea, Under Stone*, she stops short at introducing magic, secondary worlds, or other motifs of the genre. Because it lacks some of the excessive elements of fantasy, it can capture the imagination and ease the reader into the demanding genre of fantasy, a genre that requires the reader to "suspend disbelief."

Over Sea, Under Stone begins the five-book sequence. In it, we meet three of the four principal characters, all young. We also meet their mentor, Merriman Lyon, who plays a significant role throughout the series. The second book, *The Dark Is Rising*, introduces the fourth young character, Will Stanton. In the third book, the four young people are united. The

Series
Dark Is Rising

Publisher
Simon Schuster, 1989

ISBN
0020427859

TC Level
14

A Field Guide to the Classroom Library, Lucy Calkins and the Teachers College Reading and Writing Project, Heinemann, ©2002 Teachers College, Columbia University; http://www.heinemann.com/fieldguides

series, based loosely on Arthurian legend and the myths of Wales, focuses on the struggle between good and evil. It is an excellent example of "high" fantasy, containing all the elements that are characteristic of that genre. Only some of these elements are introduced in *Over Sea, Under Stone*. In the second book of the series, the sense of journey or quest is combined with other high fantasy elements-moving across thresholds into earlier times and different worlds. Only then is the reader truly introduced to the sense of the marvelous and the timelessness of characters.

Noteworthy Features

Cooper uses a syntax that is challenging, sentences that are long, some with as many as thirty-five words, and vocabulary that is unfamiliar to many younger readers. There are uncommon words like "quay" and "vicarage," place names like" Trewissick" "St. Austell" and "Kemare Head," and British spellings like "harbour" and "grey."

The story is told in third person and switches point of view among the three young characters, Jane, Simon, and Barnaby. The story moves forward in time, with only one exception-when the two boys are separated from Jane. We first follow the boys and then return to Jane and what she was doing outside during the same passage of time.

The story is filled with foreshadowing that provides tension in the story. Readers need to be alert to the inferences suggested as well as to the ties to Arthurian legend. While Cooper does include characters who speak in the Cornish dialect, their roles are not significant. The brief encounters with this dialect should not prove too difficult for a preteen or teenage reader.

Teaching Ideas

Students will better appreciate this story if they understand the typical structure and elements of the fantasy genre: the major role children play in the plot, the secondary role of adults, the quest, or search one finds (particularly in so-called "high" fantasy), and the struggle between good and evil. Although passage between two worlds or time slips and magical elements are not present in this story, they do occur in the four sequels. Since Merriman symbolizes Arthur's mentor and teacher, students would benefit from a brief review of Arthurian legend and of the role the magician played in that legend. A reader might use post-it notes or a notebook to mark those events that tie into the genre of fantasy. For example, in Chapter 1, we learn that Barnaby is an aficianado of King Arthur, Great Uncle Merry was "ancient as the hills" and had "gone on a quest." Such hints can be found throughout the story.

Teachers might use this book as an invitation to encourage readers to consider the setting-to put the book down for a few minutes and read a related text that might amplify the historical or physical setting. This story is set in Cornwall, so students might learn something about that part of the United Kingdom to better prepare them for the events that take place there. Teachers might also want to point out the British spelling used for some words as well as the name of the British currency, the pound.

Because this book is dense, students might want to discuss it after each chapter. They may note the foreshadowing and predict what such hints might lead to. For example, students may notice Barnaby's link to King Arthur, the references to Gumerry's "larger than life" size, and Jane's sense of uneasiness at seeing the yacht.

Students might keep a two-column record of the important events in the story. In the left-hand column, students can note what happened and in the right-hand column, write their reflections. For example, in reflecting on Chapter 3, when the family first met Mr. Withers, one student wrote in the left-hand column that Jane didn't like him "but didn't know why." In the right-hand column, she wrote: "Maybe he was too neat, too nice. Maybe it was the way he thought. Or maybe he was evil."

In Chapter 6, a reference is made to the book's title. It might be interesting to speculate about its possible meanings. It certainly is the key to the mystery of the place the grail has been hidden.

In Chapter 12, Hastings makes the statement: "You will find, Barnaby Drew, that the dark will always come and always win." Students may look at such sweeping statements and discuss the underlying philosophies they represent. Does this hold true in *Over Sea, Under Stone*?

If children have read other children's fantasies like *Harry Potter* and *The Lion, the Witch and the Wardrobe,* students might compare these books and note which philosophies hold true. They may even connect the struggle between good and evil to the *Star Wars* movies. Finally, students might connect such philosophies to life in general.

Book Connections

Students who enjoy this book will want to continue the series of adventures that follow in *The Dark Is Rising, Greenwitch, The Grey King,* and *Silver on the Tree*. They might also enjoy reading such popular fantasies as *Harry Potter* or *Brian Jacques Tales from Redwall: The Bellmaker, Martin the Warrior, Salamandastron.* Other books that contain similar adventures are *The Diamond in The Window* by Jane Langton, and Edward Eager's *Tales of Magic: Half Magic, Knight's Castle, The Time Garden,* and *Magic by the Lake.*

Genre
Chapter Book; Fantasy

Teaching Uses
Independent Reading; Small Group Strategy Instruction

A Field Guide to the Classroom Library, Lucy Calkins and the Teachers College Reading and Writing Project, Heinemann, ©2002 Teachers College, Columbia University; http://www.heinemann.com/fieldguides

Redwall

Brian Jacques

Book Summary

The bumbling mouse Matthias, an orphan who is a novice at the Abbey of Redwall discovers that a large army headed by the dreaded rat Cluny the Scourge is heading to conquer Redwall. As the forces of Cluny grow nearer, Matthias sets out on an epic quest to discover the famous sword of Martin the Warrior, the founder of Redwall. This search leads him to the very darkest basements of the Abbey to a terrifying climb to its roof, and even into the pit of a powerful Adder with hypnotizing eyes. The search is a race against time, because without the Sword the peaceful mice of Redwall Abby have little chance against Cluny's hordes. This book has the well-known fantasy theme of good versus evil, which will ring familiar chords with readers of the *Harry Potter* series. The book also follows the theme of the weak rising up and overcoming the strong.

Series
Redwall

Publisher
Philomel Books, 1986

ISBN
0399214240

TC Level
14

Basic Book Information

Redwall is the lynch pin in a series of at least thirteen books. The entire series is named after this book. These books are popular among fourth through sixth grade audiences. Brian Jacques, a British writer, has just written his first book outside the *Redwall* series, *Castaways of the Flying Dutchman*.

The Redwall series is unusual because there is no single character that connects all the books. Instead, they are linked by a shared setting: an imaginary world inhabited by mice, rats, stoats, badgers, ferrets, and otters. This world centers around the medieval Redwall Abbey, a huge red-stone structure that houses the Brotherhood of Mice-a pacifistic order that was founded years ago by the legendary Martin the Warrior, who overthrew the vicious wild cats who ruled a castle that once stood in the same location as Redwall Abbey. The world also centers around Salamnadastron, a hollowed-out mountain stronghold-ruled by a dynasty of Badger Lords and filled with a garrison of Hares (rabbits). Between the Abbey and the mountain there are swamps, a mountain range, plains, and several rivers.

Brian Jacques is a master at creating characters that take on meaning to the reader. Many readers become emotionally attached the mother-like Badgers, and bumbling, yet trustworthy mice of Redwall, and readers come to hate Cluny as he uses attempts to use terror tactics against the indefatigable inhabitants of Redwall.

Redwall has 351 pages, with fifteen chapters, and thre "books." Instead of titles, the chapters have small black and white pictures that hint at either the character the chapter will follow, or the setting in which the chapter will take place. There are no other illustrations except for the map at the front of the book. The book jumps from character to character, sometimes following Cluny the Scourge, and sometimes leaping to Matthias, then to the Abbot.

The subjects and settings change, as do the narrators. These can change between and within chapters.

Noteworthy Features

One problem that some readers have with the *Redwall* series is that animals speak dialects and these can be hard to read. The dialect of the Moles sounds like this; *"Yurr moles, get outten th' loight. Let'n um dog at bone thurr"* or the easier dialect of the Sparrows; *"What for ratworm want sentry?"* War beak shrugged her wings. *"Him catch Abbey, not know we come to catch back."* Any one of these sentences is not vital to the story, but obviously to read this series, readers need to begin to acclimate to the dialects in the text.

Teaching Ideas

If a teacher wants to introduce students to *Redwall*, she might begin with reading aloud even just a portion of the first chapter, as it introduces the reader to Matthias, and some important characters in his life. The teacher might nudge a child who is reading the book to make a chart of the characters, because throughout the books there are well over 50 separate encounters with new creatures, which may cause some readers to lose track. Reading aloud will also give students a taste of the dialects.

Students may choose to follow a single character's development throughout the book, using post-it notes to mark places in the text where events occur or which a character changes. The teacher may want to talk to readers and find out how the characters have changed. If a reader is following Matthias, the reader may notice that Matthias slowly grows to be more and more like his perception of Martin the Warrior. Once this student has finished the book, the teacher may encourage the student to go back over the text, and try to find places where Matthias takes on Martin the Warrior's attributes. Then the student could try and discover *why* Matthias grew to be like Martin.

It would also be worthwhile to compare *Redwall* to the *Harry Potter* books. Both are fantasy, but *Harry Potter* is more of a modern work then *Redwall*, and *Redwall* is closer to an epic fantasy then *Harry Potter*. The two series share battles between good and evil, which belong almost exclusively to fantasy, and both include characters that mature from a very childish start.

Book Connections

Redwall is, in part, another version of the famed *Harry Potter* books, with the same sense of adventure, and magic. But it is more similar to "adult" fantasy (such as the works of Robert Jordan and Terry Goodkind) than *Harry Potter*. Brain Jacques' other well known books in this series include *Mossflower*, *Martin the Warrior*, and *Marlfox*.

Genre
Fantasy; Chapter Book

A Field Guide to the Classroom Library, Lucy Calkins and the Teachers College Reading and Writing Project, Heinemann, ©2002 Teachers College, Columbia University; http://www.heinemann.com/fieldguides

Teaching Uses
Independent Reading; Book Clubs

Roll of Thunder, Hear My Cry

Mildred Taylor

Book Summary

Roll of Thunder, Hear My Cry is a story about an African American family in the 1930s. The story is centered around the Logan family and its children as they confront numerous circumstances throughout the year. For readers, their encounters shed light on what life was like for both whites and blacks in the segregated South. The book explores different themes ranging from race, socioeconomic class, and family through these lenses we see how the family approaches different scenarios.

Basic Book Information

A well-deserved 1977 Newbery Award winning book, *Roll of Thunder, Hear My Cry* is a wonderful example of historical fiction. Mildred Taylor takes the reader on a journey exploring what many African American families experienced post Reconstruction. The book is 276 pages long. Readers will understand the complex issues that Taylor explores in the novel best if they know something about what it was like in America during the 1930s. Students may need background knowledge regarding the economic turmoil that many Americans experienced as well as race relations, sharecropping, and so on.

Two books follow this one in the series: *Let the Circle be Unbroken* and *Road to Memphis*. There is also a prequel, *The Land*.

Noteworthy Features

As readers we get an inside look into race relations both between whites and blacks as well as within one's race. For example, we see that because the Logans own land they are in a different economic class than other African American families that have no choice but to be sharecroppers. We see what life was like for African Americans prior to the *Brown v. Board of Education* decision and what walking to school was like prior to schools being allocated funds to provide their students with a bus. But one of the most noteworthy features of the text is its examination of how the Logans overcome numerous problems in the face of adversity. As readers we see how they stay together and persevere against all odds.

Teaching Ideas

Teachers who confer with a child who is reading this book may want to talk about Cassie, the narrator. Throughout the story, Cassie attempts to make sense of her world. She does not quite understand the implications of confronting the store owner while in Strawberrys. Later asked to apologize to Miz Lillian Jean for walking into her, she is angered by what she perceives

A Field Guide to the Classroom Library, Lucy Calkins and the Teachers College Reading and Writing Project, Heinemann, ©2002 Teachers College, Columbia University; http://www.heinemann.com/fieldguides

Series
Logan Family

Publisher
Penguin, 1976

ISBN
014034893X

TC Level
14

Big Ma's support for this gesture. At the time she is not aware of the implications her actions could have.

Both Jeremy and Cassie are strong characters and readers should be able to generate theories about these characters and their strengths. We look to Jeremy as an example of what it might have been like to be between two worlds: the white world that he chooses not to be a part of and the black world that is weary of his motives. He is an example of what it means to go against the societal norm when he chooses to walk to school as opposed to ride the bus.

This book can also be used to discuss Reconstruction and what it meant to own land in the 1930s. A reader may want to do some non-fiction reading and inquire into the economic issues of sharecropping. Alternatively, students might research 40 acres and a Mule or find out what slaves were promised after the Civil War.

Book Connections

Two books follow this one in the series: *Let the Circle be Unbroken* and *Road to Memphis*. There is also a prequel, *The Land*.

Genre
Chapter Book

Teaching Uses
Read Aloud; Independent Reading; Partnerships; Content Area Study

A Field Guide to the Classroom Library, Lucy Calkins and the Teachers College Reading and Writing Project, Heinemann, ©2002 Teachers College, Columbia University; http://www.heinemann.com/fieldguides

Salsa Stories

Lulu Delacre

Book Summary

Like Laura Esquival in *Like Water for Chocolate*, Delacre weaves food and fiction to create a story that is as rich and sweet as a dish of Helado de Coco. The story opens with salsa music, conversation, and heavenly cooking aromas stirring through the house at young Carmen Teresa's New Year's party. It is a festive event that has gathered family and friends from many different Latin American countries.

Dona Josephina, a neighbor, comes to the party with a gift for young Carmen-a journal. The people at the party decide that this journal should be a place where they can record stories of their youth. Each partygoer, in turn, tells a separate tale of when they were growing up in their native countries. When they are done, Carmen notices that food is a common element in each of their stories. In the end, she decides to use her journal for a family and friends' cookbook. Every food that was mentioned in their stories is recorded in a recipe. The whole party is happy with her idea.

Basic Book Information

Lulu Delacre is the author of such award winning books as: *Golden Tales: Myth, Legends and Folktales from Latin America*; *Arroz con Leche: Popular Songs and Rhymes from Latin America*; and the Pura Belpre Award Honor Book, *The Bossy Gallito* (text by Lucia M. Gonzalez). Ms. Delacre is also the creator of all the artwork in *Salsa Stories*. She uses linocuts, which are carved on pieces of linoleum as reliefs and then stamped on to the page.

Noteworthy Features

Salsa Stories is set up as three books in one. The first chapter (New Year's Day) and the last chapter (Carmen Teresa's Gift) are set in the present. These chapters set the scene of the New Year's Eve party and the gift. They are written from Carmen's perspective. All other chapters are written from the perspectives of the various partygoers. Each partygoer tells their story in first person. Finally, the back of the book contains all of the actual recipes from the food mentioned in each of the stories. This is Carmen Teresa's "Book of Fantastic Family Recipes."

There are many shifts in time, place, and narrator. Every time someone at the party tells their story it is set in their respective country and told in first person. This may be confusing for some readers.

While the linocuts provide beautiful images about the events of the story

Illustrator
Lulu Delacre

Publisher
Scholastic Press, 2000

ISBN
0590631187

TC Level
12

(on approximately every tenth page) they do not provide much support for the text. The linocuts are akin to folk art. They give the book a "homespun" quality that matches the book's mood.

Salsa Stories gives readers a flavor of different Latin American cultures. It uses many phrases from the Spanish language, especially when characters speak to one another. There are also many references to different dishes from Latin America. Children who do not speak Spanish are provided support for unfamiliar words. Often, there is a direct translation in the proceeding sentence (e.g.," '*Mama que pasa*?' I asked sleepily 'What's going on?'"). Delacre uses italics whenever she uses Spanish in the text. Readers can be taught that they should pay special attention to italics and try to figure out what it means from the context and/or glossary. Children can look at the table of contents to gain further reinforcement of the book's structure. All stories, which are not told by Carmen, have a second line added in their title that tell readers who is the narrator.

Teaching Ideas

In *Salsa Stories,* it may be difficult for some readers to keep track of who is narrating. The characters are only briefly introduced in the first chapter and then, they go on to tell their own stories. At the beginning of each of these chapters the title tells who the speaker is (i.e., Abuelita's story). By pointing out the family tree that is provided on the second page, readers will be able to cross-reference the narrator's name with their place on the family tree. In a read aloud, it may be helpful to have the family tree on chart paper and refer to it at the start of each chapter. The family tree will also help students know the chronology of the stories. For example, Abuelita's (her grandmother's) story about her childhood will have taken place many years before Carmen's tia's (her aunt's) story. Teachers can discuss how the narrators on each level of the family tree will be telling stories that are roughly from about the same time in history because they share a generation.

If read in conjunction with a writer's workshop, readers may be interested in emulating both the style and structure of *Salsa Stories.* It can be wonderful when kids realize that they can blend fiction and non-fiction into a single text. Some may even attempt to combine English and another language in their pieces, using *Salsa Stories* as a model. Others may let the language of cooking and eating tell their story as Delacre does (e.g., "Our house stirs with laughter and chatter as guests arrive, one by one.").

After a read aloud of *Salsa Stories*, it may be helpful to ask about how the book is set up and why. Are these three separate stories or one larger story? Some will say that the first and last chapters provide us with the story behind the journal.

Genre
Chapter Book

Teaching Uses
Whole Group Instruction; Book Clubs; Read Aloud; Independent Reading;
Teaching Writing

Sang Spell

Phyllis Reynolds Naylor

Book Summary

Grieving over the loss of his mother, Josh, a high-school student, is hitchhiking cross-country to reluctantly begin a new life with his aunt. He hitches a ride with the wrong person and finds himself beaten up, mugged, and dumped on the side of a desolate, Appalachian road. Hurt and desperate, Josh accepts a ride from a woman driving a horse and cart. She takes him to her primitive village Canara, which is seemingly cut-off from time. Modern amenities, including electricity, do not exist in Canara, and the inhabitants claim to belong to a long lost group of people called Melungeons. They graciously accept Josh into their community, treat his injuries, and put him to work with other villagers digging ginseng root (which they call "sang"). When Josh asks the way out of the village, he is given only cryptic, puzzling answers. Panicked that he might actually be a prisoner, rather than a guest, Josh is determined to find his way back to civilization. As he tries all different paths of escape, the paths only lead back to Canara. When Josh finally resigns himself to being part of the village, joins in their rituals and celebrations, he finds that his grief and despair over his life begin to heal. His loyalty to the Melungeons is tested, and at last, Josh is free to leave.

Basic Book Information

This book is 212 pages long with 17 chapters of an average length of eleven pages. It has a setting that will be unfamiliar to many readers-a spooky mysterious town in mountains, where people live like it's far in the past.

Noteworthy Features

This story moves chronologically through time and is always seen through the main character's eyes. It is rather scary at times, slightly reminiscent of Stephen King's less flashy but realistic stories that take place in a world almost, but not quite, like our own.

One of the most interesting features of this text is the author's incorporation of the Melungeons into the story. The Melungeons, of Portuguese, Turkish, and African descent, existed as a group in sixteenth century America and claimed to have inhabited America prior to other Europeans. Persecuted for these claims, they were forced out of main American society and virtually vanished from history.

Teaching Ideas

Readers could read this book simply as an action-filled mystery, taking the story only on its surface level, but Naylor is trying to do more than just write

Publisher
Aladdin Paperbacks, 1998

ISBN
0689820062

TC Level
14

something interesting, and the challenge lies in moving readers beyond a literal understanding and into the bigger picture. This story should push readers thinking. As readers move through the text they should be asking, "What is the author trying to say?" or "What does the author want me to understand?"

Since this *is* a mystery, there is a danger that readers will lean toward pure prediction when developing ideas and theories about *Sang Spell*. However, real issues are raised about people's characters, their development, and self-knowledge. Readers could be encouraged to make inferences and grow theories about Josh's character as he is placed in the various situations and settings. How does he change? How does he grow? What do his actions say about how he is feeling?

Setting is crucial to contributing to the message of this book, and it is particularly interesting to think about why the author chose to leave Josh in a primitive village, a village inhabited by a people who "are every man who has ever lost his way, every race who has ever lost its compass." What does this group have in common with Josh? What does he have to learn from them? How does this setting echo the message of the book? And why did the author choose to have the villagers digging up roots? How does that contribute to the story?

This book is *meant* to occasionally be confusing both to the reader and the main character. For example, when Josh is asking his way out of Canara, he receives only a riddle in response-"To go forward, you must go back." The challenge posed both to readers and to Josh is to solve this puzzle. Readers might want to talk with a partner about the significance of this answer-what it could mean, why it was so confusing, and how does it relate to how Josh personally feels?

Book Connections

Among the Hidden by Margaret Peterson Haddix is another text that could be read alongside this one.

Genre
Mystery; Chapter Book

Teaching Uses
Independent Reading; Book Clubs; Interpretation

Scorpions
Walter Dean Myers

Book Summary

Twelve-year-old Jamal is a loser. Tormented by his sister Sassy, worried about by his mother, let down by Randy, his older brother who is in jail, he leads a miserable life. Not even in school does he find a haven. His teachers harass or ignore him; his classmates pick on him. Only his friend, Tito, stands by Jamal. Like so many preteens, he acts moment-to-moment without thinking of the consequences.

When Randy sends a message home through Mack, recently released from prison, that $2000 will buy him an appeal, Jamal feels obligated to help raise the money. The second part of the message from Randy, that Jamal should take over the Scorpions (the gang that Randy headed before being arrested), is what sends Jamal on the journey he should not take. As leader of the Scorpions, Jamal will have access to money that will get Randy released. But Jamal knows that trouble lies ahead, especially when Mack gives him a gun.

Tito advises Jamal to stay away from Mack but Jamal doesn't listen. Jamal keeps his meetings secret from Mama and hides the gun, but when Dwayne, the class bully, wants to fight him, Jamal decides to take the gun to school to scare Dwayne. It works. Now Jamal is afraid Dwayne will tell on him and when that happens, he denies having the gun. It doesn't stop there. Jamal and Tito, fascinated by the power of a gun, decide to "try it out." When a woman sees the two boys shooting the gun, they run into Tito's house to hide the weapon. The next day Tito shows up at Jamal's house to report that his grandmother found the gun and threw him out. Then his brother Randy gets stabbed in prison. Jamal knows he needs to act quickly to raise the needed money.

Intending to give up the gun, he makes a deal with the Scorpions to raise the money. But older boys have taken Randy's place in the Scorpions. Tito and Jamal head out to a meeting with them, Tito carrying the gun. When the two older boys start to beat Jamal up, Tito shoots them. The result: one dead, the other, patched up and arrested on possession of drugs. And Tito-good, sensitive, loyal Tito-is messed up. Unable to deal with his guilt, Tito confesses to his crime and is sent to Puerto Rico to live with his father. Jamal is transferred to a school for problem kids. There are no winners.

Basic Book Information

Walter Dean Myers is a popular award-winning author. *Scorpions* is not only a Newbery honor book, but also an ALA Notable Children's book, recommended for reluctant readers. The story is told in twenty sequential chapters and 216 pages. The chapters are numbered, not titled. Common words make up the vocabulary Myers uses, with the characters speaking in

Publisher
Harper Collins, 1988

ISBN
0064406237

TC Level
14

A Field Guide to the Classroom Library, Lucy Calkins and the Teachers College Reading and Writing Project, Heinemann, ©2002 Teachers College, Columbia University; http://www.heinemann.com/fieldguides

the dialect heard on the streets of Harlem or Detroit or Camden, New Jersey.

Noteworthy Features

The sentence structure for the most part is simple and easy to follow. When time moves forward and the scene changes within a chapter, the text is separated by a space with a centered "bullet" accenting the change. There is a great deal of dialogue which not only moves the action forward but fills pages with "white space" that tends to make reading easier. There are a few flashbacks-one that describes the crime that sent Randy to prison, and another that reviews the times his "absent father" arrived home only to make promises and take off again.

While the story is told in third person, we view the action through the eyes of Jamal, the main character. The sentence structure is varied yet easy to follow. The only difficulty the reader might have is following dialogue between two people. Myers tends to leave off most of the markers that would identify the speaker, leaving only alternating indentations to carry out that task, with an occasional "he said/she said" as a reminder.

Certain expressions-"catch you on my 'chine again I'm gonna mess you up bad"-for example, may puzzle less able readers not familiar with the dialect, but Myers includes enough detail so that the meaning becomes clear.

Myers also gives only some of the facts. We learn on the first page, for example, that Jamal and Sassy's mother is late coming home, but the reason is not revealed until the end of the chapter. Even that information requires an inference.

While there is little humor in this very sad story, there are lighter moments, as when Tito and Jamal, down by the docks, fantasize about the kind of yachts they will own some day. Or when Jamal, at the end, promises to sail down to Puerto Rico on his yacht to visit Tito. Nevertheless, it is a somber book.

Teaching Ideas

This story, so well told, deserves to be in classrooms, but especially when it is read in suburban schools, the book could be introduced with a discussion that warns against stereotyping. Yes, it could happen and it has happened-but not to everyone who lives in a city. It is the story of one boy, not an entire population. Events, similar to those that Myers describes, might happen to anyone in any situation who does not consider the consequences.

Although Jamal made many mistakes, he also tried to do the right thing. Teachers might encourage a student to keep track of actions that were positive or those that were negative. In Chapter 1, Jamal fixes supper for his little sister, but soon after, he acts in less than generous ways to her. More importantly, readers could try to empathize with Jamal's struggles, to understand his motivations, to consider how things might have worked out better for him.

It is important that readers appreciate the character Jamal and his lack of self-esteem. In the story, we learn how others-his sister Sassy, his teachers, and classmate, Dwayne-do little to make Jamal feel good about himself. But Jamal himself contributes to this lack of esteem. Teachers might encourage a reader to use post-it notes or to make notations in a reading log to note examples of the actions that make Jamal think less of himself. They might also note what Jamal did to invite those actions, such as not doing his homework. After reading a larger section of the book, the reader might consider how much others contributed to Jamal's foolish actions and what part he himself played.

Neither Tito nor Jamal had a trial, yet they were involved in a shooting. When a group of students has read the book, the group could hold a mock trial. One or more students could prepare a defense for Tito, while another group could act as prosecutor. The defense team could be responsible for preparing a list of facts that would prove Tito's innocence, while the prosecuting team could list all the actions that would prove him guilty.

Teachers might encourage a reader to reflect on whether Jamal's parents were carrying out their responsibilities, basing arguments on details the reader learned in the reading about Jamal's mother and about his father.

Is Walter Dean Myers telling us a story or a parable that carries a lesson for the reader? This is a question a teacher might ask a student to mull over after he or she has read the book, perhaps through a log entry. What parallels can students find in their own lives? The consequences may not be as dire, but students can perhaps relate Jamal's foolish acts to some they have themselves committed-which, in hindsight, they know were foolish.

Book Connections

Myers has written on this theme before, as have others. Teachers might recommend such books as Myers's *Monster* or *Somewhere in the Darkness*. They might also want to have students compare *Scorpions* with Hinton's *The Outsiders*.

Genre
Chapter Book

Teaching Uses
Read Aloud; Book Clubs; Independent Reading; Critique; Interpretation

A Field Guide to the Classroom Library, Lucy Calkins and the Teachers College Reading and Writing Project, Heinemann, ©2002 Teachers College, Columbia University; http://www.heinemann.com/fieldguides

Seedfolks

Paul Fleischman

Book Summary

There are thirteen short chapters in this book, each telling the story of a small city garden from another person's point of view. A little girl named Kim starts a garden in what was once an abandoned lot, filled with garbage and debris. She wants to be a gardener like her dead father. The garden started by Kim is discovered one by one by other dwellers of this city block who yearn for community and connection to the world of nature. Together, the gardeners create their own paradise and learn to care for each other despite their differences.

Basic Book Information

This 69-page book has thirteen chapters, ranging from three to five pages in length. Each chapter is a story told by a new character, from their own point of view. Chapter by chapter the garden and the book grow to contain many characters. Although this is a story about a garden, the book contains no sense of special garden language. Almost any reader will be able to understand how the garden develops and grows.

Noteworthy Features

Each chapter is told from a different point of view, and all are titled with the name of that character speaking in the first person. Because of the use of the first person point of view, the reader can usually easily connect to that character. Each of the characters has a different ethnic background, and all characters have experienced some form of prejudice due to their nationality, skin color, religion, gender, or age. Each of the characters mentions their experience of prejudice, in varying degrees of detail. *Seedfolks* celebrates the diversity of its characters and allows readers time to reflect upon the bias all people encounter.

Teaching Ideas

One upper grade teacher decided to use several of the chapters from *Seedfolks* as short texts to be used for writing a response to literature. Because there are many chapters that are connected yet stand alone, *Seedfolks* was a particularly good choice. He began his study of the literature by reading the first chapter, "Kim," aloud to his class. The class had previously done some work on point of view, and so the students were familiar with listening and reading to figure out who is telling the story and what impact that makes on the story itself. Since the class was already on this train of thought, it was natural for the students to pick up on the strong voice that Fleischman uses with "Kim" (and in turn with all the chapters).

A Field Guide to the Classroom Library, Lucy Calkins and the Teachers College Reading and Writing Project, Heinemann, ©2002 Teachers College, Columbia University; http://www.heinemann.com/fieldguides

Illustrator
Judy Pedersen

Publisher
Harper Trophy, 1997

ISBN
0064472078

TC Level
13

After reading the story aloud, the class listed all the places they could find that showed something about the narrator's personality. They noticed formal language and, and they listed places in the text where they found it.

The next day the teacher read the next chapter, "Ana," aloud to his class. And again, they created a chart (it became another column on the chart started the day before) of what they learned from the narrator's voice. This time the students noticed that the narrator is less proper with her speech, and seems suspicious. The teacher then pointed out that the class had started to use their observations to make guesses at what the characters, the narrators are really like. The class had started to assemble pieces of a puzzle to figure out what is going on in this book, and also to figure out what Paul Fleischman wanted them to know. The students continued this work in small groups. The groups then shared their observations with the rest of the class, which offered constructive criticism (guided by the teacher) of how well they proved their points.

Book Connections

This is one of many books that could be examined as part of a discussion on point of view. Others include any of Avi's *Poppy* series, the *Redwall* books, *Salsa Stories*, and so on.

Genre
Short Chapter Book

Teaching Uses
Whole Group Instruction; Small Group Strategy Instruction

A Field Guide to the Classroom Library, Lucy Calkins and the Teachers College Reading and Writing Project, Heinemann, ©2002 Teachers College, Columbia University; http://www.heinemann.com/fieldguides

Sisters in Strength: American Women Who Made a Difference

Yona Zeldis McDonough

Book Summary

Herein lie the simple, well-told stories of the life and adventures and achievements of eleven women: Pocahontas, Harriet Tubman, Elizabeth Cady Stanton, and Susan B. Anthony, Clara Barton, Emily Dickinson, Mary Cassatt, Helen Keller, Eleanor Roosevelt, Amelia Earhart, and Margaret Mead. Together the inspiring stories of these woman show the many different ways that a person can be great, and the many different conditions and backgrounds from which a great person can grow. The stories are not only of the accomplishments of the women, but also give a taste for their personalities and motivations.

Basic Book Information

This colorfully painted, Nonfiction picture book has about fifty pages. In it are the life stories of eleven American heroines. The one-paragraph introduction (which is not at all critical to the book) pays tribute to all the women not chosen to be subjects in this text. Each story opens with a quotation from or about the woman described and is about three pages long, illustrated along the borders and with a full-page painting to open. The paintings are in the lavishly colored folk art style. The table of contents in the beginning of the book makes it easy to find the story of any one particular woman. The book ends with a time line recording important events in the lives of all of the women in the book.

Noteworthy Features

This book is of the finest quality. The two page sketches of the women are not told as biographies only, but also as stories to listen to for their suspense and interesting details. The writing is spare but precise. The stories start not with the year of each woman's birth as in many biographies, but with an intriguing hook, for example, the woman deeply involved in some unusual task or the woman as a baby being watched by her parents. Any unusual terms within the text are explained immediately. Details from the women's lives, and even odd quotations from them make the stories vivid and lively.

The bright and lively pictures are bound to attract and hold readers. The childlike style of the art may also inspire young illustrators as well.

Teaching Ideas

These short biographies, vignettes even, are perfect to read aloud. The

Illustrator
Malcah Zeldis

Publisher
Henry Holt and Company, 2000

ISBN
0805061209

TC Level
11; 12; 13

A Field Guide to the Classroom Library, Lucy Calkins and the Teachers College Reading and Writing Project, Heinemann, ©2002 Teachers College, Columbia University; http://www.heinemann.com/fieldguides

contents of each is inspiring and interesting. Once a teacher has read one or two portraits aloud, the book could be selected by several readers to read on their own. Teachers would need to emphasize the fact that great people, men and women can inspire other great people, both men and women. Books about great women are not only for other women.

The table of contents makes the book an easy one to use as a reference as well. It would be especially interesting to put this book alongside some of the biographies in the series of *A Picturebook of Helen Keller*, [or Eleanor Roosevelt, or Harriet Tubman] to let readers compare and contrast the information and the impressions they receive about the woman from the two different texts. It may be a surprise to readers to see the way the same facts can be put together to create different impressions.

This book also provides examples of ways that children can write about other people. Since each essay in the book is short, children can easily use these sketches as examples for their own writing of biography, or even autobiography.

Readers in partnerships or clubs may be interested in following the thread of what makes these women "great.". For some, it may be that they saw social injustices and tried to address them. For others, it may be that they overcame obstacles to achieve goals. It may be useful to readers to "look back" on this book following their reading of it, to draw conclusions about these women and their impact on society.

Genre
Nonfiction; Picture Book

Teaching Uses
Reading and Writing Nonfiction; Independent Reading; Teaching Writing

A Field Guide to the Classroom Library, Lucy Calkins and the Teachers College Reading and Writing Project, Heinemann, ©2002 Teachers College, Columbia University; http://www.heinemann.com/fieldguides

Snowflake Bentley

Jacqueline Briggs Martin

Book Summary

Wilson Bentley loved snow. He even examined snowflakes as a child in the deep cold blizzards of winter. By the time he was a young man, he had decided he would find a way to photograph them so that everyone could see their uniqueness and beauty. Some people have never understood his passion, and some, even today admire and learn from his life, his work, and his photographs.

Basic Book Information

The Caldecott Medal graces the cover of this beautiful, down-to-earth, Nonfiction book. The woodcuts inside it give the feel of rustic 1920s Vermont, and warmth and appeal of the pictures may be what makes it makes it generally a popular choice even when the children know nothing of its story.

Noteworthy Features

The text is constructed in an unusual way. The story is told along the bottoms or tops of the pages, and then black-bordered columns on the sides of certain pages offer more information about the part of the story on those pages. The information on the sidebars does tend to make some readers lose the thread of the "main" story if they stop to read them while on the first read. Since the information is related to the main story and usually a bit more complicated, it might be most appropriate for readers to ignore them the first time through and instead, read them the second time they read the book. Perhaps it is easier to follow if the reader imagines, or really hears, two voices, one for the "main" text, and one for the marginal text. It might also be appropriate for readers to decide for themselves how to handle the two kinds of reading, and for readers to discuss and compare their conclusions.

Teaching Ideas

The messages of this story often make it a perfect choice for us to read aloud to children at the beginning of the year when they are learning or relearning how to use writers notebooks. Wilson's appreciation for an ordinary thing like snow-his passion for studying it and learning even more about it than anyone had ever known, his finding the patterns and beauty in its deepest structure-can inspire and serve as examples for children trying to learn how to observe, feel passionate about, study, and see patterns in the things in their own lives that may at first seem ordinary.

Illustrator
Mary Azarian

Publisher
Houghton Mifflin, 1998

ISBN
0395861624

TC Level
10

A Field Guide to the Classroom Library, Lucy Calkins and the Teachers College Reading and Writing Project, Heinemann, ©2002 Teachers College, Columbia University; http://www.heinemann.com/fieldguides

Genre
Nonfiction; Picture Book

Teaching Uses
Reading and Writing Nonfiction; Content Area Study; Independent
Reading; Read Aloud; Teaching Writing

Soldier's Heart

Gary Paulsen

Book Summary

This is the gripping account of what Charles Goddard, and soldiers like him, endured in the Civil War. Fifteen-year-old Charley enlisted with the First Minnesota Volunteers. We follow him as he develops from a raw recruit to a soldier who fights in the Battle of Bull Run and Gettysburg. Through Charley's eyes, Paulsen provides gripping descriptions, not only of the fighting and the dying but also of the character's inner thoughts and reactions to these events.

The war is finally over and Charley, now twenty-one years old, returns home wounded. We leave him resting next to the river, a Confederate pistol in his hand, the trigger cocked. But Paulsen tells us: "He eased the hammer down with his thumb and laid the pistol back on the rock next to the cheese and then sat, listening to the ripple of the river, watching the water go by, thinking of all the pretty things." It is for the reader to decide what Charley did next. Actually, from the author's note that follows, we learn the answer when Paulsen tells us that Charles Goddard died at the age of twenty-three.

Basic Book Information

An undersized, 102-page book, sentence length varies from an occasional one-sentence paragraph to sentences made up of only three words. The syntax is not complex, however, and even the longer sentences are easily processed. There are twenty-one lines per page as opposed to the usual thirty. This format, along with the action in the text, makes the book a "page-turner," attractive to the reluctant reader.

The book is divided into ten chapters, each describing an episode in Charley's Civil War experience, from his training in Fort Snelling, Minnesota, through four battles of the war and finally to his return home. A map preceding the table of contents traces Charley's journey from Fort Snelling and marks the four battles in which Charley took part. Most of the chapter titles indicate the contents of the chapter.

The only dramatic jump in time is from the Battle of Gettysburg, in 1964 when Charley is wounded-mortally, as he believes, to June, 1867, which begins: "He could remember all the sweet things when it started...." Paulsen's action-packed writing makes his many books popular with pre-teens and younger teenagers. He has written three Newbery honor books. One of them, *Hatchet*, is on the list of required reading for many sixth grade classes.

Noteworthy Features

Paulsen tells us in his author's note that the story, although fictionalized in parts, is a factual account of a Union soldier's experience. Charles Goddard

Publisher
Bantam Doubleday Dell, 1998

ISBN
0385324987

TC Level
13

did exist and did fight in the Civil War. The text, told in third person, draws occasionally from the dialect of a mid-nineteenth century Minnesotan: "Charley didn't figure to miss it or it would have near on a thousand men when it was full." Paulsen also includes necessary technical details: "He snapped three caps on the nipple to burn any oil out of the nipple hole, then took a cartridge from his cartridge box, bit the end of the paper off, poured the powder down the bore..." and some dialogue: "Better hold up there, Gamecock," that may be challenging to some sixth grade readers. But Paulsen's vivid descriptions, pacing, and word craft will motivate even the reluctant reader. Paulsen also uses an occasional four-letter word, expressed in the heat of battle.

Teaching Ideas

This book provides a realistic account of two significant battles of the Civil War. It would be an excellent selection to include in the study of that period of our country's history. Students who have learned the reasons for this war, and the part slavery played in it will have the necessary prior knowledge. Teachers might, after reviewing these facts, ask students to reflect on the information on the cover and predict the subject of this book. They might also study the table of contents and discuss the period the story spans as well as some of the topics the chapter titles indicate.

Because of the graphic nature of the text, teachers might prefer to use this book as a read aloud. While listening, students might use a two-column note-taking strategy. In the first column, they record the facts they learn. In the second column they indicate the thoughts and/or questions they have about that fact. The teacher might also have students use the strategy Stephanie Harvey recommends to categorize the "thinking." In addition to the codes that indicate Keene's text-to-text (TT), text-to-self (TS), text-to-world (TW) connections, students might use Q for questions the text raises, I for inferences they must make, *Imp* for important facts in the text and *Char* for information about character development.

Teachers might ask students to contrast the details on the battles of Bull Run and Gettysburg with the information their textbooks provide on these battles. Students might write a paragraph indicating which of the two accounts is better, defending their position with details from either or both texts.

We know from the author's note what actually happened to Charles Goddard. Before reading that part, teachers might ask students to speculate about the ending of Chapter 10, reflecting on the question: What is Gary Paulsen telling us here about what Charley did? They might discuss this question, using the "say something" approach (turn to a classmate and tell him/her what they think). Teachers might follow this discussion by reading the author's note to determine whether their prediction was correct.

Gary Paulsen' skill as a wordsmith provides and opportunity for students to "read like writers" and study his craft. For example, teachers might ask students to study his descriptions, such as the one about the uniform Charley wore: "There was a pair of black pants that were so short his calves showed, a pair of gray socks and a black felt hat. That was the uniform he received to go for a soldier the socks and pants were stout but the hat was cheap and with the first little sprinkle it sagged around his head and drooped over his face." Teachers might ask students to find examples in such text that illustrate how Paulsen "shows," that is, creates word pictures with specific nouns, strong verbs, and sparse use of adjectives and adverbs.

Book Connections

For further information on battles of the Civil War, teachers might consider Paul Fleischman's *Bull Run*, vignettes of people who took part in or witnessed the battle (available on audiotape as well as in print) or Patricia Lee Gauch's *Thunder at Gettysburg*. *My Brother Sam is Dead* by Collier and Collier and Avi's *The Fighting Ground* are two books about the Revolutionary War with young boys as main characters.

Genre
Chapter Book; Historical Fiction; Biography

Teaching Uses
Teaching Writing; Read Aloud; Content Area Study

A Field Guide to the Classroom Library, Lucy Calkins and the Teachers College Reading and Writing Project, Heinemann, ©2002 Teachers College, Columbia University; http://www.heinemann.com/fieldguides

Some of the Kinder Planets

Tim Wynne-Jones

Book Summary

This is a collection of short stories about children to whom strange and unusual things happen. Each story includes a fantastical aspect. The stories are quite short, perhaps ten pages long, and they are quirky-complex and dense enough to ignite the response of "Huh?" from children who need to be challenged. For teachers with the courage to muck-about in complex texts and worlds, this can spark grand conversations.

Basic Book Information

Some of the Kinder Planets was awarded the 1993 Governor General's Award for Children's Literature in Canada.

Noteworthy Features

First of all, the acknowledgments alone are worth looking at, "A crow likes to steal shiny bits of the world and hoard them away in its nest: pull tabs, gum wrappers, bread ties, rings. Writers are like crows. They call their nests stories." Then he goes on to say, "I would like to thank all the people from whom I have stolen stuff to make the stories in this collection, but, unfortunately, I can't remember them all."

TimWynne-Jones is a comedian writer. Some people say that Canadian and British writers both write more actively, daring readers more than many American writers. This may or may not be a justifiable stereotype but certainly this book expects an active reader.

The book includes nine stories. Teachers have especially loved "The Night of the Pomegranate," which is a less unusual and complex story than the others. Teachers have also loved "Save the Moon for Kerdy Dickus," a story that requires multiple and close readings. The title comes from a line that the narrator is told by Ky. This line is a refrain that comes up several times throughout the Ky's story. The story tells of a family-the Mori familythat lives in the country. Two days before Xmas, there is a bad ice storm and a young man comes to their door asking for help. He believes he has been transported to another planet because he is from the sticks and their house is very modern, equipped with fax machines and so forth. When this stranger who thinks he has been abducted by Martians finally leaves, he thinks they say, "Save the moon for Kirdy [ED: Kerdy?]Dickus," which is what he tells to the National Enquirer. In reality, they had said, "Save some room for turkey dinner."

Teaching Ideas

This is not a book to be read cover-to-cover. It is a good source of texts that teachers might duplicate (with permission of course) and invite students to study together. In book groups, guided reading groups or conceivably, whole-class work, students could learn the benefits of close and repeated reading.

A teacher might want to introduce any one of these texts by talking about strategies for reading difficult texts. We could tell proficient readers that all of us sometimes encounter hard texts and that sometimes, when readers approach dense texts, it can help to vary their speed. There are reasons to almost gun-it through a text, trying to hold onto some through-line and to gleam a sense of the whole story.

Some readers will ask to stop often and to talk about even very literal questions like who are the characters, where this is happening, and what's going on? These questions will require textual reference and research-and therein lies the heart and the power of these stories.

Genre
Short Story Anthology; Fantasy

Teaching Uses
Whole Group Instruction; Small Group Strategy Instruction; Read Aloud

A Field Guide to the Classroom Library, Lucy Calkins and the Teachers College Reading and Writing Project, Heinemann, ©2002 Teachers College, Columbia University; http://www.heinemann.com/fieldguides

Sort of Forever

Sally Warner

Book Summary

This is the story of friendship between two twelve-year-olds, Cady and Nana. The text examines how Cady deals with Nana's cancer and imminent death.

Basic Book Information

This book has 136 pages and thirteen chapters of an average length of ten pages. This book contains difficult issues-Cady has to deal with illness, decline, and death of friend Nana from cancer.

Noteworthy Features

A third-person narrator tells this story from Cady's perspective. Much of the story is internal; Cady goes through a whole range of emotions dealing with Nana's illness and spends a lot of time thinking about her friend and their friendship. It is often an emotional story, which helps keep the reader invested.

The text provides little challenge, but the subject matter is very serious. This book is honest about the emotions accompanying a serious illness-anger, resentment, jealousy, love, loss fear-and is therefore an emotional read. It is a book that is written to touch the reader deeply.

Teaching Ideas

Sort of Forever is a good book to read for those who like to read about really important friendships. But it is also a very hard book to read sometimes because Cady, the main character who just finished sixth grade, has a best friend who gets really sick with cancer.

This book is a good one for readers to pick up early in the year, as it is a rather short quick read for many fifth, sixth, and seventh graders. It could be a good read aloud when the class is working on developing theories about books or talking about character growth and change. An independent reader could use it in a reading project of books that have main characters who have to deal with death or main characters who have friendships that go through a lot of stress and change.

Book Connections

Other texts that deal with death of a family member or friend include: *Fig Pudding* by Ralph Fletcher, *Mick Harte Was Here* by Barbara Park (slightly easier reading level),

Bridge to Terebithia by Katherine Paterson (slightly higher reading level,

Publisher

Alfred A. Knopf, Inc., 1998

ISBN

037580207X

TC Level

13

A Field Guide to the Classroom Library, Lucy Calkins and the Teachers College Reading and Writing Project, Heinemann, ©2002 Teachers College, Columbia University; http://www.heinemann.com/fieldguides

older female main character), *Walk Two Moons* by Sharon Creech, *Jericho* by Janet Hickman, and *Toning the Sweep* by Angela Johnson.

Genre
Chapter Book

Teaching Uses
Independent Reading; Read Aloud

A Field Guide to the Classroom Library, Lucy Calkins and the Teachers College Reading and Writing Project, Heinemann, ©2002 Teachers College, Columbia University; http://www.heinemann.com/fieldguides

Speak
Laurie Halse Anderson

Book Summary

This is a story of a girl who is ostracized at school in the fall for calling the police during a party the past summer. Melinda is just entering ninth grade and this is her first year of high school. Her peers believe she called to bust the party, and she has told no one the real reason-she was raped by an upper-classman. She can't find the words to tell anyone this story, and the reader doesn't hear about it until well into the book. Obviously, this is mature subject matter and recommended for older middle school readers.

Basic Book Information

Speak is a realistic fiction novel of 198 pages written in the first person. The book is divided into four sections, each titled for the four marking periods at the high school where the main character, Melinda, attends ninth grade. These four major sections are further divided into very short sections with headings: FRIENDS, OUR FEARLESS LEADER, FIZZ ED, MY LIFE AS A SPY. These sections are very short, generally two or three pages.

Noteworthy Features

Speak is a very interesting book-it's written in first person by Melinda, a ninth-grader. She has a very strong voice in the book-you have to look for her sarcasm and humor because it comes through a lot, but is often understated. Melinda is ostracized by her classmates and former friends, but the reader won't immediately find out why. This is a book driven by a character and her thoughts in addition to the mystery of why people at her school are so angry at her.

Melinda is a very engaging narrator. Middle school students generally are very interested and entertained by her. The narrative voice is so strong and compelling and the story is so powerful that it is a fairly fast read. The subject matter and the details of Melinda's life give fuel to many conversations about character development and change across the story. Melinda is trying to make sense of, and deal with, her life and it's not always very easy for her.

Many of the characters and situations are rather stereotypical and extreme-the school changes its mascot three times during the year and each time the new mascot prompts protests. One of her teachers, who she calls Mr. Neck, is a blatant racist and bigot. The rapist is a football player and he's boorish and not at all remorseful or confused ("You liked it. I think I know what you want."), Melinda's parents are clueless, incompetent, and never around... All of this doesn't negate the interesting and complex character of Melinda, but it is a book which benefits from some discussion of perspective and critique.

Publisher
Farrar Straus Giroux, 1999

ISBN
0374371520

TC Level
13

A Field Guide to the Classroom Library, Lucy Calkins and the Teachers College Reading and Writing Project, Heinemann, ©2002 Teachers College, Columbia University; http://www.heinemann.com/fieldguides

Teaching Ideas

As mentioned above, the rather flat characters and stereotyped situations lend themselves to a study of interpretaion and critique: What is this author saying? Do you, as a reader agree with this message?

Book Connections

Another book that deals with a troubled girl trying to deal with a serious problem in her life is *Kissing Doorknobs* by Terry Spencer Hesser. This book is also written in first person, but seems more narrative than the journal-like quality of *Speak*. Ultimately, obsessive-compulsive disorder (the problem in *Kissing Doorknobs*) and rape (the problem in *Speak*) are different subjects and need to be treated differently in discussion.

Genre
Chapter Book

Teaching Uses
Independent Reading; Interpretation; Critique

A Field Guide to the Classroom Library, Lucy Calkins and the Teachers College Reading and Writing Project, Heinemann, ©2002 Teachers College, Columbia University; http://www.heinemann.com/fieldguides

Spirit of Endurance: The True Story of the Shackleton Expedition to the Antarctic

Jennifer Armstrong

Book Summary

After six long months in the middle of winter, the *Endurance* reaches Antarctica only to be trapped in the ice pack, according to one crew member, "like an almond in the middle of a chocolate bar." The freezing winter months take their toll on *Endurance*-ice squeezing all sides, on October 27th the ship is slowly crushed. It is on that day that Shackleton gives the orders to abandon ship in the middle of the frozen sea.

Shackleton, with a small group of crew members, sets out on the strongest of their lifeboats-the *James Caird* leaving the rest of the crew behind. Shackleton's plan is to get back to the whaling station over 800 miles away on South Georgia Island to find help. The *James Caird* is only 22 feet long and on the most violent ocean in the world. "The twenty-two-foot boat was often covered with ice, and the men had to crawl across the decking while the boat heaved and pitched to chop the ice away."

After an 800 mile, open-boat, seventeen-day journey, Shackleton and his exhausted crew land on the southwest side of South Georgia Island, but the whaling station is on the northeast side! The crew has to trek over jagged mountains and glaciers that had never been crossed before. Shackleton and his crew arrive at the whaling station that houses wild men, in rags and with matted beards. After three unsuccessful attempts, Shackleton finally returns to Elephant Island on a Chilean ship and rescues his crew.

Basic Book Information

Spirit of Endurance ends with a timeline delineating important dates and events beginning with Shackleton's birth and ending with his death. The names of the "Members of the Imperial Trans-Antarctic Expedition" are listed under the timeline, as is a Resource Guide-"Books for Children," and "Books for Adults." Finally, an index with the integral places and people of the expedition is found in the back of the book. *Spirit of Endurance* is an unforgettable story of courage and heroism that is beautifully written and illustrated.

Noteworthy Features

This impressive oversized book chronicles Sir Ernest Shackleton's near catastrophic attempt to lead the first expedition across the Antarctic

Illustrator
William Maughan

Publisher
Crown Publishers, 2000

ISBN
0517800918

TC Level
13; 14; 15

A Field Guide to the Classroom Library, Lucy Calkins and the Teachers College Reading and Writing Project, Heinemann, ©2002 Teachers College, Columbia University; http://www.heinemann.com/fieldguides

continent. It tells of both his and his crew's will to survive against seemingly insurmountable odds. *Spirit of Endurance* incorporates primary documents and maps as well as a number of striking paintings by William Maughan. The paintings and primary documents succeed at enriching the reader's experience.

Although Shackleton failed to cross Antarctica, he persevered against all odds and returned his crew home safely. After serving in World War I, Shackleton returned to Antarctica to pursue his dream. Shackleton died of natural causes on South Georgia Island where a monument now stands in his honor.

Teaching Ideas

Two factors make *Spirit of Endurance* a good candidate for a read aloud: its rather formidable size and the number of different occasions there are for exclamation. It is hard to hear about eating seals and surviving through arctic winters and remain silent. Armstrong's book is an especially nice selection for those teachers guilty of limiting their read aloud fare to *Anne of Green Gables* and *Little House on the Prairie*, for it may represent the kind of robust alternative that many students may have been itching to hear.

Perhaps what is most noteworthy about this historical account is its element of excitement. Jennifer Armstrong tells the story of these explorers as if the drama of their lives mattered- and that is exactly what we ask of our writers. Admittedly, Armstrong has potent stuff with which to work: snowbound arctic explorers. But, so do students-the death of a baby robin, a first hit in Little League. Their lives can be just as compelling.

What makes Armstrong's account work? Part of it is its pace. The author is not afraid to create a moment or two of tranquility during which a less skilled writer might have rushed on to the next climax. Successful writers such as Armstrong linger in between cataclysmic events to describe the landscape: the physical surroundings, for one, but also the emotional tenor of the moment. An example:

"Shackleton replied, 'We shall hang on as long as we can. It is hard enough on the men as it is. Without a ship in which to shelter from these blizzards, and in this continuous cold-' He broke off and paced the cabin. He didn't want to think about it. But as commander of the expedition, Shackleton had to prepare for the worst."

Many students would be apt to discount the importance of such descriptions. "No one will want to hear about what the grass smelled like," they might say. "It doesn't matter if I put in a part about my sister's feelings." But they are wrong. Stories that read well have rhythm, and you can't have explosions if you don't have moments of silence to go with them.

Book Connections

Spirit of Endurance may inspire further reading in the Nonfiction genre. Students can learn further about the continent of Antarctica, Elephant Island, South Georgia Island as well as do research into the first successful expedition across Antarctica. Be advised that the original book from which most of this information is derived, *Endurance*, by Sir Ernest Shackleton.

Genre
Nonfiction; Chapter Book; Picture Book

Teaching Uses
Reading and Writing Nonfiction; Read Aloud; Book Clubs; Partnerships; Content Area Study

Stargirl
Jerry Spinelli

Book Summary

As soon as the new, formerly home-schooled, tenth-grader Stargirl Caraway arrives at Arizona's Mica Area High School, things begin to change. She wears pioneer dresses and kimonos to school, strums a ukulele in the cafeteria, carries around a pet mouse called Cinnamon, laughs when there are no jokes, and dances when there is no music. Everyone in the school is stunned by her. The narrator, Leo Borlock, describes her rise to and subsequent fall from fame and popularity during the school year.

Basic Book Information

This book is 186 pages and divided into 33 chapters that are five to seven pages long. The chapters are not titled. There are no illustrations. The story is told in the first-person narrative, from Leo Borlock's point of view.

Noteworthy Features

The author Jerry Spinelli addresses the theme of adolescent conformity in this novel. Stargirl is most definitely a non-conformist, and because of this, she shakes up the students at Mica Area High School, who all wear the same clothes, talk the same way, eat the same food, and listen to the same music. She is charming, has pure-spirited friendliness, and a penchant for celebrating the achievements of other. These attributes confuse, enchant, and later infuriate the other students.

The setting of the story is a young Arizona city called Mica, established because it is home to the main employer MicaTronics (and reason why people settled there). Since it is set in the desert, there are references throughout the book to plat life, i.e. maricopas. The names of such plant life could be unfamiliar to the reader.

One of the book's characters named Archie is a retired paleontologist, who turns his home into a school every Saturday morning. He shares his knowledge, and bones, from digs that he conducted throughout the American West. Through Archie's discussions with the "Loyal Order of the Stone Bone" the vocabulary can be quite scientific, i.e. prehistoric creodont, paleocene rodent. These scientific references could be new to the reader.

In addition Archie has a fondness for speaking in Spanish to his thirty-foot tall cactus tree named Senior Saguaro, which lives in his backyard. The Spanish conversations he conducts with the plant are rarely translated in English.

Teaching Ideas

Jerry Spinelli writes about a high school microcosm where individuality is

A Field Guide to the Classroom Library, Lucy Calkins and the Teachers College Reading and Writing Project, Heinemann, ©2002 Teachers College, Columbia University; http://www.heinemann.com/fieldguides

Publisher
Alfred A Knopf, 2000

ISBN
0679886370

pitted against conformity. Through personal response work, students can focus on how the text relates to issues in their lives, grow their own angle of vision, really connect to a character, or take a stance and defend it using evidence from the text and the world. When a reader makes personal connections they deepen their understanding of the book.

Stargirl is a book that generates conversation. Whether in partnership, book club or whole class conversations, students can explore ideas/issues through talk using textual references to support their thinking. They could use discussion to help them think more deeply, develop rather than report ideas and to help them revise their own thinking by seeing something in a different way.

This story is told in the first person from Leo's point of view. Interpretive work can focus on what the reader knows and believes about a character (i.e. Stargirl, Leo), and how that knowledge can help us understand what motivates the character and explains their actions.

Jerry Spinelli is the author of more than fifteen books for young readers. An author study could focus on writer's craft, author's intent, thinking across texts, connecting characters between texts and connecting themes.

Book Connections

Many of Jerry Spinelli's books are first-person narrative accounts of a young adult male coming of age, like the character Leo in *Stargirl*. Other Jerry Spinelli books are *Maniac Magee* (Newbery Medal Winner), *Wringer* (Newbery Honor book) and *Crash*.

Genre
Chapter Book

Teaching Uses
Independent Reading; Book Clubs; Partnerships

Stealing Home - The Story of Jackie Robinson

Barry Denenberg

Book Summary

Stealing Home - The Story of Jackie Robinson is the biography of Jackie Robinson, the first black man to play major league baseball. The story recounts Robinson's humble beginnings in California, where his athletic prowess was evident at an early age. At UCLA, he became the first athlete in university history to earn major letters in four different sports during one year.

When Branch Rickey, General Manager of the Brooklyn Dodgers, decided that the time had come to integrate major league baseball, his decision to pick Robinson was not solely based on his impressive athletic skill. Rickey knew that it would take a special man, "he was equally concerned about the player's personality, background, intelligence, and desire to succeed. ...Rickey also needed someone with enough drive and determination to manage to hold[ED: ok?] his head up high despite the abuse." Jackie Robinson was his man. The book recounts the abuse that Robinson had to contend with both on and off the field. His talent and drive made him a trailblazer, who successfully integrated America's favorite past time. At Jackie Robinson's funeral, Jessie Jackson said, "When Jackie Robinson took the field he reminded us of our birthright to be free."

Basic Book Information

Stealing Home - The Story of Jackie Robinson is a Nonfiction, biographical account of
Jackie Robinson's life. The book contains black and white photographs. Barry Denenberg is an award-winning author of other Nonfiction books for children including: *An American Hero: The True Story of Charles A. Lindberg, Voices from Vietnam* and *The True Story of J. Edgar Hoover and the FBI*.

Noteworthy Features

Every chapter contains pictures from Jackie Robinson's life. The photographs help readers picture what Robinson looked like during the period of his life the chapter is discussing. Oftentimes, the pictures depict significant events that the author is writing about on a nearby page. For example, there is a photograph of Branch Rickey and Jackie Robinson signing the contract, which broke the color barrier in major league baseball in the same chapter that discusses that landmark event.

The dialogue throughout the book is very sparse. For the most part, the

Publisher
Scholastic Inc., 1990

ISBN
0590425609

TC Level
11; 12; 13

narrator describes the events of Robinson's life. In his narration of events, the author provides a lot of detail. He often cites names, titles and dates. The abundance of information contained in this book may be overwhelming for some readers. They may find it difficult to retain the details of the story throughout their reading of the 116-page biography.

Children who are not sports' enthusiasts may still enjoy this biography. Jackie Robinson's story is significant to the civil rights movement and American history. There are however, some reference to sports that children may not understand if they are not well-versed on the topic.

Many readers will be shocked by the abusive language and behaviors that Robinson was forced to endure. When Jackie Robinson first begins to play with the Dodgers, he is insulted with names like "nigger," "coon," and "darkie." The Phillies "shouted from the dugout, asking him why he wasn't home cleaning out bathrooms or picking cotton." Children may need to process these upsetting image by talking with their peers or a teacher.

Teaching Ideas

Stealing Home - The Story of Jackie Robinson contains a lot of information about Jackie Robinson's life. Readers who feel that they have to digest all of the details of the story may find a biography such as this overwhelming. It is important for readers to realize that they do not have to remember every piece of information. The story happens in chronological order from birth to death. The dates are not meant to be memorized necessarily, but instead to give readers a general idea of the progression of Robinson's life. Readers who have a hard time doing mental math to figure out his age from the dates can rely on the pictures for support.

In *Stealing Home* the narrator sometimes lets you know what Jackie Robinson was thinking at a specific moment-"Although Jackie appeared calm, he was nervous inside." Readers may wonder how the author could have known such a thing. It is important to realize that biographies are not always strictly factual. Readers may realize that there are times throughout the book when the narrator states things that he could not have gathered from traditional research. A teacher might nudge readers-individually or in partnerships-readers may want to use post-it notes to mark places in the text that deviate from "just the facts." It may be interesting for readers to speculate how the author could gain such information, i.e. is it fictional? Did he interview Robinson? and so on.

Some readers may be surprised at the widespread discrimination and abuse that most black Americans faced less than fifty years ago. For children who do not know about this period of American history, it is important for them to know that the book is historically accurate and that they are not reading a fictional account of someone's life.

Jackie Robinson not only endured prejudice from the white community, but from the Negro American League, too. "It would ruin their (the Negro league's) business" if the major league was integrated. In addition, many whites were against the integration of major league ball for economic reasons. When white major league teams were out of town, the stadium owner rented the space to black teams. The Yankees alone brought in $100,000 in revenue from stadium rental to the Negro league. It is important for readers to realize that not all whites were negative (i.e.,

Branch Rickey was a major crusader for civil rights) and that not all blacks were positive. Also, readers may want to attach post-it notes to all of the forces at work against the integration of baseball to begin to understand the complexity of the situation. The post-it notes can help them go back to those bits of information to think about some more.

Many readers may be surprised to learn that Rickie chose Jackie Robinson for characteristics other than solely his athletic ability. During the course of a character study, a reader may be interested in marking and discussing passages in which Robinson displays these other characteristics.

Book Connections

It may be interesting to read other accounts of Jackie Robinson's life for comparative purposes. Readers may notice that authors tend to focus on different aspects of Jackie Robinson's life or certain biases. Also, they may begin to notice that there is sometimes a discrepancy in the way facts and events are recorded. Reading biographies from different authors may also begin to give readers a more complete picture of Robinson's life.

This book could become part of a child's personal reading project on sports (or even baseball) and race. Alfred Slote's books about the Negro Leagues belong in such a text-set as does *Baseball Saved Us* by Ken Mochizoki and the anthologies about sports players.

Genre
Nonfiction; Biography

Teaching Uses
Reading and Writing Nonfiction; Content Area Study; Independent Reading; Character Study

A Field Guide to the Classroom Library, Lucy Calkins and the Teachers College Reading and Writing Project, Heinemann, ©2002 Teachers College, Columbia University; http://www.heinemann.com/fieldguides

Tangerine
Edward Bloor

Book Summary

Tangerine begins as Paul Fisher and his family are moving from their home in Houston, Texas, to Tangerine County Florida. The family-Mom, Dad, Paul and his older brother Eric-are moving into a sterile development that has been built over an old, slowly but constantly burning Tangerine grove. While the outside of the neighborhood looks perfect, the family soon realizes that things are not what they seem in Lake Windsor Downs. There are "muck fires" that burn, sending rancid smoke into the air, lightening storms that strike the football field during practice, and sinkholes that destroy entire sections of the local school.

Paul's brother, Erik, is a football player, and the family hero. Their entire life revolves around Erik and what he needs to fulfill the "Erik Fisher Football Dream." Paul feels left out and ignored, while at the same time he is acutely aware of how violet and destructive his brother is when no one is watching. He witnesses his brother beating people up, and ultimately, Paul knows that his brother and a friend have killed someone that Paul knows and respects deeply.

Meanwhile, Paul is finding his own place in the world. He is an incredible soccer player, and when his school (Lake Windsor High) will not allow him to play because of his bad eyesight-he wears coke bottle glasses and is almost legally blind-Paul transfers to the nearby and much rougher Tangerine High. There he finds true friends, and proves himself to a tough crowd through his patience, his humility and his commitment to doing what he thinks is right.

At the same time, Paul is battling to regain a memory that has escaped him for some time. He wonders what happened to ruin his eyesight so badly. He cannot remember, but as he watches his brother's violence and his family's reaction to him, the pieces start to come together.

Basic Book Information

This book has 294 pages and is split into three parts. Each part is then divided into separate journal entries, dated in bold and followed by Paul's first-person narrative account of the story. There is immediacy in the tone, as well as a sarcastic edge to Paul's voice. The author often uses italics to signal what Paul is actually thinking during a certain scene. The story shifts at times to the flashback of what happened to almost blind Paul, and these sections are often, though not always, signaled by an italicized first line.

Noteworthy Features

This book provides students with a character that they can truly root for, and allows for multiple points of intersection with their own lives and

Publisher
Scholastic Inc, Apple Publishing

ISBN
0780248716

TC Level
14

A Field Guide to the Classroom Library, Lucy Calkins and the Teachers College Reading and Writing Project, Heinemann, ©2002 Teachers College, Columbia University; http://www.heinemann.com/fieldguides

ethics. For example, Paul is often the brunt of jokes because of his thick, obvious glasses. Paul deals with these attacks with incredible patience and a foresight rare for someone his own age.

One overriding aspect to *Tangerine* is how Paul notices that things are not what they seem. This eats at him as he tries to find a more honest life for himself. He cannot find his truth is his own community. The house he lives in is pretty on the outside but built on destroyed and rebellious earth-an old tangerine grove that was burnt down to make room for a new modern development. His own family is perfect on the outside-one son is a good student, the other a star athlete-but on the inside they barely speak to each other. And so Paul looks to other communities of find his truth, and finds it in Tangerine County, where he meets Luis, Tino, and Theresa, three soccer players who honestly test him. Students may catch on to this theme of appearances being deceiving if they think hard about his vision problem and what it could mean symbolically.

Also, there is an element of suspense to the novel as Paul tries to figure out what happened to his eyes. It turns out that Erik sprayed spray paint in them and his family lied for years and told Paul that he stared at an eclipse too long. There memories Paul has about the incident are erratic and piecemeal-by the end of the book the reader is dying to know what happened.

Teaching Ideas

This book creates opportunities for students to study symbolism, as well as the ability to compare and contrast. The novel is a constant swirl of contrasting images and events: the different environment of Tangerine county and Lake Windsor, Paul and Erik, the way Luis' family interacts and the way Fisher family doesn't, and especially how Paul is at the beginning of the book versus where he is by the end. There are many amazing points for discussion throughout the book concerning the contrasting elements of the story as well as how students would react to different situations.

There are many story lines that students might keep track of while they read. It is important to keep the details of the robberies that erupt in Paul's neighborhood in mind, for example, in order to realize that Erik is the thief. While the book will eventually explain all of the suspenseful elements, one of the joys of this book is figuring a few things out on your own. Students may want to keep charts of the story lines and characters to keep track of what is happening.

This book also allows for moments of understanding symbolism. The Tangerine grove that Luis runs, and his new hybrid of fruit he calls "Golden Dawn" symbolize the kind of life that Paul would like to live-vibrant and demanding. At the same time the Lake Windsor development symbolizes what is wrong with Paul's life: while everything looks okay from the outside, on the inside things are rotting away.

Book Connections

In Laurie Halse Anderson's *Speak*, a girl who has been sexually assaulted learns to heal and talk about what happened to her. In Terry Trueman's

Stuck in Neutral, a boy with Cerebral Palsy struggles with not being able to communicate to the outside world.

Genre
Chapter Book

Teaching Uses
Small Group Strategy Instruction; Interpretation; Book Clubs; Critique

A Field Guide to the Classroom Library, Lucy Calkins and the Teachers College Reading and Writing Project, Heinemann, ©2002 Teachers College, Columbia University; http://www.heinemann.com/fieldguides

Thank You, Mr. Falker

Patricia Polacco

Book Summary

Young Trisha is eager to start going to school, and even more excited about learning how to read. She is surrounded by love and praise from her grandparents, and teacher mother. However, whenever Trisha attempts to read, she stumbles over every word. She becomes the brunt of every joke among her classmates, and an annoyance to her teachers. And as if school wasn't hard enough, it becomes even worse after both of her grandparents "let go of the grass" and go to heaven. Shortly after, her mother lands a teaching job in California, and she must leave her farm in Michigan. Her new school is not any better then the last, and her reading has not improved. Then, in the fifth grade, she meets her new teacher, Mr. Falker, and her life changes forever. Her life finally begins.

Basic Book Information

Patricia Polacco is a favorite author of picture books for children of all ages. Like many of her books, *Mr. Falker* is autobiographical in nature. These stories revolve around her childhood experiences with her family, her mother, older brother, and her grandparents. There are no chapter or page numbers in the book, but it is approximately 32 pages. The pages are covered in powerful pencil and watercolor illustrations done by the author, and a few paragraphs of rich text. Other titles by Polacco include, *Pink and Say, My Ol Man, My Rotten Red Headed Older Brother,* and the award winning, *The Keeping Quilt.*

Patricia Polacco lived on a farm in Michigan. When she was three years old her parents divorced and she became the "apple of her grandparents' eyes." Patricia's grandparents felt bad for her, so she received special attention whenever she was there. She believes that they influenced her life the most and this is evident in the traits of the older characters found in her books.

Growing up and attending school was difficult for her. Patricia had difficulty reading and doing math. She grew to despise school because the other students would tease her in her class. Although she was a poor student until the fifth grade, she loved to draw and was an excellent artist.

Patricia Polacco came from a family of storytellers and thus possesses a love and a talent for this. However, she did not begin her career of writing children's books until she was 41 years old. Even with such a late career start, she has written many award-winning books. She won her first award in 1988 and has continued to win awards for her creative, enjoyable and beautifully illustrated children's books. The book *Thank You, Mr. Falker* won a Parent's Choice Honor Award in 1998.

Illustrator
Patricia Polacco

Publisher
Philomel Books, 1998

ISBN
0399231668

TC Level
10

Noteworthy Features

The book opens with a dive into the family tradition of pouring honey on the cover of a book to symbolize the sweet taste of knowledge and a bee's journey to chase it. With all three generations of the family present to speak in unison, the reader is able to experience this ritual when a child becomes of age to read, and see how reading is considered a blessing to this family. This also lays the foundation for Trisha's journey to become a reader, and gives a glimpse of her excitement of what is to come through its italicized text. The end of the story then returns to this very tradition, except Trisha is much older, and now is performing the ritual independently to mark a milestone of personal achievement in her life. The book then closes with another italicized page set aside from the story. This time it is a future look at what happened to the little girl who struggled to learn to read, she has become an author of children's books, as she tells Mr. Falker thirty years later when she is able to thank him in person.

Another way that the author helps the reader understand Trisha's difficulties is by writing the words as if she is sounding them out. For example, "Beh, beh...oy, boy." This tactic vividly reminds young readers of that time not long ago when they too read in this fashion, attempting to read and make out the meaning of the letters on a page. There is also print outside of the story text, such as writing on the blackboards, writing in the books of the students in the class, writing surrounding Trisha of all the taunts made by other children. Children may want to think about why the author wrote those other words on the pages. Some decide that she wants to show how pervasive writing is in life, and how intimidating it can be for those who can't read. Some think the author's written taunts showcase the fact that the taunts were as torturous as written words to Trisha.

Teaching Ideas

It is a good idea when reading *Thank you, Mr. Falker* to have had already read several other autobiographical Patricia Polacco books to help gain a better familiarity with the characters. It might be important for them to note that good writers often write about what they know, and reflect upon life experiences in their work. They can often define themselves clearly when they can recall the events in the past that brought them to their present place. After the students familiarize themselves with the author's family members, they can more easily identify with the main character and how she felt when her grandparents passed away; they will understand the role that they played in her life. While they are reading independently, they may want to keep a journal to note the similarities in family life that they share with the author. This will encourage students to make connections between themselves and the characters in the story.

Also, while reading independently, there are many aspects of the book that children may want to focus on. They may want to choose a theme that is important to them and use post-it notes to mark places in the text where this theme appears. For example, they could focus on the roller coaster of emotions that Trisha displays throughout the story. In the beginning, she starts off as a child with great expectations about all she will do once she can read, and at the end, she again feels that sense of expectation. Students may note that the story has come full circle. Another focus could be the way that the other characters in the book see Trisha. Her grandparents see her as a bright and very special little girl because they love her. Her classmates see her as dumb and stupid because she cannot read on their level. Her teachers see her as a nuisance because she is always lagging behind the others. However, Mr. Falker sees her as a smart, brave girl who has tricked her teachers all through school because she really has a learning disability. He says, "But little one, don't you see, you don't see letters and numbers the way other people do. And you have gotten through all this time and fooled many, many good teachers!" In this book, the omniscient third-person narrator lets the reader in on all of the character's thoughts. Reading in partnerships might be an excellent way for students to share with each other their feelings about Trisha during several places in the story.

The essence of the story is a personal journey of change, growth, accomplishment, and determination. Students may want to "stop and sketch" with a buddy on what meaning they derived from the text. They can also discuss the changes that Trisha had to adjust to throughout the story, and what changes they predict that she will make in her life now that she can read. A student of mine was so moved by the story that she decided to reflect on someone that has helped change her life. A reading buddy helped her to notice that a majority of her post-it notes were focused around this idea.

Genre
Picture Book; Memoir

Teaching Uses
Independent Reading; Character Study; Author Study

The Austere Academy (Book the Fifth)

Lemony Snicket

Book Summary

In *The Austere Academy*, the three Baudelaire children go to boarding school where they are relegated to sleeping in a crab-infested hut and listening to the headmaster's bad violin concerts. New friends Isadora and Duncan help out when the evil Count Olaf, disguised as a gym teacher, attempts again to seize the Baudelaires and their fortune. Although they escape, their friends are not so lucky.

The Austere Academy is fifth in what is projected to be a 13-book series. Each book is narrated and begins with ample background information. Books can be read out of order without any major confusion, though they are best read in order.

Basic Book Information

This 221-page book has thirteen numbered chapters of eleven to twenty-four pages. Illustrations are by Brett Helquist.

Noteworthy Features

For information on characters, including that of the narrator, see *The Bad Beginning*.

The Austere Academy, like the earlier books in the series, has a dark, humorous, unlikely and eventful plot populated with quirky characters. Vocabulary is challenging but explained entertainingly in the narrator's asides. See *The Bad Beginning* and others in the series for more information.

Teaching Ideas

All of the books in the series invite study of melodrama, parody, literary devices, the role of the narrator, and vocabulary. See *The Bad Beginning* for more details.

Book Connections

The prison-like boarding school will remind readers of the school in Roald Dahl's *Matilda*. Readers might do a comparison of that book and *The Austere Academy*, and identify, in both books, the aspects of school that are being parodied.

Series
Series of Unfortunate Events

Illustrator
Brett Helquist

Publisher
Harper Collins, 2000

ISBN
00644078639

TC Level
12

Genre
Chapter Book; Fantasy; Mystery

Teaching Uses
Independent Reading; Book Clubs

A Field Guide to the Classroom Library, Lucy Calkins and the Teachers College Reading and Writing Project, Heinemann, ©2002 Teachers College, Columbia University; http://www.heinemann.com/fieldguides

The Bad Beginning

Lemony Snicket

Book Summary

In this first installment of the witty and ironic *Series of Unfortunate Events*, the three Baudelaire children, Violet, Klaus, and Sunny, lose their parents in a disastrous fire and are put in the care of a banker, Mr. Poe. Mr. Poe sends them to live with their evil and distant relative, Count Olaf. Olaf's one wish is to control the large Baudelaire fortune, and has his entire notorious theater troupe to assist him. In the end, Violet manages to escape being forced into marriage with Olaf. Olaf escapes the prospect of jail, but vows to return.

    The Bad Beginning starts the thirteen book *Series of Unfortunate Events*. The illustrator (Brett Helquist) always puts a clue to the next book in the last picture of the previous book. Each book consists of thirteen chapters, a number that Lemony Snicket seems to be fond of. Each book is narrated and begins with adequate background information. The books are best read in order.

Basic Book Information

Lemony Snicket, who was born in a small town "in which the inhabitants were suspicious and prone to riot" now lives in a city and spends his free time collecting evidence, presumably for his stories. Snicket has a very distinctive, melodramatic literary flair, as evidenced in his cautionary remarks to readers before they begin this book, "I'm sorry to say that the book you are holding in your hand is extremely unpleasant. It tells an unhappy tale about three very unlucky children. Even though they are charming and clever, the Baudelaire siblings lead lives filled with misery and woe...It is my sad duty to write down these unpleasant tales, but there is nothing stopping you from putting this book down at once and reading something happy, if you prefer that sort of thing."

    The Bad Beginning is 162 pages long, and consists of thirteen numbered, untitled chapters of nine to fifteen pages. Illustrations are by Brett Helquist.

Noteworthy Features

The Bad Beginning and others in the series can be seen both as bizarre adventure stories, and as satirical pokes at Victorian melodrama. While the characters are unusual and distinct, they are not particularly complicated, and most of the book's energy comes from the bizarre story line and the narrator's presence.

    The three children, Violet, Klaus, and Sunny, are established as stock characters. Violet, the oldest, dreams up inventions. Klaus, the middle child, is a constant reader. Sunny, the baby, has sharp teeth and likes to bite hard objects. As heroes, the three are honest, brave, loyal, clear-sighted, and

Series
Series of Unfortunate Events

Illustrator
Brett Helquist

Publisher
HarperCollins, 1999

ISBN
0064407667

TC Level
12

A Field Guide to the Classroom Library, Lucy Calkins and the Teachers College Reading and Writing Project, Heinemann, ©2002 Teachers College, Columbia University; http://www.heinemann.com/fieldguides

tireless. While others fail to see through Olaf's disguises, the children know him at once. Count Olaf, the evil stock character, has "shiny, shiny eyes" and is willing to lie, steal, torture, and kill en route to gaining the Baudelaire fortune. While the youngest or most literal readers might find Olaf disturbing, most readers will see him as a non-threatening cartoon.

The device of the narrator is what makes this humor, rather than horror. He acts as a buffer between the reader and the story, providing distance between reader and the unlucky characters. And his overdramatic way of speaking, clues the reader in to the fact that this is parody, rather than realism. Didactic, fussy, depressive, and histrionic by turns, the narrator interrupts the action to discuss literary devices and vocabulary and to editorialize about the characters and events.

Vocabulary is challenging, but the narrator steps in to define more difficult words and expressions. A constantly ironic tone allows the introduction of terms like "in loco parentis" and "posthaste" to seem more playful than daunting. The use of the word "standoffish" is typical. On the first occasion, Olaf uses the word inaccurately and the narrator offers the correct definition. On the second occasion, Klaus uses the word correctly. Concepts and literary devices are introduced in a similar way. The narrator also takes the time to distinguish the difference between "figurative" and "literal." Some of Snicket's references are aimed at a more grown-up audience. (This is true throughout the series.)

Snicket uses words as names to express positions or personality (e.g., Squalor, Quagmire, and Nero). At times, Snicket pauses the tale of the Baudelaire orphans to talk about his personal life, namely the mysterious Beatrice, his love who has died. He dedicates all of the books to his beloved Beatrice:

For Beatrice-
You will always be in my heart,
In my mind,
And in your grave.

Teaching Ideas

A *Series of Unfortunate Events* is a good choice for independent reading and for read aloud. The book provides any reader with opportunities for noticing and eventually discussing literary devices. Most listeners will be engaged by the humor and elements of suspense in these stories.

In all the books of the series, the Baudelaire children escape Olaf by, in part, doing research. Teachers might point this out and at other times in the day if the teacher was already encouraging research, he or she could refer to these children as examples.

Children reading this book may want to read ahead just to find out Count Olaf's evil plan, but if they pay close attention to small facts in the beginning, they can figure out Count Olaf's plan, and how the Orphans plan to defeat Count Olaf themselves. Some of the facts include:

Violet is right handed.

There will only be one performance, when most shows have two.

Instead of using an actress, Count Olaf uses a real judge, Justice Strauss, to play the judge and she is reading the real marriage ceremony from her law books.

A Field Guide to the Classroom Library, Lucy Calkins and the Teachers College Reading and Writing Project, Heinemann, ©2002 Teachers College, Columbia University; http://www.heinemann.com/fieldguides

One way to help a reader more completely understand what Snicket is parodying would be for a teacher to spend a little time in a conference helping a reader think about the genre of melodrama. The modern counterpart of Victorian melodrama is the soap opera. Both have characters who are either good or bad, sensational events, and moralistic outcomes.

The role of the narrator is another element worth examining. Is the narrator the author, or simply another character? How does his presence change the story? Is he trustworthy? Is he meant to be an actual person, or simply an omniscient presence?

Snicket's enjoyment of language-expressions, similes, colorful vocabulary, and literary devices-is noteworthy. In different books in the series, students might collect examples, define them, and then use them in their own writing.

Book Connections

Students can compare books in the series with books by Roald Dahl. While events are similarly fantastic in the two books and both have elements of parody, the books by Dahl involve far more character development, and the narrator has only a minor presence. In *James and the Giant Peach*, for example, the character of James undergoes a transformation, from timid boy to sociable hero.

Genre
Chapter Book; Fantasy; Mystery

Teaching Uses
Independent Reading; Book Clubs; Read Aloud

The Big Box

Toni Morrison; Slade Morrison

Book Summary

In rhyming, patterned verse, Morrison tells the story of three energetic and mischievous, but well-intentioned, children who have been locked in a box because the adults in their communities say the children can't handle their freedom.

Basic Book Information

Morrison wrote *The Big Box* with her son Slade who "devised" the story when he was nine. In addition to *The Big Box*, Toni Morrison's other works include her adult books *Sula*, *The Bluest Eye*, *Beloved*, and *Tar Baby*. Morrison won the Pulitzer Prize in 1988 for her novel *Beloved* and in 1993, Morrison received the Nobel Prize in Literature.

Noteworthy Features

As the story progresses, the way of life in the box gradually becomes more dismal and unappealing, and that can be a hard change for readers to pick up. At first, life in the box seems great, and then subtle details let the reader know how bleak it really is. Words change here and there to cue readers into the transition, "and" changes to "but" in a few repeated verses, and the presents the kids in the box receive begin to be small bits of real life, or imitations of real life. Without stopping to think or talk about these gifts and the slight changes in words, readers may miss the point of the book, at least on the first read.

It may also be hard for children to realize that the adults in the story are not doing the right thing. Adults making bad choices can be hard for children to realize, and the overly polite and slightly sarcastic tone used to describe the adults and their decisions might seem supportive to the readers. Along the same lines, the not-so-bad things that the kids in the box do may seem horrible to readers, especially if they are used to reading moralistic or religious stories in which being undisciplined is wrong.

The rhyming and rhythm and repetition of verse structure in the book, both consistent and predictable, makes it a highly supported read. Once the internal patterns of the words are understood or felt, the reader will have a lot to lean on in interpreting, understanding, and decoding the text. The book has an introductory verse, then a verse about each of the three children, and then an ending verse. Within each verse about each child, the text describes what he or she was like outside the box, the adults' decision to use the locked box, each child's protests, and finally life locked up in the box.

Illustrator
Giselle Potter

Publisher
Hyperion, 1999

ISBN
0786804165

The illustrations in the book are excellent support for both the explicit and internal content of the story. This book is especially attractive to kids if it is read aloud either by the teacher or the children, since the rhyming, lilting, detailed language can be captivating.

Teaching Ideas

If readers of this book do not catch on to its true meaning before the end, they may be left with many questions. One such question might be "why would the kids want to leave the box?" By focusing a study on this query, the reader will come to better understand the book. A second question that may arise is "was it fair for the adults to put them in the box?" In answering this question, the reader may be led to the question "Why, then, did the adults lock them up?"

Because this is a book written with a message as its center, finding that central message will undoubtedly be easier than in books without such a pointed interpretation. When the readers discuss all these questions, with or without teacher guidance, the talk might well turn into an analysis of the book. This analysis will bring in interpretation, as the kids puzzle over the author's message; and critique, as they decide if that message is a "just" one.

Although this colorful, oversized picture book may at first glance seem appropriate for young readers, we think it is best suited to middle-school readers. A fifth grade teacher might decide to read the book aloud, and to use it as the subject for conversations that last across many days. We would probably read it aloud, stopping at segment-breaks in the story and inviting children to talk in pairs and then at the end of the book, bring the whole class together for a response to the whole text. Children will probably have definitive, strong reactions. They may say the kids had a good life in the box, alluding only to the material gifts parents brought and not to the doors that swing only one way, the locks, and the irony of parents bringing a butterfly encased in glass, and an audio-tape of a sparrow's cry. They may on the other hand, pronounce the parents to be evil, not noticing that the kids who'd been locked up did have a part to play in their predicament. Among the acts that brought them into the box: One wrote on the mailbox, another sang in the classrooms, which may sound lovely, but wouldn't feel so lovely to the teacher. In any case, we can lead readers to identify an issue such as the role of the kids, the role of the parents, or the meaning of the book. Then we can have them reread the story, collecting more precise responses on that theme.

Some of the more complex questions might include:

Who is the narrator? A close look will suggest *we* refers to a different group of people at different times.

Is one child supposed to seem "worse than" another? Is putting the eggs back under the chicken seen as an offense in the setting of a farm?

Why are there three settings, one for each child? Do these represent different communities? If the point is that these commonalities each have their own names, why does Morrison write about them in ways that blur the differences? Are the crimes tailored to each community?

Is there evidence that these kids are teachable? Why does one have the parents give or take gifts?

What is the great problem with the box? Is it that kids lose the right to have fun and to work long and hard? If everything is given to them, this may not be a gift.

Why does one tell this story?

Genre
Picture Book; Poetry

Teaching Uses
Read Aloud; Interpretation; Book Clubs

A Field Guide to the Classroom Library, Lucy Calkins and the Teachers College Reading and Writing Project, Heinemann, ©2002 Teachers College, Columbia University; http://www.heinemann.com/fieldguides

The Big Wave
Pearl S. Buck

Book Summary

Kino and Jiya are two young boys who live between a volcano and the "angry" sea in Japan. Kino lives with his family on a farm on the mountaintop. And, his friend Jiya lives with his fishing family on the coast. One day, a tsunami, "the Big Wave," rears its angry head and strikes upon the shores. As Jiya escapes to safety, by joining his friend on the mountaintop, his entire family and neighbors are killed. In the aftermath, Jiya struggles to grieve his loss. He does so with the help of Kino's family who adopt him as a son. Even when Kino is offered a life of luxury from the Old Gentleman, who adopts children orphaned by tsunamis, he declines. Jiya learns that it is love and not money that makes a family. In Kino's family, Jiya learns to face his fears. As an adult, he is finally able to build a "new life in a new home on the old beach."

Basic Book Information

The Big Wave is 57 pages long and has no chapter divisions or illustrations. The Pulitzer Prize winning author Pearl S. Buck, who won the award for her novel *The Good Earth*, writes the book. Ms. Buck also received the Nobel Price for Literature in 1938.

Noteworthy Features

The Big Wave reads very much like a folk tale or fable. Children who pick up the book expecting to find a chapter book, with believable characters and a plot they can relate to, may be somewhat disappointed. The characters speak in a very formal fashion with one another. Kino's family members say things like, "Father we are not very unfortunate people to live in Japan?" and "You wanted to stay where you were in the house of the unborn. But the time came to be born, and the gate of life opened." Also, the descriptions of the characters give them a sense of two-dimensionality. Kino's father says to Jiya,"You are strong and brave" and the narrator describes Jiya as, "very beautiful even though he was pale and weary." The descriptions throughout the book portray Jiya as the embodiment of goodness and strength, a symbol, not a real person with character flaws.

The formality of the book may be due in part to the time in which it was written, 1947. As was common in this era, the family refers to each other as "son," "mother" and "father." It may cause some confusion for modern-day readers when Kino's father also refers to his wife as "mother." Other references in the book that readers may find confusing are when the Old Gentlemen says that, "The children of God are very dear, but very queer" and Setsu, Kino's sister, is described as "gay." These terms have different meanings now and children may need to have that explained to them.

Publisher
Curtis Publishing
Company, 1947

ISBN
0381999238

TC Level
10

 A Field Guide to the Classroom Library, Lucy Calkins and the Teachers College Reading and Writing Project, Heinemann, ©2002 Teachers College, Columbia University; http://www.heinemann.com/fieldguides

The characters tend to look at life very philosophically and their dialogue reflects commentary on the big issues of life and death. The book is filled with quotes such as, "We love life because we live in danger," and, "We do not fear death because we understand that life and death are necessary to each other." In the end, as in most folk tales and fables, we learn that there is a moral to the story. In *The Big Wave*, it seems to be that "Life is stronger than death" as Jiya comes to terms with his family's death and rebuilds his life by the sea.

Teaching Ideas

The Big Wave takes place in rural Japan, a setting that will be unfamiliar to most readers. During a read aloud, the children may benefit from the teacher taking pauses after certain passages and asking the children to form mental images of the story. When reading the first few pages of the book, which establish the setting, it is especially important to take the time to ensure that the children have a strong image of the locale. This is very important in order to understand how the tsunami only affects Jiya's village, and not Kino's farm, later in the book. The setting also changes throughout the course of the story and these settings will be equally unfamiliar to most readers. It may be beneficial to take pauses every time a new setting is introduced and form solid mental images of the location. If this book is being read on an individual basis or in partnerships, readers may benefit from noting scene changes with post-it notes, to help themselves keep it straight. At the beginning of the book, it may also be important to highlight that this setting does not represent what all of Japan looks like. It is important to draw attention to the book's 1947 copyright date and remind readers that much of Japan is currently very urban and modern.

The devastation of a tsunami is not an issue with which most children will be readily able to identify. Combined with the formal dialogue and dated references, children may not find the book very accessible. It may be important to highlight the universality in this story. In the book, the protagonist deals with a grave and enormous loss and then also learns what it means to be part of a family. These are issues many readers can identify with, and this can help them form connections to the text.

Readers who are having difficulty following the story could be encouraged to stop and then retell what has happened so far to a partner throughout the course of the book. The plot follows the lives of Jiya and Kino from childhood to adulthood. The story is mainly about their childhood and then there is a jump in time to their adulthood, signaled only with the words "Time passed." In addition to the difficulties some readers might have in retaining this continuous story that spans half a lifetime, there are many events that take place in this short book. Since the story is so short, readers may experience a sense of suddenness when these events occur. For instance, by page 22 the Big Wave kills everyone in Jiya's entire village. The emotional impact of "All that had been was now no more," may need to be digested by having readers reflect on the event in a retelling and a conversation.

In partnerships or during independent reading work, it may be interesting for readers to find places in the text that support Jiya's healing and attach post-it notes to turning points that climax with Jiya moving back to the shore. Many young readers of this book find incomprehensible Jiya's decision to rebuild on the same beach where his family died. It may be important for readers to see that there is a series of events that lead up to his decision, to dissipate some of their shock.

This book embodies nature; forces are given a sense of "human-ness." The ocean is often described as "angry," the volcano has a "great yawning mouth" and the " . . .Old Ocean god begins to roll in his ocean bed and heave up his head and shoulders." Readers may find some of these descriptions confusing until they focus on understanding them. It may be interesting for readers to explore whether the ocean and the volcano should be considered characters in the story.

Book Connections

While this is a fictional account, the book does give some insight into the devastation that a natural disaster can have on an entire community. The book may be a wonderful addition to the reading of non-fiction texts about tsunamis. In addition, children may like to see how *The Big Wave* compares with traditional folk tales and fables.

Genre
Fairy and Folk Tale

Teaching Uses
Content Area Study; Independent Reading; Partnerships; Read Aloud

A Field Guide to the Classroom Library, Lucy Calkins and the Teachers College Reading and Writing Project, Heinemann, ©2002 Teachers College, Columbia University; http://www.heinemann.com/fieldguides

The Birthday Room

Kevin Henkes

Book Summary

On Ben's twelfth birthday he is surprised with a room of his own for an art studio and a letter from his uncle. He hasn't heard from his Uncle Ian in ten years, not since he accidentally cut off Ben's little finger in his wood shop. Ben is faced with his mother's and uncle's estrangement as well as pressure from his parents to perform as an artist. Then, Ben and his mother go to Oregon to visit his uncle. While there, Ben meets neighbors, who bring magic and understanding to his life and his new aunt, who is pregnant. Through tragedy, Ben comes to understand himself, and his mother and uncle learn to forgive each other.

Basic Book Information

Kevin Henkes is best known for his books for younger readers, especially *A Weekend with Wendell* and *Lilly's Purple Plastic Purse*. Henkes has also written other young adult books, *Sun and Spoon* and *Protecting Marie*. This book has 152 pages, separated into five parts, and from there into chapters.

Noteworthy Features

There are some memory flashbacks, which can make confusion about how time is passing in the book. Many of the flashbacks are indicated with a chapter change or a pattern of ellipses at that point on the page. Some readers will need to be clued in to this device early on in the book, as it recurs with each memory.

Teaching Ideas

The relationship of Ben and Linnie in *The Birthday Room* is reminiscent of Jess and Leslie in *Bridge to Terebithia*; both have a very special boy-girl friendship. Book clubs may find this connection interesting and one that could be investigated in young adult literature (*Baby*, *Journey*, and *Arthur for the Very First Time* all by Patricia MacLachlan have similar relationships). Students could conduct a character study in *The Birthday Room* and it might lead readers to notice this similarity. Many of these are boy-girl relationships and readers might want to look at these across the books they've read (see *Bridge to Terebithia*, Cooney's *Burning Up*). Many early chapter books have characters that are animals, *Andy and Tamika* (by David Adler), as well as *Pinky and Rex* (by David Howe), but portray boy-girl friendships as well.

The connection with *Bridge to Terebithia* doesn't end with theme or characterization; it also extends to the writing style itself. Both Paterson and Henkes tell their stories with incredible beauty. A comparison of the writing

A Field Guide to the Classroom Library, Lucy Calkins and the Teachers College Reading and Writing Project, Heinemann, ©2002 Teachers College, Columbia University; http://www.heinemann.com/fieldguides

Publisher
Greenwillow, 1997

ISBN
0688167330

TC Level
14

style in these two books could be productive. How do Paterson and Henkes create the magical atmosphere in their books? "No one and nothing else existed. They were all alone in the universe. Together." This epiphany occurs to Ben two-thirds of the way through the book as he comes to understand his place in life and his family. Henkes has created a sense of transcendence and this is one of the connecting themes between Paterson and Henkes. Readers can look for this or other ideas between these or other books, noting similarities as well as differences.

Some students decide to study Kevin Henkes as an author. They may wonder why they all seemed to love Kevin Henkes books and set out to discover the reasons. They should probably begin by re-reading all their old favorite picture books written by Kevin Henkes and to set these alongside this new glimpse of the author. They might want to study his characters and their relationships, and make discoveries about those, despite some characters being animals

Book Connections

The following all feature special boy-girl relationships: *Bridge to Terebithia*, by Katherine Paterson; *Baby*, *Journey*, and *Arthur for the Very First Time* all by Patricia MacLachlan; Caroline B. Cooney's *Burning Up*; *Andy and Tamika*, by David Adler, as well as *Pinky and Rex*, by David Howe.

Genre
Chapter Book

Teaching Uses
Book Clubs; Independent Reading; Author Study; Character Study; Teaching Writing

A Field Guide to the Classroom Library, Lucy Calkins and the Teachers College Reading and Writing Project, Heinemann, ©2002 Teachers College, Columbia University; http://www.heinemann.com/fieldguides

The Boggart
Susan Cooper

Book Summary

Susan Cooper, who received the Newbery Medal for *The Grey King*, has written another equally interesting fantasy story. Emily and Jessup are brother and sister who travel to Scotland with their parents to see the castle that has been left to them by a long-lost uncle. The family returns home to Toronto, Canada, accompanied by the Boggart, a spirit creature, which is a part of the ancient world. The Boggart is a playful creature who likes to entertain his friends, but is perceived by the adults as being a poltergeist, or even as a psychokinetic outpouring of Emily's mind. The children work together, amidst the dangerous pranks of the Boggart, to understand what he is and needs, finally realizing that he must go home to Scotland. This story illustrates scenic Scotland, the winter in Toronto, and shows Emily and Jess' parents to be multi-dimensional and human. This realistic rendering of parents in young adult literature is unusual and convincing.

Publisher
Aladdin Paperbacks, 1995

ISBN
0689801734

TC Level
12

Basic Book Information

There are fourteen untitled chapters in this 196-page fantasy novel. Chapters frequently are chopped into parts by use of a line of asterisks, which imply either a gap in time or a change in setting. There is infrequent use of some Gaelic language and, in the beginning of the book, much reference is made to geographical sites as the family is traveling from Toronto to Edinburgh and on to Castle Keep.

The story is told in the third-person omniscient point of view, and the tone manages to be sympathetic to the perspectives of the children, the parents, and the Boggart itself.

Noteworthy Features

This fantasy story presumes some knowledge of world geography, computers, and modern technology as well as Celtic lore. If a reader has knowledge in one of these areas, then the other factors can be supported. More importantly, a reader needs to have some fantasy reading in his or her repertoire to understand the workings of this book. Even some knowledge of fairy tales is helpful, as the traditional forces of good and evil come into play between the good-natured children and "the creep" psychologist Dr. Stigmore.

When the Boggart goes into the computer and disappears into the Black Hole game, readers may feel disbelief. However, if the reader has been roped into the story and feels sympathy for Emily, Jessup, and the Boggart, this improbable event can be tempered with patience as the reader waits for the Boggart to come out safe and sound upon his return to Castle Keep in

Scotland. After all, if the reader believes in the Boggart, why not in the computer's black hole?

Teaching Ideas

Many youngsters enter the upper elementary grades with a lot of experience being caught up in the worlds and drama of realistic fiction. They read these tales as if they are true; they get lost in these stories. A book such as *The Boggart* can challenge readers to allow themselves to be equally caught up in worlds that are not at all realistic. The skilled reader of fantasy forgets "this couldn't have happened" and reads with bated breath, as if every event on the page is utterly real. It's not important that fantasy, by definition, couldn't happen. It is happening to the reader who brings that "willing suspension of disbelief." The author of this book makes such a leap of the imagination easier because the book is beautifully written with utterly believable and real characters. Readers in fifth and sixth grade would do well to be introduced to this idea because it becomes more and more important as they continue to read within the genres of fantasy and science fiction.

A teacher could introduce willing suspension of disbelief to her class by using *The Boggart* as a read aloud. Some teachers discuss with their classes the difference between movies that are not real that you are willing to believe and books in the same category. What makes a reader willingly suspend disbelief? Some classes determine that a movie's use of real things made them believe the rest. The class then constructed a theory about *The Boggart*, that the spirit Boggart would be believable if the other parts of the Boggart character were true to life. They chose to use a chart to represent the Boggart, using one side to accumulate the outlandish happenings or behavior, the other side to collect all the reasonable actions, attitudes, and facts about the Boggart. This class learned a lot about poltergeists and about understanding human behaviors. The outcome of the chart was that they believed that the Boggart as a character in this story existed; they were willing to suspend their disbelief because Susan Cooper had convinced them they could. No matter what a class determines is the determining factor that makes an unreal book believable, that class can use chart paper or post-it notes to trace those features in the text.

The Boggart would be a good introduction to Susan Cooper's style, without being overwhelmed by the Celtic myth present in *The Dark is Rising*. *The Boggart* could be used well as a read aloud book to focus upon the elements of fantasy and its links to fairy tales and legends, but to also introduce readers to many classical literary devices and the intent of the author. For instance, Dr. Stigmore represents a fantasy archetype (typical kind of character in fantasy book). Dr. Stigmore is a meddling psychologist who cannot understand that the Boggart is an aberrant creation of the mind. This is an archetype that is used in many gothic/fantasy novels, notably *Dracula* by Bram Stoker and *Frankenstein* by Mary Shelley.

The Boggart would work well as a book club selection for fifth and sixth grade readers. There is interaction with the adult characters in the book that is unusual for most young adult fiction. For instance, the parents sometimes behave in a very self-centered way, but they also change, as they defend their children from the evil Dr. Stigmore and from adolescent fears. This could set the club up for some very interesting discussions, possibly discussing

A Field Guide to the Classroom Library, Lucy Calkins and the Teachers College Reading and Writing Project, Heinemann, ©2002 Teachers College, Columbia University; http://www.heinemann.com/fieldguides

their parents' behavior and then comparing them to the novel's adults. Students can then progress from labeling what the adults in their lives and books are like to understanding why they act in these ways.

Book Connections

Susan Cooper has written many other books for readers who like this one.

Genre
Fantasy; Chapter Book

Teaching Uses
Read Aloud; Whole Group Instruction; Independent Reading

A Field Guide to the Classroom Library, Lucy Calkins and the Teachers College Reading and Writing Project, Heinemann, ©2002 Teachers College, Columbia University; http://www.heinemann.com/fieldguides

The Butterfly
Patricia Polacco

Book Summary

This is a heart-warming story of a friendship between a young girl named Monique and a Jewish girl named Sevrine. The story takes place during the French Resistance. Monique's mother, Marcelle Solliliage, has been helping Sevrine's family and other Jewish families hide from the Nazis. Then one night, a neighbor discovers the two girls playing together secretly. Terrified for their lives, Sevrine and her family have to leave the home and get out of the country. Marcelle and Monique help the family escape.

Basic Book Information

Patricia Polacco has written over 30 books such as *Babushka's Doll, Mrs. Katz and Tush* and *Thunder Cake.* She comes from a family of great storytellers, and most of the books are based on the stories that were told to her. *The Butterfly* was based on the events that occurred during the French Resistance. According to her Aunt Monique, her Great-Aunt Marcelle helped the Jews escape from the Nazis. The "Author's Note" at the end of the book is very helpful to the readers. It allows us to understand what *The Butterfly* is based on. The readers can then recognize the actual events that happened during the French Resistance.

Noteworthy Features

As she does in many of her other books, Polacco uses some foreign words and phrases such as *ma petite, Schwein . . . Judenschwein, Maman, ma cherie, vite, papillon* without offering the reader the definitions to these words and/or phrases. This may be a spot for some readers to pause and think about what the words could mean.

At the end of the book, the reader isn't certain if Sevrine and her family have escaped safely. The butterflies may be a symbol to some readers that they have, but others may not read the book this way. Children will want to talk this over.

The illustrations in the book are colorful, detailed, and full of appealing contrasts. There is also room for readers to think about how the meaning of the story is reflected in the illustrations. For example, after Monique and Marcelle help Sevrine's family escape, they are separated by a mob of people. In that picture, the mob of people seems to blend together. Clearly, you can spot Monique with her bright red coat and a terrified face. Marcelle, who is not too far away from her daughter, is wearing a blue polka dot blouse, searching for Monique. Readers may want to discuss how the drawing helps readers understand the story.

Illustrator
Patricia Polacco

Publisher
Philomel Books, 2000

ISBN
0399231706

A Field Guide to the Classroom Library, Lucy Calkins and the Teachers College Reading and Writing Project, Heinemann, ©2002 Teachers College, Columbia University; http://www.heinemann.com/fieldguides

Teaching Ideas

The class may well need to discuss symbols in this book. From the butterflies to the swastikas, objects and pictures in the story represent big important and consequential ideas. Book clubs and partnerships may choose some of the images or objects in the stories and talk about all they mean.

Certainly, this book can contribute to studies of the holocaust, French Resistance, racism, or bravery.

Because Patricia Polacco is a favorite author for many students, she often becomes the topic of an author study. Children who read and re-read several of her books are likely to notice some common elements. She often uses non-English words and phrases in her books. She tends to write about a relationship or friendship between a child and an adult. She often explains one or more cultures and cultural practices in her stories. Her books often have an autobiographical element to them. Readers will undoubtedly find many other common elements and surprises.

Book Connections

Lois Lowry's *Number the Stars*, also describes an escape from the Nazi's in a young girl's point of view. Anne Frank's *The Diary of a Young Girl* is another, more difficult to read story about a teenage girl who lives in hiding from the Nazis.

Patricia Polacco has a website www.patriciapolacco.com.

Genre
Historical Fiction; Picture Book

Teaching Uses
Partnerships; Author Study; Book Clubs; Content Area Study

A Field Guide to the Classroom Library, Lucy Calkins and the Teachers College Reading and Writing Project, Heinemann, ©2002 Teachers College, Columbia University; http://www.heinemann.com/fieldguides

The Cookcamp

Gary Paulsen

Book Summary

During World War II, a young son of a serviceman catches his lonely "mother with Casey on the couch making sounds he did not understand but didn't like." Wrought with guilt, the mother sends her son to stay with his grandmother in Pine, Minnesota. There, his grandmother runs a cookcamp for workers who are building a road to Canada. Life at this humble cookcamp is thrilling for the young boy. The burly workers are gentle giants who give the boy rides in their tractors and show him how to play cards. Grandmother is a kindly woman who has enough love in her heart to share with the entire cookcamp.

"The boy thought life in the cookcamp could just go on and on except for missing his mother." So, when the boy finally receives a train ticket back to Chicago from mother his heart leaps. Boarding the train, the young boy does not know that he will not see his grandmother until he is a grown man with a child of his own. Many years later, when he is reunited with his grandmother, he wishes "to God that all good things could go on forever and forever."

Basic Book Information

The Cookcamp is a fictional chapter book. The author, Gary Paulsen, is a three time Newbery Award winner. He has written numerous books for young adults including: *Dogsong, Hatchet, The Winter Room, The Island, The Crossing*, and *Voyage of the FROG*. *The Cookcamp* was voted an American Library Association Best Book for Young Adults.

Noteworthy Features

In the frenetic pace of today's world, this is a slow-moving story. The saying, "still waters run deep" holds true for the book, for Paulsen has done a masterful job of developing his characters, and of creating a memorable place. The cookcamp isn't a fancy place, but it is brim full of everything that matters-everything except the boy's mother.

Although an astute reader will recognize that the boy is sent away at the beginning of the book because he is witness to his mother's extramarital affair, the sexual content is not in the least bit explicit. Children who are naïve to this content matter will probably not notice the reference to these "noises."

The characters' names may be difficult for some readers to keep track of. Since the workers are Norwegian, their names, Salvang, Sven, Ole, Nels, Emil, Altag, and Gustaf may be difficult to hold on to. In addition, the book rarely refers to characters by their proper names. They often use pronouns in lieu of names, which may hinder some readers in their identification of

Publisher
Dell Publishing, 1991

ISBN
0440407044

TC Level
12

 A Field Guide to the Classroom Library, Lucy Calkins and the Teachers College Reading and Writing Project, Heinemann, ©2002 Teachers College, Columbia University; http://www.heinemann.com/fieldguides

the characters. Teachers may want to suggest to readers confused by the characters that they keep a list with a short description next to them as, for easy reference.

For the most part, the plot unfolds chronologically. A new day is usually marked as the boy wakes up in the morning. Jumps in time in the plot are not always explicit, for example, "Summer days mixed with summer nights." Some readers may be temporarily confused here and there, not realizing that much time has passed in the story.

In the last two chapters, Paulsen plays with time. When the boy is boarding the train, his adulthood is foreshadowed. Then, the last chapter, "Portrait," recounts the ninety-two years of his grandmother's life. And, finally, at the end of the chapter the boy is reunited with his grandmother as a "grown man." These large leaps of time (forward, backward, and then forward again) will be confusing for some readers.

There are some terms related to building roads such as "cat," "grate" and "treads," which are not thoroughly explained. When the boy says "Gustaf said he would take me out on the cat," some readers may picture the boy riding an actual cat rather than a caterpillar tractor. Hopefully, in the context and genre of the story, they will realize their mistake, but teachers may occasionally need to help readers notice their error.

Teaching Ideas

Readers will notice that the main characters of the book are never referred to by name. Paulsen merely refers to them as boy, grandmother, and mother. It is important for teachers to point out that this choice by the author is deliberate. Readers may speculate why the author chose to do this. Some may feel that the narrator reflects the perspective of a young boy who would never refer to his grandmother and mother by name. Other readers may have different interpretations of the reasons. These discussions may give readers more insight into the characters' relationships.

In the first chapter of the book, the boy's mother and Casey wake him up. Throughout the book, readers may notice that the boy is continually put to sleep and awakened by different events. Individually or in partnerships, readers may want to attach post-it notes to these instances in the book. It may be interesting for readers to explore their relationships and development, and the post-its make it easy to turn back to those times to develop theories. For instance, when the boy first arrives from Chicago to his new home in the forest, "the silence awakened him." Later, "the noise" and excitement are two factors that rouse the boy from sleep. The change in what wakes the boy could be a window into understanding the boy's acclimation to life at the cookcamp.

Paulsen foreshadows the boy's life when he boards the train. Readers may not be accustomed to this writing device. Paulsen writes that the boy " . . . did not know then that he would take the train with a new note on his jacket, take it back to Chicago to his mother and that Casey, Uncle Casey would be gone or that the war would end in another year or that he would see his father who came back from Europe. . . ." Readers may need to be told that the boy "did not know" about these events because this is his future that has yet to unfold. Paulsen uses foreshadowing to tell us about the boy's future before even the boy himself experiences it.

A Field Guide to the Classroom Library, Lucy Calkins and the Teachers College Reading and Writing Project, Heinemann, ©2002 Teachers College, Columbia University; http://www.heinemann.com/fieldguides

Readers who have read the prologue ("Tuning") of *The Winter Room* may notice that Paulsen is an author who values the five senses in the experience of reading a book. Paulsen does not solely rely on a visual recording of events. In *The Cookcamp*, the boy describes "smell from the biscuits seemed to fill the room, fill the world. . . ." The boy also experiences many different events through touch-he "felt her warmth through the sleeve of her dress." Paulsen also describes tastes such as "milk with the taste of tin in it;" and sound, "She sang a song in Norwegian that he couldn't understand. The small sounds seemed to be inside his head and in the pillow and in his hair." Readers may begin to see how Paulsen uses the senses to give readers a complete description of events in several of his books. This study of craft may inspire rich descriptions in young adult's writing.

In a writing workshop, it would be interesting to study the section of *The Cookcamp* before the young boy leaves. The grandmother tells the boy about "all the times of her life." This outpouring comprises only two sentences that run the length of almost an entire page, separated by commas and semi-colons. Teachers may want to model how sentences such as these would sound (like a rambling). Writers may argue that a sentence should contain one complete thought. However, at this point in the story it could be argued that the boy's grandmother's life story *is* one complete thought. There is a sense of urgency-the grandmother must tell the boy about her life before he leaves. Young writers may want to incorporate this style of writing in their own pieces to create a fast paced rhythm to their sentences.

In many ways, *The Cookcamp* is about that wonderful period of childhood when every day of life is an adventure. When the boy is a grown man at the end of the story he "wished to God that all good things could go on forever and ever." This final sentence frames the contents of an entire book. It may cause readers to reflect on the story in a different light. The line gives the story sentimentality, because it reflects on the fleeting, wonderful times in our life.

Book Connections

Gary Paulsen has written many other books for young readers as well.

Genre
Chapter Book

Teaching Uses
Teaching Writing; Language Conventions; Partnerships

A Field Guide to the Classroom Library, Lucy Calkins and the Teachers College Reading and Writing Project, Heinemann, ©2002 Teachers College, Columbia University; http://www.heinemann.com/fieldguides

The Coyote Bead

Gerald Hausman

Book Summary

This historical fiction novel is based upon American history when the Navajos (or the People) were massacred and the survivors were forced to walk to a reservation. The story starts in Canyon del Muerto, Arizona, literally meaning the Canyon of Death, in 1864. *The Coyote Bead* tells the story of Westward Expansion from the Navajo perspective. There is conflict between Native Americans and whites, and Native Americans and Native Americans. Navajos were herded like animals into reservations and the whites hired the Ute and even some Navajos to do this. This conflict is set up in the early chapters and built upon in later chapters.

Basic Book Information

The Coyote Bead is a 141-page chapter book. There is no table of contents, but there are chapters with titles although they are not numbered. The 23 chapters range from four to five pages long. The chapter titles are pulled from the text of the chapter and most often are the actual last words of the chapter. The titles themselves represent both the context and tone of the chapter. It makes sense to know the chapter title after you've read the chapter but doesn't really help scaffold the reader before reading the chapter.

The story is told in first person by a young Navajo boy, Tobachischin. He tells the story occasionally using Navajo words but continuously uses Navajo culture and perspective.

Noteworthy Features

Time usually flows at a constant predictable pace from one event to the next, though sometimes background information is added in by recounting past events. The point of view is consistent and the narrator tells the story in the present tense. The verbs are all active rather than passive which keeps the story concrete. Because the boy narrator witnesses and describes the massacres, it is easy for the reader to take on his point of view perspective.

The chapters are short making remembering the whole chapter easier. In addition to the brevity, the chapters are also confined to one topic or idea, which makes it easier for students to understand the plot and talk about it, even when several chapters have passed. The age of the boy is probably between 11 and 13, probably near the age of the reader, making him even easier to relate to, in some cases.

Publisher
Hampton Roads, 1999

ISBN
1571741453

TC Level
13

This story has sophisticated language, but often the word's meaning is embedded in the paragraphs and pages. There are Navajo words in italics that need to be remembered from page to page: "Bilagaana" is "white man" and is defined in the first chapters, but must be remembered later on.

Although the story uses sophisticated language, there are parts that are laced with humor, for example, "The blue coat leader with the yellow hair wiped his forehead with the cloth that white people use to store their seat and nose particles." This is a sophisticated humor that shows the ridiculous nature of a handkerchief, yet it is conveyed with puzzlement.

Sometimes the names of the Native American nations can be confusing and readers must consciously remember that Dineh = The People = the Navajo.

Good and evil become more complicated concepts when the white man, as well as some Native Americans, are both portrayed as being evil in different cases and for different reasons. This can easily become the topic of conversation in a partnership or book group.

Teaching Ideas

Although this book is beautifully written and excerpts from it could be used in a study of the qualities of good writing (especially the importance of writing with powerful, evocative verbs and the value of telling a story from a particular point of view), it would be a loss to read this book and focus on its craft rather than its content. The book's content becomes especially valuable because Westward Expansion has long been part of the historical canon, and usually students are taught to regard the movement west as a display of pioneer persistence, fortitude, and resourcefulness. This book helps children see that the histories they have read tell only one side of the story, and this can profoundly influence a student's understanding of America and people's treatment of Native Americans. This book can also help readers to move to a whole new level as critical readers of history.

In order to read any historical record well, a child needs to learn to read with a critical lens, asking, "Who is telling this story?" "What does the teller gain from telling it this way?" "How else could it have been told?" "What voices are left out of this story?" When this book is set alongside history textbooks or other "whitewashed" stories of Westward Expansion, incredible conversations can emerge. For this reason, we tend to recommend this as a read-aloud book (perhaps in the social studies workshop) or as the centerpiece for a book club.

Book Connections

Books on westward expansion pair well with this one, for comparisons of factual, as well as subjective, information.

Genre
Short Chapter Book; Historical Fiction

A Field Guide to the Classroom Library, Lucy Calkins and the Teachers College Reading and Writing Project, Heinemann, ©2002 Teachers College, Columbia University; http://www.heinemann.com/fieldguides

Teaching Uses
Read Aloud; Teaching Writing; Critique; Reading and Writing Nonfiction;
Content Area Study; Book Clubs; Partnerships

The Dark Is Rising

Susan Cooper

Book Summary

The second book in the sequence, *The Dark Is Rising*, introduces Will Stanton, seventh son of poor but honest parents. Will discovers on his eleventh birthday that he is the last to be born into a mysterious society of "Old Ones," a group of individuals throughout the world who are timeless (as Cooper has Merriman explain, "We of the Circle are planted only loosely within time") and whose responsibility it is to protect civilization from "The Dark."

In Will's time, the Dark is rising and it is his quest, once he learns the way of the Old Ones, to seek out six "signs" that together will drive back the forces of evil and break the spell of icy cold that threatens to destroy the land. Merriman Lyon, eldest of the Old Ones, also appears in this volume, but this time in the role of Master and instructor of Will. The personification of evil, a "Mr. Hastings" in *Over Sea, Under Stone*, now takes on the form of "The Rider," who pursues Will and strives to win him to the side of the Dark. In this volume, parts of the traditional structure of fantasy finds its way into the backbone of the story with motifs of magic, time-slip, quest, and the endless struggle between good and evil. Typical of such children's fantasy novels, it is a child who is at the heart of the story and whose courage and vision eventually overcome the evil that stalks the world.

This is the second of the five-book sequence. In it, we again meet Merriman Lyon, the mentor of the three children from *Over Sea, Under Stone*, the first book. We are also introduced to the fourth young character, Will Stanton, who will be united with the three children in the third book of the sequence. *The Dark Is Rising* is an excellent example of fantasy, containing elements that are characteristic of the genre. This novel incorporates many common fantasy elements, such as the book-spanning quest, the shifts of space and time, and the omniscient taste of magic. These motifs continue in the three books that follow.

Basic Book Information

This book was named a Newbery Honor book and Cooper's fourth book in the series received the Newbery medal. As in all the books in this series, the structure of the text is challenging. The story is told in 244 pages. Sentences are long, syntax is complex, and vocabulary is not run-of-the-mill. The chapters end on a note of suspense, leaving the reader with the question: What will happen next? or What does that mean? Characters appear in different roles at different times, and complicate the already complex plot. Only Will Stanton remains constant.

Series
The Dark Is Rising

Publisher
Simon Schuster, 1973

ISBN
0689710879

TC Level
14

A Field Guide to the Classroom Library, Lucy Calkins and the Teachers College Reading and Writing Project, Heinemann, ©2002 Teachers College, Columbia University; http://www.heinemann.com/fieldguides

Noteworthy Features

The chapters, named but not numbered, are divided into three parts: The Finding, The Learning, and The Testing. The first two parts include four chapters. The last part is made up of six chapters. The chapters fluctuate between Will's reality and a world that even he finds difficult to believe. For instance, in the first chapter, the reader learns of the ordinary affairs that go on in the Stanton family home. In the second chapter, Will crosses into a world that existed six centuries ago. Unlike the first book in this sequence, this third-person narrative is told consistently from the point of view of Will, the main character. Time markers are implied rather than stated. The time "slips" that Will experiences will at first bewilder the reader as much as they did Will. With him, we learn to adjust to the switches in time, drawing on the clues Cooper gives that imply those switches have occurred. Readers familiar with the structure of fantasy will have an easier time, for they will recognize patterns that typically are used in this genre. Vocabulary, particularly those words that typify English life, such as "manor," "liege lord," and "Midwinter day," may interfere with comprehension for less-able readers.

Teaching Ideas

Students who have read the first book of this series, *Over Sea, Under Stone*, can use their prior knowledge to follow the development in this book. Still, they would probably benefit from a discussion of the genre of fantasy and its typical patterns before beginning this book. One teacher used Sendak's *Where the Wild Things Are* to illustrate the journey pattern. Max has a quest (to regain his self esteem), travels to a different world, conquers the Wild Things (struggle against the Dark), becomes king (which restores his self esteem), then returns, his quest fulfilled (to find his supper-and it was still warm). Students familiar with it might also discuss how Arthurian legend played a role in the first book of the series. Teachers might remind students how nature plays a part in fantasy. This was evident to a degree in the first book of the sequence, and it is even more evident in this book.

Teachers might initiate discussion by using the title and cover illustration. They may want to point out that the crow-like birds are called rooks and are in fact, members of the crow family. Cooper reveals their role, messengers of The Dark, in the text. Certainly conflict is evident in the illustration. It is also not difficult to predict that the young boy is the protagonist and the man on the horse represents evil, or "The Dark." Teachers might also want to discuss the titles of the chapters, in particular, "Midwinter Eve"-the longest night in the year-and its significance in the story.

The titles of the three parts to the book become clear only after the reader gets into the story. Teachers often have students read and discuss the book, chapter by chapter. Through discussion, students can share ideas about the many inferences Cooper requires of readers. There is a great deal of foreshadowing-the static on the radio, the uneasiness of the animals in

A Field Guide to the Classroom Library, Lucy Calkins and the Teachers College Reading and Writing Project, Heinemann, ©2002 Teachers College, Columbia University; http://www.heinemann.com/fieldguides

Will's presence in chapter one, for example. Students might keep two-column notes on each chapter. In the left-hand column they might record events they consider significant, and in the right-hand column comments and questions about these events. These notes can be the basis for discussion at the end of each chapter.

Probably the most significant attribute of this story is the development of the character, Will. He grows from a shy eleven-year old, the baby of the family, into a fearless "Old One," who takes on the challenging quest of seeking the six signs that will turn back the Dark. Students might use post-its notes or make notations of pages that indicate actions or events that address this development. There are times when Will slips back into the young boy that he is in the real world, times when he senses the change in himself, and other times when his mentor, Merriman, reminds him of his calling. Students might discuss how Cooper skillfully describes this young boy through his actions as well as his inner thoughts.

This is the struggle between Good and Evil. At times, it appears that Evil will triumph. At other times, those of Good prevail. Students might want to keep a line graph in their reading logs indicating these shifts. Points when the line rises will indicate triumph on the part of the Light, while points where the line dips will indicate the Dark is winning. It should prove interesting to see the page numbers students ascribe to these shifts and to compare how each of several readers rate these ups and downs. Which is the biggest up or down? With just a word or two, students can note the significant event each point represents on the graph, thus turning this EKG-like chart of the story also into an outline of it.

Once students have finished reading the book, they might write or talk about possible explanations of the titles Cooper assigned to the three parts as well as to the individual chapters.

Cooper draws on mythology and legend for her stories. Interested students might want to research Arthurian legend and/or the mythology that provides the basis for this story as well as those that follow.

Book Connections

Students who complete this book will probably want to continue the adventures in the next book of the sequence, *Greenwitch*. They may also want to read the *Harry Potter* series, or *A Wrinkle in Time* by Madeleine L'Engle.

Susan Cooper has a website address that teachers may want to access: http://usit.shef.ac.uk/~emp94ms.html. On that site, they can find a biography of Cooper and her own comments on writing fantasy as well as pictures of the places she uses as settings for the stories.

Genre
Chapter Book; Fantasy

A Field Guide to the Classroom Library, Lucy Calkins and the Teachers College Reading and Writing Project, Heinemann, ©2002 Teachers College, Columbia University; http://www.heinemann.com/fieldguides

Teaching Uses
Small Group Strategy Instruction; Independent Reading

A Field Guide to the Classroom Library, Lucy Calkins and the Teachers College Reading and Writing Project, Heinemann, ©2002 Teachers College, Columbia University; http://www.heinemann.com/fieldguides

The Devil's Arithmetic

Jane Yolen

Book Summary

In this story, a young Jewish girl named Hannah dreads the celebration of holidays with her relatives. She finds the ceremony strange and meaningless, and she doesn't understand all the emphasis on remembering the past. Then, during the Passover Seder, she is mysteriously transported into the past, into the times of the Holocaust, and into the body of the girl after whom she is named. Gradually, she is assimilated into that life and comes to only vaguely remember her other life. Life in the village is peaceful at first, but soon she and her family and their entire village are forced onto a train for "relocation." They are moved to a concentration camp where horrible things befall them, and where Hannah learns how to survive, and when it is better not to. When she returns from her past life, she understands her relatives, and even knows things about their lives and holidays that they have never told her.

Basic Book Information

This chapter book is probably best described as historical fiction. It is 170 pages long, and is divide into untitled chapters of six to ten pages each. There is no table of contents, and there are no illustrations. At the end of the book there is a one-page explanation entitled "What is True About This Book." In it, the author explains that the characters are fictional but the details of life in the concentration camps and in those times are all horribly true. The page appears directly after the end of the book and is in the same font as the rest of the story, so it is likely that children will read it, as they should.

Noteworthy Features

This book presents the Holocaust in its horrible detail, making real the evil forced upon one people by another. Although the descriptions of the violence and death are not gruesome or gory, and the book does not detail torture or rape, the fact of the evil and the deaths and violence are quite present. A teacher will probably want to know who is reading this book, and make sure those readers have an adult to talk to about it at some point to help them process the truths they are reading.

The author brings the reader into history through the eyes of a young girl in modern times. This helps many readers make the jump into the past, because they can go right along with the character from the very beginning of the story.

If readers aren't familiar with the traditions of a Jewish Passover Seder,

Publisher
Puffin, Penguin, 1988

ISBN
0140345353

TC Level
13

A Field Guide to the Classroom Library, Lucy Calkins and the Teachers College Reading and Writing Project, Heinemann, ©2002 Teachers College, Columbia University; http://www.heinemann.com/fieldguides

the scenes in the early chapters will probably be challenging to understand. Although each of the traditions is explained a bit in the context, there are a lot of them, and a lot of new words. Readers might feel a bit overwhelmed with the newness of it. They can be encouraged to keep reading because a surprising change is about to take place-a new scene is about to take over. These readers can also be encouraged to have a conversation with a classmate or teacher who is familiar with the Passover traditions either before they begin reading, or as they read the early parts of the book.

Once Hannah is in the village of her ancestors, she too is new to the surroundings and the traditions, so things are explained for her and the reader's benefit.

At the end of the story, the character of Hannah, or Chaya as she becomes, takes the place of another woman, her friend, who is about to be executed. The book does not follow Chaya all the way to her execution, and some readers aren't sure if she was killed at all. The Epilogue involving Hannah's aunt clear this up a little, as does a part earlier in the book in which Hannah refers to her namesake as someone who died in the labor camps. Some readers however, perhaps wishfully, don't accept that Chaya has been executed for the sake of her friend-Hannah's aunt.

This is probably not the best book to serve as an introduction to the Holocaust. Rather, this one is better for students who know some of the history of the event and the facts surrounding it. The character herself knows quite a bit about it, and so for students to feel on a par with her, humanizing the facts as she is, they would be better off knowing a bit already too. Also, since this book is set in the midst of fiction, it is an odd first presentation of history.

Teaching Ideas

Some teachers like to pair this book with another book about the Holocaust for young readers entitled *Number The Stars* by Lois Lowry.

Some teachers may want to do work around the use of time in the text. Being that Hannah finds herself in a Polish village in the 1940s, students will need to understand how she got there. It is important to understand the historical setting of this story.

One teacher had students who were exceptionally interested in this time period and their book club chose to read other texts, for example:

Books with a similar theme
Books from this period of history
Books about the Holocaust
Other historical fiction texts

Book Connections

Number The Stars, by Lois Lowry.

Genre
Historical Fiction; Chapter Book

A Field Guide to the Classroom Library, Lucy Calkins and the Teachers College Reading and Writing Project, Heinemann, ©2002 Teachers College, Columbia University; http://www.heinemann.com/fieldguides

Teaching Uses
Content Area Study; Independent Reading; Book Clubs

The Fortune-Tellers

Lloyd Alexander

Book Summary

An unhappy, young carpenter wondering about his future seeks out a fortune-teller. The old man tells him truisms such as "Rich you will surely be, on one condition: that you earn large sums of money." The carpenter is overjoyed. When he returns looking for the old man, he is mistaken for the fortune-teller himself and soon people clamor for *his* predictions. He follows the pattern set by the old man and soon becomes rich and famous. As for the original fortune-teller, he was beset by problems great and small, ever since accidentally falling off his balcony and leaving his trade to the young carpenter.

Basic Book Information

Lloyd Alexander is well-known and well-loved for his chapter books including *The Cat Who Wished to be a Man* and *The Book of Three*. Trina Schart Hyman is also an award-winning illustrator and may be familiar to readers from her illustrations in *Cricket Magazine*.

Noteworthy Features

The most uncommon vocabulary in *The Fortune-Tellers*, phrases like "Scruffy old codger," "cloth merchant's shop" and "an early demise," should be fairly decipherable from their context.

Teaching Ideas

For readers at this level, the most difficult aspect of *The Fortune-Tellers* will be in grasping the humor and the logic in the prophecies. The carpenter asks if he will be famous. "No question about it," said the fortune-teller, "once you become well-known." The carpenter asks if he will marry. "You shall marry your true love," the old man replies, "if you find her and she agrees." The predictions make the carpenter very happy, and they will probably make the reader smile too, if he or she grasps what they are really saying, and what they are really *not* saying.

To help children who might otherwise misunderstand these prophesies, a teacher might read one aloud and stop to laugh and talk about it so that they will know what to expect. Inevitably, readers themselves begin creating predictions for each other; the formula seems to be captivating.

The illustrations are vibrant and colorful. Though the exact setting is not explicitly referred to, the presence of a lion near the end of the book may conjure up the stereotypical image of West Africa for some readers, but then again, in children's stories, lions tend to turn up just about anywhere. As kids read, they can try to find indicators of the setting, and if they can't find

A Field Guide to the Classroom Library, Lucy Calkins and the Teachers College Reading and Writing Project, Heinemann, ©2002 Teachers College, Columbia University; http://www.heinemann.com/fieldguides

Illustrator
Trina Schart Hyman

Publisher
Penguin Putnam, 1997

ISBN
0140562338

TC Level
9

much, they can then try to determine from the pictures which part of the world the story takes place in. The pictured artifacts, patterns on the fabrics, foods, and the language on the signs may allow them to place the story, especially if they compare these details to what they know of certain countries around the world.

The detail and energy in the pictures invites more careful scrutiny, which can pay off for those who wish to interpret the messages of the book. For example, the monkey is on every page where one can find the "real" fortune-teller. When the old man is the fortune-teller, the monkey is near him, and when the carpenter becomes the fortune-teller, the monkey is on the page with him. When readers come to the last page, they see only the monkey, the fortune-telling crystal ball, and the moon. Could this mean that we the readers are now the fortune-tellers, as we are the only ones near the monkey now? Could it mean that only the powers that be, in the sky with the moon, are the ones that hold the truth to our fortunes? Of course it could be just a series of coincidences and a cute picture at the end, but it is nearly always constructive work to find supportable meaning in texts, even where none is intended. Besides, in carefully constructed books like this one, nearly every detail, studied with consistency and care, can lead to interpretations of or perspectives into the text.

Some readers, in trying to interpret this story and others, ask the question "Why do things happen to the characters the way they do?" In other words, "Why did the author make good things happen to some characters and bad things happen to other characters?" In this case, when the reader asks why bad things happened to the old man fortune-teller, some readers come to the conclusion that it was because he tried to make a prediction for real. At just the moment when he diverged from his pattern of predicting only the indisputable, when he was really trying to predict the weather, that is when misfortune befell him. The carpenter, on the other hand, only foretold that which was certain, he didn't try to know what he couldn't know. He, unlike the old man, had good fortune. A reader could then draw the conclusion that the message of the story is that you will be better off if you don't try to speak about what you can't know. The theme of having bad fortune when meddling with fate is a classic in literature, from Greek myths to Oedipus to fairy tales from around the world.

Genre
Fairy and Folk Tale; Picture Book

Teaching Uses
Interpretation; Independent Reading; Read Aloud

The Gift-Giver

Joyce Hansen

Book Summary

Doris lives with her mother, father, and baby brother on 163rd Street in the Bronx in New York City. Her mother scolds constantly and Doris feels separated from her friends at school. Then Amir comes along and shows Doris how to be friends, to care about other people, and how to keep her family together despite tough times. Amir lives with a foster family and dreams of getting back together with his own brothers and sisters some day. Amir's sense of perspective is contagious, which helps the whole neighborhood grow closer. When Amir leaves to go live in a group home upstate, he leaves his joy of life and family with his old neighborhood.

Basic Book Information

The story is told in the first person with Doris' point of view, which immediately draws the reader into the story. Much of the book is dialogue and most of the dialogue is street vernacular. This 118-page novel has nineteen relatively short chapters. Hansen has written a sequel to this book called *Yellow Bird and Me*.

Noteworthy Features

There are far too few chapter books that present African American children as protagonists, and this book thankfully does just that. Doris narrates the story in her own voice, "Amir looked at all of us like we was crazy." Many urban children will be comfortable with this way of speaking.

While the chapters are short and the text itself is easy to read, the issues raised in the story are sophisticated. Readers should have had previous experience reading unreferenced dialogue before tackling this book, as it is a constant feature in this text.

Teaching Ideas

One teacher decided to use *The Gift-Giver* in a mini-lesson to show children that we come to know characters not only by *what* they say but also by *how* they say it. This teacher said, "Joyce Hansen has used dialogue as a way to give added personality to the characters as well as move the story along. She does this in a way that sometimes can be confusing because she has one character speak and then another, without telling you who is talking. Today when I read, we're going to look at how Hansen writes the dialogue and how the way a character speaks gives us clues as to who is speaking and what that character is like." One student responded by saying, "I've noticed that Doris

Publisher
Clarion Books, 1980

ISBN
0395294339

TC Level
12

talks a certain way, and Amir talks different. When Doris and Amir are doing the talking, that helps me keep straight who is talking." The class then set up a chart to study speakers in dialogue, finding that Doris, Amir, the twins, and Yellow Bird all spoke a little differently. They used this chart to begin a character study based upon the speech patterns of the characters. As the class studied the speech of the characters, they brought their own speech patterns into the discussion. One small group of students even tried to write their own dialogue using dialect and speech attributes.

When the author does not explicitly name who is speaking but instead asks readers to supply the identity of each speaker, the author is requiring readers to do a particular kind of inference, and this puts important comprehension demands on a reader. If the reader is closely following a text, making a movie in his or her mind of the action as it occurs, then the reader *will* know who is speaking most of the time. But if a reader is passively letting his or her eyes flow over the words on the page, without really generating a mental story, this will quickly reveal itself in a text such as this one because the reader will have no clue who is talking. An easy way to assess whether a reader is comprehending this book, then, is to ask the child to read it aloud and to supply the missing speech tags, adding, "said Doris" or "said Amir." If a child can't begin to do this, the text is probably too hard for this reader. If the reader *can* do this but it's a stretch, then this book presents important teaching opportunities. The teacher will want to emphasize really "getting the story" and the importance of envisioning what's happening and let the dialogue tags come as a result of active comprehension. They aren't the goal-the goal is active, engaged reading and knowing who is doing the talking will probably come with that. We may want to start such a reader off by our reading aloud an early section of the text and pausing to envision for and alongside the reader. After we read a paragraph, we could say, "Okay, so I'm picturing. . . . " Then we can read another paragraph and again open our minds and say aloud the thinking we're doing and we hope readers are doing as well.

The Gift-Giver can be an effective read aloud book to 5th or 6th grade classes, and an especially effective one in urban areas. This book mirrors the aspects of life experienced in the city projects which makes it a jewel both for teachers wanting to show all children that their stories are literature, and also for teachers wanting to find books that open new worlds for readers. The characters of Doris and Amir are developed in ways that make them universally appealing, and most readers will bond and identify with them.

The Gift-Giver can also be a wise choice for book clubs. Some teachers have found it helpful to ask small groups of similar readers to take on a subject of concern and read several books related to that subject. Sometimes teachers suggest that all clubs read books in which there is a strong, interesting character and then the class reads such a book aloud and discusses it together. The class might, one day, develop theories about "What kind of person this is" in their read aloud and then show evidence from the text, and in reading groups children would all do the same. Another day, in the read aloud, the class could think about times the character acts out of character, or seems to be changing, and again reading clubs could do similar work in their respective books. *The Gift-Giver* would be a great book for character book clubs, especially the character of Doris.

A Field Guide to the Classroom Library, Lucy Calkins and the Teachers College Reading and Writing Project, Heinemann, ©2002 Teachers College, Columbia University; http://www.heinemann.com/fieldguides

Book Connections

Joyce Hansen has also written *Which Way Freedom?*, a historical fiction book that deals with slavery and the Civil War and the sequel to this book, *Yellow Bird and Me*. We also recommend *Habibi* (Naomi Shihab Nye), *The Monument* (Gary Paulsen), and *Flip-Flop Girl* (Katherine Paterson).

Genre
Short Chapter Book

Teaching Uses
Book Clubs; Small Group Strategy Instruction; Read Aloud; Language Conventions

A Field Guide to the Classroom Library, Lucy Calkins and the Teachers College Reading and Writing Project, Heinemann, ©2002 Teachers College, Columbia University; http://www.heinemann.com/fieldguides

The Golden Compass
Philip Pullman

Book Summary

The Golden Compass is the first book in the *His Dark Materials* trilogy by Philip Pullman. The story continues in *The Subtle Knife* (1997) and in the recently released, *The Amber Spyglass* (2000). *The Golden Compass* is the story of Lyra, the only girl at Jordan College (a part of Oxford University). As the book opens, Lyra believes that her parents have died and she is an orphan. Lyra soon learns that her "uncle," Lord Asriel, is really her father and that her mother too, is also alive. Lyra's mother is known to the world as Mrs. Coulter, who lures children to her in order to perform a dangerous and life threatening operation on them.

This book has many elements of realism and many of fantasy. All people in the world of *The Golden Compass* have a daemon, a part of themselves that is in the form of an animal. Although the human and the animal appear as two distinct entities, they are really parts of one whole and separating them causes irreparable damage, physically, emotionally, and psychically. While Lord Asriel and Mrs. Coulter are estranged, they do continue on together with a quest to move to another universe. The two believe they can do this only when aided by the "dust" created when separating children from their daemons. Although Lyra is their daughter, she has a quest of her own, contrary to that of her parents: to keep children from harm.

This book has several simultaneous plot lines, with many literary allusions, starting on the first page with a quote from Milton's *Paradise Lost*, which explains the title of the trilogy, *His Dark Materials*. There are many learned terms used in this book, including many of existential philosophy, Christian symbolism and terms, the use of Danish and other Scandinavian myths as well as Nordic and Russian history.

Basic Book Information

This 399-page book is comprised of three parts, which are named for places in the book, Oxford, Bolvangar, and Svalbard. There are twenty-three chapters, all named for the principle event of that chapter; they do not lend much support to the reader except in retrospect. Within chapters there are shifts in time and setting, indicated by additional spacing between paragraphs and sometimes by fancy curlicues.

The story is told in the third person, with Lyra as the point of view.

Philip Pullman has also written *Clockwork*, another fantasy story based on literary and scientific principles, though shorter. Pullman in a recent review in the *New York Times* was called, "The Man Who Dared Make Religion the Villain," and the book can be seen not only as cerebral, but controversial in regards to the status quo in most fantasy novels.

Series
His Dark Materials

Publisher
Knopf, 1995

ISBN
0679879242

TC Level
14

A Field Guide to the Classroom Library, Lucy Calkins and the Teachers College Reading and Writing Project, Heinemann, ©2002 Teachers College, Columbia University; http://www.heinemann.com/fieldguides

Noteworthy Features

The character of Lyra is strongly written and it is easy for a reader to become involved in her story, wondering what will happen and trying to solve the mystery of severing children from their daemons (their other half). Because of this attraction to Lyra, it is possible that a reader can forge through many of the intricate plot twists, the information given and information alluded to in world history, physics, philosophy, and religion. There is a lot going on in this book. A proficient reader may be able to read this, using knowledge of the genre of fantasy and mythical quests, as a sole support.

Having read *Harry Potter*, *Redwall*, *The Chronicles of Narnia*, some of Bill Britain's work, Ursula LeGuin's *Catwings* and *The Earthsea Cycle* books, *The Search for Delicious*, and Lois Lowry's *The Giver* will give a reader strength in *The Golden Compass*, as it relies heavily upon fantasy archetypes (good versus evil, quest, greed, innocence, and hope). If a reader understands the structure of the story and anticipates how the genre behaves, then her reading of the book will go more smoothly. *His Dark Materials* is similar to J.R.R. Tolkein's *Lord of the Rings* trilogy in difficulty.

Teaching Ideas

The Golden Compass would make for a great book club selection for 6th grade readers who are extremely proficient and have experience with easier fantasy books such as *The Chronicles of Narnia* (C.S. Lewis), *Redwall* (Brian Jacques), and *The Dark Is Rising* sequence (Susan Cooper). If a book club has a liking and understanding of fantasy, a fantasy study could be encouraged. The archetypes of fantasy (good versus evil, going on a quest, the small versus the large) could be discovered over and over again in all of these books. *The Golden Compass* takes these archetypes one step further by making the battle between Lyra and her parents represent the battle of good versus evil. While pitting a child against its parents may seem unnatural (and it *is* in fantasy for young readers), it makes much sense in the world of the adolescent who fights for autonomy in an adult world. *The Golden Compass* also blurs the meaning of "parent" as Lord Asriel and Mrs. Coulter do not behave as parents. Rather, Lyra's parents revolve, fading in and out as she moves through the book. It is the characters Farder Coram and the bear Iorek Byrneson, who are Lyra's protectors, champions, care givers, and parents.

Pullman uses names and words that have grounding in history so an etymological study could be fun and interesting to advanced readers. Even studying the names of the characters, Lyra, similar to the word "lyrics" and "lyre," Lord Asriel, similar to "astral," or even "Aslan" from *The Chronicles of Narnia*. An investigation of the etymology, and so the hidden meaning to "Pantalaimon," the name of Lyra's daemon familiar, would be fascinating and encouraging to young linguists (Pan is known as being a Greek god, as well a being root word for many common words of today, like pandemonium). There is reference to "gyptians," made several times. The basis of this word could be from "gypsy" or from "Egyptian," and both theories could be supported and debated.

Pullman also uses this knowledge and play of words in his other books such as *Clockwork*. An author study of Philip Pullman in this respect would engage readers with a penchant for linguistics.

There is no map to the world in *The Golden Compass*, yet readers may find that having an orientation to the geography of the land is fun and helpful. One 6th grade book club that was having difficulty understanding Lyra's journey to the north decided to make their own map. "After we decided to make a map, we had to find all the information to help make it. So we re-read everywhere, searching for all the clues to the geography and we kept post-its on a chart of all the places and references to directions. Here we have Jordan College. That's one of the colleges in Oxford. I didn't know what Oxford was, but we looked that up. We figured out that's in England, so we started there," the student pointed to their map which had England, Scandinavia and Russia on it. "We know we have to make the North Pole. We're working on that now."

The reading of fantasy books could be supplemented by reading of articles from the *Horn Book* about *His Dark Materials* and any other fantasy books.

Book Connections

The Chronicles of Narnia (C.S. Lewis), Tolkein's Trilogy of the Ring, *Redwall* (Brian Jacques), and *The Dark Is Rising* sequence (Susan Cooper) are all related by genre to this book.

Genre
Fantasy; Chapter Book

Teaching Uses
Partnerships; Independent Reading; Book Clubs

A Field Guide to the Classroom Library, Lucy Calkins and the Teachers College Reading and Writing Project, Heinemann, ©2002 Teachers College, Columbia University; http://www.heinemann.com/fieldguides

The Great Fire
Jim Murphy

Book Summary

This is a Nonfictional account of the Great Fire of Chicago in 1871, a fire that consumed most of the city. Using eyewitness accounts from letters and journals, Murphy tells the story from the first flame to the rebuilding process.

Basic Book Information

The Great Fire won the Newbery Honor in 1995, and is representative of Jim Murphy's Nonfiction work: clear, factual, and riveting. This 138-page book has seven chapters that move the story along chronologically. Much of the story is narrated by actual persons who survived the fire, from their letters and other correspondence. There are numerous black and white drawings that appeared in newspapers of the time. All drawings are accompanied by captions that are in sentence form which carry the same clear voice as the narrator.

Noteworthy Features

This is a Nonfiction book with a strong narrative, creating a strong sense of story. From the moment of the first flame, the reader knows that there was a huge devastating fire, and yet the reader is driven on to find out the particulars and the human elements involved. The narrator moves the reader on, bit by bit, as the fire progresses, and then through eyewitness descriptions of people and their search for family and safety. The reader sees through the eyes of Claire Innes, a young girl, through the eyes of Alexander Frear, a man searching for his sister-in-law's family, and through Joseph Chamberlin, a newspaper reporter. These accounts work well to humanize this story, and this is a good thing, as the book contains many pages of dense expository text.

There are frequent maps of the fire's advance on the city of Chicago, which help to show the reader how extensive the fire was. Whenever a reader is confused, the reader will benefit from flipping back to the most recent map to create a better sense of the reality. Sometimes the abstract nature of the pages and pages of text can create distance from the events.

Teaching Ideas

The Great Fire is a book to use when studying the rise of urban areas, and possibly when studying Westward Expansion, as Chicago was a frontier city. Beyond its value for conveying content, *The Great Fire* is an excellent book to study as an example of well-written Nonfiction, and also as part of a study on the ways readers can read Nonfiction on a variety of levels. This

Publisher
Scholastic, 1995

ISBN
0590472674

TC Level
13; 14; 15

book can be read as a story, or used as a reference book on the Great Fire.

The final chapter of the book, called "Myth and Reality," pulls the stories of the eyewitnesses and the facts of the rebuilding together, and mixes it with the sociological reasons for affixing blame to Catherine O'Leary and to the fire department of Chicago. Murphy shows the cartoons from newspapers of the period, which show Mrs. O'Leary to be the culprit of the fire, and conveys that she was ignorant. None of this was true. Murphy points out, but does not editorialize, that the Great Fire of 1871 served to polarize the rich and the poor in urban areas, an interesting point and one which usually isn't brought up for readers until they are in college.

The Great Fire can be used in the reading workshop to show readers how to follow an expository text closely by using the story of the eyewitnesses as an anchor. A teacher working with Nonfiction reading told her upper grade students, "Jim Murphy worked hard at this book to make sure that readers would be able to understand the information. There's a lot of information on every page, and sometimes I am overwhelmed by it. One thing that Murphy has done for us, and we need to know this, is that he has given us several people to help us go through this story. The eyewitnesses that come in and out of this story are there not only to make the story believable, but also to make it interesting to us, the readers. Have you noticed that the eyewitnesses speak to us? Murphy uses their own words, and it sounds like they are talking to us right from out of the page. That makes it seem more real, and closer to us. That's what Murphy wants us to feel, so that we'll be able to stick around for all the information he's loading in there too."

Another teacher explained *The Great* Fire's use of the eyewitnesses to a small group this way, "Have you noticed that the author has used more than one eyewitness account for this book? Why do you think he's done that? You can bet he did it on purpose." A student responded, "Well of course he's using more eyewitnesses for more evidence, that's what I would do. But yesterday I noticed that while I like to know about what's happening with Claire, the girl who is running around all by herself, Kris doesn't care so much about her. Instead Kris likes to know about the guy who's looking for his family. I think maybe Murphy does that on purpose too, because he knows some readers will be girls and some will be boys." Another student disagreed, "Well, I'm a girl and I want to know about Alexander Frear, that guy who's looking for his sister. The fire keeps on catching him and he keeps on going, moving. I like that. I don't think it has anything to do with being a boy or a girl reader."

The class compiled a small chart that helped them keep track of how the author was using the different eyewitnesses for several purposes. Through this chart work, the class was also able to see that they had several purposes themselves, as readers. They decided to use their purposes for reading *The Great Fire*, and mix in their knowledge of what the author wanted them to get out of the book, too. From this inquiry, this class discovered that authors of Nonfiction have an agenda for reading their book, but that readers need to have an agenda, too. Most importantly, readers need to be able to identify these agendas.

Genre
Nonfiction; Chapter Book

A Field Guide to the Classroom Library, Lucy Calkins and the Teachers College Reading and Writing Project, Heinemann, ©2002 Teachers College, Columbia University; http://www.heinemann.com/fieldguides

Teaching Uses
Content Area Study; Critique; Reading and Writing Nonfiction

A Field Guide to the Classroom Library, Lucy Calkins and the Teachers College Reading and Writing Project, Heinemann, ©2002 Teachers College, Columbia University; http://www.heinemann.com/fieldguides

The Hobbit

J.R.R. Tolkien

Book Summary

The Hobbit begins "In a hole in the ground lived a hobbit" and so begins the most well-known fantasy work of all time. Hobbits are one of the multitudes of races in this novel. They are a short people, with tough feet, and therefore do not need shoes. There are also men, and the lithe graceful Elves, as well as the short and stout Dwarves.

The hobbit in the title is a respectable hobbit, happy to live in his home, and lives a life of ease. That is, until one day when a Wizard named Gandalf knocks on his door, and enlists the hobbit, Bilbo Baggins, to be a burglar for a party of Dwarves who seek to free their mountain stronghold from the grip of a powerful dragon.

Together the party travels across the great Misty Mountains where they encounter the Great Goblin, leader of tribes of savage cave-dwelling creatures, and are nearly killed, but Gandalf comes to their rescue, and leads the Dwarves out of the dank caves. Then Bilbo Baggins trips and falls into a hole and soon discovers himself in a large cavern, which is almost filled with water. He discovers and pockets a small ring, just before he meets a strange creature named Gollum, who lives on a small island at the lake's center. He challenges Bilbo to a riddle contest; the prize is Bilbo's life. When Bilbo wins the contest Gollum angrily attacks, and in Bilbo's rush to dodge the attack, the ring slips on his finger, and he suddenly realizes that he is invisible. Discovering the passage that leads out of the chamber, Bilbo manages to find the exit from the Goblin's caverns and tunnels. When he leaves, he discovers he is on the far side of the Misty Mountains.

With a great deal of luck, Bilbo manages to reunite with the Dwarves, but just as he begins to tell them his story, they are set upon by giant wolves, or Wargs, that are allied to the Goblins. They are sent scurrying up trees, and soon the Wargs summon the Goblins to burn them out. Gandalf makes the decision to sacrifice himself, but just in time a force of Great Eagles come upon the scene, and decide to foil their enemies, the Goblins, by rescuing the party. Soon, Bilbo wakens in a daze atop a towering pinnacle, in a Great Eagles aerie. He finds Gandalf has negotiated with the king of the Eagles, and they have agreed to send them on their way.

The Eagles set the party far south of their planned route, so Gandalf decides to take them to the home of the shape-changer Beorn. When they finally reach the home of Beorn, they negotiate, and he agrees to aid them, and gives them food, as well as new ponies. They then ride north to the path that leads through Mirkwood Forest. It is at this time that Gandalf leaves them to deal with business of his own, leaving them with one bit of advice: *Do not stray off the path*. Of course they do, and soon all of the Dwarves are captured by giant spiders who anticipate a juicy meal. Bilbo comes to the rescue. He escapes being captured by the spiders because of his magic ring, and he frees the Dwarves who flee the spiders right into the hands of the

Series
The Lord of the Rings

Publisher
Houghton Mifflin
Company, 1966

ISBN
0395177111

TC Level
14

A Field Guide to the Classroom Library, Lucy Calkins and the Teachers College Reading and Writing Project, Heinemann, ©2002 Teachers College, Columbia University; http://www.heinemann.com/fieldguides

Elves. Once again Bilbo rescues the Dwarves, who soon discover themselves at the base of the Lonely Mountain.

In a moment of supreme luck the companions discover a secret door that leads to the heart of the mountain and straight to Smaug the dragon that long ago took possession of the mountain from the Dwarves. Smelling the hobbit, Smaug decides that he is from the human town near the base of the mountain, and angrily flies out to deal with the "thieving" humans. Bard, a Human archer, is forewarned, and told of a weak spot in Smaug's armor by a courier-bird, and manages to use his last arrow and penetrate straight into the creature's heart. Finally the mountain is freed, but the Men and Elves decide to go take their share of the mountain's wealth. The party quickly forms its defenses, as they soon find themselves under siege.

Just before the allied humans and Elves attack the mountain, Gandalf comes rushing from the west, ahead of a Goblin horde. The Elves, humans, and Dwarves ally to defeat the massive horde, and once again there is a King under the Mountain.

Basic Book Information

The Hobbit is the base for the entire genre of fantasy, and some would say even science fiction. In *The Hobbit* the "adventuring party" idea, which plays a role in games like Dungeons & Dragons is introduced. Many of the races in modern fantasy are directly derived from the races that appear in this book. Elves and Dwarves in particular are copied almost exactly by authors of adult fantasy such as Terry Brooks, Margaret Wise, Tracy Hickman, and Samuel Donaldson. Goblins (though they are often called Orcs) are also often transplanted from *The Hobbit* into modern fantasy. *The Hobbit* is a must read for any student interested in pursuing further fantasy reading.

Noteworthy Features

The Hobbit is written in third person, and the narrator often inserts commentary to update readers on little tidbits of information that suddenly become important to the story. The narrator has a very conversationalist approach to telling the story with comments like, "Still, I dare say . . ." or "Quite apart from the stones, no spider has ever liked being called. . . ."

Teaching Ideas

The Hobbit is first and foremost an adventure story. It was conceived as a story that J.R.R. Tolkien told his children as a bedtime story. Still, it is a complex book and deserves thoughtful attention. It is perfect for book groups and partnership reading, and it is also the perfect book to read all alone, to be swept up utterly and completely in the other world Tolkien has created.

Some students might find it interesting to document the multitude of races, because there are nine races that play active roles throughout the story. Students can then use this information when reading other fantasy books and see how many authors have borrowed heavily from Tolkien's work.

Some students could examine Bilbo in depth, and in particular examine how he slowly becomes one of the parties' leaders. For a large section of the beginning, Bilbo is very meek and not one to take risks, but by Mirkwood he is deceiving the giant spiders and rescuing the Dwarves. Bilbo even acts *against* the Dwarves by giving the besieging Elves and Humans the Arkenstone, an incredibly precious gem, in hopes of resolving the conflict, by forcing the Dwarves to give up in exchange for the gem.

The most obvious parallels between this book and others are in the races, but parallels can also be drawn between Gandalf and Anselon as both are mysterious yet powerful protectors of their respective books' main characters.

The Hobbit and *The Lord of the Rings* may be viewed as required reading for any writer hoping to write fantasy

Book Connections

The Hobbit is closely related to *The Silmarillion,* which is the novel detailing the mythical creation of the world, and *The Lord of the Rings* trilogy, which tells the story of the magic ring that Bilbo discovered in Gollum's lair.

If a student enjoys *The Hobbit*, he or she may want to read another fantasy story such as *The Sword of Shannara* by Terry Brooks. The student may find it extraordinarily worthwhile to explore parallels between *The Hobbit* and this book.

Other fantasy books that are recommended for this level include the now famous *Harry Potter* series, and C.S. Lewis' *The Chronicles of Narnia* series. Books by Margaret Wise, Tracy Hickman, and Samuel Donaldson may also interest readers of this book.

Genre
Chapter Book; Fantasy

Teaching Uses
Character Study; Independent Reading; Book Clubs

A Field Guide to the Classroom Library, Lucy Calkins and the Teachers College Reading and Writing Project, Heinemann, ©2002 Teachers College, Columbia University; http://www.heinemann.com/fieldguides

The King's Equal

Katherine Paterson

Book Summary

As the good king dies, he sees the character flaws in his son, the next king, and tries to amend them by proclaiming that the boy cannot wear a crown until he finds and marries a woman who is his equal. The vain and arrogant prince demands that such a woman be found and when his councillors fail time and time again, he orders them cast into the dungeon. Just as they are about to be killed, the peasant girl Rosamund arrives, commanded by her friend, a magical, speaking wolf. With her intelligence and the prince's foolishness, Rosamund tricks the young man into spending a year in the mountains with the wolf and goats. If he has changed in that time, she will be his wife. With the wolf's help, he does change, and the two are married and the kingdom saved.

Basic Book Information

This book may actually be closer to a chapter book with pictures than it is to a picture book with chapters. There is quite a lot of text to deal with, and at least two out of three pages have no pictures, only text with decorated borders. However few they may be, the illustrations do seem magical and may pull in readers who might otherwise think the book is too hard for them. The book might best be displayed open to a particularly nice illustration, perhaps the double-page spread on page fifty. That page features the reforming prince facing a large wolf in the dead of winter, and may help entice boys who might otherwise leave the fairy tale for girls to read. Reading aloud the first few lines probably isn't necessary, as they are easy to read for anyone who picks up the book, and are no more intriguing than any other fairy tale.

Noteworthy Features

As mentioned earlier, the book contains a lot of text for the reader to grasp. The chapters, however, are carefully written so that each one deals with a certain section of the story. Because of this, chapter markers themselves can help children realize that a new section of the story is coming up, either dealing with new characters, a new setting, or a new problem. Expecting this can aid in comprehension of these new elements, it may be worth alerting readers to this facet of chapters-one that recurs in many books.

Teaching Ideas

Readers who are familiar with fairy tales will recognize the genre in this story. They may expect magic and know that good is rewarded while bad is

A Field Guide to the Classroom Library, Lucy Calkins and the Teachers College Reading and Writing Project, Heinemann, ©2002 Teachers College, Columbia University; http://www.heinemann.com/fieldguides

Illustrator
Vladimir Vagin

Publisher
Trumpet, 1992

ISBN
0440832543

TC Level
11

corrected or punished. They will recognize that the prince will set tasks for his councillors, that they will respond in threes, and that there will be serious and usually grisly punishment for failure. All of these elements are present in the story, and expecting them, consciously or unconsciously, will facilitate reading. This is not to say children have to memorize the elements of fairy tales before they begin, but only that if they are familiar with the genre. It may orient them better in their reading.

Many of the key phrases booking the story are repeated verbatim or close to verbatim throughout the book. Each time the councillors fail to find a wife that will be the king's equal, the king threatens that they will "be cast into the dungeon until the flesh rots and falls from their bones." Each time the wolf notes one of Rosamund's virtues, he says, "Your kindness [or wisdom, etc.] will not go unrewarded." Many of the characters have these repeating refrains, and even certain actions in the story are written similarly each time they happen. This is an element of the writing that readers' attention need not be drawn to directly; it will merely aid them as they read, since figuring out the phrases once will help them over and over again. If a reader doesn't catch on to these patterns, however, and struggles each time the same phrases appear, then perhaps we can draw their attention to the repetition.

Some readers might expect the magical wolf in the story to turn into a better prince than the one featured in the story. The reader can go back over the text and note where that expectation came into play and why. They can speculate about whether the author intended this and what its effects are on the story. This can make for an interesting discussion. Readers who don't have that reaction, on the other hand, aren't necessarily missing anything. Whichever reaction they do have can be traced.

A special element of this fairy tale is its representation of the female character as strong and intelligent, not merely a damsel in distress as in many other fairy tales. In this one, the woman takes care of her animals, the kingdom, her father, the prince and herself, all with a good attitude and songs on her lips. However, some readers might say this is a traditional female role, one of homemaker and caretaker, and that in fact, this princess bakes and cleans (and even marries an unappealing character!) for the benefit of her family and her country and is therefore not a liberated role model at all. These readers might say that the story encourages girls to sacrifice everything for others, not to be actualized women of their own. Each reader will have to decide for himself what the character of the woman in the story represents, and how her role plays out in the real world.

If readers embark upon an interpretation, they may well decide that the morality of the story is less materialistic than usual for the genre. Many fairy tales end with the poor character ending up wealthy and powerful, usually from marrying royalty-that is depicted as the ultimate reward. Although the same is true of this story, there is also mention of the fact that friendship is as prized as gold, and that learning how to do things like bake bread and make a fire with your own hands has value as well; it is not merely drudgery merely to be escaped by marrying well. This, and other elements of the story, can be discussed with the reader, who can use examples from the text to bolster her argument.

A Field Guide to the Classroom Library, Lucy Calkins and the Teachers College Reading and Writing Project, Heinemann, ©2002 Teachers College, Columbia University; http://www.heinemann.com/fieldguides

Genre
Picture Book; Fairy and Folk Tale; Chapter Book

Teaching Uses
Interpretation; Independent Reading; Critique

The Library Card

Jerry Spinelli

Book Summary

Jerry Spinelli is the author of the Newbery winner *Maniac Magee* and *Wringer*. *The Library Card* is written similarly to *Maniac Magee* in its grittiness and use of the urban landscape. The characters are a little older than Maniac and most are what would be called "At-Risk Kids"-kids at risk of dropping out of school before they graduate. The library card, in the story of the same name, is magic, something that all kids need and sometimes never get. This magical library card is the device that connects all these stories. The stories could be read on their own or together.

Because there are short stories, the genre needs to be considered. In less then 50 pages, Spinelli creates a conflict with resolution and to do this, he (the author) must compact time and action as well as description. Short stories by their length cannot contain extraneous details; everything that is there is needed and usually does convey some message or adds to the meaning of the book. Two of the stories are about boys and two are about girls.

Basic Book Information

The Library Card is 148 pages long with four chapters or parts. Each "chapter" is named for its main character. The "chapters" (really four short stories) vary from 30 to 50 pages each. There is a table of contents and separate title pages for every chapter. There are no illustrations.

Noteworthy Features

This book is intended for sophisticated readers, perhaps older, who have a broader vocabulary and world-view. The characters in this book are adolescents; they are dealing with peer pressure, popularity, the media, poverty, parent neglect, vandalism, and theft. The main characters participate and are involved in the above issues and younger readers may find little to connect to. Readers need to be willing to suspend their disbelief over the magic in *The Library Card* and "go for the ride."

The characters are complex adolescents that are neither all good nor all bad, a complexity that may be attractive to readers of the same age. The setting of each story is different and ranges from urban to rural landscapes. In this way, all readers will probably encounter some familiarity and some strangeness, but people are people no matter what the landscape. One of Spinelli's greatest strengths as a writer is the ability to communicate commonalities among different people and populations.

Publisher
Scholastic Press, 1997

ISBN
059046731X

TC Level
12

Teaching Ideas

This book could contribute well to an author study as Spinelli has written many interesting books for young adults that could be fascinating when paired up and studied together.

Character study of these four characters would also be fruitful, as the people in the books are deep and realistic. These short stories could be used for read aloud and shared reading text as well as independent reading and book club text because there is so much to be discussed in each story.

Genre
Anthology of Short Stories

Teaching Uses
Whole Group Instruction; Small Group Strategy Instruction; Book Clubs; Partnerships; Read Aloud

The Life and Words of Martin Luther King, Jr.

Ira Peck

Book Summary

The Life and Words of Martin Luther King, Jr. presents a mostly chronological biography of Martin Luther King Jr.'s life, as it related to the great historical events of that time.

Basic Book Information

This book is 96 pages long and there are photos on every few pages.

Noteworthy Features

The book begins with a forward about the assassination of King, and then backtracks so that it can provide a few paragraphs about his contribution to the civil rights movement. Chapter 1 introduces us to King as a 25-year-old on his way to Montgomery, Alabama, for a job as a minister.

The text is interspersed with over 50 photos illustrating both the joyous and the painful moments of his life. We see his wedding picture, a photo of him looking pensively out of his Birmingham jail cell to a protest outside a Montgomery courtroom, Coretta Scott King in mourning, White supremacists, and King getting his mug shot taken.

The book also brings us closer to him as a person. The book begins, "Martin Luther King felt good, real good." Here, King is not just a historical statistic-born 1929, died 1968-he is a person. While giving us a historical overview of his life, it engages us in an anecdotal story. Though many students may know of King's life, reading the language might help students appreciate why he was charismatic.

Much of the focus of this book is on the words of Martin Luther King Jr. and the ideas from which he drew those words. There are ample selections from his speeches.

Teaching Ideas

Readers will probably want to talk less about this text's literary qualities, its use of language, sentence structure, and so forth-and more about its content. Seeing the picture of a man being attacked by a German Shepherd will makes it strange for readers to *not* respond on a profoundly personal level, regardless of their personal experience with discrimination. Though overt racism has certainly declined, some students may have had personal experiences related to race and class. Because of the personal nature of these responses, some students may at first need the privacy to work through

310 *A Field Guide to the Classroom Library,* Lucy Calkins and the Teachers College Reading and Writing Project, Heinemann, ©2002 Teachers College, Columbia University; http://www.heinemann.com/fieldguides

Publisher
Scholastic, Inc., 1968

ISBN
0590438271

TC Level
12; 13; 14

these thoughts on their own. It may be helpful to allow students to simply freewrite, in a stream of consciousness form, as they read, while offering opportunities for willing students to share their entries with the class. Students can then go back to their writings to see if, in them, there are ideas worthy of following throughout the reading of the book.

Numerous inquiry projects may arise from reading this text, on topics ranging from civil rights history both here and abroad to media portrayal of race and class. Students may also be interested in researching the controversy over the case against James Earl Ray, who was convicted of assassinating of Martin Luther King, Jr. Though it may be meaningful to ask what students think about race and class as it exists today, it may be more useful to let students take ownership of such questions, and give them the freedom to come up with and answer their own questions about this provocative book.

One of the limitations of this book is its publication date, 1968. The fact that it was written in 1968 makes it a kind of historical document. It presents the reader with a number of unanswered questions. To what extent have things changed since the time of Martin Luther King Jr.? How might the author write a biography of King differently today?

The liability of considering someone of the magnitude of King is that he comes to be regarded as an inaccessible man-a saint whose every thought was pure. One would be hard-pressed to find a more compelling model of humanity at work. Students may be better able to connect with such a saintly figure if they are also introduced to King as the family man, King who had birthday parties, or even King as a little boy, as this book does. This approach may help students be able to be personally influenced by this book to take action of some kind on their own. Teachers can be there to scaffold this action.

Genre
Nonfiction; Biography

Teaching Uses
Reading and Writing Nonfiction; Independent Reading

A Field Guide to the Classroom Library, Lucy Calkins and the Teachers College Reading and Writing Project, Heinemann, ©2002 Teachers College, Columbia University; http://www.heinemann.com/fieldguides

The Lion, the Witch and the Wardrobe

C.S. Lewis

Book Summary

This is Book Two of *The Chronicles of Narnia*, but it is generally regarded as the foundational book in the series because it is here that the reader is introduced to the four children: Lucy, Susan, Edmund, and Peter. Lucy discovers another world on the other side of a magic wardrobe in a friendly professor's house and she and her siblings begin their adventures in Narnia. Lucy's brother Edmund is enchanted by the White Witch, evil ruler of Narnia who has kept the land forever in a winter without Christmas. Together with Aslan, the magic lion, Lucy and her brothers and sister work to free the land and its inhabitants of their enslavement.

Basic Book Information

This book was originally published in 1950 and this edition is its 50th year anniversary. This is a full-color collector's edition, which, interestingly, is the first time that it has appeared with the complete interior illustrations and jacket that Pauline Baynes created for the book in 1950. Some of the illustrations (especially those of Mr. Tumnus) will look familiar to older readers because they have appeared in black and white in previous editions.

About This Series

Unlike many series, it is not necessary to read this series in order. For many years, it was thought that *The Lion, the Witch and the Wardrobe* was the first in the series, not the second. Although the children are introduced in *The Lion, the Witch and Wardrobe*, reading out of order will not have a detrimental effect. Rather, it makes for a more interesting, and sometimes more challenging read. *The Chronicles of Narnia* are considered classics. The United Kingdom thinks so, too, having bestowed the prestigious Carnegie Award in 1956 to the final book in the series, *The Last Battle*.

Noteworthy Features

There is a map of "Narnia and the Surrounding Counties" before the title page and it is worth examining and referring back to as the book is read. An island called "Terebinthia" appears within the Bight of Calormen and some readers may think of *The Bridge to Terebithia* by Katherine Paterson. Indeed, Paterson mentions Narnia as a reference point for both Leslie and Jess when they create their own magical land and it is no coincidence that the names are so similar.

There are seventeen chapters in this 189-page fantasy book, which is sometimes steeped not only in Briticisms, but sayings common to the 1950s.

Series
The Chronicles of Narnia

Illustrator
Pauline Baynes

Publisher
Harper Trophy Edition, 2000

ISBN
0064409422

TC Level
12

The children speak proper English, "Do stop grumbling, Ed," and "Indeed, indeed, you really mustn't," and may seem impenetrable to young readers. Even those who have read *Harry Potter* haven't been exposed to true British colloquialisms because J.K. Rowling created an American version for readers west of the Atlantic. A few students may need help deciphering "wireless," a radio, and "row," a fight, both which appear within the first pages of the book. Probably, though, they can speed over these words without needing to know exactly what they mean.

There is sophisticated vocabulary that readers need to be encouraged to "have a go" with by relying on context clues. Sometimes children will puzzle over words because they've grown up in a modern culture, and are unfamiliar with "marmalade" and "pavilions."

Readers come to meet mythical creatures who often populate fairy tales and fantasy books: centaurs, dryads, dwarves, elves, talking animals, and bewitching witches. Lewis also incorporates some references to the Old Testament as he names the children the Sons of Adam and the Daughters of Eve. C.S. Lewis is a Christian theologian and these books can be read as allegories, with Aslan representing Christ. Unless an adult tells children that deeper meaning, it's doubtful a child will find it on his or her own. The story does not require this interpretation and most readers find abundant meaning and significance in the fantasy story itself.

Teaching Ideas

The Lion, the Witch and the Wardrobe marks another step up into higher-level fantasy for readers. Readers who have read some fairy tales and legends and perhaps fantasy books such as *The Search for Delicious* by Natalie Babbitt will find this background helps them when they turn to *The Chronicles of Narnia*. A genre study of fantasy and how it weaves in elements of other genres could be fascinating to fantasy enthusiasts. Lewis incorporates important features such as the battle between good and evil, enchantment, talking animals, magical powers, delicious foods, and believable characters. His rich portrayal of Lucy, Susan, Peter, and Edmund also affords a character study that could cross over into the other books of the series. Readers could follow Lucy, or any of the other characters, and see how they develop in the future.

There are several rather obvious lines of thinking that a reader might follow when reading this book. Early in the book, Edmund is lured onto the Evil Queen's sleigh by the taste of Turkish Delight, and after that much of the plotline involves the other three children's efforts to rescue their brother from the Queen's power. Many readers read to find out if Edmund is freed, even though he has done some things that could make readers wonder whether he is worth all the risk and effort the other children go through to rescue him. The core plot of this story is not unlike the plot of *The Wizard of Oz*. In both books a cluster of characters journey through an enchanted land en route to their goal. All such journeys have their ups and downs, their internal journeys paralleling the external ones, artifacts that do and don't accompany the travelers, and so on.

One sixth grade book club took on *The Chronicles of Narnia* as a project, and each of the club members studied a particular character (Lucy, Edmund, Peter, or Susan). During one of their meetings, the club was discussing the changes in Edmund. One member of the club said, "In *The Lion, the Witch and the Wardrobe*, Edmund is a weak and greedy boy. He just wants the candy, the 'Turkish Delight,' and to be a prince. He doesn't care about his sisters or brother. That's why Aslan dies, because of Edmund and his dumbness. But, at the end of the book Edmund seems a little different than in the first book." Another club member chimed in, saying, "Yeah, I think so. I think he's sorry. See how he acts, look at this page. . . ." Following this exchange, the club decided to make a chart for Edmund and one for each of the other characters, to follow how, or if, they change through the series.

Indeed, the club discovered that in later books, Edmund develops into a hard-working and wise young man. He has learned through his experience with Aslan's death. Susan, however, is shown to be a virtuous and open-minded character in *The Lion, the Witch and the Wardrobe*, but in later books, her character deteriorates. She becomes selfish and unwilling to use her imagination so as to be a part of the adventures in Narnia.

With the inclusion of the map of Narnia, *The Lion, the Witch and the Wardrobe* becomes part of a growing collection of books that have maps in their frontispieces. All of the *Tales of Dimwood Forest* (by Avi) contain maps, as do Lloyd Alexander books, *The Search for Delicious* (by Natalie Babbitt), the *Oz* books, and the *Redwall* books. A study of these books, which are mostly all fantasy books, could be a rich one. In each of these books, a new world is created. What do these worlds have in common? How does the skilled reader come to envision and care about these worlds and the characters who live in them? A book club or an individual may take on these maps that are present in all the books as a project, patching them together to create the whole world of Narnia. (Students can also undertake this study with the *Redwall* series by Brian Jacques.) While these books are fiction, they utilize many geographical principles that readers and students need to be acquainted with (like physical features such as rivers, mountains, oceans).

Book Connections

See above for many book connections. Edward Eager's *Tales of Magic*, including *Half Magic*, *Knight's Castle*, *The Time Garden*, and *Magic by the Lake*, is about siblings who embark on a variety of magical adventures and could be another good companion series to this one.

Genre
Fantasy; Chapter Book

Teaching Uses
Independent Reading; Read Aloud; Book Clubs

A Field Guide to the Classroom Library, Lucy Calkins and the Teachers College Reading and Writing Project, Heinemann, ©2002 Teachers College, Columbia University; http://www.heinemann.com/fieldguides

The Miserable Mill (Book the Fourth)

Lemony Snicket

Book Summary

In *The Miserable Mill*, Violet, Klaus, and baby Sunny are sent to yet another cousin, the nameless owner of Paltryville's Lucky Smells Lumbermill. Weary but stalwart, the Baudelaires work in the mill until Klaus is hypnotized by an optometrist and directed to cause terrible accidents. Violet breaks the spell and just in time, she finds out who has been behind the spell-the evil and relentless Count Olaf, of course.

The Miserable Mill is fourth in what is projected to be a thirteen-book series. Each book is narrated and begins with ample background information. At least through book five, *The Austere Academy*, the characters remain the same. As a result, books can be read out of order without any major confusion, though they are best read in order.

Basic Book Information

This 194-page book has thirteen numbered chapters of nine to nineteen pages. Illustrations are by Brett Helquist

Noteworthy Features

For information on characters, including that of the narrator, see *The Bad Beginning*.

The Miserable Mill continues in the same sensational vein as earlier installments. Adults continue to be portrayed as either evil or well-intentioned and dim, while the children remain resourceful, savvy, and loyal to each other. See *The Bad Beginning* for more information on characters.

The narrator continues to explain the varied and colorful vocabulary through asides, and to provide little tongue-in-cheek lessons on literary topics. The opening, for example, humorously describes how a book's first sentences clue the reader in to the atmosphere and (often) plot of a book. While this is a valuable lesson in reading, it is also an opportunity for Snicket to gently parody the predictability of many books. In Chapter 11, Violet must find information on hypnotism in an almost unreadable book, and fortunately recalls the value of reading the table of contents; this, again, is a sort of lesson about how to read properly.

The Miserable Mill, like earlier installments, contains literary references, many of which will be over some readers' heads. One example is the name of the optometrist, Georgina Orwell. Her talent for hypnotism ties in with George Orwell's *1984*, where a theme is mind-control.

Series
Series of Unfortunate Events

Illustrator
Brett Helquist

Publisher
Harper Collins, 2000

ISBN
0064407691

TC Level
12

A Field Guide to the Classroom Library, Lucy Calkins and the Teachers College Reading and Writing Project, Heinemann, ©2002 Teachers College, Columbia University; http://www.heinemann.com/fieldguides

Teaching Ideas

All of the books in the series invite study of melodrama, parody, literary devices, the role of the narrator, and vocabulary. See *The Bad Beginning* for more details.

Snicket has fun, as usual, with figures of speech, such as "quiet as mice" (which Snicket says would make more sense if changed to "quiet as mimes"), and expressions such as "Don't judge a book by its cover" (p. 60). Students might enjoy finding similar inaccuracies in common expressions.

Snicket's instructions on how to read an opening might be used to look at a variety of books. What are the clues for plot and for tone? How predictable are certain books? Students can compare their predictions and evaluate them for accuracy.

Genre

Chapter Book; Fantasy; Mystery

Teaching Uses

Independent Reading; Book Clubs

The Moorchild
Eloise McGraw

Book Summary

The Moorchild is a story that takes places in two worlds-one that is similar to ours and one, the Mound, which is magical. One girl, Saaski, who lives in the "regular" world was actually born in the magical one and feels very out of place in her life the way it is now. She had forgotten the other world, but in the story, she starts to remember and connect with it, partly because she learns to play the bagpipes very beautifully. Much of the book deals with Saaski's difficulty fitting in and finding a place for her unusual abilities in the "normal" world.

Basic Book Information

The Moorchild is a Newbery Honor book. It contains 241 pages with 24 chapters. The story is a fantasy and is written in a style that uses some invented language as well as slang.

Noteworthy Features

The story moves chronologically through time, describing Saaski's birth and then her life and growth as a young girl. The characters aren't terribly complex, but are interesting, particularly in relation to how they handle Saaski's "differences." The book is fairly long. There are sections where the plot is strong and active, pulling the reader into an engagement with the story line, but there are also slower parts filled with Saaski's thoughts and reflections.

Teaching Ideas

Some teachers look through their entire library and select a limited number of books to highlight at the start of the year. In September, these teachers make a point to showcase books that are fairly accessible for readers and books that teachers know especially well. In this way, we can steer children to books that are likely to be compelling, and we know enough about the books to be able to keep a close eye on a reader's journey through the book.

A number of fifth and sixth grade teachers include this book in their early-in-the-year library. Although there are reflective slow spots in the book, it's mostly plot-driven and therefore it hooks readers in quite easily. Many teachers, in September and October, have created a structure in which kids read silently for twenty to forty minutes and then meet with partners to talk about the books they've been reading. Often in these early months, we angle the expectations for this talk-time so as to hold kids accountable to a low-level "getting-it" sort of comprehension. We ask partners to retell the

A Field Guide to the Classroom Library, Lucy Calkins and the Teachers College Reading and Writing Project, Heinemann, ©2002 Teachers College, Columbia University; http://www.heinemann.com/fieldguides

Publisher
Scholastic Books, 1996

ISBN
0590035584

TC Level
13

plot of what they've read, perhaps paging through the text as they do so and scanning it.

Eventually we teach them that if they are reading a story, their retelling should weave together some mention of the characters, setting, plot, and passagethrough time. This book is well suited to this early-in-the-year emphasis on retelling, and this is another reason to promote it early on in the year. Obviously, it'll circulate through the class all year long, but we may want to put it on a "Recommended" shelf or do a five minute book promotion on the text so that it's a hot item from the start.

The biggest challenge will be *The* Moorchild's length, and a teacher may need to talk up the importance of staying with it and making good time when reading a book of this length. In general, we hope most third and fourth grade children will usually get through a book a week, and therefore would both work with readers on pace and stamina and also steer them toward far briefer books if they read only fifteen pages a day.

The book contains issues of being different and fitting in that don't take place in the world we live in, but could be nice connections to our own lives.

Genre
Chapter Book; Fantasy

Teaching Uses
Independent Reading

The Music of Dolphins

Karen Hesse

FIELD GUIDE

E **G**

Book Summary

Mila is discovered in the waters between Florida and Cuba, where she has been raised by dolphins for as long as she can remember. She is taken to a Boston University research center, where she is observed by professors of cognitive and neural systems to determine "the role language and socialization play in the making of a human being." Mila is introduced to qualities of existence that are uniquely human: language, music, dance, the arts technology, and territory. Initially desiring only to please, Mila is a willing subject. She never suspects that she may be unable to return to the sea. This is the story of her growing awareness of being "trapped in the net of humans," and her growing awareness of self. By page 118, Mila has "decided to work hard at being human so they will let me go free." Although Mila delights in certain aspects of her human existence, she ultimately decides to escape to the sea and return to her dolphin family. Here she is occasionally "startled by the fierce and sudden hunger for things left behind," but she is home. This book is about Mila's internal movement and tension between the human and dolphin aspects of her self. Although this is never fully resolved, she has made her decision.

Basic Book Information

This book is 181 pages long and divided into sixty-two short chapters. Each chapter is a new entry in Mila's journal, and the story is told in the first-person narrative from her point of view. The beginning pages of Mila's journal are printed in large, bold letters, which gradually decrease in size as she acquires greater fluency and proficiency with the English language. Her syntax changes dramatically throughout the book. Initial journal entries consist of short, choppy, incomplete sentences. Mila's writing is most fluid about three quarters into the book. When she begins to feel she can no longer live in the human world, the print gradually becomes larger and sentences grow increasingly choppy until she finally returns to the sea. The font, syntax, and fluency of entries at the end of the book mirror those of the beginning.

The story begins with an italicized passage, written from Mila's point of view before she is taken from her dolphin family. Italicized passages throughout the text detail Mila's immediate experience of the sea, and are not part of her journal. The reader is listening to Mila's inner voice. The plot is revealed on pages four and five through a newspaper article chronicling the events behind Mila's rescue. The font of both the italicized passages and newspaper article are relatively small, as is the spacing between words and lines.

Publisher
Scholastic, 1996

ISBN
0590897985

TC Level
12

319

A Field Guide to the Classroom Library, Lucy Calkins and the Teachers College Reading and Writing Project, Heinemann, ©2002 Teachers College, Columbia University; http://www.heinemann.com/fieldguides

Noteworthy Features

This book offers an excellent opportunity to heighten students' awareness of voice. As Mila becomes more human, the syntax and fluency of her writing grow increasingly sophisticated. When she begins to yearn more deeply for her ocean life, her voice echoes that of her beginning journal entries. Mila's voice also shifts in italicized passages, when she is directly experiencing or remembering her life in the sea. The inner language of her thought and feelings is markedly different from her written language. There also exists strong evidence for the existence of both dolphin and human characteristics within Mila, allowing students to cite these and easily chronicle the evolution and resolution of the primary tension within the text.

There are three italicized passages in this text, at the beginning, the middle, and the end. These are set apart from the rest of the book because they are not part of Mila's journal. Instead, they are her inner, more immediate experiences of life with the dolphins. This may confuse readers, as both the journal and the italicized passages are written in the first person narrative, from Mila's point of view. To ponder this question for a considerable length of time would detract from the story and students' attention to the big question: Will Mila go back to the sea? Instead, it might be advisable to explain to students the function of the italicized passages, so they may be fully empowered to do the interpretive work intended by the author.

A teacher may not want to spend undue time focusing on the letter Mila receives from her father on page fifty-eight. Students tend to develop theories that Mila will return to her real family. This is not part of the story and, although it is a reasonable prediction, the author's intent is not to put this question into her readers' minds. Another potential stumbling block is the newspaper article at the beginning of the book. This is written in adult language that may be difficult for some students to comprehend. They might benefit from a simplified summary before approaching the body of the text.

Teaching Ideas

During daily read aloud conversations, the teacher can gently guide students to understand and articulate that, although Mila yearns to go back to the sea, she embraces those parts of her that are human as well. The teacher might explain that when two parts of a person or community are at odds with another, it is called *tension*. Tension within and between characters is a theme continually addressed by literature, and may be illustrated and chronicled with a T-chart. The teacher can instruct students to divide their papers into two sections, dolphin and human, then cite passages and page numbers which provide evidence for each of these aspects of Mila's character. For example, the following passages highlight the ways in which Mila is becoming human:

"Dr. Beck says, If you are waiting seven days for Sandy to come back and five days are finished, how many more days do you have left to wait? Dr. Beck shows with her fingers. I say two. I like to play these games." (p.41)

"Making progress is when I talk words. Making progress is when I wear clothes. Making progress is when I sleep in a bed and eat the fish." (p.50)

A Field Guide to the Classroom Library, Lucy Calkins and the Teachers College Reading and Writing Project, Heinemann, ©2002 Teachers College, Columbia University; http://www.heinemann.com/fieldguides

"I listen to the music. It is little sounds and little sounds all put together to make something so big. It is a bird singing and a whale singing and people singing. It is so many sounds I cannot name...I love the music." (p.53)

"I am happy. I love the lessons. I love my work with the computer. With the cards. With the paper and crayons and pencils and paint. We dance. We sing. We go different places. We swim. We play games." (p.75)

"I turn the radio off and on. If I move the knob so slow, I can find music, so much music hiding in the radio...And it is all human." (p.81)

"I know seven notes on the recorder now. They say I learn fast. They say I can catch up with others my age before too long. Good. I want to catch up. I want to be with others." (p.82)

"I love to use my hands. To play games, to make the music on the recorder...I like every little thing I am learning with my fingers and toes." (p.83)

On the other hand, there exists equally strong evidence to remind the reader that Mila possesses a dolphin's sensibility and love for the ocean. She has every intention to return to the sea:

"I am splashing water on Sandy. I am so happy. I say, Doctor Beck, I can stay here and sleep here in the water room with Sandy all the time?...I do not want to go." (p.27)

"I have another family too. Dolphin family. The ones who love and care for me. The ones I love and care for. Can they see me again? I say, Sandy, can the dolphins see me again?" (p.35)

"I am not listening. I see water. Water! It is not big like the ocean, but it is not little like the pool...I go over the road and into the water, swimming and swimming in my clothes, going with the good tide. I dive in the water. The water is not good to see in. It is all clouds. But it is much water. I call my dolphin name. I call again and wait." (p.45)

"The water sings in my ears. I feel the pull of the sea. I swim a long time. I swim very far. The cold water empties the strength from my bones. Again and again I make my dolphin name in my nose, but there is no answer. I cannot find the warm sea where the dolphins wait. It is too far, and I am too alone." (p.68)

"I feel the music inside me. It says something more than just the notes, more than just the sounds. It is hearing with more than the ears. Like the way it is when I am with the dolphins." (p.76)

"I beat my hands against the locked door...I look at the hands that held the fin of my dolphin mother. My hands bleed. I am trapped in the net of the room. In the net of humans. I think I may be drowning in the net of humans." (p.110)

"When I know the language, when I know the rules, when they unlock the door, I can run back to the warm sea. I can leave my human clothes on the beach. I can leave my human thought on the beach. I will go home." (p.117)

"I want to go back to the sea, where I do not feel the crushing of my heart by the ideas in my head." (p.131)

"My music is fading. Inside me everything is fading. When I make music on the recorder it is such sad music. It has nothing to do with dolphin life." (p.151)

"I have been coming back to the sea from the moment I left it." (p.175)

A Field Guide to the Classroom Library, Lucy Calkins and the Teachers College Reading and Writing Project, Heinemann, ©2002 Teachers College, Columbia University; http://www.heinemann.com/fieldguides

Book Connections

The fiction writer, John Gardiner, has said that all stories are about one of two themes: "the human search for home," or "a stranger comes to town." This book fits the former category, as do countless books including Voigt's *Homecoming* series, both *The Great Gilly Hopkins* and *Flip-Flop Girl* by Katherine Paterson, and Spinelli's *Maniac Magee*. In *The Invisible Thread*, Yoshiko Uchida experiences a similar tension between her Japanese heritage and American upbringing. This same tension is the theme of Fritz's *Homesick*. Like Mila, Jean Fritz feels torn between two worlds.

The Great Gilly Hopkins, by Katherine Paterson, and Jerry Spinelli's *Maniac Magee* are also stories of a search for home, family, and acceptance. In *The Invisible Thread* Yoshiko Uchida experiences a similar internal tension between her Japanese heritage and American upbringing. Like Mila, she feels torn between two worlds.

Genre
Short Chapter Book

Teaching Uses
Read Aloud; Independent Reading; Language Conventions; Book Clubs

A Field Guide to the Classroom Library, Lucy Calkins and the Teachers College Reading and Writing Project, Heinemann, ©2002 Teachers College, Columbia University; http://www.heinemann.com/fieldguides

The Phantom Tollbooth

Norton Juster

Book Summary

For Milo, everything is a bore. The novel opens with *The Phantom Tollbooth*'s main character, a young boy named Milo, feeling unhappy and thinking everything is a waste of time. That day, when Milo goes home, a mysterious package awaits him in his bedroom. "FOR MILO, WHO HAS PLENTY OF TIME." "ONE GENUINE TURNPIKE TOLLBOOTH EASILY ASSEMBLED AT HOME, AND FOR USE BY THOSE WHO HAVE NEVER TRAVELED IN LANDS BEYOND." Having nothing better to do, Milo embarks on a fascinating journey.

Milo's journey takes him through the Kingdom of Wisdom, which includes the warring municipalities of Dictionopolis and Digitopolis. He goes to the Land of Expectations where he learns that if you expect everything, the unexpected never happens, gets stuck in the Doldrums where it's against the law to think, and meets the literal watchdog, Tock, who is appalled when Milo says he's killing time. Milo ends up eating his own words at the Royal Banquet in Dictionopolis, and conducts a colorful symphony for Chroma the Great, "conductor of color, maestro of pigment and director of the entire spectrum." The book ends with Milo realizing that life is far from dull; it's exciting beyond his wildest imaginations!

Basic Book Information

This fantasy book is 256 pages long, and divided into twenty chapters. The author, Norton Juster, is an architect and planner, professor emeritus of design at Hampshire College, and the author of a number of highly acclaimed children's books, including *The Dot and the Line*. The illustrator, Jules Feiffer, is also an author and has won a number of prizes for his cartoons and plays.

Noteworthy Features

The Phantom Tollbooth is a creative masterpiece and an absolute marvel in wit. Students laugh out loud while reading this book. This book should only be used as a read aloud if all students have copies of the text, as many of the jokes on words need to be seen to make sense. Take the following example concerning the Whether Man:

"...Do you think it will rain?"

"I thought you were the Weather Man," said Milo, very confused.

"Oh no," said the little man, "I'm the Whether Man, not the Weather Man, for after all it's more important to know whether there will be weather than what the weather will be."

Similarly, much of the Spelling Bee's talk is lost unless visually read since the Bee is literally spelling words as he speaks:

Illustrator
Jules Feiffer

Publisher
Random House, 1996

ISBN
0394820371

TC Level
12

"Perhaps - p-e-r-h-a-p-s - you are under the misapprehension-m-i-s-a-p-p-r-e-h-e-n-s-i-o-n-that I am dangerous," he said, turning a smart loop to the left. "Let me assure-a-s-s-u-r-e-you that my intentions are quite peaceful-p-e-a-c-e-f-u-l."

The Phantom Tollbooth ingeniously incorporates challenging vocabulary (SAT vocabulary no less), while providing context and a story line that makes learning the words fun and comprehensible. For example, the following passage teaches students the words cacophony, discord, and dissonance, while making it clear that all these words are synonyms of a word students already know, "loud."

"I am KAKOFONOUS A. DISCHORD, DOCTOR OF DISSONANCE," roared the man, and, as he spoke, several small explosions and a grinding crash were heard.

"What does the 'A' stand for?" stammered the nervous bug, too frightened to move.

"**AS LOUD AS POSSIBLE**," bellowed the doctor, and two screeches and a bump accompanied his response.

The illustrations are likewise central to the text in terms of understanding the humor and appreciating the novel more deeply. A map of the Kingdom of Wisdom is included before the opening pages of the novel, and pictures of demons in the Mountains of Ignorance aid in visualizing text descriptions.

Teaching Ideas

The Phantom Tollbooth beautifully integrates mathematics and language arts teaching. Chapter 10 affords great discussions on perspective, and contemplation of Reality versus Illusion, "You see to tall men I'm a midget, and to short men I'm a giant; to the skinny ones I'm a fat man, and to the fat ones I'm a thin man." Chapter 14 leads into wonderful connections with two-dimensional and three-dimensional geometry when Milo meets the Dodecahedron. Moreover, the road sign to Digitopolis can branch off into multiple lessons on Customary unit conversions.

DIGITOPOLIS
5 Miles
1,600 Rods
8,800 Yards
26,400 Feet
316,800 Inches
633,600 Half inches
AND THEN SOME

Chapter 15 introduces students to the concept of Infinity, while Chapter 16 offers witty insights into the study of Statistics and Averages. Milo is stunned to encounter a portion of a child, who subsequently explains that he's the .58 of the 2.58 children each average family has.

Book Connections

Along with reading the book, students delight in performing the play, *The Phantom Tollbooth*, by Susan Nanus. The script may be ordered from Samuel French, Inc., samuelfrench@earthlink.net (item number 18004, for

$6.00 each). In addition, a delightfully animated movie, *The Phantom Tollbooth*, is available in VHS format (Color, Rated G, ASIN: 6301971523, $19.98).

Genre
Fantasy; Chapter Book

Teaching Uses
Book Clubs; Independent Reading; Content Area Study

A Field Guide to the Classroom Library, Lucy Calkins and the Teachers College Reading and Writing Project, Heinemann, ©2002 Teachers College, Columbia University; http://www.heinemann.com/fieldguides

The President's Cabinet: And How It Grew

Nancy Winslow Parker

Book Summary

The beginning of the book is an overview of the Cabinet today and its functions. For the bulk of the book, each page describes a particular president's changes to the body of the Cabinet with a cartoon-like character alongside the text to illustrate the change graphically. This is followed by a description of each of the offices of the Cabinet in turn. The text of these descriptions is exceedingly small, like captions. At the end of the book is a summary of changes to the Cabinet, in table form. This is followed by maps of the United States throughout its history, to give readers an idea of the territory with which various Cabinets were concerned. Next is a chart of the approximate budgets of the fifteen Cabinet offices in 1991. Finally, there is a description of the cleaning of the room after the Cabinet meeting is over each week.

Basic Book Information

This Nonfiction picture book is forty pages long. The book has no table of contents, but it has a detailed index of the positions and position holders of the presidents' Cabinets.

Noteworthy Features

This text takes a complicated and often overlooked aspect of government and explains it carefully and precisely, even with a touch of humor. The illustrations are excellent, witty summaries of the text they accompany, and they make skimming the book much easier. The clear organization of the book allows browsing to be meaningful, and information hunting to be productive.

While not talking down to the reader, this book does not employ many technical terms and therefore doesn't require a glossary. However, understanding this book requires a basic knowledge of government in America, including a general understanding of the system of checks and balances amidst the three branches of government. A general understanding of concepts like the powers of the Constitution, reelection of presidents, resignation, and appointed positions is assumed. Of course, without understanding any of this, some knowledge can still be gleaned from the book.

There is also a one-paragraph introduction/recommendation of the book written by former Secretary of State Dean Rusk. Some children may be

Publisher
Harper Trophy, 1991

ISBN
0064461319

TC Level
12

A Field Guide to the Classroom Library, Lucy Calkins and the Teachers College Reading and Writing Project, Heinemann, ©2002 Teachers College, Columbia University; http://www.heinemann.com/fieldguides

excited to learn who he is and that he has read and appreciated the same book they now hold.

Teaching Ideas

The text includes descriptions of pressures from the general public to create certain Cabinet positions, and it describes reactions of the general public to certain changes in the Cabinet. This allows for discussions of democracy and democratic processes.

The pictures of Cabinet members show clearly the predominance of white men. Students may well notice this, and teachers can take this opportunity to open a conversation about issues of women and minorities in government.

This book can be well-used in classrooms where children often read the newspapers. Readers of articles that quote or refer to members of the president's Cabinet can use this book to educate themselves about who each official is and what his or her responsibilities are.

Genre
Nonfiction; Picture Book

Teaching Uses
Reading and Writing Nonfiction; Content Area Study; Independent Reading; Critique

A Field Guide to the Classroom Library, Lucy Calkins and the Teachers College Reading and Writing Project, Heinemann, ©2002 Teachers College, Columbia University; http://www.heinemann.com/fieldguides

The Reptile Room (Book the Second)

Lemony Snicket

Book Summary

In this installment of the tongue-in-cheek travails of the Baudelaire children, Violet, Klaus, and baby Sunny live briefly in happiness with their Uncle Monty, a herpetologist. Shortly thereafter, the evil Count Olaf, disguised as a new assistant to Uncle Monty, tries to kidnap the children and win their fortune. The resourceful trio escapes from Olaf, only to be rendered homeless once more.

The Reptile Room is second in what is projected to be a thirteen-book series. Each book is narrated and begins with ample background information. At least through book five, *The Austere Academy*, the characters remain the same. As a result, books can be read out of order without any major confusion, though they are best read in order.

Basic Book Information

This 190-pagebook has thirteen numbered chapters of nine to fourteen pages. Illustrations are by Brett Helquist.

Noteworthy Features

For information on characters, see *The Bad Beginning*.

As in the entire series, the story line is full of hyperbolic and hair-raising events. The playfully ironic opening tells the reader what to expect: "The stretch of road that leads out of the city, past Hazy Harbor and into the town of Tedia, is perhaps the most unpleasant in the world." Subsequently, Monty and the children plan a trip to Peru, a huge snake bites Sunny, Count Olaf tracks them down, threatens them with a knife and murders Monty, and the children finally succeed in convincing the clueless adults around them of Olaf's guilt. Only the most literal readers will fail to recognize these as exaggerations and impossibilities.

As in other books of the series, the narrator editorializes about events. His overly dramatic style will indicate to most readers that such statements should be understood as irony. For example, the narrator says, "It is unfortunate, of course, that this quiet, happy moment was the last one the children would have for quite some time, but there is nothing anyone can do about it now" (p. 39).

Vocabulary is fairly difficult, but can often be understood in context. What is harder to understand is often explained by the narrator. The explanations of vocabulary and literary terms are both useful and humorous. For example, on page 31, the narrator defines "dramatic irony" and illustrates it with an anecdote about veal marsala. He writes that a knife's blade glows like a lighthouse, and, to explain the simile, states that both the knife and lighthouse warn of danger (p. 59). He frequently

Series
Series of Unfortunate Events

Illustrator
Brett Helquist

Publisher
Harper Collins, 2000

ISBN
0064407675

TC Level
12

introduces comments with statements like "as you probably know," so that more knowledgeable readers will not feel condescended to, and less knowledgeable ones will not feel ignorant.

Teaching Ideas

All of the books in the series invite study of melodrama, literary devices, parody, the role of the narrator, and vocabulary. See *The Bad Beginning* for more details.

Genre
Chapter Book; Fantasy; Mystery

Teaching Uses
Independent Reading; Book Clubs; Read Aloud

A Field Guide to the Classroom Library, Lucy Calkins and the Teachers College Reading and Writing Project, Heinemann, ©2002 Teachers College, Columbia University; http://www.heinemann.com/fieldguides

The Secret Garden
Frances Hodgson Burnett

Book Summary

In *The Secret Garden*, Mary Lennox, a weak, disagreeable and recently-orphaned child is sent from India to live with her uncle in England. Lonely and struggling, she finds a secret garden by the old stone house. Her growing love of the garden proves the key to not only *her* happiness, but the happiness of her sickly cousin Colin and her grieving uncle.

Basic Book Information

The Secret Garden has 298 pages and twenty-seven titled chapters of between eight and nineteen pages.

Noteworthy Features

The Secret Garden is a beautifully-written classic. The story emphasizes character, motivation, and descriptive writing over plot and action. It will appeal to those readers who enjoy deeper explorations of character and an old-fashioned, lyrical style of writing.

The main character, Mary Lennox, will grab most reader's attention because she makes such an unlikely heroine-self-centered, bossy, and peevish. Her transformation from bratty child to altruist is gradual and accompanied by realistic setbacks. Mary's motivations are complicated and make that transformation meaningful. Growing up in India, she was both catered to and deprived of affection; in England, she learns to take care of herself and recognize the satisfactions of doing so. From there, she learns to care for the secret garden and enjoy the results. The reasons behind Colin's bad temper and self-pity, and the ensuing reasons for his recovery, are carefully developed.

In order to understand Mary's life before England, readers may benefit from some information about England's colonization of India. Some attitudes in the book are outdated, and readers should keep in mind the book's age as they read about India, Colin's illness and treatment, and the attitudes of masters and servants.

The language in *The Secret Garden* is sophisticated, and contains Indian terms, for example, "ayah" (p. 1), "obsequious" (p. 25), and "imperious" (p. 101). The Yorkshire accents and local vocabulary add another level of difficulty. For example, "Canna thy dress thysen!" (p. 26) means "Can't you dress yourself?" Readers need to have solid vocabularies and be fairly skilled at inferring meaning from context.

The earnest tone and resolutely happy ending-a "crippled" boy learns to walk-will be satisfying to some readers and too neat for others. An absence of irony, though, can be a welcome change from the highly ironic tone of much current material.

Publisher
Scholastic

ISBN
0590433466

TC Level
12

A Field Guide to the Classroom Library, Lucy Calkins and the Teachers College Reading and Writing Project, Heinemann, ©2002 Teachers College, Columbia University; http://www.heinemann.com/fieldguides

A major theme of the story is that society is largely bad, while nature is basically good. Society spoils: Mary's sociable parents die of a contagious disease; Mary's behavior is spoiled by her upbringing by those sociable parents and by her luxurious lifestyle; Colin is spoiled by being kept indoors and by too much doctoring. On the other hand, nature heals: the uneducated housemaid and her "wild" brother are sources of wisdom; the garden and its animals help turn Mary and Colin into kind, resourceful people.

Teaching Ideas

The Secret Garden provides an excellent opportunity to study character development and motivation. In addition, Mary and Colin might be compared. How are they similar and different? Do they change for the same reasons, or not?

The book concerns upper-class characters, but it also provides glimpses of the working class. What does the book say about the classes? Is this book fair?

As part of an exploration of the theme concerning nature and society, readers might look at the descriptions of the inside of the house, including Mary's and Colin's bedrooms, and contrast them with the descriptions of the moor and the garden.

Genre
Chapter Book

Teaching Uses
Book Clubs; Critique; Independent Reading

The Skin I'm In

Sharon G. Flake

Book Summary

The book is written in first-person point of view told by Maleeka Madison using the voice of a city teenager, full of slang and Black English. The story of Maleeka's growing up begins, "The first time I seen her...". This is a realistic fiction book that focuses on the hardships of fitting in at school and of being different (peer pressure). *The Skin I'm In* is an interior view of someone (Maleeka) who looks different and is insecure about herself because of it. This is also a story about a world that finds difference hard to accept and live with. The story takes place predominantly in school and the characters are kids in class, the teachers, and the principal.

This book brings up the subject of school assignments and Maleeka begins writing a diary for a slave girl during the 17th century. The teacher wants her students to "know what it feels like to live in somebody else's skin and to see the world through somebody else's eyes." The diary entries begin, "Dear Diary" and can be distinguished easily from the regular text by italics. The story moves chronologically forward, occasionally circling back to a memory of her father, "My Daddy used to always pinch it [her nose] when I was little," with overt clues to the past, like "used to." Her father is dead and any reference to him is as a memory. The diary entries crop up every few chapters of Maleeka's alter ego, Alkeema, and show a softer, more poetic side of Maleeka. This structure helps to round out her character.

Basic Book Information

Winner of the 1999 Coretta Scott King John Steptoe Award for new authors *The Skin I'm In* is 171 pages long, with 32 chapters, numbered with no titles, varying from three to nine pages in length. There are no illustrations. The print size is small with median spacing between words and lines. The main character, Maleeka, is in 7th grade.

Noteworthy Features

The story is set in an urban middle school with its first and second periods, lockers, and homework. Maleeka is a character in conflict over her life, encountering typical issues in an adolescent's life. "If I do this, will I be accepted?" she often asks. Maleeka's voice is the voice the reader hears throughout the book. She is the narrator and she talks like many city kids, not grown-up talk or proper talk. Her character is very accessible to city kids and her landscape (setting) will be familiar to them, too. Her dilemma is more universal than her language and setting: peer pressure happens in city, suburban, and rural settings. This book may be especially important for kids in urban areas who are of color. *The Skin I'm In* is a step above *Junebug* and *Junebug and the Reverend*, but very much the same kind of book. The main

Publisher
Hyperion, 1998

ISBN
0786804440

TC Level
13

characters struggle to become themselves despite their hardships and trials of the city landscape. The oral language is a strong feature of this book and will be attractive to readers as well, pulling them into understanding and to side with and root for Maleeka, "She don't even give the girl a chance to move...".

Teaching Ideas

This book is good for read alouds and for discussions to deal with peer pressure, racism, and prejudice. It would also be good for book clubs. The short chapters chunk this book well, giving a struggling reader structure to work within and so would make for a good independent read for someone moving past a book like *Junebug*.

Genre
Chapter Book

Teaching Uses
Book Clubs; Independent Reading

A Field Guide to the Classroom Library, Lucy Calkins and the Teachers College Reading and Writing Project, Heinemann, ©2002 Teachers College, Columbia University; http://www.heinemann.com/fieldguides

The Trolls

Polly Horvath

Book Summary

Not wanting to "spread the buboes around," the Anderson's babysitter calls in sick. Forced with having to find a babysitter before their trip to Paris, the Anderson's reluctantly call Aunt Sally. Pee Wee, Amanda, and Melissa are so excited to finally meet their aunt from Canada. When she arrives, the kids know they're in for an adventure by taking one look at their outrageous Aunt Sally. And, they are *not* disappointed.

Every day, Aunt Sally tells the kids an exciting new story about her family's life on Vancouver Island, such as the story of "Great-Uncle Louis who came for two weeks and stayed for six years" and Maude, who shot eighty cougars. One night, Aunt Sally tells the children the story that will forever change the family... "The Trolls." Great-Uncle Louis said that there were trolls who lived on the beach and took things that people didn't want anymore. The story recounts the night that Sally's jealousy of their father, led her to leave him for the trolls. Melissa notices a discrepancy in her aunt's story . . . it couldn't have been the trolls. . . .Because Great-Uncle Louis said that once you give something to the trolls you can never have it back." Sally sadly says that she never did get her brother back the night she left him for these mythological creatures, ". . . a lot of life was gone from the dinner table after he left . . . some acts alter things forever."

Basic Book Information

The Trolls is a National Book Award Finalist. It is also a *Boston Globe*-Horn Book Award Honor Book. Polly Horvath is the author of other books for children including, *An Occasional Cow*, *No More Cornflakes*, *The Happy Yellow Car* and *When the Circus Came to Town*.

Noteworthy Features

The Trolls is narrated in third person but primarily the story is told through Aunt Sally. Aunt Sally tells the children about their family history through stories. Often, Sally acts as the narrator by recounting the precise dialogue of the characters in the story and making commentary. " 'So,' I said one day when Edward and John and I were scrambling over boulders down by the sea, sticking our fingers in anemones and catching crabs. 'So you think there are really trolls down here among the rocks?' " Dialogue within dialogue in this story may be confusing for some readers.

It is also important to note that every time Aunt Sally tells a story the reader is transported back to the past. So, there are frequent jumps backward in time to when Aunt Sally was growing up.

There are many difficult words in *The Trolls* since Melissa likes using "fancy words." Often times, readers also have these words defined by Melissa

Illustrator
Wendy Anderson Halperin

Publisher
Farrar Straus Giroux, 1999

ISBN
0374377871

TC Level
14

A Field Guide to the Classroom Library, Lucy Calkins and the Teachers College Reading and Writing Project, Heinemann, ©2002 Teachers College, Columbia University; http://www.heinemann.com/fieldguides

in her effort to show off. For example, " 'What's a visage?' asked Amanda. 'Face,' said Melissa 'Now, shhh.'"

Teaching Ideas

In a read aloud, teachers may want to use different voices for every person in order to keep the abundance of eccentric characters straight. Readers can use this strategy when reading alone or with a partner. *The Trolls* is heavy in dialogue and speakers. Often, the speaker has to be inferred. The strategy of using distinguishable character voices, either aloud or to themselves, may help readers identify the characters. Another strategy readers may use to identify characters is by using the illustrations on the book jacket. By having pictures of the characters, it may help to visualize the story better.

There seems to be elements of both fantasy and truth in Aunt Sally's stories. When she leaves the children ask themselves, "How much of those stories do you believe? She made them seem so real when she was here. ..." Readers may ask themselves the same question as they read tales about the day grandmother got so wrapped up in a pinball game that she spent the families savings in a machine and the time Sally put a curse on the fat-little mean girl. Readers may want to collect textual support for their ideas about the fact-or-fiction quotient of Aunt Sally's tales.

Readers may notice that many of the stories parallel Melissa, Amanda, and Pee Wee's life. For instance, Melissa and Amanda find Pee Wee to be a nuisance. In the story of the trolls, Aunt Sally is mean to her little brother, too. Leaving her brother, Robbie, to the Trolls forever changes their relationship. Some readers may feel that Aunt Sally's absurd stories are a way for her to teach the children a lesson. Others may see the parallels between an aunt and her niece or nephew's lives as a case of history repeating itself. Readers may find it interesting to look into why Aunt Sally tells the children the stories she does.

The Trolls contains a lot of foreshadowing. Throughout the course of the other tales she always brings up the trolls. Readers may notice that by the time Aunt Sally tells the story of the Trolls Amanda, Melissa *and* Polly Horvath's readers are on the edge of their seats. Horvath uses teasers by telling us just a little about the Trolls but not enough. This makes readers feel the same way the kids do. ..."We *have* to make Aunt Sally finish the story of the trolls."

The Trolls is a very funny and outrageous book. Some readers may not grasp the humor in Aunt Sally's absurd musings. Readers who interpret the book literally may be confused when Aunt Sally says thing like "Haven't you noticed that Americans know nothing about Canada?...We take a solemn vow every morning of our lives not to ever tell any Americans what goes on up there. When you go to shopping malls close to the border, you see Canadians walking around looking absolutely terrified. ...They restrain their impulse to leap into shopping carts and race each other up and down the halls."

Young writers may want to study the way that quotation marks are used. Within the story, whenever Aunt Sally speaks there are quotation marks. Aunt Sally often describes the events of the story in this manner. Then, Aunt Sally also lets us know what the characters in the story say to one another by using single quotation marks within the double ones. By giving us actual

A Field Guide to the Classroom Library, Lucy Calkins and the Teachers College Reading and Writing Project, Heinemann, ©2002 Teachers College, Columbia University; http://www.heinemann.com/fieldguides

dialogue it brings her stories to life. Her eccentric characters are given their own voices.

Genre
Fantasy; Chapter Book

Teaching Uses
Read Aloud; Independent Reading; Language Conventions; Book Clubs; Interpretation

A Field Guide to the Classroom Library, Lucy Calkins and the Teachers College Reading and Writing Project, Heinemann, ©2002 Teachers College, Columbia University; http://www.heinemann.com/fieldguides

The Twits
Roald Dahl

Book Summary

The Twits is a terrible tale about two ugly old people. Their ugliness manifests itself into everything they do. First, the narrator introduces the characters and explains how they became so ugly: "If a person has ugly thoughts, it begins to show on the face. And when that person has ugly thoughts every day, every week, every year, the face gets uglier and uglier until it gets so ugly you can hardly bear to look at it." The Twits reign terror on each other, making their lives more and more miserable each day.

In between torturing each other, The Twits find time to spread their unhappiness to everyone and everything around them. Their pet monkeys, the Muggle-Wumps, are forced to stand on their heads all day long for no reason. The Twits terrorize innocent birds by spreading "Horrible Hugtight" onto the branches of trees, so when the birds land on the branch they stick and can't get away. Unfortunately, these birds end up in the weekly bird pie, the Wednesday night special. The plot starts to change when the Muggle-Wumps band together with Roly-Poly, a bilingual bird that swoops down and rescues his species. Together, the animals play a crafty trick on the Twits, leaving them to meet their timely demise.

Basic Book Information

Roald Dahl, a masterful storyteller, is the author of *The Twits*, a delightfully disgusting book about karma and revenge. Dahl has written several very popular books, such as *James and the Giant Peach*, *Matilda*, and *The Witches*.

The Twits has 76 pages with 29 chapters. The chapter titles are written in a way to give you small clues as to what will come next, without totally giving the book away. Then again, each chapter is as unpredictable as the next. Almost every page has an illustration by Quentin Blake that captures the expressions of each character.

Noteworthy Features

The text is rich with ongoing alliteration, such as "squiggly spaghetti," "filthy feathery frumps," and "fearful frumptious freaks," to name a few. Students will find this a delightful read, even if they do tend to stumble over some of the expressions.

This book contains some material that is borderline offensive. The pet monkeys speak a "weird African language," according to the author. This could unfortunately give students a negative connotation to African languages. Different does not mean weird. In addition, Roly-Poly, the bilingual bird makes this comment: "It's no good going to a country and not

Illustrator
Quentin Blake

Publisher
The Penguin Group, 1980

ISBN
0141301074

TC Level
10

knowing the language." Again, this type of subversive comment might make the reader question the values of the author.

Teaching Ideas

The short chapters make this an easy read for children. Students will want to explore the text on their own, probably imitating the voices of the characters, including the talking animals. It would also make a great book for partners to read together.

Dahl provides foreshadowing when Mr. Twit is scaring Mrs. Twit by telling her about the shrinks and "in the end there's nothing left except a pair of shoes and a bundle of clothes." Ironically, this is how the book ends. There are a few good book talks that could revolve around the use of foreshadowing.

The book has a great lead-"What a lot of hairy-faced men there are around these days." It could be used for just that-a mini-lesson on leads.

It would be interesting to explore the relationship the Twits have with one another. Do they love each other or hate each other? Is it a love/hate relationship? Can two people be happily miserable together? What about Mr. Twit-would he really have let Mrs. Twit float away from earth? What would his life be like without her, or her life without him?

Although this is a book and not a poem, readers could explore the use of alliteration and onomatopoeia. How do these techniques help make language come alive?

Another interesting discussion could revolve around the everyday habits of the Twits. Why do they have less than humanistic characteristics? Why do they like to catch birds and eat them? Readers can discuss the idea of not being accepted in society, and the impact it has on you as an individual.

Lastly, there is the topic of revenge. Did the Twits get what they deserve? Is there such a thing as karma? Were the Twits predestined to die a miserable death, because of the misery they bestowed on others? All these questions and more tend to come up in book club discussions children have.

Genre
Fantasy; Short Chapter Book

Teaching Uses
Book Clubs; Independent Reading; Character Study

A Field Guide to the Classroom Library, Lucy Calkins and the Teachers College Reading and Writing Project, Heinemann, ©2002 Teachers College, Columbia University; http://www.heinemann.com/fieldguides

The View from Saturday

E.L Konigsburg

Book Summary

A View from Saturday is the story of a group of four sixth-grade students, and their coach, who form an Academic Bowl team. It is several stories wrapped together: the forming of the team chosen by the coach, the students' friendships, their competition in the finals, and their individual histories. It is a complicated book, but, for most readers, it is very interesting and fun to figure out.

Basic Book Information

This 12-chapter book of realistic fiction is 160 pages long. It is a Newbery Awardwinner. It contains many different characters, narrators, and plots. Movement though time is not chronological and the text includes flashbacks.

Noteworthy Features

The View from Saturday is a very complex book structurally. It is essentially the story of a group of four children and their teacher (an Academic Bowl team and coach), but each character also gets to tell part of the past from his or her own perspective and flashbacks so overlapping plots are common. The reader needs to keep track of not only the story of the present (the Bowl competition), but also a variety of past events, ranging from interactions earlier in the school year, to vacations and relatives met last summer, to the thoughts of the teacher about the individual members. It is an entertaining book, and discovering the overlaps and tracking timelines are part of the challenge and accomplishment of reading it.

It is best to recommend this book to a student who is a fairly advanced reader and who has read other books with slightly simpler multiple plots and/or multiple narrators and perspectives, as well as non-chronological presentation, for example *Holes* by Louis Sachar, or *Seedfolks* or *Bull Run*, both by Paul Fleischman.

Although the structure of the book is quite complex, the breaks and changes in time and narrator are clearly marked in the text with chapter changes or with noticeable chapter breaks (marked with a new title within a chapter or three large dots). New narrators are clearly identified and introduced. Students can be taught to cue into the visual breaks to help them notice the story breaks.

Teaching Ideas

It can be a very good advanced book to use in the teaching of story elements. *A View from Saturday* has a lot to keep track of in terms of

A Field Guide to the Classroom Library, Lucy Calkins and the Teachers College Reading and Writing Project, Heinemann, ©2002 Teachers College, Columbia University; http://www.heinemann.com/fieldguides

Publisher

Aladdin Paperbacks, 1996

ISBN

068980993X

TC Level

13

movements through time, plot, and characters. It could be a good book for individuals (or even more helpful, partnerships, or book clubs) to work on not only retelling, but summarizing and placing events and characters in context. This would be a good challenge book if a very competent reader has trouble following complicated stories. It is a character-driven story, and contains much that could be used in a discussion of character development and change. This book could also be used to think/talk about perspective, since sometimes the very same events are told by more than one narrator.

It's important for readers to pay attention to how E.L. Konigsburg changes the way the text looks to indicate changes in the story-this will help them keep track of all the different stories. Teachers may want to have readers find a partner to read this book with or to have students jot notes as they read to help them keep track of all the different parts.

Book Connections

Texts that could be read alongside this one include, *Seedfolks* and *Bull Run* by Paul Fleischmam, and *Bat 6* by Virginia Woolf. Other texts that have multiple plots that overlap and intersect are *Holes* by Louis Sachar, and *The Westing Game* by Ellen Raskin.

Genre
Chapter Book

Teaching Uses
Character Study; Book Clubs; Partnerships; Independent Reading

A Field Guide to the Classroom Library, Lucy Calkins and the Teachers College Reading and Writing Project, Heinemann, ©2002 Teachers College, Columbia University; http://www.heinemann.com/fieldguides

The Wanderer

Sharon Creech

Book Summary

This is the story of 13-year-old Sophie and her cousin Cody as they travel across the Atlantic aboard the *Wanderer*, a forty-five foot sailboat. They are on their way to England from Connecticut to visit their grandfather, Bompie.

Basic Book Information

From Newbery Medal author, Sharon Creech, we have a new book, *The Wanderer*. It has 6 parts and 78 chapters, yet each chapter is small and digestible. The jacket copy explains that it is told "through Sophie and Cody's travel logs...", but that isn't immediately apparent as the reader hears Sophie's voice alone for 27 pages and 5 chapters. After page 28, Sophie and Cody alternate telling the story, many times overlapping and telling their own versions of events (two points of view).

Sophie and Cody's chapters use different fonts, which remind the reader of the two different points of views. After a while the voices become equated with the font.

There are 305 pages with 78 chapters. Chapters have titles that are extremely supportive and that refer to the setting or to major events in the story. There are 6 parts to this book: the first part, "Preparation", has four chapters; the second part, "Shakedown", has ten chapters; the third part, "The Island," has eight chapters; the fourth part, "Under Way," has thirteen chapters; the fifth part (and the longest from page 181-241), has twenty-five chapters; and the sixth part, "Land," has eighteen chapters. There are black and white drawings by David Diaz that punctuate every part-title page and every chapter-title page. Immediately to the right of the drawing is "Sophie" or "Cody" (Cody begins his narration on page 28).

Chapters are short, ranging from one to eight pages in length. Chapters are both numbered and titled. Print size is medium, with medium spacing between words, and large (double) spacing between lines.

Noteworthy Features

Dialogue is a large piece of the narrative and often it is not referenced. The reader needs to use inferring skills as well as identification of the voice of the character when she reads.

The titles of the chapters serve as guides to the book, ferrying a reader along to the end. There is a mystery to the character of Sophie; the readers wonder throughout the book what her real story is and this overwhelming sense of curiosity pushes the reader on. It is easy for some readers, as well as Sophie, to think that making a trans-Atlantic crossing in a sailboat is a

Illustrator
David Diaz

Publisher
Harper Collins, 2000

ISBN
0060277300

TC Level
12

beautiful, relaxing thing, but the reader soon finds the event of sailing to be difficult.

Some readers will be drawn to both Sophie and Cody because the story is written in a journal fashion, in the first-person point of view, and these characters seem to be speaking their words aloud.

Teaching Ideas

This book is good for read alouds because the voices of the characters are so strong. However, it might be even better for independent reading, partner, and book club situations for the same reasons. The voice is so strong, that the teacher's voice doesn't need to intercede. This book is good as an independent reading book to build stamina in book length. It is already "chunked" by chapters and is ready to go. This is also a great book for partner reading and book club because there is so much to wonder about and Creech creates many pauses with the chapter breaks, which encourage discussion.

Book Connections

Sharon Creech is also the author of *Walk Two Moons* and many other outstanding books for young adults.

Genre
Chapter Book

Teaching Uses
Independent Reading; Book Clubs; Read Aloud

A Field Guide to the Classroom Library, Lucy Calkins and the Teachers College Reading and Writing Project, Heinemann, ©2002 Teachers College, Columbia University; http://www.heinemann.com/fieldguides

The Watsons Go to Birmingham-1963

Christopher Paul Curtis

Book Summary

The Watsons Go to Birmingham-1963 tells the story of an African American family including Kenny, Byron, Joetta, and Momma and Dad who live in Flint, Michigan. They are also self-named the "Weird Watsons" due to their silly antics and humorous interactions with each other. The story is told through the eyes of ten year-old Kenny Watson. Byron, a thirteen-year-old "official juvenile delinquent," keeps on getting into trouble. Momma and Dad decide the whole family will visit their grandmother in Birmingham, Alabama. They think she will help straighten him out and take him away from his pal Buphead, whom they feel is a bad influence.

Although this work of historical fiction takes place during one of the most racially tense times in America's history, Byron and Kenny have not been exposed to racism. This changes when Kenny accidentally witnesses the aftermath of one of the darkest points in America's history-the bombing of the Sixteenth Avenue Baptist Church during Sunday school that killed four young teenage girls. It is at this point that Byron helps Kenny through this very difficult time and shows how supportive family members can be, even the Weird Watsons.

Basic Book Information

This book is the winner of the Newbery Honor, Coretta Scott King Honor, and many other awards. It is written by Christopher Paul Curtis, who also wrote *Bud, Not Buddy*.

It is 210 pages long, and divided into 15 titled chapters and an Epilogue. This historical fiction book is not illustrated. The story is told in first-person narrative, from Kenny's point of view.

Noteworthy Features

This book is marked by its use of dialogue to create a very believable, likeable family. The family members make fun of each other in a lighthearted way, such as when Dad makes fun of Momma's hometown of Flint, saying, "Folks there live in these things called igloos." Another example is when Byron gets his lips frozen to the car mirror and Dad says, "Well, lover boy, I guess this means no one can call you Hot Lips, can they?"

Despite the humorous nature of the book, it also deals with themes that many students can relate to. These include friendship and family. When Kenny is told to help the new student Rufus feel welcome, it initially feels like a burden. Rufus speaks funny, wears raggedy clothes, and never brings

Publisher
Bantam Doubleday Dell, 1997

ISBN
0440414121

TC Level
13

lunch to school. However, Rufus proves to be a true friend until one day Kenny laughs along with the other students at him. Realizing the error of his ways, Kenny despairingly tells Momma about the incident. Momma meets Rufus and his brother Cody at the bus stop and when they get off they say "Hi, Mrs. Watson, and gave her their big smiles. The three of them walked towards Rufus's house. Momma put her hand on Rufus's head while they walked." Later Rufus appears at the door of the Watsons' house and Kenny apologizes for his behavior.

Perhaps most importantly, Curtis provides a text through which the craft of writing can be explored. He begins with a humorous mood throughout the first twelve chapters. In chapter thirteen, which may be confusing to young readers, there is a definite shift in tone with the "Wool Pooh," which symbolizes and foreshadows the social evil of racism. This ominous mood is heightened in the following chapters, when Kenny goes to look for Joetta and sees the carnage from the church bombing.

Teaching Ideas

This book lends itself to a variety of mini-lessons and strategy lessons about writers' craft. It works well, especially with reluctant readers, because of its easy style. Students can be directed to view character development through language/dialogue, actions, and changes the characters go through throughout the story. A good example of this might be to notice how Byron changes. He matures from a boy who is always getting into trouble like playing with matches to one who helps Kenny overcome the devastation that results from seeing the church carnage. He tells Kenny, "You ain't got no cause to be ashamed or scared of nothing. You smart enough to figure this one out yourself. Besides, you getting the word from the top wolf hisself; you gonna be all right, baby, bruh. I swear for God." As mentioned under the previous heading, the idea of the shifting mood with the "Wool Pooh" could also be explored. It would also make for an interesting inquiry into why Curtis chose to do this in his book (to soften the blow of the bombing for younger readers? Endear the Watsons to the readers?).

The setting of this book in Civil Rights era America is one of its strongest teaching points. It would be good to use in a genre study of historical fiction. In addition, mini-lessons on setting as a crucial story element could work well because the effects the setting has on plot, characters, and so on.

Because the end of the book can be somewhat confusing due to the change from the focus on family and friends to the church bombing, a mini-lesson could be done on monitoring for sense, and re-reading to check for understanding. This would help students ensure that they have not breezed through a section that may be somewhat unclear.

Book Connections

There are several books that can be connected to this book. Other books dealing with the topic of family include Lois Lowry's *The Giver*, and Mildred D. Taylor's *Roll of Thunder, Hear My Cry*. In *The Giver*, a science fiction book, the role of family is quite different as marriages are arranged; there is no romantic love/affection between spouses. This differs drastically from Momma and Dad in *The Watsons Go to Birmingham-1963*, where the parents' affection for one another is obvious in their teasing. In *Roll of Thunder, Hear My Cry*, more similarities can be drawn. Just as the Watsons travel very far to help Byron and help support Kenny through the haunting time after the bombing, the Logans band together at a time when their land is being threatened.

Genre
Historical Fiction; Chapter Book

Teaching Uses
Content Area Study

A Field Guide to the Classroom Library, Lucy Calkins and the Teachers College Reading and Writing Project, Heinemann, ©2002 Teachers College, Columbia University; http://www.heinemann.com/fieldguides

The Winter Room

Gary Paulsen

Book Summary

Eldon, his parents, brother Wayne, and great uncles live "on a farm on the edge of a forest." Readers follow their lives through four seasons and come to know about the hardships and joys of farm life. In the spring, the air is rich with smells of thawing decay, but the family finds pleasure in an occasional dance at the local beer hall. Summer is filled with plowing work and hearty dinners to satiate appetites grown from a hard day's labor. Fall "starts off better than it ends." At the beginning, the whole family has a picnic by the lake, but soon it's killing time. The time, when animals go to slaughter and their blood and cries leave indelible marks on the family's psyches. Then, it's Eldon's favorite season-winter. This is the time when the whole family gathers in the Winter Room, known as a living room to others, to hear Uncle David's stories.

All is well, until Uncle David tells a story about himself as a young man, back when he was a woodcutter of great fame. He claims the story is true, but Wayne looking at his feeble old uncle cannot believe it so. Wayne feels like his uncle is a sham,"...he's been lying with the stories, just telling us lies." Feelings are hurt, family ties are broken, and great storytelling ends. Then, one day, Wayne and Eldon look through the opening in the barn and they see something horrible; their old uncle was wielding an axe surely too great for his strength. Then, in one magical moment, he became young again and struck the wood with "silver curves." Uncle David proved to them, but most importantly to himself, that he was the woodcutter. They never told their uncle what they saw. They didn't need to. The stories started up once again. As Uncle David spun tales that evening they listened, and they believed.

Basic Book Information

The Winter Room is written by Gary Paulsen who is the author of such books as *The Voyage of the FROG*, *Brian's Winter* and *The Monument*. He won the Newbery Honor Award for *The Winter Room*, as well as *Hatchet* and *Dogsong*.

Noteworthy Features

The book contains a prologue, which is called "Tuning." Then, the book is set up in chapters that represent the four seasons: "SPRING," "SUMMER," "FALL," and "WINTER." This straightforward division of time will give readers support as to when the events of the story are taking place. Also, the chapters are focused on the seasons themselves. So, the chapter headings also provide content focus for readers.

In addition to these chapters, there are several additional sections under "WINTER." These chapter headings correspond to the stories that Uncle

Publisher
Dell Publishing, 1989

ISBN
0440404541

TC Level
12

A Field Guide to the Classroom Library, Lucy Calkins and the Teachers College Reading and Writing Project, Heinemann, ©2002 Teachers College, Columbia University; http://www.heinemann.com/fieldguides

David tells during the winter season. It may be confusing for some readers as to why Paulsen deviates from his original order in which each season only has one chapter devoted to it.

Paulsen uses precise language and many farming terms. Readers may be able to use the context of the sentence to determine meaning, but not in all cases. The book is written from Eldon's perspective-in the language of an eleven-year-old boy on a farm. Therefore, children may need to get accustomed to the specific dialect used. Eldon says things like, "And when he laughs I get mad and take after him" and "But come fall. ..."

There are several noteworthy features in reference to time in *The Winter Room*. The book does not make any reference to the exact time the story is taking place. There are mentions of Captain Marvel comics, Sears catalogues, and wax-teeth harmonicas however, so readers may be able to infer that it took place in the second-half of the twentieth century (probably in the 1940s or 1950s). Also, the book is written in past tense.

Teaching Ideas

The Winter Room by Gary Paulsen opens with a foreword that Paulsen entitles "Tuning." In it, Paulsen says that, "If books could have more, give more, be more, show more, they would still need readers, who bring to them sound and smell and light and all the rest that can't be in books." It may be helpful for readers to see that Paulsen relays what is important for him to get across to his readers in "Tuning." Readers may see the prologue as Paulsen's intentions and values that guide his writing. Then, they may note how Paulsen fulfills his intentions throughout the text by creating a story that is rich in sound, smell, and light. It can be discussed during a read aloud that the readers have to create mental images that match his rich descriptions in order for the words to be brought to life.

Readers may look at the way that Paulsen set up *The Winter Room's* chapters as another way to see what the author values. Since "WINTER" is the only chapter that has additional subchapters and is also part of the title of the book, readers may note that this is a device that Paulsen uses to clue the reader into what he is choosing to focus on.

Paulsen uses precise language and many terms relate directly to farm life. Some urban readers may have difficulty figuring out the terminology from the context of the sentence. The context itself is often unfamiliar as well. It may be helpful for readers to understand that they can look to other resources like dictionaries if the unfamiliar word is interfering with comprehension of the story. However, readers could be encouraged to approximate meaning and read on. Sometimes the term can be figured out from the context of the book. Terms are often repeated throughout the text and with their repetition readers can build more approximate meaning.

Time is something that may be confusing to some readers. Eldon, the narrator, talks about his life on the farm in past tense. Readers can perhaps best understand how the story is told as a "retelling." In this retelling, some of the events reoccur every season, that is, "In the spring everything is soft." While, sometimes Eldon focuses on a specific event that happened one time during that season, "Come a late spring day maybe one, two years ago. ..."

Readers individually or in partnerships may want to explore why it was so important for Uncle David to prove that he could still wield an axe like the

A Field Guide to the Classroom Library, Lucy Calkins and the Teachers College Reading and Writing Project, Heinemann, ©2002 Teachers College, Columbia University; http://www.heinemann.com/fieldguides

woodcutter. Also, why he chose to do so without any onlookers.

Readers may also want to note the ways that each of the characters reacts to Uncle David's story of "The Woodcutter." Their reactions may provide readers with a window into the characters of the story. For example, readers may want to figure out why Wayne would become "raw mad" after Uncle David told the story of the woodcutter. They may note other places in the text where Wayne could not separate fact from fiction such as when he "made wings out of some sticks and two feed sacks and tried to fly off the granary roof. A fool would know it wouldn't work..." and build a theory about the character and attach post-it notes to evidence throughout the text for support.

Book Connections

Since Paulsen is such a prolific and accomplished writer of children's literature, an author study may be very interesting to do as a class. For example, by reading the *FROG* and *The Winter Room* during read aloud, discussions may be sparked about common elements in his writing. Discussions could focus on specific terminology (e.g., farming terms and nautical terms), natural settings (a farm and the sea), or the way he sets apart sentences on their own lines for emphasis and main characters that are adolescent boys. An author study may encourage children to read more of Paulsen's books. Also, children can extend the study by exploring more of Paulsen's books individually or in partnerships. Children may begin to build theories of Paulsen's writing as they may note similarities in craft and genre.

Genre
Chapter Book

Teaching Uses
Independent Reading; Read Aloud; Character Study; Interpretation

The Wise Woman and Her Secret

Eve Merriam

Book Summary

This beautifully illustrated book tells the story of a very wise woman who lives alone in the country. People from surrounding towns know of her great wisdom and travel to her home to find her secret. Once there, they abruptly demand that she reveal herself. "We are here for your secret. We have come a long distance, and we wish to get home before dark, so give it to us without delay." Amused, the wise woman will not give them an answer, but allows them to search her house and property.

Frantically, the group goes from place to place looking for the secret, never stopping for more than a minute or two at each location. Meanwhile, a small girl named Jenny trails behind the rest of the group. She curiously observes all that is around her. The group is impatient with the girl. "Don't lag, don't loiter, don't dawdle," they scold. The little girl finally approaches the wise woman and excitedly asks her several questions about a penny the rest of the group discarded in disgust. The delighted woman reveals that Jenny already possesses the secret. Her curiosity and tendency to "wander and wonder" were all she needs to receive the gift of wisdom.

Basic Book Information

The Wise Woman and Her Secret is a picture book that features lush language and illustrations and tells the message that "stopping to smell the roses" will bring wisdom and peace. Eve Merriam is the author of several children's picture books such as *Halloween ABC* as well as poetry collections such as *You Be Good & I'll Be Night: Jump-On The Bed Poems*. Her work as a poet is evident in the gorgeous language she uses throughout the text. Teachers can focus on Merriam in the beginning of the year to demonstrate how writers work in a variety of genres, showing students that Merriam writes poetry, list books, picture books, and ABC books. Eve Merriam's first book was published in the 1960s.

The illustrator, Linda Graves, has illustrated more than 25 books including *Frogs' Legs for Dinner?* Her illustrations have also appeared in major magazines.

Noteworthy Features

This 27-page picture book features idealistic, pastel illustrations that strongly support the text. True to the message of the story, if the reader looks slowly and carefully at each illustration, the wonders of nature can be discovered. A beautifully shaped leaf, curious cat or a bird preparing to take flight are just some of the surprises readers can encounter.

The illustrations could be analyzed to get deeper into the story because they are so detailed and expressive. For example, the illustrations could also

Illustrator
Linda Graves

Publisher
Aladdin Paperbacks, 1991

ISBN
067172603

be used to discuss the idea of following a crowd versus thinking as an individual. Throughout the book, the group looks like a frenzied and somewhat hostile mob than a group looking for answers. When a group member shouts out a wild theory about the woman, the others are shown joining in without hesitation. When the man shouts, "She may not be of our kind at all. Perhaps she isn't a human being like us, perhaps she is from another planet." The crowd looks both excited and enraged. "Yes, yes they began to whisper in excitement, that must be the answer that is why we can't find the secret." Students who are reading the book in partnerships or book clubs may stop to ask, "Is this book fair?" a question many readers ask as they critique their reading.

By contrast, illustrations of Jenny and the wise woman show them looking serene and content. Throughout the book they are both observing nature with a thoughtful gaze and knowing grin. Comparing the images within the same page would most likely produce a lively discussion among students, and encourage them to talk about why the illustrator chose to draw the characters so differently.

Teaching Ideas

There are many teaching points that can be explored with this book. Therefore, it would make a good choice to be a touchtone text, one that is revisited several times throughout the year. While first introduced as a read aloud in order to fully absorb the richness of the language used it could be read independently, in partnerships, or in small groups.

When first read aloud, the teacher could focus on the beautiful language highlighted by the use of metaphor. While that term wouldn't have to be used, a teacher could instead discuss how Eve Merriam helps put a picture in the reader's mind with descriptions such as "She had long, dark hair that was streaked with white, like patches of snow on the muddy spring ground," or "Her voice was soft as the fur of her cat, yet you could hear her every word from far away." During the first reading, the teacher could read these sentences a few times before showing them the illustrations and have students close their eyes and try to picture the woman. They could then discuss what they visualized with a partner. The teacher might later invite the students to try to use descriptive sentences such as these in their own writing.

There are several ways this text could lead children to write about their reading. It is important to note that in order for children to be able to write about their reading, they must first be able to talk about their reading. If studying character traits, for example, children could work with a partner to discuss their ideas about Jenny or another character. If a reader decides that Jenny is "curious," he might then go back with a partner and place post-it notes throughout the book whenever they notice Jenny being curious. They could, for instance, mark pictures of Jenny looking intently at a stick with cobwebs or when she asks the woman many questions about the found penny. The same could be done for the wise woman or for "the crowd."

This book is reminiscent of a folk tale in which a lesson has been learned, and could also be used as a reading center. A small group of children could compare *The Wise Woman and Her Secret* with folk/fairy tales and try to determine if the book would fit in with this category. Students could read through a selection of texts and decide how they would report what they discovered to the whole group. A comparison chart, summary of opinions, or oral presentation are just some of the ways children could share what they noticed in their reading.

Book Connections

Fairy tales by the Brothers Grimm such as *Hansel and Gretel, Little Red Riding Hood,* and *Rumplestiltskin* are tales where a lesson is learned. Books by Jan Brett, such as *The Mitten* and *The Gingerbread Baby* would also make good companions to this book because of the folk tale style and similar illustrations. A connection could also be made to *Wizard of Oz* because a character is seeking what she already possesses much like the characters journeying to the wizard.

Genre
Picture Book; Fairy and Folk Tale

Teaching Uses
Read Aloud; Independent Reading; Teaching Writing

A Field Guide to the Classroom Library, Lucy Calkins and the Teachers College Reading and Writing Project, Heinemann, ©2002 Teachers College, Columbia University; http://www.heinemann.com/fieldguides

The Witch of Blackbird Pond

Elizabeth George Speare

Book Summary

After the death of her grandfather, Kit Tyler leaves her home in Barbados to live with an aunt and family in the Connecticut Colony. Almost immediately, she distinguishes herself as different by jumping into the water to retrieve a doll for an anguished child. She soon realizes that this action was unusual and, as such, unacceptable to her neighbors. Kit's differences are not welcome and are, in fact, looked upon suspiciously by the strict-minded Puritans of the colony.

Kit settles into life with her aunt, uncle, and two cousins. But it is not the carefree existence she had known with her grandfather. Instead, her daily routine consists of constant, grueling work with few intermissions. Kit finds this Spartan way of life suffocating. Her only release is in the visits she makes to the meadow and to the old woman in a nearby cottage, known as the Witch of Blackbird Pond to her neighbors. When this innocent friendship is discovered, however, it casts a greater shadow of suspicion over Kit and she is accused of witchcraft.

Basic Book Information

This book is 249 pages long, divided into 21 chapters, and is not illustrated. The author is a noted writer of historical fiction. *The Witch of Blackbird Pond* received one of the two Newbery Medals awarded to Ms. Speare.

Noteworthy Features

This book should be read for the sheer power of its story. The characters are admirable, and Kit and the Witch of Blackbird Pond exemplify strong, smart, brave characters.

Some students may wonder the extent to which this historical fiction story is true. One way to explore this would be to study an excerpt from a similar text, such as Gary Bowen's *Stranded in Plimouth Plantation*.

Readers will notice that characters use the language of the time. Additionally, the book includes excerpts from a primer reader, a posted notice at the meeting hall, and a poem of a colonial poet. All of these forms of written expression provide ample insight into the mindset of the time, all with reference to the Puritan ethics readily portrayed elsewhere in the book.

Teaching Ideas

This is a coming of age story-the story of a young woman who is compelled to make decisions that will color the complexion of the remainder of her life, choices from which her future will be determined.

There are a number of other themes that are prevalent in *The Witch of*

Publisher
Bantam Doubleday Dell Books

ISBN
0440495962

TC Level
13

A Field Guide to the Classroom Library, Lucy Calkins and the Teachers College Reading and Writing Project, Heinemann, ©2002 Teachers College, Columbia University; http://www.heinemann.com/fieldguides

Blackbird Pond. These include, but are not limited to, the conflict between the individual and the community (self versus society), the role of religion in the colonization of America (tyranny versus tolerance), the nature of prejudice (fear of the unknown), and the personal choices one makes because of, or in spite of, these varied circumstances.

This book lends itself particularly well to an in-depth study of character, specifically the growth of Kit Tyler throughout the developing plot. Additionally, the changes in Kit can be compared and contrasted to some of the other characters-such as the ever-constant Mercy, or the faithful John Holbrook.

An interesting extension of this character study could be the study of author's craft as it pertains to characterization. This line of inquiry could begin with questions. How does the author play characters off one another (e.g, William Ashby vs. Nat Easton)? Are there parallels between characters or the actions of characters (e.g., Kit's decision to give up William Ashby, John Holbrook's decision to marry Mercy instead of Judith)? Do characters symbolize ideas relative to the major themes within the text (e.g., Uncle Matthew, patriot vs. Reverend Gersholm, royalist; Goodwife Cuff, religious intolerant vs. Hannah Tupper, religious tolerant; Nat Easton, independent vs. William Ashby, society's child)? How do the actions of characters signify the changes in characters (e.g., Kit's abandonment of William Ashby and acceptance of Nat Easton; Kit's decision to help Hannah Tupper)?

Book Connections

Stranded in Plimouth Plantation by Gary Bowen is another example of historical fiction that takes place during the same era as *The Witch of Blackbird Pond*. It is written in journal format by a visitor to the colony and is rife with factual information pertaining to the time period.

The Crucible by Arthur Miller is a play depicting the witch hunts that took place in Salem, Massachusetts in 1692. There are many parallels between themes and characters within this play and *The Witch of Blackbird Pond*.

Genre
Historical Fiction; Chapter Book

Teaching Uses
Independent Reading; Character Study; Interpretation

A Field Guide to the Classroom Library, Lucy Calkins and the Teachers College Reading and Writing Project, Heinemann, ©2002 Teachers College, Columbia University; http://www.heinemann.com/fieldguides

The Witches
Roald Dahl

Book Summary

In Dahl's *The Witches*, the unexpected and unimaginable are carefully interwoven. It is the story of a boy and his Norwegian grandmother. As a prelude to the story, the boy explains that "things happened to me that will probably make you scream when you read about them. That can't be helped. The truth must be told. The fact that I am still here and able to speak (however peculiar I may look) to you is due entirely to my wonderful grandmother." (The boy is never actually named in the story.) The kindly, cigar-smoking grandmother is wise and understands things that most adults would not. To help him forget his sadness, she tells her recently orphaned grandson a story about witches.

While on holiday in England, the boy accidentally gets locked in a room where a witches' meeting is being held by The Grand High Witch herself. As he peers from behind the screen, the grandmother's startling descriptions of witches proves to be true. A wicked plot to rid England of boys by turning them into mice is presented by The Grand High Witch. Another boy, Bruno, is invited to the council so that the Grand High Witch can demonstrate the effects of this formula. Just as the meeting ends and we think the boy is safe, he is discovered. Despite his attempt to escape, he is caught and turned into a mouse.

This does not seem particularly to startle the grandmother. Together she and the mouse-boy make a plan to get the bottle of Formula 86 Delayed Action Mouse-Maker and turn all the witches into mice. At this point the mouse-boy becomes the hero of the book. The boy takes to being a mouse very well and is not traumatized by the sudden change. As a mouse, the boy is even more resourceful and independent. Through his daring acts the plan is a success.

The boy and his grandmother return to Norway and share happy days together. Whether as a boy or a mouse, the grandmother takes special interest in his life. She looks after him, prepares his meals, and assures him that he is special. The grandmother asks if the boy minds being a mouse for the rest of his life, to which he replies, "It doesn't matter who you are or what you look like as long as someone loves you."

In the last pages of the book, they consider the fact that there are still more witches at large and that they are in a unique position to fight against them. They realize that as a mouse, the boy won't live forever, nor will the old grandmother, so in their remaining years they will have magnificent adventures ridding the world of witches.

Basic Book Information

The book contains 207 pages and is divided into 22 chapters. The chapters are titled. There are illustrations by Quentin Blake that prompt and guide

Illustrator
Quentin Blake

Publisher
Puffin Books, 1983

ISBN
0141301104

TC Level
12

A Field Guide to the Classroom Library, Lucy Calkins and the Teachers College Reading and Writing Project, Heinemann, ©2002 Teachers College, Columbia University; http://www.heinemann.com/fieldguides

the imagination through this fanciful tale. The story is told in the first-person narrative from the boy's point of view.

The boy and the grandmother are the central characters. Supporting characters include the Grand Witch, Bruno (who is also turned into a mouse), and the hotel manager.

Noteworthy Features

The book is very descriptive. The images of the transforming witches are cleverly etched with the words chosen by Dahl. He makes up words such as "blabbersnitch." The Grand High Witch also speaks in an accent, so all "w" sounds are written in the letter "v"-perhaps sounding slightly German if one were to pronounce it. Some of these words may be difficult for children to get the sound of. Dahl also uses Norwegian words such as *fjord* (where the mountains meet the water), names of children (Ranghild, Birgit, Harald, Leif), and *gletost* (a type of cheese). Particular English words such as drawing pins (thumb tacks) also appear.

Independence, acceptance, and caring are central themes students often end up talking about in book clubs. The boy is orphaned and turned into a mouse and throughout has the caring love of his grandmother. He has adventures-whether as a mouse or a boy-and his grandmother is there to love and support him. As a mouse he has more "control" of his environment. He is freer and less hampered by interference from adults. For example, as a boy, the manager of the hotel is telling him what to do and not do, whereas as a mouse he can do what he likes. Being small is an advantage. This may be a launching pad for children to discuss how our external environment affects us, how we react to events, and what we are able to accomplish despite or because they are little "people." The boy does not question the unfortunate events that happen to him; instead, he decides what he likes about the new situation and makes the most of it. "What I especially liked was the fact that I made no sound at all when I ran. I was a swift and silent mover." The boy is pleased to explore the new environments in which he finds himself.

Teaching Ideas

The illustrations throughout the book are well placed, and each elaborates a particular event in the text. A reader might find it intriguing to notice passages that have no illustration, but which seem, to the reader, to merit one.

In talking about Dahl's writing style, it's almost certain a child would notice Dahl's onomatopoeia (whether or not the child knows this term). Children will notice how Dahl formed words from the sounds associated with what the word defines.

The boy, the grandmother, and Bruno each undergo interesting character development. Bruno and his parents are foils to the boy and his grandmother both as individuals, their relationship, and their perspective on life.

Children might also decide to explore the meaning of certain images that are threaded throughout. For example, the grandmother's cigars are referred to frequently-it is "foul," "stinking," "vile," and "disgusting." At the same

A Field Guide to the Classroom Library, Lucy Calkins and the Teachers College Reading and Writing Project, Heinemann, ©2002 Teachers College, Columbia University; http://www.heinemann.com/fieldguides

time, there are references to her lace handkerchiefs and lace shirts-how they feel and how they look. Readers might look at how these images are used to develop an understanding of the characters.

The book can be used to consider tolerance, understanding, family ties, and the nature of unexpected situations and magic in our lives.

Book Connections

As with *James and the Giant Peach* and *The Magic Finger*, *The Witches* takes for granted that magic exists in the world.

Genre
Chapter Book

Teaching Uses
Book Clubs; Independent Reading; Interpretation; Language Conventions

A Field Guide to the Classroom Library, Lucy Calkins and the Teachers College Reading and Writing Project, Heinemann, ©2002 Teachers College, Columbia University; http://www.heinemann.com/fieldguides

Toning the Sweep

Angela Johnson

Publisher
Scholastic, 1993

ISBN
0590481428

TC Level
14

Book Summary

Toning the Sweep, written by Angela Johnson (1993) is the story of an African American girl, who is spending what will probably be her last summer with her grandmother. Her grandmother lives in the California desert and has had an important influence on Emily throughout her life. It is the story of three generations of African American women.

Basic Book Information

It is a novel of 103 pages and the chapters are approximately four to five pages in length.

This novel makes an excellent read aloud for about grades five and above. It should be placed in the classroom library of this grade and above to be chosen during independent reading.

Noteworthy Features

Though this book is short, it presents a challenge because much of the story takes place in the mind of the main character, Emily. It is not a book filled with action. It is a book filled with deep thinking and reflection. The narrator of this story is Emily, except for Chapter 10, where we get to hear the voice of Emily's mother. This book does not have many characters or scene changes.

Teaching Ideas

The teachers reviewing and studying this book in middle school felt that it would lend itself very well to a unit of study on interpretation. Such a study might go as follows:

Day One: The teacher could introduce this text to the class by asking them what they notice about the text and if they have any expectations of it based on knowledge of the author, the blurb on the back cover, the title, the picture, and so on. The teacher can then read aloud (students do not have a copy of the text) Chapter One (which is only two pages long). Students might use post-it notes or reading notebooks to write down their thinking after reading. Then, partners share of their thinking from their writing. During the share on this first day, the teacher can also gather information about story elements.

Day Two: The teacher could read aloud the second chapter and begin to focus the class on the entire text by asking a questions such as, "What do you thinking this text is really about?" The teacher could put the answers on a chart so groups can talk about the different answers.

Day Three: The teacher can read Chapter Three and stop on page eight.

The teacher can ask, "Does this new information support the theories of yesterday?" The teacher might get conversation going in partnerships that would focus on explaining how the reading today supports or changes yesterday's theories. Students could do homework that helps them to carry on this conversation (by writing, sketching, or thinking). This is a method that many teachers use to help students keep conversations going in their minds.

Day Four: The teacher can complete Chapter Three, Four, Five, and Six. The teacher might check understanding by having students retell the story up to this part. Then he might introduce a tool for growing an interpretation of a text by showing a wheel (graphic organizer) on the overhead. The teacher can ask if students can fill in the sections of this wheel with things that are important to consider talking about for the whole of this text (thus far). The class would jot down ideas (on post-its or notebooks) and then whole class could organize them on the chart.

From Then On... The teacher can continue to use the chart as a jumping off point for discussions in partnerships and/or with the whole class, helping students in revising what is on the chart as theories develop and are changed by further reading and discussion. It is important to monitor those things that are helping to develop and change interpretation as they are charted. Within a week the class may have outgrown the use of the tool, the graphic organizer, but have learned how to use what is known about the world, the text and themselves to grow a theory about a book. The teacher can repeat questions that were asked on Day Two at several points during this study. This study may take three weeks.

Book Connections

Other books that may be used in the same manner as *Toning the Sweep* are: *Bluish* (V. Hamilton), *Missing May* (C. Rylant), *Monster* (W.D. Myers), *Baby* (P. MacLachlan), *Words of Stone* (K. Henkes), *Walk Two Moons* (S. Creech), *Out of the Dust* (K. Hesse), *Journey* (P. MacLachlan) and *What Jamie Saw* (C. Coman).

Genre
Short Chapter Book

Teaching Uses
Interpretation; Read Aloud; Independent Reading

A Field Guide to the Classroom Library, Lucy Calkins and the Teachers College Reading and Writing Project, Heinemann, ©2002 Teachers College, Columbia University; http://www.heinemann.com/fieldguides

Tuck Everlasting
Natalie Babbitt

Book Summary

A beautifully written, rich and tender novel, Natalie Babbitt weaves a story that is rich in imagery and prose. This multi-layered story captures the reader from the start with a Prologue that should not be missed. Babbitt sets the reader up for purposeful reading when she paints three different engaging scenarios and warns that things can come together in strange ways.

Mae Tuck sets out to meet her sons, Jesse and Miles, for their ten-year reunion near the small town of Treegap. Winnie Foster, an only child who is watched all the time and has to obey lots of rules, is bored and very cross at constantly being confined to her yard. That evening, a stranger in a yellow suit comes by the Foster home and stops to ask a few questions. While conversing, they hear faint, surprising wisps of music coming from the wood.

Quite curious about the tinkling little melody from the wood, Winnie sets out early the next day and wanders into the wood, which is owned by her family. She unexpectedly comes upon Jesse Tuck sitting under a large tree drinking from a spring. Prior to Mae and Miles appearance, when Winnie tries to drink, Jesse stops her. Alarmed by Winnie's discovery of the spring they feel compelled to kidnap her. Even with a calm head and speechless tongue she realizes this was not what she had envisioned as running away. Suddenly Winnie is comforted from the familiar tinkling melody coming from Mae's music box. She also learns the Tuck's secret: the water in the spring is magic and has made them ageless. Shocked by this revelation, Winnie attempts to understand that the Tucks are a family frozen in time. Despite her worries about being kidnapped, Winnie loses the last of her alarm and finds them to be her friends.

Meanwhile, the man in the yellow suit has followed the Tucks home, stolen their horse, and in exchange for Winnie's return, blackmailed the Fosters in selling him their woods. The man returns to the Tucks' home and informs them of his plans to sell the spring water. When Mae attacks and kills the man to defend Winnie, she, in turn, does her best to help with Mae's rescue from jail even though it means breaking the law and disappointing her family. After a successful attempt at rescuing Mae, Jesse secretly gives Winnie a bottle of water from the spring and asks her to drink it when she's 17 so they can be married and live together forever. Although she loves Jesse, Winnie chooses to pour the water on a toad she has befriended. When the Tucks return to Treegap years later they find Winnie's grave.

Basic Book Information

Babbitt has published many other children's books including, *Phoebe's*

A Field Guide to the Classroom Library, Lucy Calkins and the Teachers College Reading and Writing Project, Heinemann, ©2002 Teachers College, Columbia University; http://www.heinemann.com/fieldguides

Publisher
Sunburst, 1975

ISBN
0374480095

TC Level
14

Revolt, The Search for Delicious, Kneeknock Rise, Goody Hall, The Devil's Storybook, and *The Eyes of the Amaryllis*. This fantasy book is 139 pages long, divided into twenty-five chapters. Readers might be surprised by some of the brief but concise chapters. The Prologue and Epilogue are a must read. Three aspects of the story that the reader must follow carefully as the plot unfolds are: Winnie's intense battle of boredom and desire to leave Treegap, Mae's strong and courageous leadership as she attempts to reunite her family every ten years, and the mysterious stranger in the yellow suit who seeks to discover and destroy the Tucks' secret.

Noteworthy Features

The strong characterization of Winnie serves as a link between the reader and this engaging story. The reader is able to identify with the motives, actions, and feelings of Winnie who is close to the same age as the book's target audience. The trust, promise, and risk taking can easily be transacted and personally connected to the reader. Upper elementary and middle school students will easily imagine themselves in this text and develop literary thinking.

As readers think alongside Winnie they will be faced with the vast possibilities and grow a greater clarity about their life as she faces her ultimate decision about eternal life. Clearly the compelling metaphor of the cycle of life is revealed when Tuck and Winnie set out to go fishing on the pond and he stages the scenario as an opportunity to explain how his family has dropped off the wheel of life and are stuck "like rocks beside the road" because they will never die. Even with the gentleness of Tuck's careful and elaborate description of the cycle of life, Winnie comes face to face with her own mortality. "Just go out, like a flame of the candle, and no use protesting. It was certainty." It is at this turning point that the reader is swept along with Winnie's anguish of everything that is happening to her. Students' self-questioning may force them out of the text and they may want to discuss the questions that will drive them back into the layers of the text: "Would I want to live forever? Will Winnie want to live forever?" Readers know that that perplexing question will have to be answered. They may find themselves wanting to answer the question for her.

As readers listen to the language of the text they will be able to glean the reoccurring literary elements of foreshadowing that Babbitt uses to craft the text in a way that makes the readers pay attention. When Winnie and Tuck were in the rowboat a bullfrog foreshadows the trouble ahead, "Across the pond a bullfrog spoke a deep note of warning." Those clues direct the reader's thinking and almost force the reader to question the text. The significant detail makes the reader notice parts of the text, which lead to questioning the plot, for example, the man in the yellow suit makes the reader notice him and realize that he is different. The superb imagery that Babbitt creates allows the reader to uncover layers of significant text and pay close attention to the beautiful language of similes, metaphors, and personification.

This story is a rich source of beautiful language and metaphorical descriptions. Natalie Babbitt begins the first chapter with beautiful words to describe the setting. The road, "wandered along in curves and easy angles, swayed off and up in a pleasant tangent to the top of a small hill, ambled down again between fringes of bee-hung clover ..." The descriptions of the cottage, "...a touch-me-not appearance," and fence, "...Move on-we don't want *you* here" are personifications. Inanimate objects are brought to life and given dialogue throughout this text. The author suggests that a toad that Winnie meets regularly at the fence can understand her and responds to her with his eyes and movements. Another example of Babbitt's use of poetic language is a description of a sunset, "the last stains of sunset had melted away...remnants clung reluctantly to everything that was pale in color...turning them blue and blurry." Characters, such as Jesse, are also described using comparisons, "he wore his battered trousers and loose, grubby shirt with as much self-assurance as if they were silk and satin."

Some vocabulary in the text is used in unusual ways, which can confuse young readers. The meaning can be drawn from the context such as, "an apologetic beard, quivering in splotches." The text includes vocabulary that may be unfamiliar to children: *rueful, jaunty, galling, crowed, retorted, self-deprecation.* One way Babbitt uses language irregularly, is in the dialogue of Mae, Pa, Miles, and Jesse Tuck, which is written in a dialect, that may confuse some young readers. Words are run together and written as contractions with apostrophes to give the reader a sense of a rural accent as in, *why'd, what're, boys'll, how do.*

Quotation marks are used in different ways in this story. Babbitt asks rhetorical questions throughout the text. Some questions are written without quotation marks, but some are written in quotation marks. Most rhetorical questions are asked by the narrator or Winnie. Some are thoughts, some are spoken by Winnie to herself or the toad. Following who or what Winnie is talking to or thinking can be confusing to some readers.

Teaching Ideas

The hauntingly real setting and tightly wound plot provide levels of interpretation. The reader can interact between the text and the author, the reader's life and concepts of the world (i.e., justice, life/death issues, and religion). As students accumulate inferences they will grow a more literal idea than what is on the page. While reading aloud the teacher can use talk to develop thinking (think alouds) and push others to talk. By pausing and asking, "So what?" at critical parts of the text, student responses can bring important ideas to the text and fill in what is literally not on the page. "So what if someone looks the same for 87 years? So what if the stranger is following Winnie and the Tucks? So what if Winnie doesn't keep the Tucks' secret?" These questions can be springboards for partnership conversations. These can be collected in notebooks and then used to decide what's worth exploring again. Webs can be created about issues, talked about and then moved back to other texts with similar issues to develop interpretation and intertextuality. During discussion, the teacher might encourage students to consider and negotiate the text by what is justifiably provocative, compelling, and accountable to the text. A simple framework can be designed to organize thinking (i.e., I think...Evidence in the text...What I know about the world...). This is an excellent book to develop the literary thinking necessary to lean into the "Aha!" moments of interpretation.

A Field Guide to the Classroom Library, Lucy Calkins and the Teachers College Reading and Writing Project, Heinemann, ©2002 Teachers College, Columbia University; http://www.heinemann.com/fieldguides

Tuck Everlasting is a wonderful story for considering issues based on point of view. The characters are strong in their beliefs and have plenty of personal experience that brings them to their perspectives on the possibility of eternal life. This text would work well in a class read aloud where children take turns reading dialogue so they can feel the emotion behind the interactions. This would also reinforce the role of the narrator in this story and help readers distinguish between rhetorical questions and dialogue.

Natalie Babbit's use of rich language can help students get pictures in their minds and sketch. This is a way to support their understanding of qualities of good writing through reading. The imagery is developed and can be tracked throughout the entire book.

Book Connections

This magical novel and *The Fall of Freddie the Leaf*, an *Allegory* [Ed: ital ok?] by Leo Buscaglia, *A Taste of Blackberries* by Doris B. Smith, *The Bridge to Terabithia* by Katherine Paterson, and *On My Honor* by Marion D. Bauer confront the reader with the perplexing but inevitable issue of death and the cycle of life. The mood, tone, and reoccurring line of thinking in these books demand that the students read closely into the text and themselves.

Genre
Fantasy; Chapter Book

Teaching Uses
Language Conventions; Character Study; Interpretation; Read Aloud; Book Clubs

Vanishing

Bruce Brooks

Book Summary

Bruce Brooks is well known for his fiction as well as his non-fiction: he has written *Boys Will Be*, *Everywhere*, and *The Moves Make the Man* (which won the Newbery Honor in 1985). *Vanishing* is the story of Alice, an eleven-year-old girl, in the hospital on a hunger strike. She is on strike against the treatment her divorced parents have given (or not given) her. Her mother is an alcoholic; her father is a wimpy man living with his mother, a woman who has never been able to be more than grumpy. Alice has nowhere to turn but to the hospital she was admitted to for a serious bronchial infection. While there she meets Rex, a boy in the children's ward with her who has cancer. Alice experiences fasting hallucinations where she floats above her body and detaches from reality. Alice prefers these times, seeing them as the time when she has control over her body. At Rex' death, Alice realizes how important life is, and that it cannot be controlled.

Basic Book Information

This is a short book, consisting of 103 pages, and yet it is very complex because of the characters and plot. Despite its length, this book is not for young readers. The themes of body control, eating disorders, depression, death and dying are present and should be considered fare for mature readers.

This book is told in the third person with Alice's point of view. This technique helps the reader to feel objective while at the same time identifying strongly with Alice. There are fifteen chapters of varying length. There are occasional chapters written in italics that depict Alice in her hallucinations. These italicized chapters appear to be happening in the present and might confuse a reader who is not sure what the italics indicate.

Noteworthy Features

This book contains many sophisticated themes such as rebellion against parents, dysfunctional parenting, alcoholism, divorce, death, and suicide. Alice is very outspoken and her language contains vernacular and colloquialisms, though never crossing into profanity.

There are many scene changes that happen quickly. Alice has memories of living with her father and her mother while she is in the hospital. These shifts may call for some explanation or time for conversation if readers are to understand them.

Teaching Ideas

Vanishing is a book that is full of setting changes that can create confusion

Publisher
Harper Tempest, 1999

ISBN
0064472345

TC Level
14

for the reader. Because of this, it is an excellent choice for a read aloud or for a study of setting. One teacher decided to read this book aloud to her class twice. "We've read *Vanishing* through and decided that it is pretty hard book. One thing that you noticed is that there are a lot of changes in the scenes as the book goes on. I thought we could read it again, since it is so short, this time, reading it looking for all those scene changes and trying to figure out why Bruce Brooks did this. All authors combine the elements of story in a way that helps us to make meaning of the overall story. You can bet that Brooks did all these scenery changes for a reason. Especially since he does it so often. That's not by coincidence! Let's figure it out!"

The class decided to stop and respond to the text every time there was a scene change. This class had learned to respond to text in a variety of ways, by saying something to a partner, by jotting some thoughts in their notebooks, and by sketching quickly an impression. The students had determined what best suited them as readers over the span of the year, and so their responses were according to their needs. This meant that the students were listening very carefully, and signaling the teacher to stop when they perceived a scene change. They became very adept at finding these scene changes.

During the end of the book discussion, one student noticed, "Every time there was a scene change, there was also a change in the plot. When I was noticing the scenes and the setting more I could see where there were changes. I didn't get that Alice moved from her mother's to her father's, then she went on the plane and then she was in the hospital on the first read. When you read it the first time I didn't see that and it all got mixed up in my mind, it seemed so weird and kind of dumb. Now I can see the story has parts and I can keep track better. By understanding the scene Alice was in, I can understand Alice better."

Some teachers work with their students on retelling with this book. One found that students needed to improvise in order to retell the story of this book, that some needed to create two-layer timelines to help them recount events. Another middle school teacher had students create character timelines. Both timelines helped because of the complex characters and scene changes.

This book usually generates powerful discussions. Asking questions such as, Who's voice is heard here? Who's missing? Is the narrator trustworthy? can push those discussions even further.

Book Connections

Chicken Soup for the Teenage Soul has many short stories that can relate to the theme and content of this book. *Cut* by Patricia McCormick also explores control and body image as well as self-mutilation. *Mind's Eye* (by Paul Fleischman) is also is set in a hospital and relies on the many scene and setting changes to develop the characters.

Genre
Chapter Book

A Field Guide to the Classroom Library, Lucy Calkins and the Teachers College Reading and Writing Project, Heinemann, ©2002 Teachers College, Columbia University; http://www.heinemann.com/fieldguides

Teaching Uses
Book Clubs; Read Aloud; Character Study

What You Know First

Patricia MacLachlan

Book Summary

What You Know First tells the story of a little girl and her family who are preparing to move away from the only home the girl has ever known. The farm she lives on is located on the prairie and holds some of her most cherished memories. The young girl reflects on all of the things she loves about this place and how she will say goodbye to them. The sky, the grass, and her tree, are all a part of her and hard to part with. The little girl wants to find a way to hold on to these things so she can share them with her baby brother when he grows up. She is determined to find a way to take these memories with her.

Basic Book Information

Patricia MacLachlan is the author of many well-loved novels and picture books, including *Sarah, Plain and Tall,* winner of the Newbery Medal; it's sequel, *Skylark,* and *All The Places To Love,* illustrated by Mike Wimmer.

Noteworthy Features

The dark, serious, dramatically cropped engravings on these pages lend the book an adult air, which attracts some children and repels others. The small amount of text per page may, for some children, counterbalance the sophisticated air lent by the illustrations. On the other hand, some children see the format of the copy on the page and think the book is poetry, and therefore (sadly) intimidating to read. In most classrooms, especially at the beginning of the year, this book could use an introduction or a promotion or at least a link to another book (perhaps one of MacLachlan's many others) to get it off the shelves and into children's hands.

What You Know First is really more a meditation than a story. It is the thoughts of a girl-a reader can only tell it is a girl from the pictures, not the text, so conceivably it could be a boy-as she adjusts to the fact that she is moving away from the place she loves.

This book is laden with farm-specific vocabulary and images, so, like any book, readers unfamiliar with the places described will undoubtedly have a harder time picturing it, and possibly understanding it, than other readers. Passages that describe the pipits feeding or the geese sky-talking may give some readers pause.

Some of the more interesting facts about this story are based in its creation. Patricia MacLachlan was born on the prairie, and to this day carries a small bag of prairie dirt with her wherever she goes to remind her of what she knew first. One day, shortly after a move to a new home MacLachlan felt unstable. She was having a hard time adjusting to her new surroundings and missed her old home. She was having trouble writing as

A Field Guide to the Classroom Library, Lucy Calkins and the Teachers College Reading and Writing Project, Heinemann, ©2002 Teachers College, Columbia University; http://www.heinemann.com/fieldguides

Illustrator
Barry Moser

Publisher
Harper Collins, 1995

ISBN
0064434923

TC Level
8

well. At that very time she was to speak to a fourth grade class at the Jackson Street School and worried about what she would say to them in this state of mind. She wound up discussing heavily the topic of "place and landscape" and showed the students her bag of prairie dirt from where she was born. The children were very involved in the discussion because they could relate. Five were foster children, disconnected from their homes. One boy had recently lost everything he had to a fire in his home. Another told her that he was moving in a few days to a place he'd never been. MacLachlan suggested to these students that maybe she should take her prairie dirt and toss it in her new backyard so that the two places could mix together. The children's reactions to this were so strongly against this idea, fearful that the dirt might blow away. One small girl suggested placing the dirt in a bowl and keeping it on the window so that it would be a constant reminder of "what you knew first." When MacLachlan left the school she went home to write this book.

Teaching Ideas

This book starts right in the middle of her thoughts, with no explanation of the characters, situation or setting. If children are confused by this opening, or by books in general that open this way, it may help them to learn that all readers feel that sense of missing knowledge when a book starts in the middle like that. We can tell children that authors know the reader will be wondering about the details of the situation, and the authors use that to get the reader to read more in order to get their questions answered. In order for the words to make sense as the reader does read more, he or she has to read carefully and hold in mind the questions raised by the text. In this case the questions are probably the following: Who is the "I"? Where is it she won't go? Why?

In this book, some of the reader's questions are answered almost right away. It becomes clear that the place the girl doesn't want to go to is a new house, a new place, a land she's never seen. That quick answer to the reader's early question provides some support for the reader unused to reading with questions. For that reason, this book might make a good transitional read for kids who aren't yet able to read fantasy and other-world-type books that require the reader to hold in mind a lot of unanswered questions.

The book leaves some questions for readers to puzzle over, to discuss in groups or reread and think about. The narrator asks to herself why they must leave at all, and the reader may well try to figure that out from the story. It seems the family must leave for monetary reasons, but students can debate over the possibilities that are hinted at in the book.

Like many of MacLachlan's books, this one has a tone of nostalgia for the "good life," one where people live side by side with natural beauty and in perfect harmony with the land. The tone itself can provide fodder for discussion, especially if the tone in this book is compared to the tone in another book that presents another perspective on farm life-one that shows some of the hardships or negative aspects of country living.

This book could appear in a basket with multiple copies. Whether a teacher wishes to introduce Memoir, Poetry or an Author Study of Patricia MacLachlan's literary work, or if a teacher would rather discuss the beautiful

A Field Guide to the Classroom Library, Lucy Calkins and the Teachers College Reading and Writing Project, Heinemann, ©2002 Teachers College, Columbia University; http://www.heinemann.com/fieldguides

language and vivid vocabulary or even the structure of this text, it would make a great mentor text. Not only is it a wonderfully structured book, but it can even be used to ease the anxiety of that new child that appears at each of our classroom doorways in the late winter or early spring. Surely a child such as this could immediately feel comforted after reading the first page ("I won't go, I'll say, To a new house, To a new place, To a land I've never seen").

This book also provides an outstanding opportunity for introducing the concept of studying artifacts in Memoir. The young girl will "take a twig of the cottonwood tree...take a little bag of prairie dirt." One can almost picture the girl sitting with these artifacts later in life and all of her original memories come flooding to her mind:

Or maybe
I'll live in a tree.
The tall cottonwood that was small when Papa was small,
But grew faster than he did.
Now it has branches
And crooks where I can sit
To look over the rooftop,
Over the windmill
Over the prairie...

Book Connections

Patricia MacLachlan is the author of many well-loved novels and picture books, including *Sarah, Plain and Tall,* winner of the Newbery Medal; it's sequel, *Skylark,* and *All The Places To Love,* illustrated by Mike Wimmer.

Genre
Picture Book

Teaching Uses
Read Aloud; Independent Reading; Critique; Teaching Writing; Partnerships

When I Was Puerto Rican

Esmeralda Santiago

Publisher
Random House Inc., 1993

ISBN
0679756760

TC Level
13; 14; 15

Book Summary

Esmeralda Santiago writes a memoir of her childhood and youth growing up in rural Puerto Rico. One of eight children, her family lives in poverty. Despite her parents' constant bickering and separations, there is abundant love and tenderness throughout the tears and laughter. Esmeralda learned at her mother's hands the proper way to eat a guava, the sound of tree frogs in the mango groves at night, the taste of the delectable sausage called *morcilla*, and the formula for ushering a dead baby's soul into heaven. The story moves to New York City. From the barefoot, carefree, and endless days of work on the island to the tenements of New York City, everything changes-different language, different schools, different everything. The courage of Esmeralda is alive in the honest telling of this memoir. She shares with her readers the combination of cultures that makes her story, her life, so remarkable.

Basic Book Information

Esmeralda Santiago's first book is richly crafted. It begins with a prologue that introduces the reader to the author's unique style. Each chapter begins with a Spanish quotation meant to teach a lesson: "Truth, although severe, is a true friend." And it is then translated into English-supporting the crossing of these two beautiful cultures. The book ends with an epilogue that can leave the reader with a thirst for more. A glossary of Spanish words helps the reader get a clearer picture of the language, the foods, the culture, and geography of Puerto Rico.

Noteworthy Features

The book is written in the first person, as a memoir. Esmeralda tells her story as she sees it. Her craft allows the reader to feel, smell, taste, hear, and see her life in these two different worlds. She shares with her readers the person who she has become as a result of her early barrio experiences on the very rural island. The clear details of the land and family she grew up with become a part of the reader's understanding, as she tells her story with a craft that is unmatched. The story of her immigration into New York's culture is told with a power that is at the very heart of her craft. This book should be used with older students as many chapters contain sophisticated material that is realistically and often explicitly told. The book is 274 pages long, with fifteen chapters. The widespread use of Spanish words as well as the sophisticated vocabulary makes this book appropriate for older and fluent readers.

Teaching Ideas

When I Was Puerto Rican is a must for any memoir genre study, in reading workshop or writing workshop. As many of the chapters can stand alone, parts of this work could be used at any grade level from intermediate grades through adult. A focus on crafting might begin with observation and envisionment techniques. The reader could study closely how this author brings her characters life with meticulous details and close observations. Sketching might be employed in the early listening of parts of these chapters. It allows readers to hold onto more of the text.

Another possible study might be an investigation into Nonfiction work. The reader might focus predominantly on Puerto Rico, its land and culture. Charting the information can be one focus as the reader moves through the text. Contrasting this information with the world the reader knows will lead to further inquiry about different ways of living. Ways of holding onto information from difficult texts might be fact-finding. The challenge of determining what is important in this kind of reading is another conference that the teacher might have with a reader. Tools, such as sketching to hold onto ideas, might help a reader to get a fuller picture of the island life. Holding the reader accountable might require some strategies for note-taking or chunking information. Teaching children to re-read to understand the text is another strategy that this text might encourage. Having questions in mind as one reads is also important when the text is dense and chock full of ideas.

Another use for this text is an in-depth interpretation study: Who should read this story? Whose voice is missing? Whose story is it? What is the author really saying? This could be coupled with a study of Latino authors or possibly a study of different cultures. The forum for this work could be in a unit where students were learning to think and talk in the company of others. Reading clubs and large group work would enrich the reading beyond what independent reading can do.

Book Connections

Other memoirs readers might enjoy include Toni Morrison's *Bluest Eye*; Maya Angelou's *I Know Why the Caged Bird Sings*; Gary Soto's *Short Stories*; Jimenez's *The Circuit*; Eloise Greenfield's *Child Times*; and Jean Little's *Little By Little*.

Genre
Nonfiction; Memoir; Chapter Book

A Field Guide to the Classroom Library, Lucy Calkins and the Teachers College Reading and Writing Project, Heinemann, ©2002 Teachers College, Columbia University; http://www.heinemann.com/fieldguides

Teaching Uses
Teaching Writing; Content Area Study; Book Clubs; Character Study;
Interpretation; Critique

Yolanda's Genius
Carol Fenner

Book Summary

Yolanda's family has moved from urban Chicago to suburban Michigan to be rid of violence and drugs. As Yolanda struggles to find friends, Andrew, Yolanda's baby brother, plays his harmonica and gets into trouble with the "Dudes," a gang that sells drugs to the suburban kids. Andrew's harmonica is his way of communicating with the world and after the Dudes break it he retreats into silence. Yolanda, who knows what a genius Andrew really is, defends his lack of progress in school and determines to show the world Andrew's genius. Through Yolanda's own genius, she gets her brother to meet and then play on stage with a famous blues artist at the Chicago Blues Festival. The family heads back to their new home in Michigan, Andrew set with a music teacher for geniuses, Mother with renewed hope for her children, and Yolanda with a sense of dignity and self-worth.

Basic Book Information

Yolanda's Genius won the Newbery Honor in 1997 as well as being selected as the ALA's Notable Children's Book of the year. It is a 208-page realistic fiction novel with eighteen chapters, which portrays urban and suburban life for adolescents with candor and sensitivity. There is plenty of street talk and some suggested profanity as one boy says, "Get off my effin' foot," to Yolanda. Fenner doesn't sugarcoat her characters or their language and behavior and this is just what makes this book so strong, but may be worrisome to some adults. The story is told in the third-person narrative, with Yolanda as the point of view. This helps to moderate any potential negative messages, as Yolanda is a strong character: bright, responsible, and motivated to protect her family from harm.

Noteworthy Features

Part of what makes this story so real is the true-to-life speech patterns used by the characters, and especially Yolanda's thoughts. However, for readers not familiar with city street talk this may be confusing, and some introduction to this language will be helpful. The strong character of Yolanda will be an aid to many readers. She is a bright student who gets straight As and is sometimes referred to as the Teacher's Pet. Her command of language is immense and she acts as interpreter for much of the vernacular used.

The story line is very involved, swirling from school to home, from Shirley (Yolanda's new friend), to Aunt Tiny from Chicago. Again, the strong character of Yolanda can mediate some of this difficulty. A character study of Yolanda would enhance a struggling reader's attachment to Yolanda, thereby helping the story to hold together better.

Teaching Ideas

This is a great read aloud for fifth and sixth grade classes. *Yolanda's Genius* brings many issues to the front, like drugs, self-esteem, racism, suburban prejudice, violence, and special education. Fenner does a great job bringing Yolanda to life, making it possible to consider and talk about real life issues.

Yolanda's Genius is a book full of issues and interwoven with many stories. It is the plot structure that can make it difficult for many readers. Upper grade teachers like to use this book as a read aloud in order to identify the plot structure and to teach some supportive strategies for handling it. A sixth grade teacher decided to use *Yolanda's Genius* as a read aloud because it had a similar plot structure to many of the advanced chapter books that her students were reading. The students were having difficulty staying on top of all the stories going on within the book. "*Yolanda's Genius* is our read aloud and I've chosen it to help us all know and deal with books that have complicated plots. *Yolanda's Genius* has a plot that is sort of like a big rug, it has many threads that go through the whole rug, sometimes mixing with the other threads. [Here she held up a colorful rag rug that the class used to sit on during independent reading time.] There is the story of Yolanda. She is the main character or protagonist of the story, and she narrates the story. The story is of a time in her life when she moved to a new town. Yolanda's story is in the present, but like all of us, she has lots of memories. These memories come back and get woven into the present story to help us understand Yolanda's overall story."

The teacher and the class went on to use this picture of the story lines to help define all that was going on in the book. They called this plot structure the "rug plot," using this to help them identify and understand similar plots in other books.

Genre
Chapter Book

Teaching Uses
Independent Reading; Read Aloud

A Field Guide to the Classroom Library, Lucy Calkins and the Teachers College Reading and Writing Project, Heinemann, ©2002 Teachers College, Columbia University; http://www.heinemann.com/fieldguides

Index